Signs from the Unseen Realm

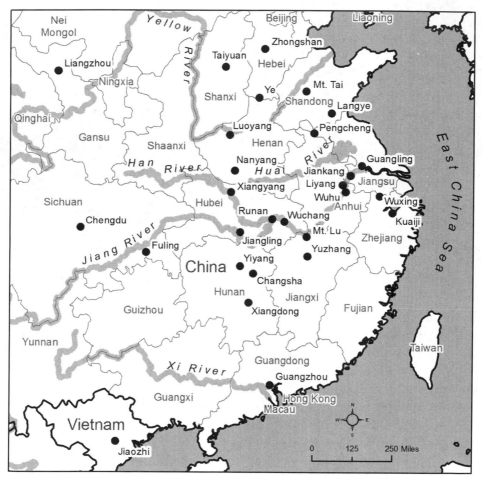

Map prepared by Jacob Thornton

CLASSICS IN EAST ASIAN BUDDHISM

Signs from the Unseen Realm

Buddhist Miracle Tales from Early Medieval China

A translation and study by
ROBERT FORD CAMPANY

A KURODA INSTITUTE BOOK
University of Hawai'i Press
Honolulu

Library of Congress Cataloging-in-Publication Data

Campany, Robert Ford
Signs from the unseen realm : Buddhist miracle tales from early medieval
China / a translation and study by Robert Ford Campany.
p. cm. — (Classics in East Asian Buddhism)
Includes bibliographical references and index.
ISBN 978-0-8248-3602-3 (cloth : alk. paper)
1. Wang, Yan, 5th cent. Ming xiang ji. 2. Buddhist legends—China.
3. Miracles (Buddhism)   I. Wang, Yan, 5th cent. Ming xiang ji. English.
II. Title.   III. Title: Buddhist miracle tales from early medieval China.
BQ5775.C6C36 2012
294.3'44320951—dc23
2011038216

ISBN 978-0-8248-9682-9 (paperback)

The Kuroda Institute for the Study of Buddhism and Human Values
is a nonprofit, educational corporation founded in 1976. One of its primary
objectives is to promote scholarship on the historical, philosophical, and
cultural ramifications of Buddhism, which it publishes, in association with
the University of Hawai'i Press, in its Studies in East Asian Buddhism series.
To complement these scholarly studies, the Institute also makes available in
the present series reliable translations of some of the major classics of
East Asian Buddhism.

Designed by Santos Barbasa Jr.

**Kuroda Institute
Classics in East Asian Buddhism**

The Record of Tung-Shan
William F. Powell

Tracing Back the Radiance: Chinul's Korean Way of Zen
Robert E. Buswell Jr.

*The Great Calming and Contemplation: A Study and Annotated
Translation of the First Chapter of Chih-i's* Mo-ho chih-kuan
Neal Donner and Daniel Stevenson

*Inquiry into the Origin of Humanity: An Annotated Translation of
Tsung-mi's* Yüan jen lun *with a Modern Commentary*
Peter N. Gregory

*Zen in Medieval Vietnam: A Study and Translation of
the* Thiền Uyển Tập Anh
Cuong Tu Nguyen

*Hōnen's Senchakushū: Passages on the Selection of
the Nembutsu in the Original Vow*
Senchakushū English Translation Project

*The Origins of Buddhist Monastic Codes in China:
An Annotated Translation and Study of the* Changyuan qinggui
Yifa

*The Scriptures of Wŏn Buddhism: A Translation of
Wŏnbulgyo kyojŏn with Introduction*
Bongkil Chung

*Personal Salvation and Filial Piety: Two Precious Scroll Narratives of
Guanyin and Her Acolytes*
Wilt L. Idema

*Signs from the Unseen Realm: Buddhist Miracle Tales
from Early Medieval China*
Robert Ford Campany

In memory of
John R. McRae

Contents

Preface

This book concerns a collection of Buddhist miracle tales, *Mingxiang ji* 冥祥記, or *Records of Signs from the Unseen Realm*, written at the end of the fifth century CE by the scholar-official Wang Yan 王琰. In part 1, I introduce the work and its author, exploring the nature and genre of the text, its religious themes, narrative tropes, and social and religious contexts. Part 2 offers an annotated translation and selective commentary. Here I would like to say briefly why I think these sorts of texts deserve to be considered more carefully than they have been so far by scholars of Buddhism, historians of Chinese religions, and anyone else interested in the comparative study of religion or religious literature or in using miracle tales as sources for religious history.

In the study of Buddhist texts, the overwhelming share of attention has been paid to sutras—those texts purportedly preserving the words of the Buddha. This attention is certainly justified. Sutras (and commentaries to them) were often the places where new, important ideas or practices were announced. They were studied, chanted, cited, preached, visually illustrated, and ritually revered as virtual embodiments of the Buddha's presence, even if they were probably read for their content by ordinary Buddhists much less often than we might think. Some of them are classics that rank among the world's most compelling works of religious literature. When read with care, sutras offer clues about the religious contexts in which they were produced. But sutras that were translated from Indic languages into Chinese can tell us little about how Buddhism was lived and practiced in China. Hence Michel Strickmann's characteristically provocative statement, published twenty years ago: "It might be thought perverse to claim that Chinese Buddhism remains a largely unknown subject."[1] Sutras composed in China, on the other hand—long dismissed as "apocryphal" but increasingly valued by historians of Chinese religions (if not yet by large numbers of scholars of Buddhism)—testify to ways in which Buddhism was taken up and responded to there. But even these indigenous sutras, valu-

---

1. "The Consecration Sūtra," 75.

able and underresearched though they are, tell us little of how they were received or understood, or of how religious practice changed in light of them. When we read sutras, whether translated into Chinese or indigenously composed in that language, we often unconsciously assume that, once they were available in a given period and region, people were somehow automatically "influenced" by them, took up their teachings in their entirety, and proceeded to act accordingly. But, for many reasons, this was probably not the case very often—certainly less often than we imagine. If we want to know, then, how Buddhism was lived and practiced in early medieval China—if we want to know how it worked as a religion, and not merely how it was presented as a philosophy, an assemblage of doctrines, or a body of scriptural literature—we must turn to texts of other genres.[2]

In addition to histories and biographies, which themselves merit more attention (and more hermeneutically astute attention) from scholars than they have so far received, one of these other genres is that of miracle tales. Historians often dismiss such texts as sources because of what they take to be the contaminating presence of the miraculous. In my view, the miraculous elements of these narratives are part of what the historian should seek to understand. They, too, if read with the right questions in mind, constitute important historical evidence, not necessarily of what happened but of what some people believed and wanted others to believe had happened—itself a matter of considerable historical interest. Further, as I argue in the pages below, miracle tales, like hagiographies, bear invaluable witness not only to the content of the collective memory of religious groups but also to the social processes by which collective memory was shaped, transmitted, and preserved. What one person or family felt to have been a miraculous occurrence was simply that one person's or family's experience and would have remained such unless others, having heard the story, had responded by circulating it along social networks until it wound up in a compilation such as Wang Yan's. Such a story was, in a literal sense, socially fashioned, an artifact of collective memory. It is because of these social networks of narration, estimation, and circulation that we possess miracle tales at all. And it is this densely social quality that makes them important sources for the history of religion.

When read with care, the stories show us many of the ways in which people in China responded to the teachings of sutras. They do so not only by virtue of the behaviors and practices they depict but also in the narrative forms they take. These tales enact some of the most typical narrative sequences in terms of which Buddhism's efficacy was argued to audiences and readers in early medieval China. It would have been one thing to say the equivalent of "Buddhism is true," "the Buddha is powerful," or "the

---

2. Or of course to art, architecture, and other aspects of Buddhist material culture, which are not of central concern here except insofar as they number among the aspects of Buddhist life about which miracle tales inform us.

soul survives death and undergoes karmic reward or punishment." It was quite another to embed these and many other assertions in narratives that conveyed to readers—perhaps in ways that only narrative can—"that our task, as agents, is to live as good characters in a story do."[3]

Historians of the early period of Buddhism in China have tended to focus on the great translators and the groups surrounding them. The historian's searchlight, trained on the foreign translator-monks and their closest assistants, has left other members of the surrounding audience in relative darkness. Meanwhile, these same historians have lamented our lack of knowledge of lay Buddhism during this period. It may in fact have been the initially small, family- or locale-based groups of literate laypersons that are so often glimpsed in the miracle tales—each of them associated with one or more monks as a source of teaching and a field of karmic merit and linked to one another by networks of patronage, intermarriage, government service, and the exchange of letters—that were most instrumental in spreading the religion in its early centuries in China. And the miracle tales suggest that no activity was more central to the religious life of these groups than the zhai 齋, or abstinence ceremony, held twice a month and (for longer periods) three times a year in lay households— gatherings of anywhere from a handful to fifty or more laymen and women, along with invited monks and nuns who were expected to offer sutra recitation and preaching in addition to the opportunity, by their acceptance of offered meals, for the lay hosts to earn karmic merit. Through the tales, then, we may be glimpsing the social contexts in which Buddhism gained its earliest demographically significant foothold in China.

The miracle tales also illustrate how these same groups wrestled with tensions between Buddhism and non-Buddhist[4] religious traditions, practices, assumptions, and values. I think we must learn to read these tales not as "expressions" of an organic, holistic Buddhist tradition but as artifacts of how certain aspects of that tradition were taken up and responded to by Chinese people in light of religious alternatives.

In three sentences that have had a profound impact on the study of medieval Chinese religious history, Erik Zürcher famously remarked concerning certain "misunderstandings and distortions" of Buddhist ideas that he felt were reflected in appropriations of them in early Daoist scriptures: "But perhaps such misunderstandings and distortions were also widely spread among the simple Buddhist believers themselves. Perhaps we are—as so often happens—handicapped by the fact that we can only observe Buddhism and Daoism at the very highest level, that of the religious

---

3. Nussbaum, *Love's Knowledge*, 3–4. For insightful considerations of how Buddhist narratives conveyed values in supple, complex ways, see Hallisey and Hansen, "Narrative, Subethics, and the Moral Life."

4. Throughout, I will sometimes use the term "indigenous" as shorthand for elements of Chinese religious ideology and practice that demonstrably predated the earliest known Buddhist activity in China.

'professionals' and their written texts—the tops of two pyramids. We may consider the possibility that at a lower level the bodies of the pyramids merged into a much less differentiated lay religion, and that at the very base both systems largely dissolved into an indistinct mass of popular beliefs and practices."[5] It happens to be precisely the midlevel lay religion here referred to, between the "indistinct mass" at the base and the professionally distinct peaks, that the miracle tales emanated from and thus inform us of. And if we learn anything from the tales, it is that the lay religion they reflect was hardly "less differentiated." The people who circulated these tales were keenly aware of ways in which their religious practices and commitments placed them at odds with aspects of non-Buddhist Chinese religious culture, as will be seen below.[6]

The miracle tales are rich historical sources precisely because *they both reflect and were attempts to persuasively shape* what these groups of early Chinese Buddhists thought and did. In the pages that follow, I offer a translation of the largest miracle-tale compilation from this period in order to make it available to a wider audience. I sketch a number of inferences about religious life that I think are warranted by the stories. And I discuss the grounds and procedures on which I believe such inferences are justified. If this book accomplishes nothing else, I hope it will at least serve to draw more attention to these unjustly neglected texts.

---

5. "Buddhist Influence on Early Taoism," 146.

6. In this respect I also disagree with Teiser's critique of the "schizophrenic" or "artificial bifurcation of the worldview of Chinese folk religion," in which matters are imagined as "the grafting of Buddhist branches onto an inhospitable Chinese trunk" (*The Ghost Festival*, 169), at least to the extent that Teiser's alternative is to posit a "folk religion" that, as Zürcher memorably phrased it, amounted to an "indistinct mass" of beliefs and practices. I will adduce evidence that some of the tales translated here clearly wrestle with perceived tensions between older, indigenous understandings and relatively newly imported Buddhist ones, and that the makers of these tales were keenly aware of these tensions. Indeed, some of the material Teiser presents in the above-mentioned book evidences awareness (not only in China but also in India) of tensions between Buddhist and non- or pre-Buddhist approaches to certain problems and areas of life (for one of many examples, see p. 176). Perhaps by the eighth and ninth centuries many of these tensions had been more or less smoothed out, but the same cannot be said—or at any rate should not be assumed—for the fifth century. Responses to perceived religious differences are not exclusively located in the uppermost echelons of religious writings, and on the other hand what Teiser calls "folk religion" is—by the evidence he himself cites—not a homogeneous mass in which religious and ideological differences play no role.

Acknowledgments

A generous summer fellowship from the Provost's Office of the University of Southern California allowed me to work on this book in concentrated fashion during the summer of 2009. That summer I spent four productive weeks at the International Research Institute for Advanced Buddhology at Soka University 創価大学 in Hachioji, Tokyo, Japan. I am grateful to Soka University, as well as the director of the institute, Dr. Teranishi Hirotomo 寺西 宏友, and members of its distinguished research faculty, including Professors Kanno Hiroshi 菅野博史 and Karashima Seishi 辛嶋靜志, for the opportunity to conduct research there. My longtime friend and colleague Jan Nattier, who was also at the time on the institute faculty, moved mountains to smooth my way there and gave freely of her time and extensive knowledge despite her hectic schedule. Another old friend and colleague, John R. McRae, helped make my stay in Hachioji memorable and fun.

After moving from Los Angeles to Nashville, Tennessee, and Vanderbilt University, I was able to return to the manuscript in the summer of 2010 while in residence at two excellent facilities in Kyoto, Japan: Otani University 大谷大学, where Professor Robert F. Rhodes and Mr. Hino Jungo 日野純悟 in the Academic Services Office provided generous assistance and accommodations, and the Italian School of East Asian Studies, where director Dr. Silvio Vita and administrator Ms. Yamamoto Makimi 山本真紀美 helped to make my work pleasant and productive.

I am grateful to have had the chance to present aspects of this project to audiences at the Association for Asian Studies, Soka University, Wellesley College, the University of Southern California, the International Association of Buddhist Studies, and Princeton University. Several colleagues kindly took time to offer helpful comments on all or part of my manuscript. These include Jan Nattier and the two readers for the Kuroda series, Daniel B. Stevenson and Stephen F. Teiser. I also profited from discussing particular passages with Steve Bokenkamp, David Knechtges, Terry Kleeman, Chiew Hui Ho, and Chang Chao-jan. Thanks to all of these colleagues this is a much better book than it would otherwise have been.

Back at Vanderbilt in the fall of 2010, I received indispensable assistance from Ms. Yuh-Fen Benda at the Jean and Alexander Heard Library in acquiring sources rapidly as I completed the manuscript. Tracy Miller gave expert help in locating a suitable image for the book jacket. Jacob Thornton, GIS coordinator at Vanderbilt University, created the map. I would like to extend heartfelt thanks to the supportive colleagues and friends who have helped make my transition to Vanderbilt and Nashville a very happy one, among them Lisa Shortt Dunlop, Linda Leaming, Peter Lorge, Tracy Miller, Carol Quinn, and Ruth Rogaski. I am most grateful to the College of Arts and Science at Vanderbilt University for a generous subvention to support the publication of this book.

Pat Crosby and the staff at the University of Hawai'i Press were once again simply fabulous to work with. Pat is a treasure among editors and a lovely human being.

This project was conceived during a conversation at a Paris café in the summer of 2008 with my colleague and friend Dr. Sylvie Hureau, *maître de conférences* at the École Pratique des Hautes Études. Over the months I worked on the manuscript I benefited from many conversations with Sylvie about this and other texts. We read some of the *Mingxiang ji* stories together, and she devoted some sessions of her EPHE seminar to the text. I am grateful for her kind assistance and her friendship.

Several weeks before the manuscript went to press, a dear friend and colleague, John R. McRae, died. As an inadequate gesture of gratitude for his unwavering support over many years and his immense learning, humor, and good heart, I dedicate this book to John's memory.

Conventions

In the list of sources for each translated item, when citing Lu Xun's compendium, *Gu xiaoshuo gouchen*, and the recent Japanese work *Hōon jurin no sōgōteki kenkyū*, edited by Wakatsuki, Hasegawa, and Inagaki, what I provide are page numbers, but when citing Wang Guoliang's edition of the text, *Mingxiang ji yanjiu*, what I give is the serial number of the item in his ordering, not the page number. I have generally based my translation on the *first* of the texts listed as "source texts." Most often this is a quotation preserved in Daoshi's *Fayuan zhulin*. When deviating from this and preferring a reading found in another textual witness to the same story, I indicate in a note the alternate version or versions I am following. In cases where similar narrative material is reproduced elsewhere but not attributed directly to *Mingxiang ji*, often in significantly different wording, or else in the case of different stories in which the same protagonists appear, I list most of the relevant passages known to me under "additional texts." When translating from a text in the Taishō canon, I have often departed from the punctuation given in that edition, usually without indicating this in my notes.

Stories are arranged in the approximate chronological order of the events they depict, to the extent that this can be determined. In this I have largely followed the ordering used by both Lu Xun and Wang Guoliang in their respective editions.

Following many stories, I append a section—longer or shorter depending on the case—titled "comments." Here I record observations on the stories and certain of their details, or else I provide background to something mentioned in a tale. These comments inevitably reflect my own interests, predilections, and limitations as a reader. They trail off toward the end of the series of stories because I typically comment on themes or ideas at first mention but not later, so as to avoid needless repetition.

Generally, when the Chinese text translates the meaning of an Indic term, I translate it, and when the Chinese transliterates, I render the equivalent term in romanized Sanskrit. But I do not follow this rule consistently: *fa* 法, for example, is consistently rendered here as "Dharma," not as "law," and the various transliterative terms meaning "monk" are all alike simply rendered as "monk." (I have not distinguished in my translation between those various terms, principally *shamen* 沙門 for *śramaṇa*, *biqiu* 比丘 for *bhikṣu*, or *seng* 僧, since in this and similar texts they are used interchangeably.)

When a person or monastery is mentioned in the text and I have no information on him, her, or it, I remain silent; when I do have information, I indicate this in a footnote.

All dates given fall in the Common Era (CE) unless noted. When Chinese dates are given within the translation text, Western conversions appear in square brackets.

When quoting modern scholarly works, I silently convert all romanizations to Pinyin and all English spellings to American English, except in titles of modern publications.

In translating office titles I generally follow Hucker, *A Dictionary of Official Titles.* For converting Chinese to Western dates I have followed Fang Shiming and Fang Xiaofen, eds., *Zhongguo shiliri he zhongxi liri duizhao biao.* For converting weights and measures I have followed Wang Li, *Wang Li gu hanyu zidian*, 1807–1815.

When the translated text mentions a person's age—but only when the person in question is quite young—I convert the age into Western terms. Then as now in Chinese and some other East Asian cultures, age was counted from conception, not birth, and newborns started at one year of age.

I have preferred to use English spelling of Sanskrit terms in cases where the latter have been recognized as standardized English. Thus, except when giving the titles of modern published works, I have written "sutra" instead of *sūtra* and "sangha" rather than *saṃgha* or *saṅgha*.

I cite different sorts of Chinese primary sources differently. These citation conventions are explained in the bibliography.

Florian Deleanu has made the important point that, if one wants to prepare a good critical edition of a Chinese Buddhist canonical text, it is necessary to collate at least two editions: the one found in the very widely used *Taishō shinshū daizōkyō* 大正新修大藏經 (on the basis of which a digital edition with excellent search capability, CBETA Dianzi Fodian 電子佛典, has also been made available—one that has been invaluable in the preparation of this translation) and the one included in a relative newcomer on the scene, the *Zhonghua dazangjing* 中華大藏經, published in Beijing from 1984 to 1996.[1] The reason is that, while each of these editions is based on several earlier versions of the canon, each incorporates some versions that

---

1. See Deleanu, "The Transmission of Xuanzang's *Yogācārabhūmi*," esp. 25–26. This article also contains (pp. 7–13) the best guide to the maze of available editions of the Chinese Buddhist canon and should be consulted by anyone undertaking close work on any text from those compilations.

the other does not; to use only one edition, then, is to ignore some of the available textual witnesses. Deleanu's point is well taken. However, I have not attempted to provide a truly critical edition of the text of *Mingxiang ji*. This is because I do not believe, given the nature of the genre to which it belongs and the ways in which it was preserved for us to read (topics discussed in part 1), that such an enterprise is possible if it entails the goal of recovering a supposed urtext that flowed from Wang Yan's brush; nor do I believe the effort is otherwise worth the payoff. Some random spot-checks of *Mingxiang ji* excerpts in the Taishō-edition *Fayuan zhulin* against their Zhonghua-edition counterparts yielded no textual variants that significantly altered the plot or even the terminology. For the purposes of this study I have therefore relied on the Taishō edition. I cite the *Zhonghua dazangjing* edition only when it relates to textual variations being discussed.

Signs from the Unseen Realm

PART I

Signs from the Unseen Realm and Buddhist Miracle Tales in Early Medieval China

Introduction

As far as we know, a minuscule number of monks and laymen of foreign extraction, often with the help of Chinese assistants, began translating Buddhist scriptures from Indic languages into literary Chinese in the middle of the second century of the common era.[1] Buddhist-inspired visual imagery was deployed in various places throughout China around this same time.[2] But in this earliest period, the audience for the translated texts was vanishingly small, and the Buddhalike images that have been unearthed seem to be examples of the cross-culturally attested use of imported bits of exotic cultures as apotropaic devices—things deemed powerful not necessarily because the sacred knowledge and soteriological practices behind them were well understood but precisely for the opposite reason.[3] Not until well into the fourth century was Buddhism in China anything more than a "tiny exotic plant flowering on the ruins of the Han

---

1. For the most up-to-date study, see Nattier, *Earliest Chinese Buddhist Translations*. Zürcher, "Earliest Chinese Buddhist Texts," long the best available study of the early translations, is still well worth consulting. My blanket characterization should be qualified: some of the earliest translators (such as Zhi Qian 支謙 and Kang Senghui 康僧會) were not themselves immigrants from Western lands; they were born in Chinese-held areas. (Kang Senghui's parents were Sogdian. Sources disagree on Zhi Qian's ancestors' immigrant status.) Of the earliest translators, only An Xuan 安玄 (from Parthia), Zhi Qian, and probably Kang Mengxiang 康孟詳 were laymen; An Shigao 安世高, the earliest of them all, has been argued to have been a layman (see Forte, *The Hostage An Shigao*), but the argument has not been widely accepted. See Nattier, *Earliest Chinese Buddhist Translations*, 39–40. The others were monks.

2. See Wu, "Buddhist Elements in Early Chinese Art"; Abe, *Ordinary Images*, 11–101; Bai, "Religious Beliefs," 993–1025; and Wang-Toutain, "Entre spéculation métaphysique et dévotion," 609–611. The best recent survey of Buddhist-themed art in China in this earliest period may be found in Rhie, *Early Buddhist Art of China*, vol. 1.

3. Numerous examples are discussed, for instance, in Helms, *Ulysses' Sail*.

1

empire," in Erik Zürcher's vivid phrasing.[4] Not until that time, it appears, was Buddhism practiced by significant numbers of Chinese.[5]

It seems to have been late in the fourth century that literate Chinese men who wanted to promote Buddhist values and practices began circulating, recording, and collecting records of miraculous events.[6] These events were thought to demonstrate the power of the Buddha, bodhisattvas, monks, and nuns; to prove the efficacy of Buddhist devotional practices; to illustrate the veracity of Buddhist claims; and to warn of the consequences of violating Buddhist norms. It may be that monks and nuns numbered among the earliest recorders of such tales, but in all cases of which any record survives—and with the important exception of compilations exclusively devoted to biographies of monks and nuns—the compilers were Buddhist laymen of the gentry classes. These texts also clearly assume an audience that is not only nonmonastic but also potentially skeptical of Buddhist teachings or relatively new to Buddhist norms. They are not written in technical language for religious "insiders," and the things of which they seek to persuade readers are a subset of basic Buddhist teachings, not finer points of doctrine or advanced aspects of practice.

The resulting works deploy an already established Chinese literary genre—that of "accounts of anomalies," or *zhiguai* 志怪—for the purpose of propagating Buddhist ideas and values.[7] Although Buddhist sutra, avadāna, and jātaka literature is full of narratives of marvelous deeds and miraculous events, it had seen nothing quite like the miracle tales that were fashioned and collected in China. Among the closest analogues in Indian Buddhist literature were some of the ghost stories recounted in the *Petavatthu*, or *Stories of Hungry Ghosts* (perhaps second c. BCE, with a fifth-century CE com-

---

4. "Earliest Chinese Buddhist Texts," 293. Zürcher's *The Buddhist Conquest of China* remains the best overall study in any language of Buddhism's formative centuries in China. On the question of when and how Buddhism ceased being merely a "tiny exotic plant," see in particular pp. 71–75—although this is a portrait that I will try to complexify below. Tsukamoto Zenryū's *History of Early Chinese Buddhism* in Leon Hurvitz's translation presents a wealth of translated historical material, and Tang Yongtong's *Han Wei liang Jin nanbeichao fojiaoshi* remains useful.

5. And perhaps not for several more centuries by significant numbers of nonelite Chinese, although—in ways I will not pause to discuss here—this is notoriously difficult to determine. On the fourth-century date of inception of ordination of Chinese men as monks (other than a single earlier known case, that of Yan Fodiao 顏佛調, disciple of the translator An Shigao—and not to be confused with the Zhu Fodiao who figures in our text), see Kieschnick, "Buddhist Monasticism," 552.

6. Such records may have been compiled earlier than the fourth century, but if they were, no such works from that period have survived.

7. On the *zhiguai* genre in this period, see Li Jianguo, *Tang qian zhiguai xiaoshuo shi*; Wang Guoliang, *Wei Jin nanbeichao zhiguai xiaoshuo yanjiu*; and Campany, *Strange Writing*. For a similar, recent view of the generic origins of Chinese Buddhist miracle tales, see Martin, "Buddhism and Literature," 903–910 (although I do not agree that any contemporary authors saw a difference between some *zhiguai* tales and miracle tales on the basis that the latter, unlike the former, were held to reflect "reality," *pace* what Martin says at p. 908).

mentary), but, even there, the tales are set in the distant time of Gautama Buddha (with some mentions of earlier Buddhas), and that text draws most of its rhetorical authority from this prestigious association. In these older, South Asian Buddhist genres, it is the placement of the recounted events in the sacred past time of a Buddha (as well as the Buddha's knowledge of characters' karmic conditions from times long prior to that) that legitimates the messages conveyed.[8] As a genre, the Chinese miracle tales work very differently. They situate events in the everyday world of relatively recent times familiar to their audience—but then they introduce extraordinary elements into that world, elements that demonstrate the veracity of Buddhist claims and the power of Buddhist devotion, but without the need for a Buddha who can trace the hidden threads of karma through numerous past lives. In the miracle tales it is the very closeness between the assumed reader and the textually depicted world that works to legitimate the claims made in the texts: *this event happened to someone very much like you, in the presence of named witnesses, at a particular place and time in your country*. If "every genre has its own orientation in life,"[9] then this can serve as a rough, initial summary of the orientation of the miracle-tale genre.

Those tale collections of which any parts survive from the pre-Sui period may be listed in chronological order as follows.[10] *Responsive Manifesta-*

---

8. Not to mention that jātakas, in particular, typically recount the previous lives *of Buddhas*, and avadānas focus on the past lives of characters in the stories (knowable—at least according to the most prevalent view—only to a Buddha), while with miracle tales we are in an entirely different world: the world of the everyday as known to the reader of the text. I therefore disagree with Verellen ("Evidential Miracles in Support of Taoism," 230), who sees Chinese Buddhist miracle tales as "a major step in the continuation and adaptation of the Indian devotional genre [of avadānas]." Instead, I see miracle tales as a quite distinct genre, based on indigenous literary precedents that naturally dealt with many of the same topics and concerns as the avadānas. Recent work on avadāna and jātaka texts includes Shirkey, "The Moral Economy of the *Petavatthu*"; Rotman, "Monks, Merchants, and a Moral Economy"; Rotman, *Divine Stories*; Khoroche, *Once the Buddha Was a Monkey*; and Salomon, *Ancient Buddhist Scrolls from Gandhāra*, 35–39, 139–140. Unfortunately, work on the very extensive, early-attested, and datable Chinese versions of these texts has barely progressed beyond the monumental initial effort of Chavannes, *Cinq cents contes*.

9. Bakhtin and Medvedev, *The Formal Method in Literary Scholarship*, 131.

10. Other, similar works written in this period that are now completely lost (i.e., of which not a single verifiable item remains in any extant collectanea) include *Buxu Mingxiang ji* 補續冥祥記, or *Signs of the Unseen Realm Supplemented and Continued* by Wang Manying 王曼穎, on which more below; *Zhengying zhuan* 徵應傳 by Zhu Juntai 朱君台 (listed in the preface to Huijiao's *Gaoseng zhuan* 14.418b2); and a work titled *Xiangyi ji* 祥異記 by an unknown author, of which, depending on how one sorts out the conflicting attributions in collectanea, no actual excerpts may in fact survive. On these works see Li Jianguo, *Tang qian zhiguai xiaoshuo shi*, 419–420, 385–386, and 420, respectively. The numbers of stories or textual items listed indicates the number of *extant* items, not the (often much larger) number once likely contained in the text in question (see below for further discussion). I use "stories" and "items" interchangeably here: both terms refer to discrete textual units—in the cases of these texts, almost always discrete narratives. (The parallel terms in modern Chinese discussions of similar texts include *ze* 則 and *tiao* 條.) For details on these texts, as well as transla-

tions of Avalokiteśvara (Guangshiyin yingyan ji 光世音應驗記, 7 stories plus preface) was first written by Xie Fu 謝敷 in the late fourth century and then, after having been lost, reconstructed from memory by Fu Liang 傅亮 in the early fifth century; like two other texts listed below, it exclusively contained tales of the Bodhisattva Sound Observer's[11] miraculous, compassionate rescues of devotees from extreme distress. It was also a source for the text translated in part 2 of this volume. *Records Proclaiming Manifestations* (Xuanyan ji 宣驗記, 35 stories), plausibly attributed to Liu Yiqing 劉義慶 (403–444 CE),[12] contains miracle stories of several types and is the most similar to (and also may have been a source for)[13] the text focused on in this study. Sometime in the first half of the fifth century, Zhang Yan 張演 compiled *Continued Records of Avalokiteśvara's Responsive Manifestations* (Xu Guangshiyin yingyan ji 續光世音應驗記, 10 stories plus preface), a second collection given over solely to stories of Sound Observer's miraculous interventions. *Records of Miraculous Responses* (Ganying zhuan 感應傳, 2 stories) was compiled by Wang Yanxiu 王延秀 in the mid-fifth century. Xiao Ziliang 蕭子良 (d. 494) compiled a work seemingly titled *Records of Verifications of the Unseen Realm* (Mingyan ji 冥驗記), of which only two stories now survive.[14] *Records of Signs from the Unseen Realm* (Mingxiang ji 冥祥記), the subject of this book, was assembled by Wang Yan 王琰 around 490. In 501, Lu Gao 陸杲 (459–532), a personal acquaintance of Wang Yan, compiled *More Records of Avalokiteśvara's Responsive Manifestations* (Xi Guanshiyin yingyan ji 繫觀世音應驗記), containing 69 items plus a preface; this is the third and largest of the tale collections exclusively devoted to miracles credited

tions and studies from later texts of the same genre, see Kominami, "Rikuchō Zui Tō shōsetsushi no tenkai to Bukkyō shinkō"; Gjertson, "The Early Chinese Buddhist Miracle Tale"; Gjertson, *Gods, Ghosts, and Retribution*; Gjertson, *Miraculous Retribution*; Stevenson, "Tales of the Lotus Sūtra"; and Campany, *Strange Writing*, 68–97. Wang Guoliang's "*Mingxiang ji* xiao kao" on the *Mingxiang ji* is superseded by his monograph on that work. Other works will be cited below.

11. Except when giving the titles of tale collections, when referring to the bodhisattva Avalokiteśvara (rendered as Guangshiyin 光世音 in the twenty-third chapter of Dharmarakṣa's translation of the *Lotus Sutra* [Zheng fahua jing 10.128c–129c] and as Guanshiyin 觀世音 in the twenty-fifth chapter of Kumārajiva's translation [Miaofa lianhua jing 7.56c–58b], the latter usage reflected throughout most of *Mingxiang ji* and later often shortened to Guanyin 觀音, which became the standard form) I will render his name thus, so as to avoid possible confusion. It would be preferable to refer to this bodhisattva in a way that more closely captured the sense of his name in Chinese in this period and text, but close English equivalents are too bulky to be used frequently.

12. He is already mentioned as the compiler of a text by this title in Lu Gao's *Xi Guanshiyin yingyan ji* 8 (Makita, *Rikuchō kōitsu Kanzeon ōkenki no kenkyū*, 29), dating to 501. On this work see Li Jianguo, *Tang qian zhiguai xiaoshuo shi*, 368–372.

13. Unless perhaps the two works drew on one or more sources in common. See below for a discussion of the implications of China's early medieval manuscript culture for gauging direct intertextual borrowing. On the overlaps between *Xuanyan ji* and *Mingxiang ji*, see Wang Qing, "Jinyang Wangshi de jiashi menfeng," 151, and Liu Yuanru, *Chaoxiang shenghuo shijie*, 257–258.

14. See Li Jianguo, *Tang qian zhiguai xiaoshuo shi*, 395.

to Sound Observer.[15] *Citations of Marvels* (*Jingyi ji* 旌異記, 12 stories) was written by Hou Bo 侯白 late in the sixth century. Finally, *A Record of Signs and Marvels* (*Xiangyi ji* 祥異記, perhaps 2 extant tales) was circulated by an unknown compiler sometime in the sixth century.[16] All told, this material adds up to over 260 tales and four compilers' prefaces—a sizeable remnant of a body of writing that was once perhaps many times larger.[17]

In this book I provide a translation and study of Wang Yan's *Records of Signs from the Unseen Realm*.[18] At 129 extant items plus a substantial preface, it is by far the largest miracle-tale collection to have survived from this era, and in terms of the types of tales it contains, it is also the most representative of the genre. No manuscript copy or integral version of the text survives from premodern times. Rather, like many other texts from the early medieval period—especially compilations of discrete, relatively short narrative or descriptive entries—it has been preserved in the form of quotations in medieval collectanea. By far the most important of these, though hardly the

---

15. On the relationship between Lu Gao's and Wang Yan's compilations, see Sano, "Ō En *Meishoki* to Riku Kō *Kei Kanzeon ōkenki*."

16. *A Record of Responsive Manifestations by Relics* (*Sheli ganying ji* 舍利感應記, listed in *Sui shu* at three scrolls) was compiled by Wang Shao 王邵 during the Sui—thus postdating the period treated here. A couple dozen notices are quoted or summarized from this text in *Fayuan zhulin* 40.602ff. and *Guang hongming ji* 17.213b ff. On its context, see Wright, *The Sui Dynasty*, 135–136; Chen Jinhua, *Monks and Monarchs*; and Wang-Toutain, "Le bol du Buddha," 75–78. It is symptomatic of Sinology's privileging of narrowly political history that, in the only other entire English-language book on the Sui (Victor Xiong, *Emperor Yang of the Sui Dynasty*), the great imperial project for the distribution of Buddha relics in the years 601–604 goes unmentioned. Modern Sinologists may think that the story of the Sui polity can be adequately told without reference to its legitimizing sponsorship of the sacralization of its territories via the implantation of Buddha relics, but many of the shapers of Sui polity would have disagreed.

17. Bibliographic records in *Sui shu* and *Tang shu* give only numbers of *scrolls* for each title, not numbers of *discrete stories*, and since there was no uniform calligraphic style or manuscript format it is impossible to gauge accurately from such figures the number of stories once contained in any given text. However, it is sometimes obvious that what survives of a text can represent at most only a small fraction of its earlier content. For example, Wang Yanxiu's *Ganying zhuan*, from which only two tales survive, is listed in the *Sui shu* catalogue (*Sui shu* 33.980) as containing 8 scrolls. Only 12 stories survive from Hou Bo's *Jingyi ji*, but it is listed in the same catalogue as running to 15 scrolls. Only 35 stories from Liu Yiqing's *Xuanyan ji* survive, yet that work is listed in the same catalogue as containing 13 scrolls—to which we may compare the 129 extant items from Wang Yan's *Mingxiang ji* and a listing in the same catalogue at a length of 10 scrolls. It is also likely that other texts like the ones in this list once existed in this period but were lost before they could be excerpted in collectanea or were simply not chosen for quotation. Several candidate titles—though not as many as one might expect—may be found in the same section of the *Sui shu* catalogue. And, finally, it is extremely likely that many other such texts were compiled but never circulated widely enough to be recorded in other texts that did survive. Such texts are thus now lost to us unless some turn out to be recovered in future excavations of Six Dynasties tombs, in cave temple chambers, or in the manuscript holdings of Japanese monasteries.

18. In the pages below I will often abbreviate the title in English to *Signs from the Unseen Realm* or simply *Signs*.

only one I have drawn on, is *A Grove of Pearls in the Garden of the Dharma* (*Fayuan zhulin* 法苑珠林), completed by the monk Daoshi 道世 around 668 CE. This extraordinary compendium is organized into one hundred topical sections (*pian* 篇) unevenly divided over as many scrolls (*juan* 卷). The topics covered range from the three worlds and cosmic time schemes to mouth-washing techniques.[19] To quote Stephen Teiser's summation:

> Unlike many Chinese encyclopedias, each section of *Fayuan zhulin* begins with a narrative portion (*shuyi bu* 述意部) in which Daoshi provides an elegant and often philosophical introduction to the section. His metaphors and allusions here are largely non-Buddhist. Each section then contains extracts from varied sources, which are usually cited by name. A major part of these sources are Indian texts in Chinese translation, but Chinese canonical and non-canonical texts, historical records, second-hand reports, as well as Daoshi's own testimony, are also included. Each section ends with tales of the karmic causes of miraculous events (*ganying yuan* 感應緣). These "verifications" (or "evidence," *yan* 驗) of karmic laws are culled from a variety of Chinese sources, and usually narrate events which occurred on Chinese soil.[20]

It is in these latter, "verification" subsections that a great many quotations from Wang Yan's text, other Buddhist miracle-tale collections, and various other genres are located.[21]

We have, then, no independent access to Wang Yan's *Mingxiang ji* apart from the ways in which it is quoted in Daoshi's and other compendia assembled from the early Tang onward. One implication of this is that, barring a future discovery of early manuscript versions,[22] our characterizations of this work (and all others similarly preserved) will always be to some extent tentative. It remains possible that Wang Yan's autograph text—which ran to ten scrolls (the length mentioned in his own preface and also the length given in the *Sui shu* catalogue, completed by 656)[23] but whose number of discrete stories is unknown—contained some items differing in emphasis or surprising in content when compared to the roughly 129 items (plus a few additional fragments) that Daoshi and other compendium

---

19. For a complete listing and translation of the section titles and a summary of the contents of each (as well as its location in the work), see Teiser, "T'ang Buddhist Encyclopedias." *Mingxiang ji* is not cited in *Jinglü yixiang*—not surprisingly, since that text, as indicated by its title, does not draw excerpts from miracle tales but only from sutra and vinaya texts.

20. "T'ang Buddhist Encyclopedias," 119–120.

21. I discuss the key notion of "verification" further below.

22. As was the case, for example, with the three earliest extant tale collections concerning Sound Observer, found in a manuscript dating from the twelfth century in a monastery in Kyoto in 1943. On these texts see Makita, *Rikuchō kōitsu Kanzeon ōkenki no kenkyū*; Campany, *Strange Writing*, 68–69, 77–78, 85–86; Campany, "The Real Presence"; and Campany, "The Earliest Tales of the Bodhisattva Guanshiyin."

23. See Twitchett, *Official History under the T'ang*, 87.

makers chose to include.[24] However, an unusual number of intratextual references have been preserved among the extant excerpts, a fact that indicates the work is at least fairly well represented in them.[25] Moreover, we do have Wang Yan's preface to attest to the general purpose that guided his own work of tale collection, and what it says corresponds quite well to the content of the surviving tales.

Wang Yan and the Making of *Mingxiang ji*

No biography of Wang Yan survives. The longest narrative we have about his life is his own preface to *Records of Signs from the Unseen Realm*. That document, combined with a few laconic mentions of him in other texts, allows us to construct only a rough chronological sketch.

His clan, originally hailing from Taiyuan in the north (in present-day Shanxi province), was probably among the masses of people who migrated southward in the first several decades of the fourth century. His ancestors' and father's personal names are not recorded. There was a famous Wang clan based in Taiyuan, "only slightly less prestigious than the Wangs of Langye,"[26] but whether Wang Yan was descended from it is unclear, and in any case such descent claims were less significant in his time than one might think.[27] Judging from remarks he makes in his preface, he must have

---

24. A possible example would be the Wang Huan story discussed briefly in Appendix 1, although we must always bear in mind that the misattribution of excerpts to texts was a frequent occurrence. On the possibilities and perils of reconstructing texts from this period based on extracts preserved in printed collectanea, see most recently Dudbridge, *Lost Books of Medieval China*; see also Owen, "The Manuscript Legacy of the Tang."

25. For example: (1) One of two stories about Yu Falan (item 11) refers to the other (item 15). (2) The end of item 33 mentions the previous sequence of six stories and says that they are based on the earlier compilation of Fu Liang. (That string, incidentally, suggests, though it hardly proves, that Wang may have organized his text thematically—grouping all Sound Observer tales together, for example—and that within each theme he ordered the items chronologically.) (3) The second of two stories about Shi Daojiong refers to the other one as having come ahead of it in the text. (4) The long narrative of things seen in the afterlife in item 44 is tied off with the statement: "The rest of what [the protagonist] saw more or less resembled what was seen by Zhao Tai 趙泰 [item 5] and Xiehe 屑荷 [item 45], so I do not record them in any further detail here. Only these two bits [of description] are different, so I have recorded them here in detail."

26. Mather, "Intermarriage as a Gauge of Family Status," 215.

27. See Chittick, *Patronage and Community in Medieval China*, 92–93. At least two Wangs of past eras from Taiyuan number among the protagonists of the stories Wang Yan collected in *Mingxiang ji*, but if he understood them to be his own distant ancestors, he does not indicate this in any extant passage. Wang Qing, "Jinyang Wangshi de jiashi menfeng," 143–148, offers the "hypothesis" (*tuice* 推測, p. 144), based on the fact that Wang Yan's family lived briefly in the Wuyi area of Jiankang, that he was in fact descended from the Jinyang 晉陽 branch of the Taiyuan Wangs, which, if true, would have a number of very interesting implications, including a long-standing feud between his own clan and that of Fan Zhen (on whom see below) and a line of descent that included Wang Guobao 王國寶. Wang's suggestion, while fascinating, remains highly speculative.

been born around 454.[28] From that same document we know that he spent his infancy and early boyhood in Jiaozhi 交趾, a large commandery whose administrative seat was located northeast of today's Hanoi in northern Vietnam. Jiaozhi at the time was a thriving maritime commercial center, relatively peaceful when compared with war-plagued central China. It was also a place where foreign merchants, diplomatic officials, and intellectuals gathered, and Buddhism flourished there. Zürcher calls it a "borderland halfway between the centers of Chinese and Indian civilization,"[29] though it was probably relatively sinicized by the mid-fifth century. He Jingsong has argued that, in the early centuries of the common era, Buddhism was older and better established in Jiaozhi than in central China.[30]

Sometime between 461 and 463, according to the preface, Wang Yan and his family returned to the southern capital in Jiankang and then relocated again in 471 or so to the area on the outskirts of Jiankang known as Wuyi 烏衣. He must have developed a relationship at this time with a monk at the nearby Duobao monastery 多寶寺 in the capital, for he speaks of having entrusted his beloved Sound Observer image to this monk and temple for safekeeping while he traveled about the southeast. He mentions having passed through the gorges of the middle Yangzi region in 478–479 and having returned to the capital in that year, recovering his image at the monastery. The date of this recovery (in the middle of 479) is significant, for this was the year in which the Southern Qi dynasty supplanted the Song. It would seem, then, that Wang Yan was in the capital during these momentous political events. An obscure manuscript speaks of his having been on the personal staff of the Qi crown prince, Xiao Zhangmao 蕭長懋 (d. 493), in the early Yongming period (thus around 483), and of having petitioned around this same time—with what success we do not know—to have another small prefecture joined to the one whose revenues supplied his salary, on the ground that his family was poor.[31] Taken together, the above scraps of information suggest that Wang Yan was from a relatively insignificant family but that he was a client of powerful members of the Qi royal family.

We next hear of him as a participant in a debate in 489[32] on the im-

---

28. I here concur with Li Jianguo, *Tang qian zhiguai xiaoshuo shi*, 415, and Wang Guoliang, *Mingxiang ji yanjiu*, 3.

29. See *The Buddhist Conquest of China*, 51, and cf. 43.

30. See He, "Han Wei liang Jin nanbeichao shiqi," and the briefer study by Huang Guoan, "Zhongguo fojiao zai Jiaozhi."

31. The manuscript, titled *Wansui tongtian jintie* 萬歲通天進帖, a copy of a text written in 697 during the reign of Empress Wu Zetian, apparently exists only at the provincial museum of Liaoning. See Wang Guoliang, *Mingxiang ji yanjiu*, 3, 59–60. This document is also available online at: http://www.zgyb.org/beitie/wangsengqian001.htm (consulted on June 25, 2011).

32. Not 487, the date for these events given by Liu Yuanru, *Chaoxiang shenghuo shijie*, 200. (On p. 261 of the same work she gives the correct date.)

mortality of the soul. A passage preserved only in the *History of the Southern Regimes* (*Nan shi*) recounts that Fan Zhen 范縝, a member of the famous literary salon of Xiao Ziliang 蕭子良, prince of Jingling and the younger brother of the crown prince,[33] was resolutely anti-Buddhist, while his patron was a devout Buddhist. The prince and his guest, the passage says, entered into a debate in which Xiao Ziliang challenged Fan to explain why some people turn out to enjoy high status while others do not, if such a discrepancy is not due to "cause and result" (*yinguo* 因果), that is, karma. Fan responded that it is simply a matter of chance, like the seeds carried from trees by the wind: some happen to fall in elevated places, others in muck and mire, and there is no need to invoke karma to explain why. Xiao Ziliang, the passage says, "thought this very strange" but could not prevail upon Fan to relent. Fan then wrote and circulated a *Treatise on the Extinction of the Soul* (*Shenmie lun* 神滅論), arguing that the soul, or spirit (*shen* 神), being merely a function (*yong* 用) of the body, must perish with it at death and cannot survive independently to be reborn, as Buddhists in China argued. This treatise caused a stir, and Xiao Ziliang assembled monks to dispute it, but they, too, failed to convince Fan Zhen to back down from his position.[34] This is the point at which the passage suddenly mentions Wang Yan: "Wang Yan, [whose family hailed] from Taiyuan, then authored a treatise [*zhu lun* 著論] ridiculing Zhen, saying, 'Alas for Master Fan! He has never once realized where his ancestors' spirits are!' His intention was to stymie any further retort from Zhen. [But] Zhen replied, 'Alas for Master Wang! He realizes where his ancestors' spirits are, but he cannot sacrifice animals to serve them!' Their barbed exchanges were all of this sort."[35] The passage concludes by

---

33. The most extensive studies of this salon and the discussions centered there may be found in Jansen, *Höfische Öffentlichkeit im frühmittelalterlichen China* (on the debates), and Mather, *The Age of Eternal Brilliance* (on the large body of poems produced by three of the principals). See also Pan, *Zhongguo jushi fojiao shi*, 187–191, and Zürcher, *The Buddhist Conquest of China*, 439 n149.

34. Passages in the *Liang shu* (and see also Liebenthal, "The Immortality of the Soul," 340, 376, and Lai, "Emperor Wu on the Immortal Soul") indicate that Fan Zhen wrote and circulated this treatise early in the Liang years (that is, in or shortly after 502), but this *Nan shi* passage clearly has Xiao Ziliang (d. 494) reacting to it. Either Fan wrote more than one treatise on this theme, therefore, or his old work continued to arouse controversy and opposition more than a decade later at the Liang court. Substantial portions of the treatise are quoted in *Liang shu* 48.665–670. On these and similar debates in this period, see Jansen, *Höfische Öffentlichkeit im frühmittelalterlichen China*; Balazs, "Der Philosoph Fan Dschen"; Lai, "Emperor Wu on the Immortal Soul"; Liebenthal, "The Immortality of the Soul"; Tang Yongtong, *Han Wei liang Jin nanbeichao fojiao shi*, 334–337; and Ch'en, *Buddhism in China*, 138–142. For insightful comments on a treatise on the relation of body and spirit by Shen Yue (the most renowned literary figure among Xiao Ziliang's famous "eight friends") that surpasses these debates in sophistication, see Tian, *Beacon Fire and Shooting Star*, 229–233.

35. *Nan shi* 57.1421–1422.

saying that Xiao Ziliang then sent Wang Rong 王融 (468–493)[36] to re-
monstrate with Fan, saying that, in obstinately holding to the "obviously
baseless" (zi feili 自非理) position that the spirit perishes at death, he
risked not only "harming the 'teaching of names'" (mingjiao 名教) but
also disqualifying himself from high office.[37] Fan Zhen reportedly
laughed this off.

    For our purposes, what is significant is that we see Wang Yan weighing
in heatedly on the pro-Buddhist side in this ongoing debate, aligning himself with the powerful Xiao family and the unnamed monks summoned by
Xiao Ziliang to argue against Fan's position. The passage does not indicate
that Wang Yan was personally among the group surrounding Xiao Ziliang—unlike Fan Zhen, who is clearly said to have been present.[38] I know
of no other passage linking Wang Yan directly to Xiao Ziliang or his salon.
Wang's treatise does not survive.

    The next extant mention of Wang Yan comes in Lu Gao's More Records
of Avalokiteśvara's Responsive Manifestations (Xi Guanshiyin yingyan ji 繫觀世音
應驗記), a compilation completed in 501.[39] In one of the miracle stories collected there, Wang Yan is named as the cousin of a certain Wang Lian 璉,
who knew personally the two protagonists of the story. Wang Yan is also
identified in the passage as the "old acquaintance" (jiu 舊—or perhaps we
should understand jiu here as "client" or "patron")[40] of compiler Lu Gao; as
currently or recently serving as the governor (taishou 太守) of Yi'an 義安, a
commandery not far to the west of and up the Mian/Han river from Xiangyang, site of an important garrison headed from 498 by Xiao Yan 蕭衍, a
distant member of the Qi royal house who was very soon to seize power and

---

    36. Wang Rong was a loyal client of Xiao Ziliang and wrote cycles of songs to accompany
some of his patron's Buddhist treatises. He died in 493 as the result of a failed attempt to
place Xiao Ziliang on the throne of Qi upon the death of Emperor Wu. For studies of his life
and works, see Mather, The Age of Eternal Brilliance, vol. 2; Mather, "The Life of the Buddha
and the Buddhist Life"; and Mather, "Wang Jung's 'Hymns.'"
    37. On the sense of mingjiao 名教, which, though often treated as simply synonymous
with Confucianism, was more complex than that, and which should be understood in dy-
adic opposition to "naturalness" (ziran 自然) or "the learning of the obscure" (xuanxue 玄
學), see Zürcher, The Buddhist Conquest of China, 86–87; Mather, "Individualist Expressions
of the Outsiders," 202–203; Yü Ying-shih, "Individualism and the Neo-Taoist Movement,"
136–137; Campany, "Two Religious Thinkers," 181; and Campany, Strange Writing, 278–279,
357–358.
    38. Nor is Wang Yan mentioned in any of the poems emanating from this group, which
have been admirably collected and studied in Mather, The Age of Eternal Brilliance. (Also excellent on early Chinese Buddhist poetry is Martin, "Buddhism and Literature," 929–951.)
None of the texts studied by Mather mentions Wang Yan.
    39. On Lu Gao, who also compiled a work titled Traditions of Monks (Shamen zhuan 沙門
傳) in thirty scrolls, now lost, see Tian, Beacon Fire and Shooting Star, 69–70, 120–121. Tian
dates the preface of this work to 499 (p. 121), but it mentions Qi Zhongxing 1 (501–early
502) as the year in which the compilation was completed.
    40. See Chittick, Patronage and Community in Medieval China, 8.

found the Liang dynasty;[41] and as having authored *Mingxiang ji*.[42] From this we know that Wang Yan must have compiled *Signs* no later than 501. Extant excerpts from the work mention dates as late as the third year of the Qi Yongming reign period, that is, 485. Another excerpt says that a certain Yuan Kuo 袁廓 (see item 119) was "the present librarian [in the editorial service] of the heir apparent," that is, in the service of Xiao Zhangmao, who died in February 493. We thus have a window of time between 485 and 493 when we know *Mingxiang ji* was compiled, and, as Antonello Palumbo has suggested, it is perhaps possible to narrow the date still further to around 490[43]—just after Wang Yan's bitter exchange with Fan Zhen, which must have helped motivate him to assemble these verifications of Buddhist teachings.

Our surviving information on the latest period of Wang Yan's life is found in an entry in the *Sui shu* bibliographic catalogue. He is listed there as the author of a *Chronicle of the Song* (*Song chunqiu* 宋春秋) in twenty scrolls. This listing identifies him as prefect (*ling* 令) of Wuxing 吳興 under the Liang.[44] From this we know that he must have lived past the year 502 and that he was on good terms with—if not a member of—the extensive patronage network that helped put Xiao Yan in power.[45] The same catalogue lists him as the author of *Mingxiang ji* in ten scrolls, but that listing adds no information on his official appointments.[46] Given his date of birth and the absence of any further mentions of him in the surviving record, Wang Yan probably died in the first or early second decade of the sixth century.[47] Without this *Sui shu* catalogue entry, we would not know that he lived to see the founding of the Liang.

So much, then, for the chronological and geographic framework of his life, insofar as we are able to piece it together. What were Wang Yan's reasons for compiling *Signs from the Unseen Realm*? What was he trying to accomplish? To begin with, we must not discount the extent to which

---

41. See ibid., 80–84. For a detailed recent account in English of the rise and reign of Xiao Yan, see Tian, *Beacon Fire and Shooting Star*, 15–76.

42. *Xi Guanshiyin yingyan ji* 40 (Makita, *Rikuchō kōitsu Kanzeon ōkenki no kenkyū*, 43). A version of the same story, also mentioning the protagonists' personal acquaintance with Wang Yan's cousin, appears as item 123.

43. See Palumbo, "Dharmarakṣa and Kaṇṭhaka," 176–177 n26, an article of which I became aware—thanks to the author's kindness—just prior to submitting this work for publication. For other (and concurring, if less detailed) comments on the date of the text, see Li Jianguo, *Tang qian zhiguai xiaoshuo shi*, 415.

44. *Sui shu* 33.958. Even if the statement that he held this office in the early Liang is inaccurate, there are other good reasons for surmising that Wang Yan lived into at least the first decade of the Liang dynasty.

45. On which see Chittick, *Patronage and Community in Medieval China*, 79–94.

46. *Sui shu* 33.980.

47. All scholars who have discussed Wang Yan's probable date of death place it in the early Liang. See for example Cao Daoheng, "Lun Wang Yan," 27; and Li Jianguo, *Tang qian zhiguai xiaoshuo shi*, 415.

compiling a dossier of reports designed to vindicate Buddhism was an enterprise likely to win favor for the compiler in the social networks headed by the politically powerful Xiao family, founders (in different family branches) of both the Qi and Liang dynasties and highly visible supporters of Buddhism. Wang Yan's textual sparring with Fan Zhen before the eyes of Xiao Ziliang and his circle can be seen similarly. To point this out is not, however, to discount Wang's clear account of his Buddhist piety in the preface to the work. I translate the preface below and offer further comments on it there. Here I want to consider what it tells us about Wang Yan's reasons for compiling the work.

The preface opens with a narrative of Wang's lifelong relationship to a small votive image of the Bodhisattva Sound Observer that he was given as a child by a monk in Jiaozhi. Twice the image appears to him in important dreams that spur him to save it from theft or recover it after it has been lost. He also recounts an occasion on which it miraculously gave off light. With the statement, "Today I regularly make offerings to this image," and the claim that it (or his activity of making offerings to it) acts as a vehicle for his own deliverance from sin and rebirth, he shifts to the present time. Wang then says that it was in reflecting on his personal history with this image that he decided to compile *Mingxiang ji*: "Turning over in my mind the incidents involving the image, I was deeply moved, and so I tracked down more such signs and visions and stitched them together to make this record."[48] Later in the document he appears to say that he intends his collection of cases to persuade skeptical readers to "take refuge"—that is, to perform the ritual act by which one declared oneself a follower of the Buddha, his Dharma, and the Buddhist community. In short, we might say that the primary karmic reason for Wang Yan's authorship of the text was his personal relationship with his votive image of Sound Observer, and that his primary stated aim in writing was to persuade readers to become devout Buddhists like himself.

What sort of text did Wang Yan write in order to accomplish this aim? He wrote a collection of historical cases—relatively brief narratives of incidents alleged to have actually occurred, assembled in his work because, taken together, they constituted a dossier of evidence for the truth of Buddhist claims about the unseen world, the soul's survival of physical death, karma, rebirth, the efficacy of devotional acts, and the perils of slandering the Dharma or violating the sanctity of Buddhist images and sutras. The work amounted to an episodic history of "signs" of Buddhism's spiritually responsive efficacy in China from the beginnings up to the present.[49] Wang

---

48. Translating *yan ci weidi zhui cheng siji* 沿此徵覯綴成斯記. The wording is the same in all extant versions.

49. It is possible that Wang arranged his items chronologically to stretch from the prestigious beginnings under Han emperor Ming to very recent times (and including his own experience as narrated in the preface). It is also possible that he arranged the stories in no particular order, simply adding items as he collected them.

was not the first author of a dynastic history to collect historical cases of anomalous events in a separate work for the purpose of making religious and moral arguments: a century and a half earlier, Gan Bao 干寶, author of a well-received *Jin Annals* (*Jin ji* 晉紀), had famously done the same thing with his *Records of an Inquest into the Spirit World* (*Soushen ji* 搜神記), and some other compilers of "accounts of anomalies," or *zhiguai*, also wrote dynastic chronicles.[50] None of this is surprising, since the collection and recording of accounts of anomalies was understood at the time as a branch of history and not as a free-form genre of "fiction" in the modern sense.

The title Wang Yan chose for his work announced its participation in the *zhiguai* genre and told readers what, in general terms, they could expect it to contain.[51] Readers would have assumed from its title that *Mingxiang ji* would be a record (*ji* 記) of cases in which the true nature of the hidden world (*ming* 冥) had been indicated by striking, anomalous, portentous events—that is, by signs (*xiang* 祥).[52] *Xiang* 祥 is a word emanating from divination: since Eastern Zhou times it had denoted phenomena understood to carry some nonobvious meanings that must be unlocked by a hermeneutic method or an interpreter. The collection and interpretation of portents was arguably the single most important way in which new imperial regimes justified their assumption of power, since portents were said to

---

50. Among them are Wu Jun 吳均 (469–520), compiler of *Xu Qi Xie ji* 續齊諧記; Zu Chongzhi 祖沖之 (429–500), compiler of *Shuyi ji* 述異記 (a chronicle he compiled, now lost, is listed in *Sui shu* 35.1075); and Dai Zuo 戴祚 (flourished late in the Eastern Jin period), compiler of *Zhenyi zhuan* 甄異傳. On these texts and compilers see Li Jianguo, *Tang qian zhiguai xiaoshuo shi*; Wang Guoliang, *Wei Jin nanbeichao zhiguai xiaoshuo yanjiu*; Wang Guoliang, *Liuchao zhiguai xiaoshuo kaolun*; Takeda, *Chūgoku no setsuwa to kōshōsetsu*; Liu Yuanru, *Chaoxiang shenghuo shijie*; Liu Yuanru, *Shenti, xingbie, jieji*; Liu Yuanru, "Xingjian yu mingbao"; and Campany, *Strange Writing*, 67–68, 83–84, 87–88. On Gan Bao and the arguments advanced in *Soushen ji*, see ibid., 146–150, and Campany, "Two Religious Thinkers." For the argument that most texts of the *zhiguai* genre collected reports of anomalies for the purpose of *demonstrating actual regularity* in the workings of the unseen world and its relations with living people, see Campany, *Strange Writing*, and Liu Yuanru, "Xingjian yu mingbao," where essentially the same view is articulated, apparently independently (although *Strange Writing* is cited once in passing in a way that does not engage any of its central arguments). In *Shenti, xingbie, jieji*, 15–16, Liu Yuanru notes the overlap between her work on *zhiguai* and my own but seems to suggest that the notion that some works in that genre argued for "regularities" (*chang* 常) was not only her own "discovery" (*faxian* 發現) but also was absent from my own work, whereas in fact a substantial portion of *Strange Writing* (to wit, 343–394), not to mention other studies, some of which predated her work (ranging from two studies of return-from-death accounts [published in 1990 and 1995] to one focused on ghost narratives [1991] and two focused on Buddhist tales [1993, 1996], and most recently "Two Religious Thinkers" [2005]—all are listed in the bibliography) argued just this point.

51. On the structure of most titles of works in the *zhiguai* genre, see Campany, *Strange Writing*, 28–29. For a recent, parallel discussion, see Liu Yuanru, *Chaoxiang shenghuo shijie*, 203–204.

52. That the work would contain a string of many particular cases, rather than one big anomalous event, was implied by the phrase *xiang ji*, since readers would have associated *xiang* with omens that were usually collected in series.

reveal the mandate of Heaven.[53] In the case of *Mingxiang ji* and other Buddhist miracle tales, however, the "signs" collected in the text are not subtle
mysteries requiring specialist decoding:[54] their meaning is evident to most
any reader—although, as we will see, such texts have their ways of steering
the reader toward the desired inferences.

   If *Mingxiang ji* is a compilation of "signs," or *xiang*, what about the *ming*
冥 of the title? Leon Hurvitz, in translating Tsukamoto Zenryū's history of
early Chinese Buddhism into English, rendered *Mingxiang ji* as "Record of
Mysterious Good Fortune,"[55] but this is an undertranslation. *Ming* here is
not as a property of the signs themselves; it names that of which they are
signs, that which is revealed, elucidated, or made manifest in the signs collected in the text. *Ming*'s root meaning is that which is hidden, dark, or
obscure. That it is a *realm* so denominated in this case—the realm of spirits, gods, Buddhas and bodhisattvas, the dead, the afterlife, in short, the
whole teeming cosmos of beings we normally do not see but which (this
and similar texts argue) is no less real for being normally invisible to us—is
made clear by the content of the work, which consists not of subtly mysterious portentlike clues or anomalies of just any kind but of miracles that
demonstrate, or show forth the existence and *modus operandi* of, an unseen
order of things. This nominal use of *ming* found precedent in a chapter
title of *Huainan zi* (second c. BCE) and also in other early medieval works,
including Tao Hongjing's *Zhou shi mingtong ji* 周氏冥通記, or *Master Zhou's
Communications with the Unseen World*. Similar terms include *xuan* 玄 (dark,
obscure), indicating the obscure but ultimate realities or principles of the
cosmos, and *you* 幽 (hidden, concealed), as used in the title of the fifth-
century *zhiguai* collection *Youming lu* 幽明錄, *Records of the Hidden and Visible
Worlds*—records, that is, of instances where these two worlds visibly and
vividly intersected.[56]

   Finally, there is the *ji* 記 of the title. This generic suffix signals that,
rather than being a treatise or discourse (that is, a *lun* 論), Wang Yan's text
is a *record* of historical cases.[57] As we will see, it is every bit as argumentative
as any essay, but it presents its arguments in narrative form. It does not
systematically set forth the principles of the unseen realm, but, taken as a

---

53. See among others Lippiello, *Auspicious Omens and Miracles*; Goodman, *Ts'ao P'i Transcendent*; and Wechsler, *Offerings of Jade and Silk*.
   54. A few of them do, however, carry political significance; see items 41, 63, 108, and
109.
   55. As for example in Tsukamoto, *A History of Early Chinese Buddhism*, 201.
   56. The titular parallelism increases if we read the *ming* in *Youming lu* verbally, so that
the title would connote "records of cases in which the hidden world (*you*) became clearly
visible (*ming*)." *Ming* is often used adjectivally, as for example in Buddhist sutras, to describe
persons who are "benighted" or "in the dark," but in the nominal usages discussed here it
has no such negative connotation—though it does have a slightly baleful one in some settings, as did most other references to the dead and the afterlife in China in this period.
   57. On the *lun*, or "discourse," as a rhetorical form, see most recently Schaberg, "Prose
and Authority," 506–509.

whole, its stories limn the shape of that realm almost as surely as a systematic exposition could, and much more vividly. *Mingxiang ji*, then, is a collection of miracle stories. Each story narrates events that contravene an implied everyday perspective on how the world normally works; that is to say, each story narrates *extraordinary* events—there is the *xiang* element again.[58] The shape of these events reveals the nature of the other world, and the intended effect is cumulative: a single account of what was seen by a protagonist who dies and returns to life, for example, might be taken as a chance event or one individual's fanciful invention or delusional imagining; a succession of a dozen or more such accounts—each of them tied to a particular, named Chinese protagonist more or less like the text's presumed reader—inexorably suggests that what these protagonists experienced is the way the afterlife really is. Each narrative affords a particular glimpse of the workings of the unseen world, as a forest clearing at night is suddenly illuminated by successive flashes of lightning.

The shapers of these stories were acutely aware that some readers and hearers would doubt their veracity. That is why they equipped many of them with numerous *confirmatory devices*—narrative turns and details that not only reinforce the sense that the events really occurred but also demonstrate that they can only have been due to the causes posited for them in a Buddhist worldview (rather than being accidental, say, or due to the intervention of indigenous gods). For example, a woman donates devotional canopies for use during rituals in a Buddhist temple. A man appropriates the fabric and has it made into waist sashes. Soon he falls seriously ill, and the text specifies that "the sores started at the points on his waist where he had worn the sashes" (item 75). Or a man conversing about the afterlife with a deceased friend who is visiting him in ghostly form is told, as their

---

58. Teiser and Stone write: "'Miracle' in English implies a divine intervention that temporarily suspends the natural order. Stories of the kind referred to here [i.e., stories of striking, anomalous events involving the *Lotus Sutra*], however, describe events that, while remarkable or even awe-inspiring, are nonetheless presented as instances of a universal—and therefore eminently natural—causal law" ("Interpreting the *Lotus Sūtra*," 34). The point is well taken. On the other hand, while the events depicted in *Mingxiang ji* and similar texts are certainly presented as instantiations (and indeed verifications) of karmic law, they are also, *from both protagonists' and implied readers' points of view*, presented as surprising, shocking, paranormal, and strange—as interruptions of the ordinary, normally apparent everyday course of things. As a rough, preliminary characterization we might say that these events as depicted in such texts are "miracles" not in an ontological sense ("nature" does not get "suspended") but in an epistemological one: they alert characters in the stories and hearers and readers of the stories to the existence of beings, places, and states of affairs normally hidden from their view. To put it another way, the workings of karma and "stimulus-response" (*ganying*, on which more below) may be asserted in Buddhist texts to be as inexorable as clockwork, but they did not seem that way to many people (in early medieval China and in many other places and times), as a glance at any of the narratives below will instantly and powerfully convey: hence the persuasive need for the stories collected in such texts. With this qualification, I see no reason not to continue to refer to the narratives of this genre as "miracle tales."

conversation ends, that they will meet again in three years. The story con-cludes, "He did indeed die three years later" (54). Such details represent attempts to control how the story would be received: other possible expla-nations for the reported events are preemptively discounted in favor of the one the narrative's makers preferred.[59]

What we know of Wang Yan's life tallies with the contents of *Signs from the Unseen Realm* in several respects. First, although his clan was of north-ern origin, he, like many of his contemporaries in the official classes, spent his entire life in the south—including, in his case, an early boyhood in far-southern Jiaozhi—and he served two southern dynasties. It is therefore no surprise that the non-Chinese invaders of the northern provinces during his era are portrayed in an extremely negative light in the tales. They are shown—here as in many other Chinese texts—as barbaric, rapacious, im-pious, and cruel. If this work were our only evidence we would have little idea that any rulers of the northern dynasties practiced any form of Bud-dhism. Wang's service as governor of Yi'an in the last few years of the fifth century almost certainly would have put him in command of defensive op-erations against elements of a massive force led south from Luoyang to the banks of the Han river by the Tabgatch Wei ruler Yuan Hong (Emperor Xiaowen) in the winter of 494–495 and again in 497–498.[60] Many of the stories he collected portray ethnic Chinese desperately fleeing for their lives in the face of such incursions and being tortured or executed if cap-tured.[61] Secondly, given Wang's personal devotion to his image of Sound Observer, it is no surprise to find that tales of that bodhisattva's dramatic rescues of supplicants in distress are the most frequent type of narrative to have survived from his collection. Third, and for the same reason, it is no surprise to find that miraculously responsive images often figure in the stories he compiled. Fourth, a great many of the stories he collected fea-ture people who die and return to life, telling of an afterlife in which souls survive the death of the body; or dead people who return as ghosts to visit the living; or people who have visions of the persons they were in former lives; or people who recall details from their former lives—all of these story types clearly meant to refute the claim by Fan Zhen and others that no part of us survives death to be reborn.[62] Finally, the large majority of protago-

---

59. Similar devices can be found in Wang Yan's own preface, as well as in items 2, 3, 23, 72, 77, 78, 86, 87, 100, and 107, among others. This rhetorical device also appears in avadāna literature, as for instance in the story of Koṭikarṇa, where the protagonist visits the realm of hungry ghosts, learns information from certain ghosts he meets there, and later upon visit-ing their hometowns finds the information strikingly confirmed (e.g., buried treasure is found exactly where the ghost said it would be). See Rotman, *Divine Stories*, 47–60, and Cha-vannes, *Cinq cents contes*, 2:245–257, 4:172–174.

60. See Chittick, *Patronage and Community in Medieval China*, 76.

61. For a good recent treatment of what the author aptly terms "the construction of the North and South" via texts, and the radical dependence of such constructions on authorial points of view, see Tian, *Beacon Fire and Shooting Star*, 310–366.

62. As pointed out by Cao Daoheng, "Lun Wang Yan," 31, and others.

nists are midlevel officials like Wang himself. This is hardly an accident. Nor does it allow us to conclude that such officials and their families were the only lay practitioners of Buddhism in China at the time. But what it does point to is the likely sources of most of his stories. Wang must have learned of the stories he collected through networks of narrative exchange in the decades leading up to the 490s. It is to those networks that I now turn.

Miracle Tales and the Communities That Exchanged Them

In this section I will make three points: the stories found in *Mingxiang ji* were mostly compiled by Wang Yan from various sources, not invented by him from whole cloth; they were collectively fashioned by many parties; and most of them are accounts of events claimed to have happened to one or more named individuals. I begin with this last point.

Early medieval Chinese Buddhist miracle tales constitute, as I said above, a subset of the genre known as *zhiguai*, or "accounts of anomalies." One particular feature of the miracle-tale genre must be made clear at the outset to avoid misunderstanding: the stories are not parables or fables; like fables, they are marshaled to make doctrinal or moral points, but unlike fables they are not presented as having been *made up* for this purpose. Rather, each story claims to represent someone's personal experience as relayed via a relatively short chain of transmission. Each, that is, to use (somewhat loosely) the terminology of folklore studies, is a memorate:[63] a second-, third-, or fourth-hand narrative of events portrayed as having happened to someone in particular, and (I would add) a narrative that engages issues of sufficient importance to sustain the interest of narrative communities across multiple links in the chain of transmission.[64]

Ethnographic accounts afford a closer glimpse than most historical

---

63. I here cite a few folklore studies I have consulted, although some of them strike me as conceptually confused: Dégh and Vázsonyi, "The Memorate and the Proto-Memorate" (I follow this article in expanding the category "memorate" beyond first-person narratives); Dégh, *Legend and Belief*; Tangherlini, "It Happened Not Too Far from Here"; and Honko, "Memorates and the Study of Folk Beliefs." One of the founders of folklore studies, C. W. von Sydow, apparently imagined it possible for there to be purely personal narratives that had nothing "poetical" in them, with "poetical" elements being added later by other narrators. I reject this dichotomy. *The key differentia for my purposes is not whether an account is "poetical" or not; all stories are "poetical" all the way down. It is, instead, a matter of how close an extant version of a story is to parties personally present at or involved in the recounted events.* Is the account connected by a chain of personal relations and narrative exchanges to the perceived events themselves and the circle of people involved in the event, or is there no such connection? This connection is important, in my view, *not* because it allows us to reconstruct "what really happened" but because it allows us to tie a story to a particular community of narrators and audiences who regarded it as at least a possibly credible account of events.

64. On the interest that is necessary to sustain the exchange of narratives, see below and Barbara Smith, "Narrative Versions, Narrative Theories."

materials of the initial formation of memorates; their connection to specific, local beliefs and practices; and how they are sometimes taken up by writers for translocal dissemination. I here present one example. Although this one is unusual, as memorates go, for its reflexive quality (in that the eventual recorder of the memorate is also its protagonist), we will see further on that its reflexive quality makes it an appropriate choice for our purposes.

In the 1970s, an anthropologist, Stanley Brandes, wrote of a fieldwork experience he had in a village in the state of Michoacán, Mexico. Chatting with two friends while waiting for a baptism service to start in a nearby church, he offered them each a cigarette, then took one for himself. After lighting their smokes, he used the same match to light his own, muttering, "This means bad luck, but I'll do it anyway." Asked to explain his statement, the anthropologist said that some of his countrymen believed it was bad luck to give more than two lights from the same match, because the third person was liable to misfortune, even death. At this point in his narrative he mentions to us readers—though apparently he did not mention to his friends—a legend that was employed to explain this belief, tracing it back to World War I trench warfare, when the third party to use a match risked being targeted by enemy gunfire. In any case, his Mexican friends dismissed the belief and custom as nonsense, and the anthropologist agreed. The three of them were then called in to the baptism. During the service, the anthropologist recalled that he had left his shoulder bag and camera case outside, but when he rushed out to retrieve them, they were already gone. "By nightfall, the course of events was clear, at least to the people of [the village]," Brandes explains. "It had been negligent of me to leave the bag outside the church, but the theft would not have occurred had I not lit my cigarette with that over-used match. The incident provided unmistakable confirmation of the superstition to which I had introduced them."[65] Five years later, Brandes returned to the village to find that the story of the match and the stolen bag, far from having been forgotten, was spontaneously recounted by many who had attended the baptism that day and even by some who had not been present. While not everyone in the village knew the story, many did, and not only did they tell it with gusto and relative accuracy, they also drew on it to justify their new custom of not lighting more than two cigarettes from a single match. "A memorate had been born," concludes Brandes—a story told secondhand and thirdhand that was on its way to becoming a "true legend" that would be more or less codified as it spread farther in space and time from its original circle of witnesses and that might continue to be cited as a local explanation of the new belief and custom involving matches.[66]

And then, in some cases, along comes a writer interested in collecting

---

65. "The Creation of a Mexican Memorate," 163.
66. Ibid., 163–164.

stories such as these for translocal dissemination, to make a set of points to readers elsewhere. In the above example, that role is played by the anthropologist himself. Whether or not people in the village of Tzintzuntzan are now, almost forty years on (as I write these lines), still lighting only two cigarettes per match and telling the story of the theft of Brandes's bag to explain why, the story they told back then is preserved, frozen in time and distributed, via the mechanisms of printing and academic-journal distribution, across geographic and linguistic borders to make points about things other than the use of matches. In the case of *Mingxiang ji*, this role of writer and translocal disseminator was initially played by Wang Yan, who gathered up stories from as early as three centuries before his own time. It was successively played by the medieval scholarly intermediaries who selectively anthologized Wang's stories to make points of their own. And now, in a way no one in early medieval China could have foreseen, this same role is also being played by me, making yet other points to you.

Works in the *zhiguai* genre, as well as hagiographies, were compilations of previously circulating material, however much it is true that the compilers selected and shaped their material. Of this there can be little doubt.[67] Wang Yan, far from trying to hide the compilative nature of his text, states it plainly: "I tracked down more such signs and visions and stitched them together to make this record." The sewing metaphor in the last phrase (*zhui cheng si ji* 綴成斯記) clearly points to a process of collecting and arranging existing material. But the best indications that *Mingxiang ji* was compiled of material from many sources, and the best clues as to what those sources were, are found in the work itself.

At least eighteen stories in the text say something about how they came to be transmitted.[68] One of the most striking examples is the lengthy story of Zhao Tai (item 5). In its opening, the story tells of how the protagonist died, then revived to tell of what he saw in the other world. The phrase "Tai said that when he first died" opens a frame around the protagonist's account of his terrifying spirit-journey. These are all features typical of return-from-death narratives, a common story type in the text (on which

---

67. For further discussion, see Campany, *Strange Writing*, 179–199; Campany, *To Live as Long as Heaven and Earth*, 102–108; Campany, *Making Transcendents*, 8–22; and Liu Yuanru, *Chaoxiang shenghuo shijie*, 256, 355. Unfortunately, in Liu's only citation of my work in her most recent publication (ibid., 355 n19), she attributes to me precisely the view that I have been opposing in print for the past fifteen years, namely, that *zhiguai* texts were freestanding creations rather than selective compilations. She uses *Strange Writing* as a straw man to represent what she calls, in a moment of reverse Orientalism, a "Western" valuation of independent creation over compilation and editing, even though, in the book she here cites (and in my subsequent statements on the genre), I have argued the same position she does.

68. As Stephen Bokenkamp points out (personal communication), this is the sort of string of characters often omitted by editors, so the fact that eighteen such passages survived is striking. For another recent discussion of the likely sources of Wang Yan's material, see Wang Qing, "Jinyang Wangshi de jiashi menfeng," 149–154.

more below). The last thing Zhao reports of his experience in the purgatories is a parting message from an official there: "As he was about to depart, the supervisor said, 'Having seen what the retribution for sins in the purgatories is like, you should inform the people of the world, causing them to do good. The [effects of] good and evil deeds follow people like shadows and echoes. Can one afford not to be vigilant?'" These lines make explicit the charge that, in a sense, underlies all the miracle tales: *Having seen these things, go and warn others.* The seeing, even if it amounted to just one person's experience, has collective implications. It is not simply a private affair. The frame around Zhao Tai's account of his experience now closes, and we move back to the setting in which—and the means by which—he answered the charge he had been given: "At the time, the friends and relatives listening to Tai's account numbered fifty or sixty. Tai himself wrote an account to show to people of his day. This occurred on the thirteenth day of the seventh month of the fifth year of the Taishi period [269]. Tai thereupon, on behalf of his grandfather, grandmother, and two younger brothers, invited members of the sangha and hosted great gatherings for [the bestowal of] fortune. He commanded that all his sons and grandsons mend their ways and observe the Dharma, and he encouraged them to practice with vigor." We here catch a glimpse, first, of the sizeable audience gathered to hear the protagonist's initial telling of his tale: fifty or sixty friends and relatives. Zhao then, in addition to performing acts of merit (for the benefit of specific family members) and exhorting his relatives to more vigorous practice of the Buddhist precepts, creates a written account (*zi shu ji* 自書記) to be circulated more widely.

We have other explicit mentions of documents written by persons situated close to miraculous events. In the conclusion to item 116, we read: "These events happened in the last year of the Taishi period [471–472]. Someone in the monastery who was fond of accounts of such affairs [*qi si hao shi zhe* 其寺好事者] made a detailed record of these matters [*yi ju tiao ji* 已具條記]." Item 91, after recounting the story of a monk's self-immolation, mentions an eyewitness, one Zhang Bian, who "recounted [the events] in detail in a eulogy." Item 39, on the heels of a story in which a group of workmen catch sight of a spirit-monk on a mountain from a great distance, adds: "One of them who was able to write circulated an account of the whole matter." Such written documents of various genres, treasured by families and circulated among friends and sympathizers—by those with some *interest* in telling, preserving, and spreading the narrative—doubtless formed a major source of material for Wang Yan and other compilers of miracle tales.

Often, as in the cases of Zhao Tai and Zhang Bian, the person mentioned as a transmitter of the tale is also said to have been an eyewitness to events recounted there, or at least to have been personally acquainted with the protagonist. Item 11, for example, set sometime during the years 280–289, recounts a miracle that occurred in the home of one Di Shichang. The monk Yu Falan (himself the protagonist of another *Mingxiang ji* tale), a personal acquaintance who was often invited to merit-making meals at Di's home, is implied to have been present at the time. The tale closes by saying that "Falan spoke of these events to his disciple Fajie, and Fajie spoke of it often, so that there were many religious and lay who heard about it." It is unclear from such a passage just how the story finally reached Wang Yan himself. But what is clear is that the early links in this chain of transmission started with someone who was a personal acquaintance of the tale's protagonist, someone implied to have been present during the miraculous event, and that a second, younger, named individual was instrumental in spreading the story more widely. What is more, the layman-monk relationship is mentioned as the nexus of transmission, suggesting that the often-described merit meals hosted by lay families were perhaps a context in which monks recounted miracle tales as part of the discourses on Dharma they were expected to deliver on such occasions.[69] Similarly, in item 28 a monk, Zhi Daoshan, is said to have been acquainted with a man who, on his advice, had invoked the Bodhisattva Sound Observer when falsely imprisoned. The man miraculously escaped. The story ends by saying that Daoshan, for his part, later crossed the Yangzi river and "told of this incident in detail to the layman Xie Fu"—Xie Fu being the compiler of the earliest collection of Sound Observer miracle tales. Item 33 ends by noting that this same Xie Fu had personally known a monk who experienced one of the bodhisattva's miraculous interventions.[70] Item 65 ends by naming a monk who, though not claimed to have witnessed the recounted miraculous events himself, had grown up in the same hamlet as the protagonist, had given him the lay precepts, had heard him tell of the miracle, and had been at his bedside when he died. In some cases (e.g., items 42, 60, and 111) the story simply names eyewitnesses without specifying to whom they spoke concerning the recounted events.

On the other hand, sometimes a narrator is mentioned as having recounted a story without having witnessed the events in question. Item 102, for instance, names a monk who recounted miracles during his travels through the Jiangnan region at the end of the Yuanjia period—just the time when Wang Yan himself had been born. Perhaps a family member or older acquaintance orally relayed this tale to him when he was gathering

---

69. Compare the suggestive discussion in Rotman, *Divine Stories*, 23–30. It would be tempting to speculate—though at this writing I know of no direct evidence for the notion, whether in this text or in other sources—that some of our tales were first recorded by monks, whether in full or telegraphic form, as prompts for their discourses in lay households and in sermons to lay and monastic audiences. We do at least know that monks often told such tales, although, again, it is also telling that all extant compilations are the work of laymen. So far as we can glean from *Mingxiang ji*, the use of pictures played no role in these narrative exchanges (*pace* Mair, *Painting and Performance*).

70. For a study of Xie Fu as a representative of Eastern Jin lay Buddhism, see Ji, "Dong Jin jushi Xie Fu kao."

material, or perhaps a written record of it came into his hands. We find similar passages in items 4, 31 (where the transmitter is Xi Chao, author of the well-known treatise *Essentials in Upholding the Dharma* [*Fengfa yao* 奉法要], discussed further below), and 121. There would seem to have been little point in including the names of past persons who recounted the story unless those names had come attached to the tale in Wang Yan's sources, whether written or oral.

In item 86 we find the following scenario: miraculous events befell a certain family; a neighbor of that family "transmitted [this story] to" (*chuan yu* 傳於) another named individual, one Dongyang Wuyi; "and there were many who saw the events at the time." Now, Dongyang Wuyi was himself the compiler of a collection of anomaly accounts, *Qi Xie's Records* (*Qi Xie ji* 齊諧記).[71] It is unclear when he died, but we know that he held office during the Song, and this story is set in Yuanjia 9 (432), about twenty years before Wang Yan was born. It seems likely, then, that Dongyang Wuyi, a man who took enough interest in tales of anomalies to have made his own collection, left a record of the story he had heard from the neighbor of the protagonist—even though such a story does not number among the fragments attributed to *Qi Xie ji* that happen to have survived—and that Wang Yan had seen, heard, or somehow come into possession of that record (or someone else's permutation of it) and included a version in his own collection. Another *zhiguai* compiler, Liu Jingshu 劉敬叔, who might have been a much older contemporary of Wang Yan, is twice mentioned (in items 21 and 56) in *Mingxiang ji*, once as having personally seen a particular numinous copy of a sutra and once as having witnessed the miraculous events narrated in a tale.[72] Again it seems plausible that records or oral transmissions made by Liu Jingshu (or some intermediate versions of these) were Wang Yan's source for these tales. In the case of the two earlier collections of stories involving Sound Observer miracles, we know that they were Wang Yan's source for a handful of tales, since he refers to the compilers by name in his text and there is close overlap in wording—with complete overlap in content—between his versions of the stories in question and those found in the twelfth-century manuscript. One mention of them is particularly interesting for our purposes: one Xu Rong, protagonist of the miracle tale in question, later served in Kuaiji, where Xie Fu heard him speak of his

---

71. On this text and the meaning of its title, see Li Jianguo, *Tang qian zhiguai xiaoshuo shi*, 387–389; Zhou Ciji, *Liuchao zhiguai xiaoshuo yanjiu*, 109–110; and Campany, *Strange Writing*, 80–81, 87, 151–152. That it was quite current and intertextually referred to during Wang Yan's years is indicated by the fact that Wang's contemporary, the famous literary figure Wu Jun 吳均 (469–520), titled his own *zhiguai* collection (on which see ibid., 87–88) in a way indicating its generic derivation from Dongyang's text.

72. Liu Jingshu was the compiler of *A Garden of Marvels* (*Yiyuan* 異苑). On him and this work, of which relatively many excerpts survive, see Li Jianguo, *Tang qian zhiguai xiaoshuo shi*, 372–381; Zhou Ciji, *Liuchao zhiguai xiaoshuo yanjiu*, 98–108; Liu Yuanru, *Shenti, xingbie, jieji*, 133–185; and Campany, *Strange Writing*, 78–80.

experience. Next, the same passage names two individuals, a monk and a layman, who were eyewitnesses to the recounted miracle. They in turn spoke of it to Fu Liang, the son of a friend of Xie Fu and the man who re-compiled from memory the stories Xie Fu had gathered after the latter's text was lost. The story (item 32) concludes by stating: "What they said matched what Rong had said." In addition to relaying Wang's source for the story, then, this passage also claims veracity for its account of events by noting the matching testimony of multiple independent witnesses.

Wang mentions family relationships as the conduits for some of his tales. In item 122 he reveals that the wife of his wife's great-grandfather had been a witness to a miraculous healing. In item 123 he says that his cousin, Wang Lian, was a personal acquaintance of the two protagonists of that tale of a miraculous intervention by Sound Observer. Both statements are made in the first person. Elsewhere, when Wang mentions that the pro-tagonist of a tale was still living at a certain place at the time he was compil-ing his text, we may surmise that Wang had spoken personally with the informant, had received a written communication from him, or knew someone who had.[73]

If, then, *Mingxiang ji* is a compilation of preexisting stories, whose sto-ries were they? Who made them, and who transmitted them? We have al-ready seen many hints in the discussion above, but here I want to step back from the details and sketch a more general answer. Once it is clear whose stories these were, we will also be in a position to see why they constitute such invaluable evidence for the history of Buddhism in China, as well as why Wang Yan and others were so keen to collect and circulate them.

I begin by returning to the case of Zhao Tai mentioned above. After relating how Zhao, on returning from his tour of the purgatories, "himself wrote an account" of his experiences "to show people of his day," item 5 continues as follows: "When his contemporaries heard that Tai had died and revived, and had seen in detail [the results of] sin and merit, they came in succession to ask him about it. At the time, some ten people, in-cluding Superior Grand Master of the Palace Sun Feng, a native of Wucheng, and Marquis Within the Passes Hao Boping of Changshan, gathered at Tai's home and asked in great detail about what he had seen. All went away fearful, and all became observant of the Dharma." Within the frame of Zhao Tai's story, these lines depict the reception of that story by others and its impact on them. A small community of interlocutors

---

73. One other feature of the text may preserve traces of its nature as a compilation. Six items (19, 25, 26, 69, 84, and 91) end with ellipses, indicated by the markers *yun* 云 or *yun yun* 云云, meaning "and so on" and signaling that the text at this point breaks off from its quota-tion or paraphrase of another document. It is impossible to tell, however, whether these el-lipses were included by Wang Yan in his own work or by (for example) Daoshi in his selective quotation from Wang's text. This is a technique Daoshi is known to have used elsewhere. The variant endings of item 84 in various sources suggest that there, at least, the ellipsis was added by Daoshi.

forms around Zhao Tai. Moved by fear to heightened religious observance, these persons doubtless tell his story to others, and those persons to yet others, and so it spreads along narrative networks until a version of it comes to be selected and transcribed by Wang Yan. It is because of this *narrative community* that the story was deemed to matter. Until these other people heard it, were impacted by it, and responded in ways that led (among other things) to their mention here, it was simply one person's story of his experience. But because of their responses and subsequent actions it became a narrative that was collectively fashioned and spread along social networks. It became, in other words, an artifact of collective memory. It is also because of this same narrative community—along with the compilative work of Wang Yan and others (including the others who drew on Wang Yan's compilation in making their own)—that the story survived for us to read today. It is this narrative community, this *community of estimation*—a dispersed community of people who received, sized up, commented upon, retold, were moved by, remembered, and helped to preserve stories—that left traces in the text of the sort seen above. Only occasionally does it rise to the surface of the text in an explicit mention,[74] but this community of storytelling and of estimation underlies all the extant stories and is itself a primary reason we have them to read.[75]

It is necessary to remind ourselves constantly of this community, because the stories recorded in a text such as *Mingxiang ji* come to us largely devoid of any extratextual context. The transactions involved in getting our hands on such a text today—omitting for a moment the educational contexts that equip us to read the language in which it is written and spark in us the interest in doing so—often stop at the commercial and technologically assisted acts of buying a book, making photocopies, or downloading an electronic file. It is easy to forget that the stories preserved in the text did not begin their lives in a social vacuum. They were socially made, socially exchanged and transmitted, and socially preserved by countless

---

74. Particularly explicit examples may be seen in items 20, 84, 90, 91, and 99.

75. Social networks of relation and communication were centrally important in ways to which I have not done justice here, and certainly as much in Buddhist circles as elsewhere. For more on the theme, see Connery, *The Empire of the Text*, 162–169; Chittick, *Patronage and Community in Medieval China*; Hureau, "Réseaux de bouddhistes des Six Dynasties"; Ji Zhichang, "Dong Jin jushi Xie Fu kao," 59–62; and the discussion of epistolary exchanges between Huiyuan and Kumārajīva in Hureau, "Translations, Apocrypha, and the Buddhist Canon"—an example of a sort of exchange that was probably quite common, remarkable in this case only in its level of sophistication and importance and (thus) its relative state of preservation. Among historians of Chinese literature, there has sometimes been a tendency to assume that interest in things "strange" or "miraculous" must have been almost uniquely situated in the lower reaches of society; one agendum for research is then to account for the presence of such phenomena in literary materials—a presence deemed quite surprising. For a recent example, see Xie Mingxun, *Liuchao xiaoshuo benshi kaosuo*, 1–104. This is a set of assumptions I reject here. The social circles portrayed in, and generative of, Buddhist miracle tales in this period were almost exclusively elite ones.

individuals, most of whom we will never know by name. I refer not only to the protagonists and others mentioned in the tales—many of them surely the initial sources of early versions of the stories we now have—but also and especially to all the other hearers, tellers, and recorders of the stories that stood between the protagonist and Wang Yan.

Making and recounting stories is, after all, quintessentially a social transaction. In the first place, every oral telling of a story is a performance undertaken by a narrator for an audience, and hence involves at least two parties. Barbara Smith remarks of narrative, "As in any social transaction, each party must be individually motivated to participate.... Each party must have some *interest* in telling or listening to that narrative."[76] Listeners in conversational settings play important roles in shaping the narrative as it unfolds. In the case of "living narrative"—the sort of exchange that constitutes much of everyday social interaction among individuals—story making occurs during story telling. It is not something one person does alone; it is something two or more parties do together, with interlocutors literally helping to shape the story as it is told.[77]

Then, once someone wrote a story down, it was still by way of social networks of document exchange that a written record came to be transmitted and preserved until it came to the awareness of Wang Yan, who copied it— with what alterations we usually have no way of knowing—into his text. Such written versions, many of them probably disseminated along epistolary networks, preserved in personal and family collections of papers, and included in writings about localities, and some of them possibly appended to copies of sutras (a practice documented from the seventh century), must have formed Wang's main source of material.[78] But, as we have seen, Wang also indicates in a few cases a likely path of oral transmission to his own ears.

Even written texts were not transmitted in a social vacuum. In a manuscript culture such as that of early medieval China, the only way to acquire a text was to make a copy of someone else's copy, pay someone else to do

---

76. "Narrative Versions, Narrative Theories," 232–233.

77. In ways documented extensively in Ochs and Capps, *Living Narrative*; Mattingly, *Healing Dramas and Clinical Plots*; and Mattingly, "Emergent Narratives," among others.

78. For recent studies of epistolary culture in the period, see Richter, "Letters and Letter Writing"; Richter, "Notions of Epistolarity" (though this latter article is taken up with an analysis of Liu Xie's chapter on the genre of the letter rather than with actual epistolary practice); and Schaberg, "Prose and Authority," 513–516. The role of epistolary exchange in the formation of Buddhist networks and the dissemination of the new religion in China is a rich topic that has yet to be studied carefully. (See the suggestive comments, for example, in Zürcher, *The Buddhist Conquest of China*, 214; 395 nn144, 151, 153; and 396 n171.) On newly emergent writings about locales during this period, see Chittick, "The Development of Local Writing." The best overall study of writing technologies and practices continues to be Tsien, *Written on Bamboo and Silk*. On the circulation, collection, and storage of manuscripts, see Drège, *Les bibliothèques en Chine*. On miracle tales appended to sutra copies, see Stevenson, "Buddhist Practice and the Lotus Sūtra," 136; Verellen, "Evidential Miracles in Support of Taoism," 237; and Demiéville, "Une descente aux enfers sous les T'ang," 75–76.

so, or buy a copy made by hand by another person. In our age, when books are fixed into stable form by being printed, their reproduction and use governed (most of the time) by the legal and moral concept of intellectual property, it is hard for us to appreciate, to quote Xiaofei Tian, "just how differently, how vigorously, and indeed how aggressively, a medieval Chinese reader related to literary works." She continues:

> In modern times, we can still be changed by our reading, but we usually do not change our reading materials. In the age of manuscript culture, however, a scribe—a particular sort of reader—could participate actively…in the reproduction of the works of…one of the greatest classical Chinese poets [for example], and the scribe might have been just about any literate person….To the degree that [readers] were engaged in the production of manuscript copies by copying, editing, altering, and revising, we are no longer talking about the readers' reception of a stable text, but about the readers' dynamic participation in the very process of creating a text that is essentially protean.[79]

Having been written on paper or silk, therefore, stories continued to be socially produced in a literal sense—perhaps not to the extent that oral narratives were, but to a much greater extent than we usually imagine, in ways that go beyond the reception of a fixed work to include the alteration of the text itself.[80] This holds true of whatever manuscript material Wang

---

79. Tian, *Tao Yuanming and Manuscript Culture*, 8–9. Tian also recounts the—to us at least—remarkable story of a monk who wrote a set of twenty-four quatrains, only to have the draft taken away "as soon as I put down my brush" (pp. 7–8). The monk then from time to time saw some of the poems written on the walls of his monastery or heard them chanted by people. "They were all full of errors." Later, he "happened to get hold of a complete copy" of the poems, but "the style was uncultivated and vulgar, the tone base and low." So the monk revised them: some he kept, others he excised, and some he augmented and edited, producing a new version of the set of poems. They were, to be sure, in some sense still "his" poems— he still recognized them as "his," after all—but we might almost speak of a "primary" author collaborating (often unwittingly) with numerous unnamed "secondary" and "tertiary" authors to produce a work that, even after the primary author revised it, existed in no singular, stable form anywhere.

80. On the other hand, just as each oral telling of a story is its own performance at the same time that it might be possible to speak, with careful qualification (and some oversimplification), of each of these as performances of "*the same story*," each manuscript in early medieval China was, to an extent likely to startle us, a unique performance of something that we might still, with much qualification, want to call "the same text." Cf. the thought-provoking phrasing in Tian, *Tao Yuanming and Manuscript Culture*, 21 (emphasis added): "Each manuscript and printed edition is *a unique historical performance* by copyists, editors, commentators, woodblock cutters, and book collectors who one after another leave their traces on it and therefore change it." Fair enough, except that the fact that it is still possible for Tian to refer to an "it" that is changed speaks, I think, to the need to develop finer tools for characterizing what a text is across or apart from its many "performances." Each performance may be "unique," but each is a performance of something whose irreducibility to the performed occasion is signaled in the very same phrase.

Yan may have seen as he did his work; each text that came across his desk had been shaped by many hands, just as the story recorded in the text had been orally shaped by untold numbers of speakers and interlocutors prior to being written down. It also, of course, holds true of Wang Yan's own work: whatever text he may have left was inexorably altered by chains of later copyists until it reached, for example, a compendium maker, a man such as Daoshi. In the translation in part 2 we will see cases where Daoshi, in different sections of his massive work, quotes different versions of the same *Mingxiang ji* story. We might read such cases as attesting to the sorts of alterations texts underwent in the course of their transmission in the manuscript culture of medieval China. There are other possibilities as well. The observed variations (sometimes simply a matter of a word or phrase, sometimes more significant or extensive) may in some cases have been introduced by Daoshi or his assistants. They may even have been introduced by Wang Yan himself: in a manuscript culture, even an autograph text was probably never truly "finished" until the author had died. It is easy to imagine successive versions of a text being circulated among acquaintances during an author's lifetime while he still continued to produce updated versions of it (not to mention the changes others may have introduced).

All of this underscores that the stories compiled by Wang Yan (and many others like him) were collective products in the most literal sense. To be sure, Wang played an authorial role in choosing or altering the wording as well as—perhaps most importantly—in selecting material for inclusion in the first place. But the narratives he incorporated into his text were products of collective mentality and collective memory. They were made and transmitted by narrative communities extending through generational time and across geographic space, both before and after him. One of the things the narratives show us is how such memories were formed and preserved.

The collective nature of the making of the stories in *Mingxiang ji* means, in turn, that we may read those stories as evidence about religious practices, attitudes, and dispositions that were fairly widespread—if not throughout all or even most of Chinese society at the time, at least far beyond Wang Yan's studio. The stories are artifacts of narrative exchange and social memory, and that is precisely what makes them valuable as material for the history of religions—much more valuable, in fact, than if they were the sole invention of a single author. We may not be able to conclude from these narratives "what actually happened" at the level of events at this or that time and place, but we may infer a great deal about what many people believed had happened—and what they wanted others to believe.

Wang Yan and other miracle-tale compilers hoped to reinsert their texts into future chains of narrative transmission so as to disseminate the ideas and values urged in the tales and to shape readers' dispositions in ways that would generate more miracles and more stories about them. The propagation of narratives was intended to impact readers and hearers in ways that would replicate the sorts of "signs" such narratives are about and thus also generate more stories of such signs. Zhang Yan, the compiler of the second-earliest collection of Sound Observer tales, speaks of having been moved to create his own text by reading an earlier one by Fu Liang. Lu Gao similarly speaks of having joined his own collection of stories to his two predecessors'—and he explicitly invites readers to add further miracle tales to his text.[81] Wang Yan's own compilation was continued, in a sense, in the now-lost *Buxu Mingxiang ji* 補續冥祥記, or *Signs of the Unseen Realm Supplemented and Continued* by Wang Manying 王曼穎, who corresponded with Huijiao concerning the latter's *Traditions of Eminent Monks* (*Gaoseng zhuan* 高僧傳).[82] The compilers, then, were well aware of the spiral-like relation between their texts and their readers' dispositions. This may seem an obvious point, but it takes on more complexity when we consider the extent to which the recorded tales themselves both model and reflect this process.

Just as many *Mingxiang ji* stories mention details that inform us as to the sorts of narrative networks that provided compilers with their source material, so too do many depict the sort of dispositional impact that hearing a miracle story (or witnessing a miracle outright) could produce on hearers and readers. Item 59, for example, tells of how one Shi Changhe died and then returned to life to tell of what he had seen. His story makes clear, among other things, that his ability to claim truthfully, "I do not eat fish or meat, I drink no alcohol, I regularly recite sutras, and I succor those who are sick and in distress" was a reason why he was allowed to return to life. The story closes by saying: "The future monk Zhi Fashan had at that time not yet left the household. It was because he heard what Changhe recounted that he formed the resolve to enter the path." Many such passages are scattered throughout the text.[83] We can read them as both descriptions of the sorts of responses some people had to these stories and prescriptions for the sorts of responses the compilers hoped their readers would have.

This text, like almost every text of the *zhiguai* genre from the pre-Tang period, is written in a decidedly literary (as opposed to colloquial) but workmanlike prose, with little or no metric structure (i.e., no prosodic phrasing). The language of the text, like that of other *zhiguai* compilations, most closely resembles the prose of histories (both official and pri-

---

81. On these passages see Campany, "The Real Presence," 266–267.

82. See *Guang hongming ji* 24.275a–b and Li Jianguo, *Tang qian zhiguai xiaoshuo shi*, 419–420. Wang Qing, "Jinyang Wangshi de jiashi menfeng," 147–148, following suggestions by earlier scholars (e.g., Cao Daoheng, "Lun Wang Yan," 27), presents an intriguing but self-admittedly very speculative argument that Wang Manying was none other than Wang Yan's son. He similarly suggests (p. 147) that Wang Manying, compiler of the miracle-tale collection *Ganying zhuan*, may have been Wang Yan's father or at least an older-generation close relative.

83. Similar statements of the dispositional impact of stories—or protagonists' own experiences—may be found in items 5, 6, 16, 23, 24, 25, 30, 35, 43, 50, 72, 92, 98, 118, and 124.

vate), but it is somewhat less compressed and elliptical, and it contains more constructions approximating oral speech patterns.[84] Neither the phrasing nor, with the exception of the relatively few technical terms that are sprinkled here and there, the vocabulary of *Mingxiang ji* seems to owe any noticeable debt to Chinese Buddhist sutra literature.[85] It would even be fair to say that, judged on the basis of its language alone, *Mingxiang ji* shows relatively little sign of being a Buddhist text. It is Buddhist by virtue not of its language but of its content and its rhetorical goals. When compared to other *zhiguai* texts, the only way in which it is distinctive—aside from its clearly pro-Buddhist agenda, which (as indicated above) is shared by a few other texts of the genre—is in how frequently it mentions the sources and paths of transmission of its stories and the number of internal cross-references that survive in quotations from it.

I close this section with brief comments on the sorts of historical inferences that are and are not possible on the basis of texts such as *Mingxiang ji*, in light of the above considerations. The stories in such a text, as we have seen, represent crystallizations of social memory and collective representation. They are records of consequential things that certain groups of people maintained to have occurred. To say that they strongly reflect the interests of these groups would be an understatement. They also encode certain assumptions about what their audience already knew. For all of these reasons, they do not permit us to recover "what really happened" *in this or that particular case.* But they do allow us to grasp what someone was trying to persuade others of, what a group of people *held to be the case* about what happened. They bear witness to, because they participated in and were produced by, the social processes by which stories of miraculous events were formed, shared, and preserved.

Second, given the pressure of audience expectations on storytellers and collectors, we may justifiably read these texts as evidence of practices and understandings that were rather broadly shared in their authors' time, at least in the sorts of social circles in which Wang Yan moved. Even if not everyone would have believed or approved of their contents and claims (and obviously many did not), they would nevertheless have recognized the types of figures, practices, and scenarios found there. Since the narratives were attempts to persuade an audience, and since that audience would have needed to be familiar with the scenes, the settings, the patterns of

---

84. Excellent discussions of the prose style of these and similar works in their literary and historical contexts may be found in Zhou Junxun, *Wei Jin nanbeichao zhiguai xiaoshuo cihui,* and Yoshikawa Kōjirō, "The *Shih-shuo Hsin-yü* and Six Dynasties Prose Style." Zhou focuses on *zhiguai* texts as sources for the history of the Chinese lexicon in its transition from ancient to medieval times; his comments on how the language of *zhiguai* texts compares to other contemporary genres are therefore sparse.

85. On the specialized Buddhist vocabulary of *Mingxiang ji* and a few other early Buddhist *zhiguai* texts, see the short list of terms in Zhou Junxun, *Wei Jin nanbeichao zhiguai xiaoshuo cihui,* 41–44, and the discussion at 423–446.

relationship and action described in the stories in order for the portrayals to have been convincing, we can assume that, in these respects, our texts give a relatively accurate portrayal of how things were. Naturally, claims made about this or that event would likely have been contested and controversial, supported by some but denied by others, and indeed I will present evidence that this was so. But the essential point is that the *sorts of contexts and circumstances* in which events were said to have occurred would have been familiar to readers. Through the texts, then, we catch glimpses not of the historicity of this or that specific occurrence but of the environments in which these types of occurrences were held to take place and how people responded to them.[86]

The Idiom of Buddhism Represented in the Tales

From the point of view of the history of Buddhism, the miracle tales bear witness to a particular style of the religion that arose in early medieval China. Before I elaborate on this statement, a preliminary methodological note is in order.

There is a way of imagining and writing the history of religious traditions—a way so common that we tend to forget that there are alternatives—that pictures them as holistic entities, living organisms that grow over time while maintaining a singular core "essence" throughout their entire trajectory of "development." In the case of traditions that have traveled across several cultures, the use of these organic, holistic metaphors for traditions is often accompanied by a tendency to measure the authenticity of the later, traveled forms of the tradition against its putative originals in the home country.[87] I prefer to think of religious traditions as constantly changing repertoires of resources created and used by participants in imagined communities of identity, discourse, and practice. The repertoires consist of vast arrays of resources (ideas, words, values, images, action patterns, stories, prototypes, persons, texts, strategies, goals, methods, collective memories) created over many generations. At any given time, communities avail themselves of certain of the tradition's resources while ignoring, merely assuming, or opposing others, all the while developing a characteristic style or idiom based on selections from the total array of repertoire elements. One thing this means is that, in the case of a large, complex, mobile tradition such as Buddhism, whether we view it synchronically or diachronically, it is always a matter of plural Buddhisms united not by a common "essence" but by a certain family resemblance of clusters of repertoire elements, as well as by the very idea of Buddhism as an imagined community. This seems to me

---

86. The structure and some of the phrasing of these two paragraphs are adapted from Campany, *Making Transcendents*, 21–22.

87. A tendency which, in the case of the study of Buddhism, has been trenchantly criticized in Sharf, *Coming to Terms with Chinese Buddhism*, 1–27, 132–133.

less a fashionably postmodern ideological assertion than an approximation of the empirically existing stuff of traditions and the actual ways in which people, texts, ideas, and all the rest relate to them.[88]

One thing the early medieval Chinese miracle tales show us, then—because they reflected it, participated in it, emanated from it, and were written with its participants in mind as their primary audience—is a particular style or idiom of Buddhism in action, a style that was practiced in the centuries after Buddhism's introduction to China. When compared with other idioms of Buddhism both in China and elsewhere, this one can be succinctly described as follows.

For one thing, it is profoundly lay oriented. The very genre of the miracle tale, in its concerns and in the worldview and competencies it assumes in readers, not only seems to have been created by laymen but also presumes a lay audience. Most of the protagonists in the tales are members of the gentry. Although monks and (to a lesser extent) nuns appear often in the stories—frequently occupying a central place in the narrative—they are seen largely from a lay point of view. Many of them are either wonderworkers or, when viewed negatively, lackadaisical keepers of monastic discipline. When lay protagonists temporarily die and journey to the underworld, they often are reported as having encountered monks there who acted as influential advocates for them before the underworld magistracies—testimony to the aura of exotic spiritual power that clung to monks in many laypersons' eyes. And when laypersons perform the periodic abstinence ceremony, or *zhai* 齋,[89] with appropriate sincerity, or invoke the Bodhisattva Sound Observer with sufficient concentration, it is often a mysterious monk who appears in response to their act.

The overriding concern of the Buddhism we see reflected in these texts is how to draw upon Buddhism's practical efficacy in life and after death. It is a Buddhism in which karma, rebirth, and practices such as devotion to protective bodhisattvas and the making and venerating of votive images are uppermost. It could hardly be more different from the abstract discussion and detached, emotionally cool "pure conversation" (*qingtan* 清談) carried out in certain genteel circles, of which we read so much in histories of Chinese Buddhism.[90] At its doctrinal and functional heart, instead, is the mechanism of "stimulus-response," or *ganying* 感應, a Buddhist overlay on a variety of older Chinese ideas[91] according to which—to reduce

---

88. For further discussion of these ideas and the sources and reflections on which they are based, see Campany, "On the Very Idea of Religions"; Campany, *Making Transcendents*, 39–87; and Campany, "Two Religious Thinkers."

89. Discussed further below.

90. To put the matter in other terms, it is thus a locative, not a utopian, style of Buddhism. For elaboration of the distinction, see Campany, "Two Religious Thinkers."

91. On reflection, however, it seems to me that the more relevant indigenous notion is not *ganying* but *ling* 靈, or "spiritual efficacy"—the attested responsiveness of the god of a particular temple to offerings and supplications.

it to its essentials—appropriately sincere, intense, and sufficiently repeated acts of conscious devotion and supplication, acting as the stimulus, will
elicit strikingly immediate and concrete responses from the Buddha, bodhisattvas, or spirit-beings supplicated, just as immoral or impious actions
will necessarily elicit retribution.[92] In short, the stimulus of intense devotional acts triggers miraculous responses.

The Buddhism reflected in the tales is an identifiably Greater Vehicle,
or Mahāyāna, Buddhism only in a limited set of aspects. These include the
prominence of devotion to a few specific bodhisattvas; the mention of specifically Mahāyāna sutras (including some Perfection of Wisdom sutras,
the *Lotus*, and the *Śūraṃgama*), along with the attribution of miraculous
agency and sanctity to copies of these; and a detectable if muted emphasis
on the visionary transmission of knowledge. (More will be said on all these
topics below.) The grand doctrinal emphases typically associated with
Mahāyāna Buddhism—the discourse of enlightenment, of emptiness, of
nonduality—are, on the other hand, scarcely mentioned.[93] Vimalakīrti,
the famous exemplar who, though a layman, mastered specifically
Mahāyāna insight into emptiness and nonduality, is never spoken of.[94] The
early Mahāyāna emphasis on the bodhisattva path as the preferred one for
practitioners, and the austere style of practice that tended to go with it, is
quite foreign to the world depicted in the tales.[95] Even the foundational

---

92. For a discussion of the wide range of Buddhist senses of *ganying* and some of their
indigenous Chinese precedents, see Sharf, *Coming to Terms with Chinese Buddhism*, 77–133. I
discuss the concept further below as it relates to early medieval miracle tales. For a work that
gathers copious out-of-context textual material on both pre-Buddhist and Buddhist notions
of moral retribution in China without much by way of analysis, see Liu Difan, *Tang qian guobao xitong de jiangou yu ronghe*.

93. Compare the dedicatory inscription attached to a self-produced copy of the *Scripture on the Ten Kings* by a devotee who identified himself only as "an old man of eighty-five,"
discussed in Teiser, *The Scripture on the Ten Kings*, 127–128: "He is entirely without prayers,"
the old man wrote of himself. "[Since] original nature is truly empty, there is no pleasure for
which to pray." As Teiser comments, "The very act of praying for a stipulated end assumes
the permanence of the one who prays and the reality of the result, be it the extinction of suffering or the arising of enlightenment," but the old man's invocation of emptiness instead
throws "the whole process of prayer into doubt" (128). My point is that such doubt, based on
the confrontation of devotional actions by the teaching of emptiness, is never once raised in
Signs from the Unseen Realm and its early medieval counterpart texts, and is indeed unimagi-
nable in them, however much it may have figured in the ruminations of their compilers.

94. On the reception and prevalence of the *Vimalakīrti Sutra* in southern China in the
fourth and fifth centuries, see Demiéville, "Appendice II: Vimalakīrti en Chine," and
Mather, "Vimalakīrti and Gentry Buddhism."

95. Bodhisattvas abound, of course, but they are beings from whom one seeks help, not
beings one aspires to emulate—with two exceptions (items 82 and 113), where individuals,
both of them laymen, are mentioned as having taken bodhisattva vows. On the bodhisattva
path in early Mahāyāna, see Nattier, *A Few Good Men*, and Boucher, *Boddhisattvas of the Forest*.
On the taking of bodhisattva vows in early medieval China, see Funayama, "Rikuchō jidai ni
okeru bōsatsukai," and Hureau, "La cérémonie de réception."

Buddhist teaching of impermanence is seldom broached,[96] and that of no-self, or *anātman*, never is; instead we find an overriding concern to argue the survival of the soul after death and its fate at the hands of a decidedly nonempty afterlife. When stages of spiritual advancement toward awakening are mentioned at all—and they seldom are—it is a question only of the arhat path, presumed to be an exclusively monastic pursuit.[97] It is not as if the communities from which these stories emanated were unaware of some of these ideas; the *Sutra in Forty-Two Sections*[98] had already expounded clearly and centrally on concepts such as no-self and impermanence, and most of the sutras whose recitation, copying, or miraculous preservation are mentioned in the tales speak eloquently of emptiness and nonduality. But the style of Buddhism reflected in the miracle tales placed its emphasis elsewhere, and if notions of emptiness and nonduality are not completely inconsistent with the Buddhist preoccupations of the tales, they are also not very relevant to them.

As I have noted, the principal route to religious advancement portrayed in these tales is karmic merit, not the quest for "sudden" spiritual awakening or the realization of nonduality. But the Buddhism of the miracle tales gives even greater weight to sin and its punishment than it does to the eventual path-related benefits of amassing merit. In this respect, it differs from the Buddhism of the avadāna tales introduced into China from greater India, which focus much more tightly on the almost inconceivable (if temporally distant) benefits of apparently simple acts of service and devotion. As one textbook notes: "The avadānas promote Buddhism as a feel-good religion. Minimal effort is promised maximum rewards in terms of mundane and supramundane pleasures: a long, scenic joyride through saṃsāra before going out in a blaze of glory. The rich can buy their way into nirvāṇa; the poor can get there with a bow."[99] To put it simply, while avadāna tales seem concerned primarily to illustrate the power of service

---

96. Impermanence as a phenomenon is mentioned in passing in items 9, 35, and 126 of *Signs from the Unseen Realm*, though it does not rise to the level of the main idea conveyed in any of these stories. It also underlies several scenes in which souls recently returned from their temporary sojourns in the underworld are reluctant to return to their already decomposing bodies. Xue Huiqi, in a discussion purporting to treat the themes of "illusion and impermanence" in "Buddhist *zhiguai*," spends almost all of her space sketching these Buddhist doctrines in general terms and then adduces a single dream narrative from *Youming lu* that is supposed to illustrate how the themes play out in miracle tales. See Xue, *Liuchao fojiao zhiguai xiaoshuo yanjiu*, 68–70.

97. See items 64, 101, and 124.

98. The date of this text is notoriously controversial, but some form of it seems to have existed by the end of the Later Han (220 CE). The extant version almost certainly contains later modifications, but there is no reason to assume (absent further evidence) that it differs radically from earlier versions. See Zürcher, *The Buddhist Conquest of China*, 29–30; Sharf, "The Scripture in Forty-Two Sections," which provides a useful introduction, bibliography, and translation; and Heng-ching Shih, *The Sutra of Forty-Two Sections*.

99. Robinson, Johnson, and Thanissaro, *Buddhist Religions*, 72.

and devotion in advancing practitioners on a long-range, multilifetime path, Chinese miracle tales seem more concerned with showing how these same activities allow laypersons and monastics to avoid punishment and reap rewards in this or the very next lifetime. It may seem a fine distinction, but to sample these two bodies of literature side by side is to sense a real difference in emotional tone. I doubt that anyone who reads the tales translated here would describe the Buddhism reflected in them as predominantly a feel-good religion, if only because of the proportion of space they allot to the baleful consequences of violating the norms they emphasize. The overriding emotional tone is not assurance but anxiety.

Finally, two things whose scarcity of mention in the tales is even more surprising are the cult of Buddha relics and stupas—mentioned only a very small number of times in *Signs from the Unseen Realm*—and the notion of the decline of the Dharma and associated apocalyptic ideas, mentioned in passing only once.[100]

The miracle tales reflect, then, a geographically and historically particular idiom of Buddhism in its first few centuries in China. This idiom of Buddhism has been seldom studied, and so a translation and study of miracle tales from this period is timely. Much scholarly focus has been trained on the dates of translation of the great sutras, on the doctrinal contents of these texts, their reception in China, and the early attempts to relate their central ideas to indigenous analogues. However, as Erik Zürcher has pointed out, such a "purely philological approach . . . treats the history of a religion as a history of texts"[101]—and only a limited range of texts at that. If we are justified in taking the miracle tales as representing a particular early idiom of Buddhism in China, then it is an idiom that remains to be well understood. Zürcher sums up the gentry Buddhism of the fourth and early fifth centuries in the following phrases—"Emptiness and Saintly wisdom," "the retribution of sins," and "the immortality of the soul"—but in the circles from which the miracle tales emanated and at which they were aimed, emptiness did not play a large role, and wisdom (if by this is meant insight into the most profound truths expounded in the great sutras) was largely seen as the preserve of full-time monastic practitioners. Zürcher continues:

---

100. Item 4 mentions the interment of a monk's bones under a stupa, item 17 implies that a nun's bowl and robe were interred as relics of possession, and item 21 portrays a family as treasuring a relic and a sutra copy together in the same chest. The notion of the decline of the Dharma is mentioned in item 77. On the prevalence of apocalyptic expectations in certain Buddhist circles in this period in China, see Zürcher, "Prince Moonlight," and Strickmann, "The *Consecration Sūtra*," 86–89. Recent studies of the textual sources on cults of relics in early medieval China include Faure, "Les cloches de la terre"; Strong, *Relics of the Buddha*; Shinohara, "Ji shenzhou sanbao gantong lu"; and Campany, "À la recherche de la religion perdue."

101. *The Buddhist Conquest of China*, 72. Compare the similar remarks in Strickmann, "The *Consecration Sutra*," 75–80.

Among the sophisticated Buddhist gentlemen of the fourth century, both monks and laymen, we very seldom hear emotional outbursts about the Buddha's endless love and compassion. Their Buddhism has a distinctly rational and intellectual flavor; its ideal is not the quiet surrender to the power of a super-human savior, but in the first place the realization of Zhuangzi's "equality of all things"; the pursuit of the wisdom of the sage who "reflects" 照 all phenomena without ever leaving his state of trance-like non-activity.... This hybrid Buddhism...came into being as soon as the Chinese intelligentsia, *Daode jing* in hand, set out to find its own way in the jungle of Buddhist metaphysics.[102]

A close study of *Signs from the Unseen Realm*, the largest and most representative of the early miracle-tale collections in China, suggests that Zürcher's portrait, vivid though it is, needs to be made considerably more complex. We might begin by noting that there existed, in fact, not one unitary "gentry Buddhism" in early medieval China but several coexisting idioms of Buddhism in which various groups and levels of persons participated (and in more than one of which any given individual might participate). In some circles there was indeed emphasis on the sorts of discussions Zürcher describes here. But in others, reliance on superhuman saviors was indeed a key component. Far from seeking Zhuangzi-like equanimity, participants in the idiom of Buddhism reflected in the miracle tales wanted to convey the message that afterlife punishment is real and horrific, something very much to be feared. The Buddhism of these circles was at once a rational and an emotional affair.[103] To its practitioners, texts such as the *Daode jing* were largely irrelevant except insofar as they represented obstacles to be contended against, and Buddhist metaphysics, too, was irrelevant, whereas Buddhist cosmology—with its purgatories, heavens, and Pure Lands—was very much in the foreground. If its practitioners entered "trance-like" states, it was not to assume a posture of nonactivity but to summon a response from a living, active, personal being or to receive a transmission of sacred knowledge from the unseen world. In short, the particular sort of "hybrid Buddhism" so aptly characterized by Zürcher in many ways resembled third- and fourth-century explications and applications of the *Daode jing* and *Zhuangzi* much more than it represented the sort of Buddhism seen in the miracle tales. Zürcher's "hybrid Buddhism" was a thoroughly antilocative affair, whereas the Buddhism of the miracle tales was just as thoroughly locative. In some important respects the Buddhism of the miracle tales resembled the Daoism of the *Scripture of Great Peace* (*Taiping jing* 太平經) and the early Celestial Masters much more than it did the Bud-

---

102. *The Buddhist Conquest of China*, 73–74.
103. As an example of the emotional aspects of lay Buddhist piety in this period one may cite Wang Yan's contemporary Wang Rong's 王融 "Songs of Joy in the Dharma" (*Fale ci* 法樂辭*), translated and studied in Mather, "The Life of the Buddha and the Buddhist Life."

dhism of the Perfection of Wisdom sutras or the *Vimalakīrti Sutra*.[104] Like those Daoisms, it featured a cosmos full of beings exquisitely responsive to human conduct and intention; an inexorable moral law backed by stern afterlife retribution and a watchful, infallible divine bureaucracy; opposition to local sacrificial religion; and frequent rites of confession and communal assemblies by means of which the rules of the collective divine order were reaffirmed. Antinomianism, the transcendence of the bounds of moral and bureaucratic order, indifference to one's fate at the hands of that order: all these were firmly rejected.

In these same respects, the Buddhism of the miracle tales also overlaps considerably with a subset—but only a subset, as we have seen—of the Buddhist sutra literature circulating at the time. Superhuman saviors figure importantly in the *Lotus Sutra*; a focus on the afterlife and on karmic retribution characterizes the Pure Land sutras; and the divine bureaucracy is portrayed in detail in such early translated, cosmology-focused sutras as the *Da loutan jing*.[105] To this extent, the miracle tales collected in *Mingxiang ji* and similar texts can be read as evidence for the uptake and mobilization in Chinese society of major themes at work in certain sutras. The miracle tales deploy these themes in a different genre and a different sort of literary language, but the themes are consistent with the emphases found in these sutras.

If we view what is normally referred to as "Buddhism" in early medieval China not as a monolith but as a vast repertoire of elements and of multiple, quite different idioms, some of which meshed harmoniously and others of which were in tension with one another, we can see the miracle tales as largely representing (and helping to construct) a particular idiom that may be characterized as I have here. This is not, however, to say that the individuals mentioned in the tales and the persons who had a hand in circulating them *necessarily* were ignorant of, disdained, or opposed more wisdom-oriented or monastic-oriented Buddhist idioms. It is not the case that religious repertoire elements and idioms always (or even usually) map neatly onto demographic segments: thus we should not expect to find a "wisdom camp" and a "miracle camp." The same individual who gave or listened to lectures on the doctrine of emptiness, based on Perfection of Wisdom sutras, may also have relayed a story of a miracle involving those same sutras. Indeed our text contains evidence that this was sometimes

---

104. Compare Jonathan Smith, *Drudgery Divine*, 117–118. This may be one reason, incidentally, why (as is discussed in the next section) our text spends relatively great effort attacking Celestial Master Daoism and none attacking "dark learning": Celestial Master Daoism was a rival for the same ideological and functional territory occupied by the miracle tales, while "dark learning" was not.

105. Translated by the early fourth century, although the identity of the translator is uncertain. See Boucher, "Dharmarakṣa and the Transmission of Buddhism," 21. Similar in content is the *Qishi jing* 起世經 (preserved as texts no. 24 and 25 in the Taishō canon), but it was not translated until a century after *Mingxiang ji*.

so.[106] But one did not use miracle tales as a platform for expounding on emptiness; and what is more, the doctrine of emptiness, if followed rigorously, could be seen as undercutting the entire edifice of karma and influence-response on which miracle tales were based.

Miracle Tales and the Sinicization of Buddhism

The miracle tales constitute invaluable evidence of the process of the sinicization of Buddhism—that is, the ways in which the foreign religion was introduced into China and explained, justified, and sometimes accommodated to Chinese audiences.[107] This is because, as texts, they attempted to *effect* certain aspects of sinicization at the same time that they *reflect* aspects of this complex process. I find it useful to think of them as having done so at two levels.

At the more basic level, each story contributed to the enterprise of "making Buddhism Chinese" and "making China Buddhist" simply by virtue of constituting a piece of historiography. Each story shows, for example, how some practices from the Buddhist repertoire (invoking Sound Observer, feeding monks, or venerating an image) were deployed—with striking results—at an identified place on Chinese soil by a named Chinese individual in a way that impacted a particular community; or it shows how some assertions from the Buddhist repertoire (involving the afterlife, or the dead, or the Pure Land, or the sanctity of Buddha images) were confirmed as true—in striking ways—at an identified Chinese place in the presence of named Chinese individuals. This most basic mode of sinicization may be likened to the claiming and marking (through narrative, architecture, ritual, and other means) of particular sacred sites on the landscape as Buddhist. In the miracle tale genre, it is particular stretches of Chinese social history—and sometimes also particular places on the land—that are being similarly claimed and marked as Buddhist. Miracle tales are, among other things, a means of sinicization via historiography. They helped domesticate Buddhism through the narrative demonstration of its responsive efficacy on the home territory and in the home society—in the lives of individuals their audience may have known or heard of, or at least individuals whom their audience would have recognized as being more or less like themselves.

At a subtler level, the miracle stories participated in the sinicization of Buddhism by negotiating a series of complex arguments, adjustments, and counterpositions at those places where elements in the Buddhist reper-

---

106. See items 22, 25, and 90, for example.

107. As distinct from the topic of Buddhism and *sinification*, or "the long-range enterprise of Han Chinese civilization to overwhelm, incorporate, and pacify the peoples within its ever-increasing cultural sphere," as noted in McRae, *Seeing Through Zen*, 110–111. Other than its portrayal of Central Asian non-Han peoples, discussed elsewhere in these pages, *Signs from the Unseen Realm* has little to say about sinification in McRae's sense.

toire rubbed up against elements in the repertoires of other imagined communities. Here "sinicization" may be thought of not so much as a compromising modification of Buddhist teachings to fit the Chinese context but, rather, as an unyielding and self-conscious clarification of the points where Buddhist teachings sharply conflicted with elements of non-Buddhist religion—with a none-too-subtle critique of the latter always implied. Again a methodological prelude is necessary here.

Cultures, societies, and religious traditions can be helpfully seen as contestational fields in which diverse groups assert claims and attempt to persuade others to their points of view. In contrast to an organic model of religious traditions that sees them as "chang[ing] glacially over time as the result of impersonal processes,"[108] developing according to their own internal logic, I prefer to see them—as mentioned above—as repertoires of resources developed by particular (if to us often obscure) historical agents in pursuit of various goals. Further, each repertoire element can be seen as a response—whether by intention or in effect—to alternative assertions, goals, practices, and priorities. The components added over time to any religion's repertoire of resources are each of them *contrastive* in nature. In addition to whatever intrinsic rationales may be given for a repertoire element—rationales that explain it in terms of cosmological and other beliefs internal to a community—it is also almost always the case that it will carry extrinsic meanings or functions as well, serving to differentiate those who uphold it from those who do not, usually by tacitly or explicitly elevating practitioners to a position hierarchically superior to specific religious others. We understand the myriad texts, claims, practices, and priorities of a religious tradition more completely when we see how they each constituted alternatives to other possibilities. Religious texts, in short, are not simple reports of matters on which there was consensus: they deploy *arguments* against rival positions, and they are attempts to persuade readers.[109]

This ongoing contestation—a primary driving force in the origins and development of every religious tradition and in the production of new texts, images, practices, sacred places, and narratives—can take many forms, not all of them overtly oppositional. To give even a partial list of places in *Signs from the Unseen Realm* where such contestation rises close to the surface of the narratives is to survey ways in which, at the level of communal narrative exchange, Buddhism as a body of practices and norms[110] was being situated vis-à-vis numerous other Chinese alternatives.

For example, every tale in which Buddhist monks or nuns are por-

---

108. Lincoln, *Theorizing Myth*, 18.

109. For further elaboration of these points, with discussion of supporting literature, see Campany, *Making Transcendents*, 39–61; Campany, "The Meanings of Cuisines of Transcendence"; and Campany, "On the Very Idea of Religions."

110. Or, more accurately, that selection from among all available Buddhist repertoire elements that the makers of these tales saw as essential to their imagined version of Buddhism.

trayed as working wonders by virtue of their enhanced spiritual powers[111] implicitly positions these holy persons against an indigenous type—the wonder-working transcendent (*xian* 仙), or seeker of transcendence—and the two repertoires of attributed feats match up almost completely. Taken cumulatively, these stories in effect deny that transcendents had any paranormal powers that Buddhist monastics lacked. This is an aspect of these stories that might not be evident if we had no knowledge of the parallel stories of transcendents or if we viewed the tales only as internal expressions of an organically developing Buddhist tradition in pristine isolation from its cultural and religious surroundings. To examine these stories at closer range is to marvel at the narrative creativity and degree of awareness of the rhetorical targets that went into shaping them. The pro-Buddhist makers of these tales knew their audience and its competencies very well. One story (item 7) tells of a monk on a mountain who seems to possess all the traits of a transcendent-in-the-making and is even said to have lived to the age of 140—but is implied to have died as a karmic consequence of having injured a duck in his youth. Karma is thus argued to trump longevity arts. Another story (60) again portrays a monk as keeping a transcendence-inducing dietary regime that would have been familiar (at least by hearsay) to many readers, but, rather than ending with his ascent of a mountain and departure as a transcendent, this story ends by having the monk quite definitively die: laymen climb the mountain to venerate his skeletal remains. A third story co-opts a member by marriage of the Ge 葛 clan in the southeast—famous for producing seekers of transcendence—into the role of Buddhist laywoman (89).

Similarly, several stories explicitly show Buddhist teachings, techniques, or practitioners to be superior to those of the Celestial Master Daoist tradition (items 44, 65, 67, 70, 77, 86, 87)—whether the setting is one of direct exorcistic combat or a matter of which tradition works better when it comes to dispelling demons, extending life span, avoiding afterlife punishment, or securing the birth of sons. One narrative argues Buddhism's efficacy over that of a now-obscure tradition called the Way of Pure Water (17). Sacrificial cults to local gods, an ancient mainstay of Chinese religion, are a frequent target. Buddhism is narratively portrayed as more efficacious than the style of veneration of ancestors (81, 124) or of household gods (84) that had been prevalent for centuries before the first translations of Buddhist texts into Chinese. Non-Buddhist worries about ritual purity and impurity come under attack in favor of karmic merit (35, 65). Some stories seem to be attempting to insert Buddhism as a mediator into old patterns of dynastic legitimation (41, 63, 108, 109). Even a staunch classicist from the Wang family of Langye is shown converting to Buddhism, thus co-opting a member of this famous clan while at the same time argu-

---

111. E.g., in items 8, 9, 10, 15, and 107. Cf. Campany, *Making Transcendents*, 39–61.

ing Buddhism's superiority to the tradition of learning that placed Confucius at its head (105).

Significantly, the power of spirit-mediums (*wu* 巫) and invocators (*zhu* 祝) to peer into the unseen world and effectively call down spirits is not questioned in *Signs from the Unseen Realm*, despite the common assumption that "according to Buddhism only the Buddha and *arahants* (those who have realized nirvana) have this power, and they are no longer around."[112] This power is, rather, co-opted: what spirit-mediums see in these stories bears out Buddhist claims about what is happening in the unseen world of spirits (items 65, 71, 86, 99, 124). Stories depicting ancient stupas, images, or temples lying underground in effect argue that Buddhism is not foreign to China at all (10, 45, 55), thus negating one of the most often-cited grounds on which Buddhism's opponents urged its expulsion from China.

Sometimes a single story engages in this sort of contestation on multiple fronts. Item 65, for example, takes aim at no fewer than four targets: it argues the superiority of Buddhism over sacrificial cults as well as over Celestial Master Daoism, while also affirming the teaching of karma over the practice of afterlife "plaints" and dismissing concerns about ritual purity in the service of household gods.

In all these ways, *Signs from the Unseen Realm* and other miracle-tale collections from this period at once served to domesticate the still somewhat foreign religion—situating it in a matrix of other possibilities more familiar to some readers—and to mount a running argument for its superiority to specific other options, one aspect at a time. To see a more detailed example of such cross-repertoire domestication and contestation at work, consider the following four episodes in the text.

First: A man who has temporarily died is taken on a tour of the purgatories. He encounters a female relative whom he fails to recognize because she is covered in sores. She explains that, before her death, she "did not believe in karmic retribution" (*bu xin baoying* 不信報應), but that she is now being punished with constant suffering in the purgatories for having whipped her servants too severely. She then adds, "Previously I called for your elder sister to come here, hoping she could replace me [*qian huan ru jie lai wang yi zi dai* 前喚汝姊來，望以自代—or, more literally, 'hoping to use her as a replacement for myself'], but this proved to be of no benefit and only made matters worse."[113]

Second: A relatively young man named Sun Zhi, who has died, during one of several periodic ghostly visits to his living family, recounts that his maternal grandfather was currently serving as magistrate of Mount Tai (widely known as an administrative processing center for souls of the re-

---

112. Obeyesekere, *Imagining Karma*, 41.
113. Item 119.

cently dead)[114] and in that capacity had asked him why he had come early—why, that is, he had died before his allotted time. He says that he replied to his grandfather, "My paternal uncle had me sent here to be punished as a replacement [*dai* 代] for him." He goes on to tell of how the grandfather ordered the paternal uncle's arrest and set him, Zhi, free from further punishment, expediting his rebirth as a human being.[115]

Third: A certain Chen Anju falls ill and dies, then returns to life and tells of what he experienced in the purgatories. One thing he says is that, upon his arrival before the dark magistracies, a nobleman asked him why he had come, saying that it was Anju's uncle, not Anju, who had been scheduled to die, but that Anju must have died due to the uncle's having "filed a plaint" (*gao su* 告訴) against him. We are also told that the uncle in question, who had been allowed to adopt Anju because no sons had been born into his branch of the clan, had enthusiastically "served the spirit-mediums of profane gods," whereas Anju, a devout Buddhist, had sworn never to sacrifice animals as offerings. Anju relates that while he had been released to return to life, an order had been issued for the uncle's immediate arrest.[116]

Fourth: A man named Guo Quan, thirty years dead, appears first to his son-in-law, then to his daughter, explaining that he "has been reproached for something" (*you zhe shi* 有謫事) and asking them to host an assembly of forty monks on his behalf; the merit from this act, he implies, will extricate him from the difficulty. The anxious daughter and son-in-law follow the ghost's instructions, and they promptly receive word that Quan has been pardoned.[117]

In the first two stories, dead individuals do something that the dead were typically imagined as doing in Chinese culture at the time: they attempt to draft other persons—in both cases, their own relatives—to serve as "replacements" or "substitutes" (*dai* 代) for them in the afterlife, the notion being that such replacements would undergo the punishment or perform the forced labor that the fearsome otherworld bureaucracy required. That bureaucracy was believed to care little who ended up receiving the punishment or doing the labor, as long as someone did. The second two stories mention "plaints" or "reproaches": these legal proceedings were among the mechanisms that the dead used to "summon" the living into the otherworld to serve as their replacements. These are phenomena well documented not only in texts transmitted from this period but also in its material culture: objects including ginseng roots and figurines fashioned from lead or clay have been recovered from tombs; they were buried with the

---

114. See Campany, "Return-from-Death Narratives," 106–111, and Raz, "Daoist Sacred Geography," 1403, 1418–1419.
115. Item 26.
116. Item 65.
117. Item 80.

dead to serve as their substitutes if needed, along with legal writs intended to protect the living from plaints that might in the future be filed by the tomb's dead occupant.[118] This practice was paralleled by early medical techniques in which objects were used as substitutes for a patient's own body, to trap demonic pathogens.[119] In the historical background was a body of legal precedent stretching back to Qin times according to which members of an extended family could be held accountable—and punishable—for the crimes of one of its members.[120]

Virtually all readers of *Signs from the Unseen Realm*, and most hearers or readers of these tales prior to Wang Yan's recording of them, would have been familiar with the beliefs and practices referred to in these stories. Premised on this familiarity, the stories argue against the culture of replacements and plaints. As an alternative they offer karma, which, insofar as punishment for sins is concerned, applies only to individuals (although the fortune that follows meritorious acts can be transferred to others, as the fourth story clearly implies), permitting of no substitutes to receive punishments one has oneself incurred.[121] The stories not only depict the culture of replacements as not in fact working as the dead hope it will, they further show dead relatives who try to avail themselves of it being punished more severely for the attempt. At the same time, these stories offer a Buddhist way of countering the culture of replacements and plaints that rivals earlier and contemporary Daoist—particularly Celestial Master Daoist—ways of doing so. The main features of Daoist defenses against plaints—the use of petitions, writs, and talismans—are disparagingly mentioned elsewhere in *Signs*.

This is an example of the extrinsic and contestational nature of ele-

---

118. Figurines, ginseng roots, and grave-securing writs buried for this purpose are discussed in Seidel, "Geleitbrief an die Unterwelt," 166–167, 170–171; Nickerson, "The Great Petition for Sepulchral Plaints," 244–246; Nickerson, "Taoism, Death, and Bureaucracy," 146–155; Verellen, "The Heavenly Master Liturgical Agenda," 317–319; Kleeman, "Land Contracts and Related Documents," 5; Cedzich, "Corpse Deliverance, Substitute Bodies, Name Change, and Feigned Death," 29; Mollier, *Buddhism and Taoism Face to Face*, 84–85, 160; Bai, "Religious Beliefs," 1040; and Chen Guofu, *Daozang yuanliu kao*, 283–284. (For a broader overview of miniature or sometimes life-sized human figures placed in tombs in this and earlier periods, see Wu, "On Tomb Figurines.") The danger of intrafamily "replacements" being seized to serve out terms of punishment in the other world is discussed in Bokenkamp, *Ancestors and Anxiety*, 130–131, 145–148. Such themes surface elsewhere in the extensive tale literature from our period: for an example in which a man summoned to death is invited to nominate a "replacement" for himself, see Campany, "Return-from-Death Narratives," 96–97, and for examples in which dead individuals are depicted as seeking replacements for themselves in the afterlife, see Campany, "Ghosts Matter," 22.

119. See, for example, Harper, *Early Chinese Medical Literature*, 170, 244.

120. See Pulleyblank, "The Origins and Nature of Chattel Slavery," and Lewis, *The Early Chinese Empires*, 232–234.

121. Note that as long as the practice of invoking "substitutes" persisted, Buddhist texts continued to make this argument; that is, the argument does not stop even when Buddhism is relatively well installed in Chinese society. For an example dating from around 800, see Teiser, *The Ghost Festival*, 176.

ments in the repertoires of religious imagined communities. A scholar focusing only on the workings of doctrines internal to the Buddhist tradition might be inclined to note the operation of karma in these four stories and leave it at that. But the point of the stories is not simply to show karma at work. It is, much more precisely, to juxtapose the workings of karma with a different set of assumptions in order to highlight the conflict between them and then, in each story's outcome, to demonstrate that it is karma that is the correct teaching.

Incidentally, these stories were not the first texts in this period to make this argument, though they were among the first to use experiential accounts as evidence. The Buddhist layman Xi Chao 郗超 (336–377), in his *Essentials in Upholding the Dharma* (*Fengfa yao* 奉法要), had argued the same point, although referring more to imperial law codes and precedents than to the extension of these to relations between the living and the dead.[122] Citing a passage from the *Bannihuan jing* 般泥洹經 (a text that was probably the work of Zhi Qian, who died around 252),[123] he wrote: "When the father has done wrong, the son will not receive [punishment] in his place [*bu dai shou* 不代受]; if the son has done wrong, the father will not receive [punishment] either. The one who has done good himself reaps the fortune from having done so, and the one who has done wrong himself undergoes its baleful results."[124] After quoting this passage, Xi Chao exclaims, "How perfect are these words! They agree with the heart and accord with reason." As Stephen Bokenkamp has shown, Xi Chao had personal motivation to feel thus: the Shangqing Daoist revelations vouchsafed to Yang Xi between 364 and 370 had indicated that Chao's father, the Jin court official Xi Yin 愔, was involved in otherworld lawsuits that also implicated Chao. The sutra's words on karma, Bokenkamp notes, "must have seemed 'perfect words' indeed to one so burdened with post-mortem familial entanglements."[125]

The Narrative Shape of the Miraculous

Each *Mingxiang ji* story narrates events that contravene an implied everyday perspective on how the world normally works. Each tale is distinctive,

---

122. Xi Chao appears as the source of a miracle tale in item 31, where more information on him is given in a note. The same issue had already been raised in the early-fourth-century anonymous polemical text *Zhengwu lun* 正誣論 (see *Hongming ji* 1.8a10ff. and Link, "*Cheng-wu lun*," 151; cf. Zürcher, "Buddhist Influence on Early Taoism," 140).

123. I mean in particular the work titled *Bannihuan jing* that is now preserved as Taishō 6. See Nattier, *Earliest Chinese Buddhist Translations*, 126–128.

124. *Hongming ji* 13.87b, trans. Zürcher, *The Buddhist Conquest of China*, 169. Zürcher treats the last phrase as not included within the sutra passage being quoted by Xi Chao, but it is in fact found in that passage: cf. *Bannihuan jing* 181a–b.

125. Bokenkamp, *Ancestors and Anxiety*, 170. On Xi Yin's difficulties, see pp. 113–118. (Note that Bokenkamp adopts an alternate reading of the family's surname as Chi.) On the larger relationship between individual and collective (including family) notions of retribution, see Maeda, "Between Karmic Retribution and Entwining Infusion."

mentioning dramatis personae and other details that appear nowhere else in the text. But the reader quickly notices that the extraordinariness featured in *Signs from the Unseen Realm* has been channeled into a relatively small number of narrative patterns. However broad and variegated may have been the spectrum of anomalous occurrences people imagined, experienced, or talked about in Buddhist circles in early medieval China, more than 100 of our text's 129 extant tales fall into one of only seven distinct story lines—seven kinds of narrative frames onto which the fabric of the miraculous was stretched by the collective work of story formation and social memory. I will first enumerate these seven types and then pause to reflect on this patterning of the extraordinary.

The most frequent story type in *Signs from the Unseen Realm* is that in which a person in dire distress calls on the Bodhisattva Sound Observer for help and is swiftly saved. (Devotion to this bodhisattva is an important aspect of the Buddhism reflected in these stories, as discussed in the next section; here I am concerned to characterize a particular *type of story* that features this bodhisattva.) These stories in every case unfold as follows.[126] The protagonist finds himself in a situation of extreme peril—typically a disaster while traveling, pursuit by hostile troops or bandits, false imprisonment and impending execution, wildfire, grave illness, or the like. He repeatedly and with a concentrated mind recites the bodhisattva's name or the chapter of the *Lotus Sutra* (often circulated as an independent text known as the *Sound Observer Sutra*, or *Guan[shi]yin jing* 觀[世]音經) dedicated to extolling this bodhisattva's power to respond to precisely such entreaties. He is then dramatically rescued, often by a being (a suddenly appearing strange monk, sometimes even a wild animal) implied to be either an envoy or an expedient transformation of the bodhisattva. There are thirty-one such stories in the text, along with two other stories (plus Wang Yan's preface) of miraculous manifestations of devotional images of Sound Observer.[127] These tales are among the compilation's clearest narrative embodiments of the principle of stimulus-response (*ganying*). They also testify directly to the impact the *Lotus Sutra* had on the forms taken by Buddhist devotion in China, at the same time that they helped shape such devotion there. This is so because the chapter of the *Lotus Sutra* devoted to this bodhisattva explicitly promises this sort of help to those who call for it in the specified ways. The

---

126. On this story type in this and other texts in early medieval China, see Campany, "The Real Presence," and Campany, "The Earliest Tales of the Bodhisattva Guanshiyin."

127. Such stories of miraculous intervention are found in items 13, 28, 31, 32, 33, 42, 46, 47, 48, 49, 50, 51, 52, 53, 58, 61, 62, 70, 73, 74, 85, 88, 93, 96, 97, 98, 103, 106, 120, 123, and 129. Devotional images of Guanshiyin are featured in Wang Yan's preface and in items 127 and 128. These stories were drawn from the same networks of narrative exchange that informed the three separate collections of Guanshiyin tales mentioned above, whose compilers, as we have seen, are mentioned explicitly in *Mingxiang ji*. Li Jianguo (*Tang qian zhiguai xiaoshuo shi*, 416) grossly understates the number of stories concerning Guanshiyin in our text as "ten-odd."

stories are, among other things, attestations of the veracity of the sutra's promises, and the authors were clearly acutely aware of this function, since they sometimes mention or even quote the *Lotus* chapter explicitly.

In the second recurring type of tale, the protagonist dies and, after a short span of days, returns to life and tells of what he saw in the afterlife. Nineteen stories take this form,[128] and they constitute, on average, by far the longest tales in *Signs from the Unseen Realm*. This is because they provide extensive narrative tours of the "earth prisons" (*diyu* 地獄), or purgatories, in which sinners were punished in countless gruesome ways for their karmic faults prior to their next rebirths. These return-from-death stories, in all their graphic detail, were obviously intended to warn Chinese readers of the terrible fate awaiting them if they transgressed Buddhist law. They also domesticate (and authenticate) the purgatories by tying firsthand descriptions of their horrors to particular, named, Chinese protagonists. As discussed above, certain of the details in these stories also contest elements of indigenous afterlife beliefs and modes of relation between the living and the dead, offering Buddhist alternatives. In addition to the system of purgatories itself, there is one motif in these stories that powerfully resonates with many other Buddhist texts and norms: when the dead protagonist's spirit returns to its family home and is confronted with its decaying, smelly corpse, it often balks at reentering its former body and has to be nudged in by accompanying envoys from the unseen world. Behind this motif there lay a large literature on impermanence, graveyard meditations or mental visualizations on death and decomposition, and "contemplation of the impure."[129]

A third tale type similarly informs readers of the detailed workings of the afterlife, but here a different narrative mechanism is used: a deceased individual returns briefly (or sometimes periodically) to visit living relatives or friends. The primary reason given for the dead party's visit—and the function, as well, of the story itself—is to warn the living of the real existence and fearsome nature of the purgatories, the gravity of sin, and the urgency of proper Buddhist practice. Like return-from-death narratives, these tales of ghostly visitation contest certain aspects of indigenous afterlife-related beliefs and practices, as discussed above. Thirteen stories take this form.[130]

---

128. Items 5, 6, 23, 30, 35, 44, 45, 59, 65, 66, 72, 77, 92, 104, 105, 110, 118, 119, and 125.

129. On this old body of techniques, mentioned in many scriptures translated before the late fifth century and in Xi Chao's *Fengfa yao*, see *Chanfa yaojie*; *Chan yao jing*; Demiéville, "La *Yogācārabhūmi* de Sangharakṣa," 354, 356, 361, 406, 410, 413, 420; Zürcher, *The Buddhist Conquest of China*, 33, 170; and Wilson, *Charming Cadavers* (focusing on the gendered aspects of these meditations). The relationship between this narrative motif and the above-mentioned Buddhist notions and practices is also noted in Liu Yuanru, *Chaoxiang shenghuo shijie*, 181–182.

130. They are items 18, 22, 26, 37, 38, 54, 68, 78, 80, 81, 102, 115, and 124. This story type is a Buddhist twist on an indigenous type, an example of which can be seen in *Soushen houji* 6.19.

A cluster of three tale types stresses the wonders performed by or associated with monks and nuns possessing enhanced spiritual powers. It is especially in these groups of tales that we see the extent to which, in the collective memories and communally circulated narratives compiled in *Signs from the Unseen Realm*, certain monks and nuns inspired awe because of their perceived ability to tap into realms far beyond the ken of ordinary persons. Eighteen tales narrate the wondrous feats of a particular named monk or nun (this is the fourth tale type); many of these ascribe more than one anomalous deed to their monastic subjects.[131] Most of these narratives treat individuals who are also the subjects of hagiographies in Huijiao's *Traditions of Eminent Monks* (*Gaoseng zhuan*), and in fact our text was an important source drawn on by Huijiao in his compilation.[132] Eleven tales feature the sudden appearance of strange, unnamed monks at abstinence gatherings (fifth tale type).[133] Three stories also present monks as mysterious figures of wonder but focus as much on their numinous mountain settings as on the monks themselves (sixth tale type).[134]

In a seventh type of tale, the protagonist makes a direct assault on the Buddha or his words and consequently suffers a gruesome punishment that the tale graphically recounts. Seven tales of this type survive in our text. The crimes mentioned in them include the theft of jewels or coins from votive canopies or even from Buddha images (items 75, 79, 116), the theft of metal images for use in forging currency (111), the unwarranted abridgment or effacement of sutras (83, 121), and the attempt by a Daoist libationer to exorcise the Buddha from China altogether (86).[135]

What are we to make of this *typing* of miracle tales? Why do we not find a broader repertoire of story types in *Signs from the Unseen Realm*? Indeed, why do we find story types at all? Why is it not the case that each tale is unique not just in the characters, setting, and circumstances it describes (for each tale *is* unique in these respects) but in its basic plot structure? And who was responsible for creating these types in the first place—for directing the narrative shape of the miraculous into just these particular channels?

Beginning with this last question will clear a path toward answering

---

131. Items 4, 8, 9, 10, 15, 17 (nun), 29 (nun), 40, 41, 55, 56, 60, 64, 76, 91 (self-immolation), 99 (nun), 101, and 107. Two additional items (11, 12) focus not on wonders performed by monastic subjects but on wonders experienced by them.

132. On the relationship between these two texts, see Shōji, "*Meishoki* ni tsuite"; Wright, *Studies in Chinese Buddhism*, 102–103; Shinohara, "Two Sources of Chinese Buddhist Biographies," 129–146; Liu Yuanru, *Chaoxiang shenghuo shijie*, 202–221; Wang Qing, "Jinyang Wangshi de jiashi menfeng," 164–156; and Xu, "*Mingxiang ji* ji qi sengren xingxiang," 103–108.

133. Items 11, 16, 19, 20, 27 (solo visit), 29 (cf.), 43, 76, 108, 109, and 113. Two stories (18, 19) focus on other sorts of anomalies during *zhai* gatherings, and item 95 refers to Piṇḍola.

134. Items 7, 14, and 39.

135. Again, such stories are widely distributed in other texts; cf. *Xuanyan ji* 4, 34, and 35, for example.

the others. It is tempting to pin this and all other aspects of the narrative shaping of such tales as these on the end-stage authors of the collections—in this case, on Wang Yan. But as we have seen, Wang Yan and others like him were *compilers* of narrative material already in circulation. To be sure, he must have reshaped that material in the act of selecting certain tales for inclusion and in the ways he told the stories—although it is difficult for us to establish exactly how he did so, since very few texts that we can be certain of having constituted his sources survive independently for us to compare his own treatment to. But it is easy for us, influenced by modern models of authorship, to make too much of this reshaping by end-stage collectors.

The primary fashioners of these story types were instead, as we have seen, not identifiable individuals but the countless, mostly anonymous tellers of stories in networks of Buddhist acquaintances and communal, ritual relations in the two centuries prior to Wang Yan's compilative activity. As Natalie Zemon Davis writes of another premodern body of tale literature from a very different place and time, "The 'stuff of invention' was widely distributed throughout society."[136] In general, emergent narratives are socially formed from the very beginning; stories circulated in society are fashioned in the context of social interactions involving multiple parties, and it is in part this intensely social nature of narrative formation and narrative exchange that ensures the typedness of stories, exerting the steady pressure of group expectation and precedent on the idiosyncratic.[137] People in any given social and cultural setting often tell the same types of stories repeatedly; each telling is in some way a variation on a type, but the types themselves are relatively stable and of limited number. As Linda Garro and Cheryl Mattingly explain, "Learning how to tell a story is a cultural matter, guided by a culture's notions of what constitutes a proper story, who can tell what kinds of stories in what kinds of circumstances, and the like."[138] The types of stories people tell in any given place and time are shaped by collective expectations and cultural patterns, but they also shape these in turn; "narratives shape action just as actions shape stories told about them, and...stories suggest the course of future actions as well as giving form to past experience."[139] Some narrative patterns may play such an important role in a culture that they number among its "key scenarios," "cultural schemas," or "root paradigms": typical patterns of action and narrative in terms of which many of the culture's relations, transactions, and

---

136. *Fiction in the Archives*, 111.

137. On this point see further Mattingly, "Emergent Narratives"; Mattingly, *Healing Dramas and Clinical Plots*; Barbara Smith, "Narrative Versions, Narrative Theories"; Davis, *Fiction in the Archives*; Ochs and Capps, *Living Narrative*; and Campany, *Making Transcendents*, 8–22.

138. "Narrative as Construct and Construction," 25. Cf. Chatman, *Story and Discourse*, 94–95.

139. Garro and Mattingly, "Narrative as Construct and Construction," 17.

events are framed and enacted.[140] In Buddhist contexts in China, any story types built on the notions of karmic retribution or *ganying* would certainly be candidates for "key scenario" status.

Stories tended to come in types, then, in part because they were socially formed, each society at any point in time favoring certain patterns of narrative. But there is another reason for the typing of narratives, having to do with their rhetorical function—the way in which they persuade and move their audience. The stories collected in *Signs from the Unseen Realm* were promulgated to persuade readers about the nature of the unseen cosmos they lived in, and the limited number of their types contributed to this effort. We tend to think of a good story as dramatically innovative, of "literature" as the endless pursuit of novelty, but the repetition of narrative patterns in a traditional society such as that of early medieval China, though it may have lessened the impact of any one story taken individually, wore deeper grooves in audiences' expectations and responses on topics of vital importance. "Stereotypes...convey enormous amounts of cultural information in an extremely condensed form," Jane Tompkins writes. "Their familiarity and typicality, rather than making them bankrupt or stale, are the basis of their effectiveness as integers in a social equation."[141]

There is one other reason why stories of the sort preserved in our text tend to group themselves into types. Narrative typing necessarily follows from the evidentiary stance of these tales—that is, from the fact that they were claimed to report certain individuals' personal experience in a manner designed to convince readers of the veracity of the report. Some of the stories in *Signs from the Unseen Realm*, for example, seek to convey information to the reader concerning the afterlife. These tales' particular way of doing that is not to quote scriptures that place discourses on this matter in the mouth of the Buddha, a figure who, however authoritative, stood distant in time and space. It is instead to cite people—ordinary people, people more or less like the readers of the text, not shamans or spirit-mediums—who had lived in China in recent centuries or decades and who told of having toured the afterlife personally. As a matter of simple narrative logic, in order for ordinary, living human protagonists' impressions of the afterlife to have become known to others, there was really only one possible story type: the protagonist must die, visit the realm of the dead, then revive and tell his tale to an audience in this world. Similarly, to document specific instances in which the Bodhisattva Sound Observer saved Chinese individuals from distress, only one basic type of tale was logically possible: the individual protagonist's identity having been established, he or she must be narratively emplaced in dire circumstances and then extricated by what is either explicitly stated or implied to be the bodhisattva's swift response.

---

140. See Ortner, "Patterns of History," esp. 60–63.
141. Quoted in Ebersole, *Captured by Texts*, 11–12.

Religious Themes in the Text

Having just discussed the recurrent story lines in *Signs*, I intend here to outline the major religious concerns and interests evident in the text. My aim is not to give a thorough treatment of any of these religious themes taken singly, but simply to provide an overview of what the most salient themes in the text are.

Ganying 感應. The single most important organizing concept in *Signs* is that of *ganying*, or "stimulus-response," which is both a religious notion, constructed on cosmological underpinnings, and an engine of plot. *Mingxiang ji* and other miracle-tale collections are, in a sense, nothing more or less than compilations of specific instances of stimulus-response. I do not propose here to survey pre-Buddhist Chinese precedents to this concept.[142] In basic terms, it can be understood as the idea that elements of the unseen world respond—often strikingly, visibly, miraculously—to the stimulus of human devotional activity and karmic merit or lack thereof. Alternatively, the *gan* in the phrase, as well as the *ying*, may be understood as characterizing the actions of unseen beings: they sense or feel (*gan*) what humans do and respond (*ying*) accordingly. The essential claim bound up in the idea of *ganying*, then, is twofold. On the one hand, miracles do not occur haphazardly: in one way or another they are elicited by human action and intention. Humans and the Buddhist pantheon and cosmos are bound tightly together via the mechanism of stimulus-response. On the other hand, *ganying* implies that the Buddhist unseen world is exquisitely responsive: it is not aloof and indifferent like the Heaven of Zhuangzi or Xunzi among classical thinkers, nor is it capricious in its responses, as lesser spirits or local gods were sometimes thought to be. Explicit references to *ganying* and similar terms are sprinkled throughout the text, and I usually point them out in comments or notes, but in a larger sense the entire work is a thoroughgoing application of the notion of *ganying* to the writing of what amounts to a case-by-case religious history.

Devotion to the Bodhisattva Sound Observer. As noted above, the most heavily populated story type in extant excerpts from *Mingxiang ji* is that in which devotees in distress successfully call on the Bodhisattva Sound Observer to save them. Devotion to this bodhisattva, with his impressive protective powers, seems to have exploded in popularity in China during the fourth and fifth centuries. Paul Harrison has shown that in Lokakṣema's translations of Mahāyāna sutras, produced ca. 180 CE, Mañjuśrī, the bodhisattva commonly associated with wisdom, is virtually

---

142. Sharf, *Coming to Terms with Chinese Buddhism*, 77–136, provides one such survey, to which may be compared the brief sketch in Liu Yuanru, *Chaoxiang shenghuo shijie*, 212–214.

omnipresent, while Sound Observer is almost invisible.[143] Something seems to have happened in China between roughly 200 and 400 to stimulate new reliance on Sound Observer and the circulation of hundreds of tales recounting his miraculous interventions. The likeliest explanation is twofold. First, these were the centuries in which the two earliest translations of the *Lotus Sutra* became available in China: the first, by Dharmarakṣa, in 285[144]—a translation whose importance in shaping the modes of piety portrayed in our text cannot be overstated—and the second, by Kumārajīva, in the first few years of the fifth century. It is in a chapter of that sutra (a chapter that, as we know from the Dunhuang manuscripts, also circulated widely as an independent text) that Sound Observer's remarkable powers were famously—and apparently newly—extolled. His powers to save beings were also promulgated in a great many other, briefer sutras and texts from other genres in these centuries in China, many of them indigenously composed,[145] but most of these were probably inspired by and modeled on the *Lotus*. Second, it was surely by means of the many dozens of stories of his miraculous rescues of those who called on him that these powers—as well as the sutra chapter promising them to devotees—were so widely and effectively announced in China. *Signs from the Unseen Realm* and other texts before and after it, therefore, responding to the *Lotus Sutra* chapter, both reflected and contributed to the popularity of this bodhisattva in China.

As I have argued elsewhere, there had never been a deity quite like Sound Observer in China, one who (in this early period) combined strikingly immediate, concretely salvific responsiveness to those who called on him, on the one hand, with a lack of local cult sites on the other. He was

---

143. Harrison, "Mañjuśrī and the Cult of the Celestial Bodhisattvas." The one exception comes in the translations of the larger *Sukhāvatīvyūha* produced by both Lokakṣema and (separately) Zhi Qian, where this bodhisattva is portrayed as (1) a being to whom devotees should turn for protection from corrupt local officials and (2) the future successor of Amitābha in the latter's Buddha-field, rather than (as is the case in most other early translated sutras) simply being mentioned in passing as a member of the audience for a sermon by the Buddha. (In both roles he is often, though not always, paired with the Bodhisattva Mahāsthāmaprāpta; the latter is predicted to succeed him as the Buddha of what is presently the field of Amitābha.) See Nattier, "Avalokiteśvara in Early Chinese Buddhist Translations." Sound Observer's role as Amitābha's successor, however, does not explain the particular shapes his popularity took in China in these centuries, unlike his portrayal in the *Lotus*, on which his image and function in China were for the most part clearly (and sometimes explicitly) based.

144. See Boucher, "Dharmarakṣa and the Transmission of Buddhism," 24. Nattier writes, "It seems clear that it was through the work of Dharmarakṣa—specifically, through the twenty-third chapter of his *Lotus Sūtra*, the *Guangshiyin* [*p*]*umen pin* 光世音普門品—that this bodhisattva first gained widespread appeal in China." "Avalokiteśvara in Early Chinese Buddhist Translations," 206.

145. For sources, see Campany, "The Real Presence," 233 n1. On illustrations of this text—giving as vivid a sense of the devotion inspired by this bodhisattva as do the stories—see Murase, "Kuan-Yin as Savior of Men."

portrayed as an exquisitely responsive divine being who did not need to be supplicated by means of offerings presented at any temple or shrine. Invoking him was a mental and vocal act that could be carried out anywhere, even in a prison cell or on a boat in midstream.[146] The early compilers of tales about Sound Observer were acutely aware that written accounts of the bodhisattva's miraculous responses helped propagate faith in him and thus stimulated more divine responses in an ever-widening spiral; Lu Gao, compiler of the largest such text to have survived and a contemporary of Wang Yan, even invited readers of his text to add their own reports to his, so that "as these divine marvels are transmitted through the world, the ranks of the faithful will swell."[147]

   The abstinence ceremony (zhai 齋). In modern studies, the word zhai 齋 (the term most often used to render Indic terms such as poṣadha, upoṣatha, and upoṣadha into Chinese) is often rendered as "vegetarian feast," "maigre feast," or simply "feast," or else as "fast."[148] These renditions are too narrow an understanding not only of the content of the zhai but

---

146. See Campany, "The Real Presence," 252–256.
147. See ibid., 267.
148. These terms refer to observances carried out by monastics and by laypersons (somewhat differently) centrally involving the confession of sins, the recitation of sutras, discourses on Dharma, and the recitation of monastic or lay precepts. The monastic observances were generally held on the fourteenth or fifteenth of each lunar half-month and the lay observances on the eighth, fourteenth, fifteenth, twenty-third, twenty-ninth, and thirtieth days of each month (in effect, four times per month). In addition, three "long zhai" were sometimes held during the first fortnight of the first, fifth, and ninth months. See Hureau, "Preaching and Translating on Poṣadha Days," 102; Hureau, "Buddhist Rituals," 1213–1230; Martin, "Les Bouddhistes laïcs," 537–553; Gernet, Buddhism in Chinese Society, 257–259; Hureau, "Bouddhisme chinois"; Soymié, "Un calendrier de douze jours"; Soymié, "Les dix jours de jeûne de Kṣitigarbha"; Ji Zhichang, "Dong Jin jushi Xie Fu kao," 69–72; and, for a useful study of the lay practice of inviting monks and nuns to their households, Shinohara, "Taking a Meal at a Lay Supporter's Residence." The eight prohibitions upheld by laity during these periods forbade killing, stealing, sexual intercourse, lying, drinking alcohol, using perfumes and flowers, sleeping on high beds, and eating after noon. On the "long zhai" see Forte and May, "Chōsai," usefully emphasizing the wide variety of meanings attached to the terms zhai and changzhai in Sino-Japanese Buddhist texts. Studies of the sorts of ritual documents associated with these periodic observances along with other ritual performances denoted by the term zhai, most of which documents (zhaiwen 齋文 and yuanwen 願文, with considerable debate over the proper usage of these terms) postdate the Mingxiang ji by at least two centuries, include Hao, "Guanyu Dunhuang xieben zhaiwen de jige wenti"; Hao, "Dunhuang xieben zhaiwen ji qi yangshi"; Tai, "Shilun zhaiwen de biaoyanxing"; Tai, "Wei wangzhe yuan"; Magnin, "Donateurs et jouers en l'honneur du Buddha"; Wang Sanqing, Cong Dunhuang; Wang Sanqing, Dunhuang fojiao zhaiyuan wenben; Zhang Guangda, "'Tanfo' yu 'tanzhai'"; and Teiser, "Ornamenting the Departed." On confession, which was a key element of zhai observance but was also practiced in many other contexts, see the widest-ranging available study, Kuo's Confession et contrition, as well as the more narrowly focused works by Wang Juan, Tang Song guyi fojiao chanyi yanjiu and Dunhuang lichanwen yanjiu, and Sheng Kai, Zhongguo fojiao chanfa yanjiu.

also of its significance. For laity, to reduce it to the essentials, the *zhai* (or, as it was often referred to, *zhaijie* 齋戒, "practicing abstinence and [adhering to extra] prohibitions") was a cluster of periodic practices centering on confession, the feeding of monks and nuns, abstention from eating after noon and from sexual activity, and attendance at nocturnal recitation of sutras, all in a special ritual space featuring a Buddha image. This bundle of practices, which I usually render (not wholly satisfactorily) as "abstinence ceremony," constituted a periodic intensification of lay Buddhist practice, in that laymen and laywomen temporarily behaved more like monks and nuns without taking monastic vows. Note that while feeding monastics was an important element of this cluster of practices, it was by no means the only or even the most essential element, and this is why I avoid "feast" as a translation of *zhai*.[149] Monks and nuns practiced their own set of abstinence observances, but in the miracle tales we see this cluster of activities almost exclusively in lay settings. Something of the importance of the abstinence ceremony in Buddhist life—despite the paucity of modern studies—may be inferred from the fact that these practices are the third topic Xi Chao discusses in his *Fengfa yao*, immediately after the triple refuge and the five lay precepts.[150] A reading of the miracle tales similarly indicates how central they were in lay Buddhist life.

From the tales we glean details about those practices. Given the lay orientation of the tales, it is not surprising to find that, in them, the abstinence ceremony is portrayed as a gathering, ritual meal, and attendant instruction and scripture recitation hosted in lay homes for monastic and lay

---

149. Examples of the contrary practice may be seen in Teiser, *The Scripture on the Ten Kings*, 21–22 and passim. More recently (in his "Ornamenting the Departed"), Teiser has alternated between "feast" and "ritual" as translations for *zhai*. In my opinion, the former is too narrow to cover the range of activities denoted by the term, at least in miracle tales and similar genres of texts. (If, for example, a Protestant church service that included instrumental and vocal music, prayer, a sermon, scriptural readings, a celebration of the Eucharist, a baptism, and community announcements were also customarily followed by a communal meal, as it was at the Virginia church I attended as a boy, would future historians be wise to term such occasions in their entirety "feasts"?) Teiser's latter translation, on the other hand, is misleadingly broad, since *zhai* denotes (again with the generic qualifier just mentioned) not just any Buddhist rite but this particular cluster of activities. (Funerals, the conferral of monastic vows or of lay precepts, ceremonies for consecrating images or opening monasteries, bathing Buddha images, processions: these are just a few of the other important Buddhist activities that we would also, in the context of current English usage, want to call "rituals" but that were not per se labeled *zhai*, although the performance of confession, the temporary observance of extra precepts, the recitation of scriptures, and the hosting of a meal or donation of food and distribution of the resulting merit often figured in the ensemble of activities they included. We read of *zhai* for such occasions.) In a personal communication, Teiser has proposed rendering *zhai* as "'ritual' in the broad sense of any Buddhist ceremony overseen by monks involving donation by a lay or monastic [person] and the transfer of merit or assigning of benefits." Such usage perhaps fits the Dunhuang liturgical documents on which Teiser bases his suggestion, but it is too broad to match the phenomena the term is used to describe in the (much earlier) miracle tales treated here.

150. See *Hongming ji* 13.86 and Zürcher, *The Buddhist Conquest of China*, 164–165.

guests. If *Mingxiang ji* were our only source, we would hardly guess that such practices were just as often carried out in monasteries. Careful preparations are described: sprinkling and sweeping the space, as well as setting out incense, flowers, sutras, and images. Often a special hall or room in the household, containing an altar and reserved for this purpose only, is mentioned; some well-off families even seem to have had more than one of these *fatang* 法堂 or *zhaitang* 齋堂.[151] Nocturnal recitation of sutras is mentioned and seems to have been the exclusive task of invited monks. Circumambulation is also described, probably of the image in the *zhaitang* while sutras were recited. One story mentions "purifiers," or *jingren* 淨人, serving food to monastic guests in a layperson's home during the ceremonial meal; these monastery personnel would sometimes have accompanied monks and nuns to lay homes. Every mention of these observances in *Mingxiang ji* describes both laity and monastics as attending, and it looks as if the gatherings were the major way in which some Buddhist laypersons interacted with monks and nuns. A few particular sutras are mentioned as having been recited during the observances, and occasionally they are described as having been dedicated to particular bodhisattvas—Sound Observer and Samantabhadra—who are prominently described in sutras such as the *Lotus* as serving to protect pious laypersons from harm. One story mentions that a layman composed a liturgical text for use during these rites, and several of these texts are preserved from as early as the Jin.

We know that the abstinence ceremony was performed on certain days of each month and at certain times of year. But the tales suggest that it was also performed on an occasional basis, and they inform us as to some of the circumstances that could prompt such a performance and the results it might have been hoped to bring about. The observances are described, for example, as having been sponsored by a layman on account of his recent conversion to the observance of Dharma, or as performed in hope of healing or as preparation for the host's own imminent death. They are mentioned together with public recitation of the *Sutra of the Oceanic Dragon King* as a cure for extreme drought. The merit from sponsoring them is portrayed as saving protagonists from afterlife punishment they would otherwise have to undergo; it lengthens life spans; it produces fortune for the troubled dead. They are sponsored as gestures of thanks and to fulfill vows. Especially intense piety can be indicated by a layperson's unusually exacting adherence to the abstinence restrictions, often accompanied by vegetarianism and sutra recitation.

We also glimpse through the tales the cosmological context of these observances. Sutras—though to what extent these include translated as well as indigenously produced sutras remains a question for further research—speak of a system in which four celestial kings (*si tianwang* 四天王)

---

151. On this architectural use of the term *zhai*, which was new in this period, see Zhou Junxun, *Wei Jin nanbeichao zhiguai xiaoshuo cihui*, 57–58, 143.

or their representatives descend on the days of the observance to conduct tours of inspection and note the meritorious or sinful actions of the human populace.[152] They also speak of "spirits of goodness" or "beneficent spirits" (*shanshen* 善神); indeed the indigenously composed *Consecration Sutra* (*Guanding jing* 灌頂經) mentions them no fewer than thirty-nine times. Usually they were said to be sent from the heavens to protect those who do good and to abandon those who do evil deeds. In particular, they encircle and protect those who obey the precepts or who, even when sleeping, think on them; the indigenously composed *Sutra of the Four Celestial Kings* (*Si tian-wang jing* 四天王經) imagines five spirits per precept encircling and protecting the lay practitioner, for a possible total of twenty-five. This divine underpinning and rationale for the practice of the abstinence ceremony is not mentioned in the tales as often as one might expect, but it is occasionally glimpsed in them. One tale pictures the *shanshen* as residing specifically in the heart/mind, and not only that of human beings but also of animals.

It is this cosmological and divine context implied for the abstinence ceremony—the hovering presence of divine beings just beyond the veil of ordinary sight—that sets up a further aspect of how these observances are represented in the miracle accounts: as a portal between the seen and unseen worlds. They are portrayed in the tales as "stimuli" (*gan*) that elicit divine "responses" (*ying*). When, in a body of stories, the same narrative pattern recurs repeatedly, we know something important is being said. In our tales the following scenario recurs numerous times: an abstinence ceremony is under way when a strange monk appears; often he is dirty, wears a frayed robe, breaks the order of seniority in seating, and otherwise blatantly violates regulations. The scenario then branches: either the lay host recognizes or suspects the strange guest is a "spirit-monk" (*shenseng* 神僧) and pays appropriate obeisance, sometimes then being rewarded for doing so, or else he fails the test and watches in chagrin as the monk leaves in a way that manifests his divine nature (often by suddenly ascending into the sky).[153] We need not understand all these mysterious figures to have been Piṇḍola, who is mentioned by name only once in *Mingxiang ji* (in item 95, which is not a story of this type), though certainly the story type echoes narratives found in the mid-fifth-century *Method of Inviting Piṇḍola* (*Qing Bintoulu fa* 請賓頭盧法).[154] But what these stories clearly show is that prop-

---

152. See, for example, *Shi ji jing* 世記經 (section 30 of *Chang ahan jing*, 20.134b–135a); *Da loutan jing* 4.298b; *Fangguang banruo jing* 7.46a and *Daoxing banruo jing* 2.431b–c (although here only their protection of those who uphold the sutra is mentioned, not their inspection of merit and sin); and in particular *Si tianwang jing*, an indigenously composed sutra. More research is needed to determine whether the motif of the kings' periodic inspection of sin and merit is found in translated materials or only in sutras produced in China.

153. Items 11, 16, 19, 20, 27 (solo visit), 29 (cf.), 43, 76, 108, 109, and 113. Two other stories (18, 19) focus on other sorts of anomalies during *zhai* gatherings.

154. On Piṇḍola, see the note to item 95. See also Lévi and Chavannes, "Les seize arhat

er, suitably pious performance of the abstinence ceremony was argued to constitute a stimulus powerful enough to draw forth this sort of miraculous response from the unseen world. Other story patterns similarly suggest that contact between the seen and unseen worlds was unusually open on the days of abstinence observance. These are the days, for example, on which several stories depict dead family members as periodically returning to visit their living kin, warning them of retribution for sins and urging them to stricter practice.

The net effect of these motifs is to portray the heightened devotional concentration that was the abstinence ceremony as capable—not automatically, but on certain rare occasions—of penetrating the veil of the unseen. The dedicated time and ritual household space of these observances might open a portal through which normally unseen but ever-present beings passed into fleeting visibility, impacting witnesses in ways recorded in the tales.

The spirit-monk.   Many miracle stories mention a mysterious type of figure sometimes termed a "spirit-monk" (*shenseng* 神僧) but more often left unlabeled. In one common story type, as we have seen, the spirit-monk appears as an uninvited, strange guest during abstinence meals hosted for monastics by laity. Elsewhere a monk suddenly appears before a layman to inform him that the piglet he has just sacrificed was his reborn son, then just as suddenly vanishes (item 34); a "person in a monk's robe" is glimpsed by timber cutters on a mountain slope as he flies through the air (39); two unfamiliar monks suddenly appear, dispense advice to a stubborn layman, then vanish, and the protagonist is later told that one of the spirit-monks he saw was Piṇḍola (95); and an entire group of monks suddenly appears during an abstinence observance, their bodies partially protruding from the walls of the chamber, then just as suddenly disappears again after delivering a message to the protagonist (98). In several return-from-death stories, the protagonist is unexpectedly met before the purgatory courts by an unfamiliar monk who serves as legal advocate and guide; or else he is aided by a monk he knew in life, who now continues to serve as his spiritual advisor in the other world (as amusingly portrayed in item 23). All of these motifs underscore the extent to which, from the lay point of view represented in these tales, some monks and nuns were viewed as extraordinary beings with impressive spiritual powers. The unseen world was busy with the activities of many types of beings, and one of these types was spirit-

---

protecteurs de la loi"; Strong, "The Legend of the Lion-Roarer"; and Shinohara, "Taking a Meal at a Lay Supporter's Residence," 28–34. On the *Method of Inviting Piṇḍola*, which existed no later than the end of the fifth century (see *Chu sanzang jiji* 4.23b24), whether or not it was really translated by Huijian 慧簡 (also credited with "translating" the *Consecration Sutra*), see Lévi and Chavannes, "Les seize arhat protecteurs de la loi," 216ff.; Strong, "The Legend of the Lion-Roarer," 76, 79–81; and Shinohara, "Taking a Meal at a Lay Supporter's Residence," 29.

monks who might suddenly arrive to give advice, offer protection, accept an invitation to a ritual meal, or simply allow themselves to be glimpsed as they carried on their devotions, meditation, and chanting in the unseen world.[155]

Critique of monastic laxity. Five stories in *Mingxiang ji* prominently mention afterlife punishment of monks for lax observance of monastic precepts.[156] Either the protagonist is himself a monk who dies and returns to life to tell of what he saw, or else a layperson dies, tours the purgatories, and tells of having seen monks being punished for their lapses. In other stories, we see a deceased monk returning to visit a living colleague, warning him to stop eating meat (68); or a nun gruesomely punished for destroying sutras (83); or a monk divinely warned against the same sin (121). Keeping in mind that these stories were exchanged among both laypersons and monks but told from a largely lay viewpoint, we can read these motifs as amounting to a lay critique of monastic laxity. Just as laypersons took the lead in advocating for a vegetarian diet (on which more below), so, too, in stories such as these did they call upon monks and nuns to uphold the monastic precepts.

Images. The fashioning and ritual veneration of images of the Buddha and of bodhisattvas is mentioned often in our text, suggesting that such activity was a major aspect of Buddhist devotion in the circles from which these stories emanated.[157] Only a few of these mentions occur in passing;[158] in most cases images, when referred to, play a major role in the narrative, which goes to show that images were not merely incidental accompaniments to devotional action: they were companions, they were the

---

155. See the discussion in Xu, "*Mingxiang ji* ji qi sengren xingxiang," 112–117.

156. These are items 6, 66, 110, 118, and 125. For a brief discussion of negative images of monastics in *Mingxiang ji*, see Xu, "*Mingxiang ji* ji qi sengren xingxiang," 109–112.

157. On the religious meanings and functions attached to fashioning and venerating images, see Sharf, "Production of Buddha Images"; Brown, "Expected Miracles"; Shinohara, "Changing Roles for Miraculous Images"; Liu Shufen, "Art, Ritual, and Society" (on communally sponsored votive stelae that often incorporated images in their design); McNair, *Donors of Longmen*; Ma, "Buddhist Cave-Temples and the Cao Family"; Soymié, "Quelques representations de statues miraculeuses"; and the still valuable work by Soper, *Literary Evidence for Early Buddhist Art*. The most complete and up-to-date survey of early Buddhist art in China may be found in Rhie, *Early Buddhist Art of China*, vols. 1 and 2.

158. As in stories 26 (an image is mentioned as being carried in procession in the festivities surrounding the celebration of the Buddha's birth on the eighth day of the fourth month), 40 (a monk is mentioned as making temples and fashioning images), 43 and 98 (images mentioned as being set out in preparation for *zhai* observance), 52 (frequent making of images is mentioned to indicate a village's particular degree of piety), and 124 (a monk is mentioned as fashioning a large image in a temple where he resides). Items 108 and 109 commemorate the donation by Song Empress Dowager Lu Zhao of an image of the Bodhisattva Samantabhadra to a temple.

subject of dreams and visions, and they were regarded as being alive with the presence of the august beings they represented.

In his preface to the collection, Wang Yan tells the story of his own lifelong Buddhist piety largely in terms of his intimate and deeply emotional relationship with a small metal image of Sound Observer. He tells us that he had been given the image as a boy by the monk from whom he received the five precepts. Even during periods of his adult life when he had to leave the image in the care of a monastery due to official travel, he worried about losing it and sometimes saw it in his dreams.[159] Already in the first story of the collection, purporting to relate how Buddhism first came to China, we are introduced to the central role images will play: the Han emperor's envoy, we are told, returned from India with sutras, images, and monks, and among the images is a portrait of the Buddha made from life for King Udayana—providing an authenticating visual link from the Han court back to the "true form" of the founder of the foreign religion.[160] Other tales portray people as fashioning images to replicate the forms of spirit-monks or bodhisattvas they have glimpsed in visions or dreams.[161] Conversely, the Buddha's body, seen in a vision, is said to exactly resemble images currently in use in China (item 82), just as the true form of Sound Observer is said to resemble images of him now carried in processions (48). Images, like sutras, are reported as having miraculously survived fires unscathed.[162] We find mention of the bathing of images and the affixing of coins to them as devotional acts (45, 75). The notion that some Buddha images made under the reign of the Indian ruler Aśoka might be recovered from under the soil of China is referred to in one tale (45). A man is described as wearing a small image of Sound Observer on his head for protection while traveling (51). A not-quite-completed Sound Observer image that had been fashioned by a monk appears in a dream to comfort him in prison; on returning to his quarters he finds that the image had broken free from its mold.[163] Monks and laypersons who ardently desire to make

---

159. Compare *Xuanyan ji* 32, in which a devotee who for years took solicitous ritual care of an image suddenly lost it and was disconsolate, blaming himself and thinking constantly on it. One hundred days later it reappeared on the same altar as before, emitting light, causing the protagonist and his family to redouble their devotional practice.

160. On this image, see comments to item 1.

161. In item 19, a householder makes an image of the spirit-monk who visited his household during the abstinence observance. In item 53, a man fashions an image based on the radiant form of Guanshiyin he had seen while requesting help in distress.

162. In item 36, only those homes containing sutras and images are spared when fire sweeps through a city, while the rest burn. In item 86, a lay Buddhist who is persuaded to convert to the Way of the Celestial Masters is ordered to destroy his images and sutras, but they miraculously survive the fire he sets in his oratory.

163. Item 58. Compare *Xuanyan ji* 3, in which a metal image appears, rubs the body of a sick devotee, and thus cures him on the seventh day of an abstinence ceremony dedicated to Guanshiyin.

an image of the Buddha or a bodhisattva but lack the means or materials to do so are rewarded with the miraculous provision of materials or the sudden appearance of a completed, fully adorned image.[164] Meanwhile, pious converts to Buddhist practice are portrayed as destroying their household images of non-Buddhist gods (23, 65), and theft or disrespect of Buddhist images brings down dire punishment, graphically described.[165]

Dreams, visions, and spirit-mediums.   Several scholars have pointed to the importance of dreams, waking visions, and trancelike visualization practices (or narratives of these) in early Mahāyāna scriptures.[166] The religious world reflected in and shaped by *Signs from the Unseen Realm*, as adumbrated by the work's very title, is one in which oneiric and visionary experiences are considered channels of communication to the hidden world of spirits, ghosts, bodhisattvas, heavens, Pure Lands, and purgatories. In his preface, Wang Yan recounts not one but two dreams in which vital information about the status of his beloved Sound Observer image was conveyed to him. The first story of the work presents the very advent of Buddhism to China as having been occasioned by an emperor's dream. The work contains many other dream narratives.[167] In some of them, the dreamer undergoes surgery; in others, he encounters ghosts, spirits, or bodhisattvas; in still others, he receives knowledge via divine revelation.[168] Dreaming is a mode of real contact with other beings, not a mental event merely internal to the dreamer. In waking visions, meanwhile, protagonists in *Mingxiang ji* are depicted as receiving accurate predictions and

---

164. Item 55 narrates the divine response granted to a monk who lacked material to finish constructing a Buddha image. In item 112, a nun twice finds metal images that have spontaneously appeared in response to her piety: one is an image of Maitreya; the other is unspecified. Item 114 tells of the divine provision to a layman of material needed to complete an image. In item 128 we read of a laywoman who had long desired to fashion a metal image with her own hands and then venerate it for the rest of her life, but who had not found the means; suddenly one day a five-foot-tall, painted metal image of Guanshiyin appeared on the altar in her home.

165. In item 111, theft of small metal images is divinely punished; item 79 recounts the punishment suffered by a man who stole crystals that had been affixed to an image as adornments. Monks were certainly not exempt from a similar fate: item 116 tells of how a monk who filched the pearl from between the eyes of a Buddha image was divinely chastised. In item 75, a man steals the coins that had been placed by passersby on a Buddha image in a temple; he pays the expected price for this sacrilege. In item 127, a man who "venerated the Dao and ridiculed the Buddha" habitually treats Buddha images with disrespect, then grows ill. A friend advises him to make an image of Guanshiyin to atone for his sin. He does so and recovers. For a useful study of indigenous precursors to some of these Buddhist motifs, see Delehaye, "Les antécédents magiques des statues chinoises."

166. See Beyer, "Vision Quest in Early Mahayana"; Harrison, "Mediums and Messages"; Harrison, "*Buddhānusmṛti*." On the revelation of Buddhist sutras (etc.) in China, see Campany, "Buddhist Revelation and Taoist Translation."

167. I am preparing a separate study of these.

168. See, for example, items 5, 23, 33, 48, 55, 58, 61, 63, 70, 73, 80, 81, 85, 87, 90, 95, 100, 114, 115, 118, 122, 123, 124, and 127.

warnings, being healed, having revelations of new sutras and teachings bestowed on them, and solving various other problems.[169] And the text displays a somewhat surprising attitude toward spirit-mediums. Although *Mingxiang ji* does not shy from engaging in religious contestation, it never challenges the ability of spirit-mediums to "see" beings in the spirit world. Rather, in the miracle tales we see such specialists confirming Buddhist assertions.[170]

Rebirth.   At least eight stories in *Mingxiang ji* directly address the doctrine of rebirth so central to Buddhist cosmology and ethics, so startlingly new on the Chinese scene, so at odds with the cult of ancestors and the patrilineal descent system. Seven of these are centrally concerned to provide some sort of confirmation or proof of rebirth: a protagonist recalls details from his previous life (item 3), recognizes an object possessed in a former life (57), or retains abilities acquired in a former life (69); an accomplished master discerns the past lives of two of his disciples (8); a protagonist who temporarily dies recalls his former lives before returning to life (45). A spirit-monk informs the head of a household that the piglet he has just sacrificed was his own son recently reborn (34). In one remarkable story, a layman is granted a waking vision of who he was in his two previous lives—in both instances women (117). Few of these stories (8, 34) deal with cross-species rebirth; in most cases it is a matter of humans reborn as other people. Items 3 and 124 emphasize that an individual is reborn into different families in each lifetime, whereas items 45 and 57 envision people reborn (either as people or as domestic animals) into their previous families. None of these stories is especially well attuned to what we normally think of (surely too simplistically) as standard Buddhist teaching, in which successive rebirths as a human being would be very hard to attain and in which knowledge of one's own or others' previous lives is a feat of which only highly advanced practitioners are supposed capable.

Vegetarianism.   It is well known that vegetarianism was not standard Buddhist practice in India or in the earliest period in China. Rather, the standard was that monks and laypersons were not to kill living things and were not to accept meat that had been slaughtered specifically for them, a norm reflected in Xi Chao's *Essentials in Upholding the Dharma*, for example.[171] Over time, however, strict vegetarianism came to prevail as a norm for both monks and laity in China. Valérie Lavoix has shown that it was

---

169. See items 2, 27, 29, 67, 84, 87, 89, 90, 94, 95, 100, 112, 114, and 122. Visionary receipt of new sutras (as seen in items 2 and 84) is particularly important as one way in which indigenously composed, or "apocryphal," sutras may have been constructed. See further Campany, "Buddhist Revelation and Taoist Translation."

170. As in items 65, 71, 86, 99, and 124.

171. See the translated passage in Zürcher, *The Buddhist Conquest of China*, 165.

probably laymen in China who took the lead in this.[172] In *Mingxiang ji* we do not find a univocal position on this question, but we do see early signs of the insistence in China on total abstinence from meat and fish. The stories show—and themselves also *were*—ways in which stances on meat eating were being worked out by many parties in the fourth and fifth centuries.

One story reflects the old norm: a man temporarily dies and is gruesomely punished for having fished and hunted (compare item 45 in this respect); he is warned that he may kill no living thing, not even an ant, and that of fish and meat it is permissible to eat only the flesh of those animals that have died naturally (item 92). Other tales mention total abstinence from meat and fish as a mark of unusually diligent practice, such as a layman who is said from age sixteen to have adopted a vegetarian diet, practiced the abstinence ceremony, and chanted two particular sutras regularly (25), or another who temporarily dies and is treated well during his tour of the purgatories due to his pious practices, one of which is that he eats no fish or meat (59), or a monk whose especially assiduous regimen includes a vegetarian diet (126). One story implicitly criticizes the culture of sacrificing animals to serve deceased family members and suggests that living descendants cease graveside offerings altogether (as requested by the ghost of the deceased) and keep a vegetarian diet (124).

Three other tales, however, display a deeper unease with meat eating and constitute examples of the sorts of narratives through which the new, stricter norm was being worked out. In one of them, a man who has died, seen the horrible punishments of the purgatories, and returned to life thenceforth practices a vegetarian diet (item 6). In another, a family is bereaved of a child; several months later, the head of the household sacrifices a piglet for the ceremony welcoming the arrival of a new local supervisor, at which point a spirit-monk suddenly appears to inform him that he has just slaughtered his reborn son (34). A dead monk appears to a living monk whom he knew while alive, revealing that he has been reborn in the purgatory of hungry dogs because of having eaten meat while alive; he has returned for the purpose of warning his friend to desist (68). The second of these tales may have had the most emotional impact, but the third one represents the most explicit departure from earlier norms in its clear claim that meat eating is not only a sin, it is a sin that is punished in a specially dedicated purgatory where carnivores become food for hungry dogs.

Sutra copies as sacred objects; sutra recitation as a powerful act. It is well known that many Mahāyāna sutras attempt to reinforce their perceived sacrality by incorporating instructions said to have been spoken by

---

172. See "La contribution des laïcs au végétarisme." For more general treatments, see Kieschnick, "Buddhist Vegetarianism in China," and Kieschnick, "Buddhist Monasticism," 563–564. Unfortunately I have been unable to gain access to Pu, "Kindness toward Animals in Early Chinese Buddhist History."

the Buddha on how they are to be ritually treated and revered, and by claiming many other powers for themselves. *Mingxiang ji* documents the sympathetic reception of such claims in China. One story tells of a ghost who appears to its family to thank them for sponsoring sutra recitation, since, because of it, the dead man has been reborn in the heavens (item 22). Another shows sutra recitation as guaranteeing rebirth in the Pure Land (126). Treasured copies of sutras miraculously save themselves from loss or destruction when their owners flee hostile troops or burning houses (21, 36). They miraculously appear when they have been mistakenly left behind and are needed for the correct performance of observances (24, 25).[173] All of these motifs both reflect and argue for the view that sutras are powerful, responsive agents and that reciting and venerating them will elicit striking effects.

Authentic origins. Many *Mingxiang ji* stories seem concerned to show that the terms in which Buddhism was practiced in China were authentic—that is, true to putative Indic originals. We sense an anxiety surrounding this issue that is similar to that expressed in many other Buddhist texts from the period in China. The anxiety becomes evident already at two points in Wang Yan's preface, where he asserts that Buddha and bodhisattva images made in China can move and emit light as long as they "match in kind the marks on the bodies" (*lei xing xiang* 類形相) of the beings they represent, and also where he alludes to the discovery of purported "Aśokan images" along the southeast coast of China. Item 1, a version of the famous legend of Buddhism's introduction to China due to a dream of Han emperor Ming, picks up the theme: the very structure of the story shows a concern to "match" Chinese images and practices to Indic originals; when the Han envoys return from the West with an image of the Buddha, it resembles what the ruler had seen in his dream. This story mentions the portrait of the Buddha legendarily commissioned by King Udayana, again arguing that Buddha images in China were true likenesses of their subject. Pilgrimages to India to retrieve sutras and images from their prestigious homeland are recounted in several stories, starting with this first item. Other tales recount direct, revelatory transmission of Sanskrit scriptural material to Chinese people in mediumistic trancelike states or via spirit travel—another mode of access to authentic originals. Similarly, one story (48) says that the "true form" of Sound Observer seen by a man in a vision resembled the images of that bodhisattva used in processions in China—a

---

173. Studies of these and related themes in a variety of contexts and sources include Schopen, *Figments and Fragments of Mahāyāna Buddhism*, 25–62, the classic early work on the subject; Jan, "The Power of Recitation"; Kuo, "La récitation des noms de Buddha"; Tsiang, "Embodiments of Buddhist Texts"; Stevenson, "Tales of the Lotus Sūtra"; Stevenson, "Buddhist Practice and the *Lotus Sūtra*"; and Campany, "Notes on Sutra Texts." For a convenient table of sutra-related miracles recounted in *Mingxiang ji*, see Liu Yuanru, *Chaoxiang shenghuo shijie*, 250–251.

direct authentication of Chinese iconographic styles. Accounts of stupas, relics, and images found underground in China, meanwhile (as seen in items 10, 45, and 55), in effect argued that China had been Buddhist since ancient times—yet another means of authentication. In several passages (e.g., in items 33, 45, 65, and 115), miraculous events or things seen in visions or afterlife tours are "matched" to promises made in translated sutras. Such passages authenticate the sutras by demonstrating their efficacy on Chinese soil, but they also authenticate the Chinese miracles by showing how they instantiate specific sutra verses.

PART II

Translation:
Signs from the Unseen Realm

PREFACE[1] BY WANG YAN 王琰

As a child I lived in Jiaozhi.[2] There was a Dharma master Xian 賢法師 there, a wise and virtuous monk from whom I received the five precepts.[3] I was given a metal image of Sound Observer[4] to make offerings to. Its form was different from those of today; on the other hand, it was not very old. It was of the type that was produced during the Yuanjia period.[5] Its casting was done so skillfully that it seemed to be the actual [bodhisattva].[6] I took it with me to the capital. At the time I was still a boy, and with my two younger brothers I practiced my devotions assiduously without flagging.

Later we were carrying out renovations and, living in dilapidated quarters, I worried at not having a secure room in which to set up the image. So I consigned it to the Nanjian monastery 南澗寺 in the capital.[7] At the time everyone was contending to find metal to melt down for cash, and thieves sought metal images as material for their cauldrons. By this point the image had been at the temple for several months. One afternoon I fell asleep and dreamed I saw the image standing at the edge of the altar. I thought this extremely strange. Dusk had already fallen, but I rushed to

---

1. Source texts: *Fayuan zhulin* 17.411a–b (section "honoring Buddhas" [*jing Fo* 敬佛]); *Ji shenzhou sanbao gantong lu* 2.419a; *Fayuan zhulin* 14.388c (section "Honoring Buddhas" [*jing Fo* 敬佛]); Lu, *Gu xiaoshuo gouchen*, 373; Wang Guoliang, *Mingxiang ji yanjiu*, 67–68; Wakatsuki, Hasegawa, and Inagaki, *Hōon jurin no sōgō teki kenkyū*, 117–121. The first three sources often differ in wording, with the second and third seemingly compressed paraphrases of the first. I follow *Fayuan zhulin* 17 except where noted. Additional texts: *Guanyin cilin ji* 2.90b.

2. A large commandery established during the Han and spanning parts of what are now Guangdong and Guangxi provinces, as well as northern and central Vietnam. It was an important center of Buddhism in China from earliest times, as discussed in part 1.

3. The five precepts, taken by Buddhist laity, are injunctions to abstain from killing, lying, stealing, consumption of alcohol, and sexual misconduct.

4. On this bodhisattva, very important in the religious world reflected in our text, see part 1.

5. The Song Yuanjia period (under Emperor Wen) lasted from 424 to 454.

6. On the significance of this statement, see the comments to item 1 below.

7. This monastery is mentioned in the *Gaoseng zhuan* biography of Daojiong 道冏 (12.407a), a monk who, significantly, figures in our text below.

the monastery and brought the image back home. That same night a dozen or so images were stolen from Nanjian monastery.

Long afterward there was another incident in which the image gave off light one night. It illuminated an area of about three feet around it. The light sparkled and dazzled the eyes. My brothers and I, along with household servants, over ten persons, all saw it together. I was still young at the time and did not manage to write down an account of it, but someone else wrote of it. They omitted the month and day, but it happened in the autumn of the seventh year of the Song Daming period [463].

At the end of the Taishi period [471–472], I moved to Wuyi.[8] A monk with whom I was acquainted temporarily lodged this image in Duobao monastery 多寶寺.[9] I then traveled in the Jiangdu region,[10] while this monk went into Jingchu.[11] I no longer knew where the image was. Ten years went by. I often worried that, because of these circumstances, my relation with the divine treasure would be severed. But at the end of the Shengming period of the Song [478–479], I was traveling through the gorges[12] and, passing through Jiangling, I saw this monk and learned from him where the image was. That same year I returned to the capital. I paid a visit to Duobao monastery and inquired about the image, but the abbot, Master Ai 愛公, said that no such image had been consigned there. I left and mulled it over, fearing that this monk harbored malicious intent and that I would lose the image. I was deeply saddened. That night, however, I dreamed I saw a man who said to me, "The image is at Duobao. Master Ai simply forgot about it. You will recover it." In the dream he then led me to the monastery and personally opened up the sanctuary.[13] There I saw the image very distinctly, on the east side among many other small images. The next morning I returned to the temple, telling Master Ai of what I had seen in my dream. So he opened up

---

8. A rather exclusive area of the southern capital, Jiankang (present-day Nanjing).

9. This monastery, situated north of Jiankang, is mentioned several times in *Gaoseng zhuan* (e.g., 7.372b, 8.376a, 11.402a) and elsewhere in *Mingxiang ji* as well. *Hongzan fahua zhuan* 1.13b19–20 says that it was founded in Yuanjia 5 (428), along with a Duobao stupa 多寶塔, by a certain Liu Fo'ai 劉佛愛 of Pengcheng. On *Hongzan fahua zhuan* see Stevenson, "Tales of the Lotus Sūtra."

10. That is, the region surrounding the southern capital at Jiankang and the lower reaches of the Jiang river.

11. An old double name for the region of Chu in the south, comprising modern Hubei and Hunan provinces, well upriver from the Jiankang area. The term denotes one (large) area of land, not two putatively distinct areas Jing and Chu, as seen for example in the title of an early medieval work on regional customs, *Jing Chu suishi ji* 荊楚歲時記, on which see the recent discussion in Chapman, "Carnival Canons," 50–115.

12. That is, the famous three gorges of the Yangzi river; Wang Yan is here traveling upriver from the southern capital area, heading west.

13. "Sanctuary" here translates *dian* 殿, literally "palace," which, judging from the context, must mean the liturgical center of the monastery, kept closed except during ceremonies. Later, *dian* came to be often used to refer to an entire temple, as is common today, but here it is clearly an inner chamber, housing sacred images, that is meant. I do not believe this was common usage at the time. On the layout of monasteries during this period, see Li Yuqun, "Classification, Layout, and Iconography."

the sanctuary for me, and there indeed was the image, on the east side, just as I had seen in my dream. So I took it home. This was on the thirteenth of the seventh month of the first year of Jianyuan [16 August 479].

Today I regularly make offerings to this image. It will always be for me a vehicle[14] [for salvation].[15] Turning over in my mind the incidents involving the image, I was deeply moved, and so I tracked down more such signs and visions and stitched them together to make this record.

For receiving and mirroring the feelings of intimacy, there is nothing that surpasses the ceremonial image.[16] Many auspicious confirming signs[17] emanate from them.[18] The sutras say that whatever is molded, carved, drawn, or sketched, if it matches in kind the marks on the body[19] [of the

---

14. Literally "a bridge" (*jinliang* 津梁), here as elsewhere at the time used metaphorically for things or activities that were seen as conveying beings toward soteriological goals. See *Hanyu dacidian*, 5.1191 (particularly meanings 3 and 4).

15. It is perhaps possible to understand the subject of this sentence not as the image but as the activity of making offerings to it. In a strict sense, of course, both the image and the act of offering were required to generate merit and thus advance toward the salvation of oneself or others.

16. "Ceremonial image" translates *yixiang* 儀像. Although this term is not listed in *Hanyu dacidian* or Mochizuki's *Bukkyō daijiten,* and although Wakatsuki, Hasegawa, and Inagaki say that the term is unattested (*Hōon jurin no sōgō teki kenkyū*, 120 n16), it in fact appears in a number of contexts in works collected in the Buddhist and Daoist canons, where it clearly (and simply) denotes an image used in ceremonies—often but not necessarily an image installed in a ritual environment such as a temple, shrine, or altar. Examples include *Hongzan fahua zhuan* 5.24c6; *Chu sanzang jiji* 10.76a2; *Xu gaoseng zhuan* 9.495b6 and 22.617b23; *Fozu tongji* 42.385b14; Du Guangting's *Daojiao lingyan ji* 3.5b7, quoted in *Yunji qiqian* 117.15b9; and *Wudang fudi zongzhen ji* 2.10b5. As for the initial phrase, *fu jing jie jinqing* 夫鏡接近情, both *jing* and *jie* must be read as verbs ("to mirror" and "to receive"); the feelings (*jinqing* 近情) are the object, and "the ceremonial image" is the subject. (I reverse the order of the verbs because doing so produces better-sounding English.) *Jinqing* 近情 is attested from the Western Jin as denoting the feelings of human intimacy; see *Hanyu dacidian*, 10.736a. Wang Yan is making an aesthetic argument about the emotional power of images. My thanks to Stephen Bokenkamp for discussing this passage with me.

17. *Rui yan* 瑞驗.

18. Alternatively, we are entitled, I think, to understand the referent of the *ci* 此 in this sentence (*Fayuan zhulin* 14 and *Ji shenzhou sanbao gantong lu* give *shi* 是), rendered above as "them"—the thing from which auspicious confirming signs emanate—not as the image per se but rather the intimate, emotional relationship between the image and the human subject.

19. *Lei xing xiang* 類形相. Here and throughout, "bodily marks" translates the Chinese *xiang* 相, an indigenous term among whose meanings was the art of physiognomy and the somatic markings on which it was based, and which was often used to render the Sanskrit term *lakṣaṇa.* This notion of the special, divine, identifying somatic features of Buddhas recurs multiple times in *Mingxiang ji* and figured importantly in the devotional culture it represents. Here the point is that if human-made images correspond properly to this series of markings, the images will become imbued with the power of the being thus represented. On the bodily marks, see *Mouzi lihuo lun* 牟子理惑論 (collected in *Hongming ji* 1.2c), trans. and discussed in Pelliot, "Meou-tseu," 296–297, and in Keenan, *How Master Mou Removes Our Doubts,* 81–83; de Jong, "L'épisode d'Asita dans le Lalitavistara"; Wayman, "Thirty-Two Characteristics of the Great Person"; and *Xiuxing benqi jing* and *Taizi ruiying benqi jing,* both of which are early-translated texts containing lists of the bodily marks.

divine personage being represented], can move and emit light. In the recent two cases of images of Śākyamuni and Maitreya in the Western regions that gave off light and functioned like the beings they represent,[20] they must surely have possessed the correct marks.[21] Today's images in China, modeled on these Western ones, also manifest divine responses frequently. Here, too, in recent years there have been many cases of responses to people's stimuli in which, by the conduits of mere wood and stone, anomalies from the unseen world[22] have appeared. The images need not be beautifully rendered in order for them to have this capacity. Thus even sinking stone has been known to float on the deep, a transformation truly manifested in Min and Wu,[23] and ordinary metal has been known to secrete liquid in response to disasters, as in the Song[wang monastery] in Peng[cheng].[24] Although other manifestations of this sort arrive by a profusion of means and are thus difficult to evaluate, I have collected here enough examples to serve as a basis for persuading [the reader] to take

---

20. Preferring *ruo zhen* 若真 (in *Fayuan zhulin* 14 and *Ji shenzhou sanbao gantong lu*) to *ruo ming* 若冥 (as given in *Fayuan zhulin* 17), although I believe the two phrases function synonymously here.

21. "Must surely have possessed the correct marks" translates *gai de xiang* 蓋得相; the wording is identical in all versions. The wording of the sentence perhaps suggests that Wang Yan has two particular examples in mind, but at this writing I have not been able to ascertain what they might have been. It is also possible that he simply means all cases in general of Western images of the present and future Buddhas. For a comparable yet in some ways quite different early medieval Chinese passage—written, like this one, by a Buddhist layman—on the relationship between visual representations and that which they represent, see Tian, *Tao Yuanming and Manuscript Culture*, 29–31.

22. "Anomalies from the unseen world" translates *youyi* 幽異; the wording is identical in the three versions.

23. This line might alternatively be read to mean "to announce the transformation of Min and Wu," "transformation" (*hua* 化) in that case being taken to mean the religious conversion of these regions.

24. Wang Yan here obliquely refers to two events around which several stories had collected. The first is the reported recovery of two "Aśokan images"—stone images of former Buddhas purportedly commissioned and executed during the reign of that Indian monarch—when they miraculously floated ashore on the southeast coast of China. This story is again alluded to in summary fashion in the story of Liu Sahe below (item 45), and there it is significant that the images are said to bear faithful reproductions of the bodily marks of their divine subjects. (See *Gaoseng zhuan* 13.409b–c; *Fayuan zhulin* 12.379c and 13.383b–c, the latter citing another collection of Buddhist miracle tales, later than *Mingxiang ji*, to wit, *Jingyi ji* 旌異記 [on which see Campany, *Strange Writing*, 90]; *Ji shenzhou sanbao gantong lu* 2.404b; *Bianzheng lun* 7.540a; and, for a list of anomalies involving these and other such images, *Guang hongming ji* 15.202a–203b. For brief discussions, see Shinohara, "Two Sources of Chinese Buddhist Biographies," 163–164; Liu Shufen, "The Return of the State," 327; Campany, *Strange Writing*, 333–334; and Zürcher, *The Buddhist Conquest of China*, 277–280 [and cf. 243–244].) The second is the reported excretion of sweat by a metal image in the Songwang 宋王寺 monastery in the city of Pengcheng. The image was understood to be responding thus to the outbreak of military hostilities that included attacks on monks. (See *Fayuan zhulin* 14.388b–c and 15.400b–c; *Gaoseng zhuan* 13.412b; *Ji shenzhou sanbao gantong lu* 2.419a; and *Fozu tongji* 36.344b.)

refuge of his own accord.[25] In the case of manifestations involving sutras and stupas, the meanings and proofs are of the same sort [as those of images]. But the cases are not all of one sort, so I have followed each branch to its tip rather than exhaustively investigating its root.[26] The result is the work *Records of Signs from the Unseen Realm* (*Mingxiang ji* 冥祥記) in ten scrolls, which I here make available.

Comments

We see here a striking instance, recounted in the first person, of the emotional intimacy that sometimes attended devotion to images. Wang Yan speaks of his attachment since childhood to his small metal image of the Bodhisattva Sound Observer: it appears to him in dreams, he sees it emit light, he presents offerings to it, he exercises great solicitude for its safety, and he is devastated by the prospect of losing it. Miraculous responses on the part of such images are, he tells us, triggered by two things. Primarily they are set in motion by acts of devotion, which provide the "stimuli" (*gan* 感) for images' "responses" (*ying* 應). Also, the images should resemble the special bodily marks of the beings they represent: this resemblance, Wang implies, further facilitates miraculous responses. Yet they need not be made of precious materials to be efficacious. It was the series of miraculous responses by his own image that led him to compile this record of similar phenomena involving not only images but also other modalities of the miraculous.

Wang mentions the theft of images. At times when metal was in short supply, devotional images made of metal were an attractive target for thieves. The boom in the production of devotional images also contributed

---

25. That is, to take refuge in the three treasures (Buddha, Dharma, sangha), the fundamental ritual action taken—at least in theory—by everyone counted as Buddhist. (One first bowed to Buddha, Dharma, and sangha—the religious community—then prostrated oneself, joined one's hands, and confessed sins. Then, facing a teacher, one said three times the formula, "I take refuge in the Buddha, I take refuge in the Dharma, I take refuge in the sangha." The teacher then pronounced the five basic regulations of a layperson (prohibitions against killing, stealing, lying, committing adultery, and drinking alcohol) and asked if the novice was able to observe them. The novice answered in the affirmative. See Hureau, "Buddhist Rituals," 1209–1210.) The wording of this sentence is difficult and varies across the textual witnesses. I read *zi* 自 with *Fayuan zhulin* 14 rather than *mu* 目 with *Fayuan zhulin* 17 or the Song edition of *Ji shenzhou sanbao gantong lu*.

26. I take "following each branch to its tip" (*ji qi mo* 繼其末, a phrase appearing only in the two *Fayuan zhulin* witnesses) to mean something like: "I have recorded the details of each case separately rather than lumping them together, generalizing, or abstracting from the details to paint a general picture." "Not exhaustively investigating the root" (*bu jin qi ben* 不盡其本) I take to mean something like: "I have recorded reported historical instances here rather than either investigating the sources for each report exhaustively or writing a treatise on the metaphysical, epistemological, and soteriological bases for such phenomena in general." Note that this latter phrase appears only in the *Ji shenzhou sanbao gantong lu* witness, and then only in the Song, Yuan, and Ming editions of the canon. (In translating I follow the Song edition.)

to metal shortages, prompting the government at certain points to prohibit the founding of new icons. This theme recurs in items 58 and 111 below.

1[27]

Han emperor Ming 漢明帝[28] dreamed he saw a divine personage,[29] his body sixteen feet[30] tall and the color of yellow gold, his head surrounded[31] by a radiance like sunlight. He made inquiries among his ministers. Someone told him, "In the West there is a deity who is called Fo 佛.[32] His form is similar to what Your Majesty dreamed of. Might it have been he?" With this, the emperor dispatched envoys to India.[33] They copied sutras and secured images [of the Buddha] and displayed these in China. From the emperor to the princes and marquises, everyone [at court] venerated and served them. When they heard that when people die their essence and spirit do not perish, they were all beside themselves with fear.[34] At first, when the envoy Cai Yin 蔡愔 brought the monks Kāśyapa Mātaṅga and [Dharmaratna][35] back from the Western regions and showed the portrait of Śākya[muni] Buddha[36] made for King Udayana 優填王,[37] the emperor treasured it, and it resembled what he had seen in his dream. He commissioned craftsmen to make several images based on the portrait and had these installed in the Qingliang Tower of the South Palace, at the Gao-

---

27. Source texts: *Ji shenzhou sanbao gantong lu* 2.413c; *Fayuan zhulin* 13.383b (section "honoring Buddhas" [*jing Fo* 敬佛]) (these two witnesses are identical except for a few variant readings supplied in one but not the other); Lu, *Gu xiaoshuo gouchen*, 375; Wang Guoliang, *Mingxiang ji yanjiu*, 1. Previously translated in Maspero, "Le songe et l'ambassade de l'empereur Ming," 113, a translation I have consulted in preparing my own. Discussed: Zürcher, *The Buddhist Conquest of China*, 22.

28. Liu Zhuang 劉莊 reigned as Han emperor Ming from 58 to 75 CE.

29. Here and throughout, "divine personage" or "divine man" translates *shenren* 神人.

30. Here and throughout, I take the unit of measure *zhang* 丈 during this period as equivalent to 2.45 meters and thus roughly equivalent to 8 English feet. A *chi* 尺 was one-tenth of a *zhang*.

31. Both versions have *xiang pei* 項佩; I understand *xiang* (literally "the nape of the neck") as synecdochic for the head and shoulders, and I take *pei* as functioning verbally as "to be surrounded by." Maspero, "Le songe et l'ambassade de l'empereur Ming," 113, translates: "dont le cou et les épaules avaient l'éclat du soleil."

32. Fo 佛 (pronounced "but" at the time [see Pulleyblank, *Lexicon of Reconstructed Pronunciation*, 96]) was the graph most commonly used to render the term *buddha* in Chinese, from the earliest translations of An Shigao forward.

33. Here and throughout, "India" renders Tianzhu 天竺.

34. My translation departs slightly here from Maspero's.

35. Only one monk is named in this version of the story (in both the *Fayuan zhulin* and *Ji shenzhou sanbao gantong lu* versions, which are identical up to this point), but the word *deng* 等 following his abbreviated name indicates a plural number, and other versions mention Dharmaratna 竺法蘭 as the second monk brought back by the Chinese envoy.

36. Here following the variant (*fo* 佛) supplied in *Fayuan zhulin*, rather than the *yi* 倚 given in that text as well as in *Ji shenzhou sanbao gantong lu*.

37. See comments below.

yang[38] Gate, and at the imperial tombs at Xianjie, and he made offerings to them there. Additionally, he commissioned to be painted on the walls of the White Horse monastery [Baima si 白馬寺][39] a procession of a thousand chariots and ten thousand horsemen circumambulating a stupa three times, as is recorded in many accounts.[40]

Comments

Erik Zürcher has shown that this story of Buddhism's introduction to China—a story that, with varying details, appears in numerous other texts, including the *Sutra in Forty-Two Sections*—is probably "apocryphal" and likely does not predate the middle of the third century.[41] I want to approach it, however, not from the standpoint of whether it faithfully reflects the precise course of first-century events but from that of what it tells us about how "Buddhism" and its arrival in China were narratively construed—how the very complex and almost infinitely numerous specific phenomena summarized in a phrase such as "Buddhism's arrival in China" were gathered up into an imagined unity and narratively and metaphorically constructed as a discrete event. There is much to say by way of an answer, despite the story's brevity.

First, Buddhist history, and religious history in general, is usually recounted in terms of doctrines affirmed or denied. Religious history, on this common model, is the history of ideas or beliefs. Only one doctrine is mentioned in this narrative, however, although it is depicted as the most startling thing about the newly introduced religion: that "when people die their essence and spirit do not perish."[42] For the most part, the story of the

---

38. Maspero surmises this must be an error for Kaiyang 開陽, which would tally with the parallel narrative in the *Mouzi lihuo lun*.

39. Situated in Luoyang, the White Horse monastery was one of the most famous Buddhist temples in China, although it may not have existed as early as this story implies. There were other monasteries by this name in other areas. See Zürcher, *The Buddhist Conquest of China*, 22, 31–32, 69; Wang Yi-t'ung, *A Record of Buddhist Monasteries*, 173–176; Li Yuqun, "Classification, Layout, and Iconography," 636–638; Rhie, *Early Buddhist Art of China*, 1:13–15; and, for a recent reconsideration of the many "White Horse monasteries" in China, see Palumbo, "Dharmarakṣa and Kaṇṭhaka."

40. The scope of the final phrase (which is worded the same in both witnesses) is ambiguous: it is not clear whether the phrase "as is recorded in many accounts" refers to the circumambulation scene or to the whole narrative given above. In the latter case we would (with Maspero) understand something like, "These events are recorded in many accounts." Some have understood this and similar descriptions of the temple to imply that the mural scene depicted the division of the Buddha's relics among eight kings (a common subject of stupa art). Others have suggested that it depicted Emperor Ming and his retinue venerating the stupa.

41. *The Buddhist Conquest of China*, 22–23.

42. For more on this idea and the debates surrounding it, see part 1. This idea would in fact hardly have been shocking news to any but a tiny number of elite Chinese at the time. Rebirth was indeed a novel idea (though arguably not one entirely lacking at least approximate indigenous precedents), but spiritual survival of physical death was the default assumption at the time on the part of most Chinese, usually challenged only by staunch classicists.

coming of "Buddhism" is a matter of the arrival of new sacred texts, devotional images, and skilled practitioners. Secondly, it is significant that this importation happens by imperial command. Emperors and their courts saw the management of religion as lying within their proper purview. That the coming of Buddhism was here imagined as the result of imperial decree both foreshadows and reflects the tension between the authority of the imperium and the prerogatives of the monastic community. This tension would continue throughout much of Chinese Buddhist history, especially in the early medieval period.[43]

Thirdly, it is striking that already in this early narrative construction of Buddhism's arrival in China we find a reference to the body of legend, related in many sources, surrounding the image of the Buddha fashioned for King Udayana.[44] The basic story line, of which there are as many variations as there are extant textual witnesses, runs as follows. At some point after his awakening, Gautama Buddha ascended to the heaven of the thirty-three gods[45] to preach to them and to his mother. The king,[46] to assuage his sorrow at the Buddha's temporary absence, commissions an image to be made of him. When the Buddha returns to earth via a celestial staircase—a favorite subject of Buddhist art—he is shown the image and asked to comment on the desirability of making such likenesses of his person. He extols the great merit of fashioning or commissioning such images and of paying them proper devotional attention. In some versions the image rises to greet the Buddha on his return, and the Buddha predicts an important role for this particular icon after his own final departure into *nirvāṇa*. For our purposes, the important thing about the mention of this legend cycle in our story is that it shows the extent to which Buddhist proponents were concerned to trace not only the words and teachings of their sutra texts but also their modes of religious practice and their iconography back to purported Indic originals. (This same concern for verisimilitude was seen above in Wang Yan's observation that the casting of his image of Sound Observer "was done so skillfully that it seemed to be the actual bodhisattva.") The Udayana image and all subsequent purported copies of it were seen as links back to the actual physical form of the Buddha, and this linkage served to authenticate all manner of visual productions in Central

---

43. See Hurvitz, "Render unto Caesar"; Ch'en, "Anti-Buddhist Propaganda"; Ch'en, *The Chinese Transformation of Buddhism*, 68–124; Zürcher, *The Buddhist Conquest of China*, 254–285; Wright, *Studies in Chinese Buddhism*, 112–123; Hureau, "Réseaux de bouddhistes des Six Dynasties"; and Despeux, "La culture lettrée au service d'un plaidoyer."

44. The following summary draws on Soper, *Literary Evidence for Early Buddhist Art*, 259–265, and Campany, "À la recherche de la religion perdue," 11–19. See also Skilling, "*Dharma, Dhāraṇī, Abhidharma, Avadāna*"; Carter, *The Mystery of the Udayana Buddha*; and McCallum, "The Saidaiji Lineage," the last two of which came into my possession only as I was finishing the writing of this section, thanks to the kindness of Donald McCallum.

45. For more, see the note to item 8 below.

46. In some versions there is another king, Prasenajit, involved as well.

Asia, China, and beyond, just as sutras' claim to preserve the actual words of the Buddha served to authenticate the teachings conveyed in those texts, and just as the claim that a sutra had been translated from an Indic-language original served to authenticate its contents as in fact a transmitted record of the words the Buddha had spoken on some occasion during his lifetime. Such was the dominant mode of authentication, based on an appeal to geographic and temporal origins, though we will see already in the next item that there were alternative modes of authentication in China.

Note, finally, that the whole process is said to have started because of a dream. Dreams in early medieval China were often viewed as not only prognosticatory—with an entire genre of manuals for deciphering their strange symbolic language—but also as real encounters between the multiple souls of the sleeper as they wandered outside the body and other beings in both the seen and unseen worlds.[47] That is why it made perfect sense for the Han emperor to be portrayed as treating his dream as an indication of real phenomena in the world, rather than as a mere figment of his own somnolent mind.

2[48]

During the Han[49] there lived one Ding Cheng 丁承, styled Deshen 德慎, a native of Jiyin.[50] During the Jian'an period [196–219] he served as district magistrate of Yingyin.[51] At that time the women of commoner families on the northern border [of the district] were going to an outside well to draw their water. A Westerner[52] with a long nose and deep-set eyes passed by the well and asked one of the women for a drink of water. After drinking it he suddenly vanished. The woman developed pains in her belly; they worsened, causing her to cry out in pain. After a while, she suddenly stood up and began speaking Western speech[53] and gesturing. Members of several

---

47. See Campany, "The Dreamscape of Early Medieval China."

48. Source texts: *Fayuan zhulin* 18.417a–b (section "honoring the Dharma" [*jing fa* 敬法]); Lu, *Gu xiaoshuo gouchen*, 401; Wang Guoliang, *Mingxiang ji yanjiu*, 2; Wakatsuki, Hasegawa, and Inagaki, *Hōon jurin no sōgō teki kenkyū*, 121–123. Additional texts: *Chu sanzang jiji* 5.40b18–23; *Kaiyuan shijiao lu* 18.674c23–28. Previously translated and discussed in Campany, "Notes on Sutra Texts," 44–45.

49. *Fayuan zhulin* gives Jin, not Han, but I follow Wang Guoliang in emending the text to accord with *Chu sanzang jiji*.

50. A commandery located in what is now Dingtao district, Shandong province.

51. The text gives this place name as Ningyin 凝陰, which is otherwise unattested. Wang Guoliang suggests that *ning* 凝 is an error for *ying* 穎; I emend accordingly. Yingyin was a district established during the Han in what is now Xuchang district, Henan province.

52. "Westerner" translates *huren* 胡人. *Hu* was a generalized, often derogatory designation for all manner of non-Han, non-Chinese-speaking peoples to the west of China—people of Central Asian or South Asian origin. For an intriguing argument concerning its use to designate a particular Indic script, see Boucher, "On *Hu* and *Fan* Again."

53. "Western speech" translates *huyu* 胡語, literally "the speech of Western barbarians." Some South Asian spoken language is intended, but the passage is no more specific than that.

dozen families in the town gathered to watch her. The woman called for paper and brush to be brought, as if intending to write. Upon obtaining a brush she at once wrote in Western script, horizontally, some characters looking like an *yi* 乙, others like an *yi* 巳.[54] After filling up five sheets of paper, she spread them out on the ground and directed that someone should read what she had written. There was no one in the town who could read them.[55] But there was a boy of ten-odd years whom the woman pointed out, saying he could read it. When the boy was shown the writing, he read it aloud in Western speech. The bystanders were all astounded, not knowing what to make of it. The woman then told the boy to rise and dance. He stood, and they began moving their feet quickly about and clapping their hands in concert. After a while they both stopped.

All of this was reported to Deshen. Deshen summoned the woman and boy and on questioning them was told that they both had suddenly [at the time of these events] become unconscious. Wishing to confirm the event, Deshen sent a messenger to take the text to a monastery in Xu[56] and show it to a Westerner who had long dwelled there. The Westerner was shocked and said, "This is a missing part of a Buddhist sutra. Since the way [to India] is long, I had feared I would never obtain it. Although I had been able to recite [parts of] it orally, I did not have the entire text [in memory]. This is precisely the part of the text I had been missing." So the messenger left it there to be copied.

Comments

Just as the history of Buddhism has often been written as a narrative of the succession of doctrines and "schools," so the story of its eastward spread has often been told as a matter of the translation of texts from Pali, Sanskrit, and other South and Central Asian languages into Chinese.[57] As this and some other miracle tales make clear, however, textual transmission was sometimes claimed to occur by means of a kind of spirit writing. The geographic distance that had to be surmounted in carrying texts across the Himalayas and the Central Asian deserts, as well as the linguistic distance between two very different tongues, is here collapsed via an immediate, automatic, miraculous event. Direct revelation supplants or supplements scho-

---

54. This is mildly interesting as a sheer description of what "Western scripts" looked like to a Chinese person unable to read them.

55. It is also possible to read this line as meaning that there was no one in the town who *was literate.*

56. Today's Xuchang city in Henan province.

57. One recent development in scholarship is the progressive demonstration of just how complex a process and how large a range of activities our word "translation" covers in the case of the rendition of Buddhist scriptures into Chinese in these early centuries. See, for example, the works of Daniel Boucher; Funayama, "'Kanyaku' to 'Chūgoku senjutsu' no aida"; Funayama, "Masquerading as Translation"; Zacchetti, "Teaching Buddhism in Han China"; and the articles gathered in nos. 1–2 of vol. 31 (2008) of the *Journal of the International Association of Buddhist Studies.*

lastic translation and arduous geographic travel. The trance-copyist's identity as a "commoner" and a woman functions (along with the response by the "Westerner") to authenticate the revelation *as* revelation: it is not random spiritual noise, nor a clever forgery by a learned, interested party, but rather a piece of an Indic sutra that had been missing in China until it was thus conveniently delivered by this mysterious yet content-neutral mechanism.[58]

With the phrase "wishing to confirm the event" (translating *yu yan qi shi* 欲驗其事), we see the first explicit mention in *Mingxiang ji* of the crucial notion of "confirmation," "verification," "proof," or (in Verellen's phrasing) "miraculous corroboration,"[59] most often captured in the word *yan* 驗. This sort of "confirmation" is one of the most important rhetorical devices deployed in our text.

3[60]

During the Jin there lived one Yang Hu 羊祜, styled Shuzi 叔子, a native of Taishan.[61] He was a noted minister under the Western Jin and was known throughout the country. When he was four, he asked his nursemaid to get the ring he had played with before. She said, "You never had such a thing. How could I get it?" Hu said, "I was playing with it by the east wall. I dropped it among the mulberry trees." The nursemaid said, "Then you can go and look for it yourself." Hu replied, "But this is not the same residence as before. I don't know where it is." Later he went out through the gate and walked about to have a look around, heading east. The nursemaid followed him. When he reached the home of the Li 李 family, he entered the compound, went to the east wall among the trees, and picked up a small ring. Members of the Li family were shocked and resentful. They said, "Our son previously owned this ring. He loved to play with it. He died suddenly at age six. After he was gone, we didn't know where the ring was. This was our son's possession. What do you mean by taking it?" But Hu had taken the ring and run away with it. The Li family thereupon made inquiries about

---

58. For further examples, see Campany, "Buddhist Revelation and Taoist Translation," and for further reflection on the significance of this motif for Buddhist understandings of the nature of "Buddhism," see in particular pp. 20–21.

59. See "Evidential Miracles in Support of Taoism," 222.

60. Source texts: *Fayuan zhulin* 26.479b–c (section "[karmic effects from] past lives" [*su ming* 宿命]); Lu, *Gu xiaoshuo gouchen*, 375; Wang Guoliang, *Mingxiang ji yanjiu*, 3; Wakatsuki, Hasegawa, and Inagaki, *Hōon jurin no sōgō teki kenkyū*, 162–165. Additional texts: *Duyi zhi* 獨異志 (a Tang collection of anomaly accounts cited in *Taiping guangji* 387.1; this item, the first in a section on "recollection of former lives," is a brief retelling of the childhood episode recounted here); *Soushen ji* 15.11 (also a retelling of the childhood episode; the two versions are compared in Cao Daoheng, "Lun Wang Yan," 35).

61. There is a biography of Yang in *Jin shu* 34.1013–1025, and the gist of the childhood story is included there (see 1023–1024). The area of Taishan is located in what is now Fei district, Shandong province.

it. The nursemaid told all that the boy had said. Members of the Li family were both happy and sad. They then sought to have Hu returned to them as their own son. The matter was discussed in the village for a while; later, the talk died down.

When Hu had grown up, he often suffered from head colds.[62] A doctor wanted to administer a treatment. Hu said, "When I was three days old, my head was facing a window behind me. I could feel the wind blowing on the crown of my head. In my mind it bothered me, but at the time I could not yet speak. Since the illness originated so long ago, there is no way to cure it now."

Later, when Hu was serving as commander-in-chief in Jingzhou and defense commander in Xiangyang, he made a series of significant donations to several monasteries on Mount Wudang.[63] When someone asked him why, he made no reply. Only later, in the course of a confession and repentance ceremony,[64] while setting forth the [karmic] causes and effects [of his actions],[65] did he say, "I have inherited the many sins I amassed in my former lives. Therefore, in order to try to save myself, I am making donations my utmost priority."

Comments

This story acts as a confirmation of the reality of rebirth. But more specifically, what is dealt with here is the relation between the teaching of rebirth and the family system. The story frames the problem quite starkly, even if no clear resolution is offered: If a boy of one family can be demonstrated to have been reborn into it from a different family, then whose son is he? In a patrilineal society in which the cult of ancestors played a central role, this was no idle question.

The last paragraph, depicting a layperson's awareness of his karmic legacy across many lifetimes, ties in with the theme of the first. If you remember your past lives, then you remember the many sins you committed in them, and you therefore feel a more urgent need to gain merit in this present lifetime. There was ready to hand a set of practices our text is prepared to recommend for dealing with this crushing karmic burden: confession and repentance (*chanhui* 懺悔), which, along with the periodic

---

62. This is perhaps too modernizing a translation of *toufeng* 頭風, insofar as the term *feng*, "wind," was often used in ancient and medieval medical texts to refer to almost any unseen pathogen, from wind to demonic beings. Elements of Indic medical thought introduced with Buddhism added yet further layers of medical theorization to "wind." See Unschuld, *History of Ideas*, 25, 67–73, 150–151. "Wind" could have a range of divergent meanings even in a single medical text, as evidenced in Tessenow and Unschuld, *Dictionary of the Huang Di nei jing su wen*, 117–120.

63. We know that Wang Yan himself served as governor in this same region at the close of the fifth century.

64. *Chanhui* 懺悔; see comments.

65. *Xu shuo yinguo* 敘說因果, an element of the confession ritual.

abstinence practices with which they were often combined, were certainly among the most important devotional activities in the lives of both lay and monastic Buddhists in early medieval China.[66]

4[67]

During the Jin there lived the monk Shixing 仕行,[68] a native of Yingchu-an.[69] His original surname was Zhu 朱. He had far-reaching ambition, broad and deep knowledge, and cultivated his mind according to the teachings; neither glory nor disgrace could move him. In his day the sutras were not complete: there were only rough translations,[70] with gaps and summaries rather than word-for-word renditions, so that the meaning was often unclear. In the fifth year of the Ganlu period of the Wei [260], he set out from Yongzhou 雍州[71] and reached as far west as Yutian 于闐,[72] seeking scriptures as he passed through all the realms along the way. Most of the monks and laymen of the Western regions practiced the Lesser Vehicle,[73] and when they heard that Shixing sought the *vaipulya* sutras,[74] they all thought it strange and did not give him the texts. They said, "You do not know the correct Dharma, and these will lead you astray." Shixing responded, "The sutras say that after a thousand years the Dharma will spread eastward. If you doubt that this was the Buddha's saying, then let us test it with the utmost sincerity." With that he set afire a pile of wood and poured oil over it. When the smoke and flames were at their peak, Shixing picked up the sutras and, weeping and bowing his head, uttered this vow: "If these

---

66. Studies of confession practices include Kuo, *Confession et contrition*; Wang Juan, *Tang Song guyi fojiao chanyi yanjiu*; Wang Juan, *Dunhuang lichanwen yanjiu*; and Sheng Kai, *Zhongguo fojiao chanfa yanjiu*.

67. Source texts: *Fayuan zhulin* 28.491a–b (section "numinous anomalies" [*shenyi* 神異]); Lu, *Gu xiaoshuo gouchen*, 376; Wang Guoliang, *Mingxiang ji yanjiu*, 4; Wakatsuki, Hasegawa, and Inagaki, *Hōon jurin no sōgō teki kenkyū*, 182–188. Additional texts: *Chu sanzang jiji* 7.47b–c; *Gaoseng zhuan* 4.346b; *Lidai sanbao ji* 6.65a; and others listed in Wakatsuki, Hasegawa, and Inagaki, *Hoon jurin no sogo teki kenkyu*, 187. Discussed: Zürcher, *The Buddhist Conquest of China*, 61ff.; Campany, "Notes on Sutra Texts," 63 n45. Among the other achievements credited to Shixing was the authorship of a *Record of the Han* (*Han lu* 漢錄), which is quoted numerous times in *Lidai sanbao ji*.

68. *Chu sanzang jiji*, *Gaoseng zhuan*, *Lidai sanbao ji*, and *Ji shenzhou sanbao gantong lu* all write his name as 士行.

69. A commandery at the time, its seat in what is now Xuchang county, Henan province.

70. Translating *wei you xiao pin* 唯有小品; see the note in Wang Guoliang, *Mingxiang ji yanjiu*, 76 n3.

71. An ancient designation for a large area of what is now Shaanxi province.

72. One of several Chinese names for Khotan, a region situated south of the Tarim Basin in Central Asia.

73. See comments.

74. The expression is *fangdeng zhujing* 方等諸經, a reference to the *vaipulya* ("extensive" or "expanded") class of Mahāyāna sutras that were large in scale and taught many doctrines rather than focusing on one central idea. See Mochizuki, *Bukkyō daijiten*, 4326b–4327b.

[sutras] emerged from the golden mouth,[75] they should be disseminated and spread across the land of Han. Let all the Buddhas and bodhisattvas bear witness!" With that he threw them onto the fire, causing it to flare up brightly. When the smoke had cleared, it became evident that the words of the texts were all intact, and both the wrappers and the labels were as before. The entire nation reacted with joy and reverence. So he stayed behind to make offerings and sent his disciple, Farao 法饒, back with the Sanskrit texts. Farao returned to Chenliu, the Junyi 浚儀 and Cangyuan 倉垣 monasteries. When these texts were translated, they amounted in all to ninety sections and two hundred thousand words. The layman Zhu Shulan 竺叔蘭[76] of Henan understood the texts' distinctive language and was very good at conveying the flavor of the Dharma. He personally participated in the translation, and today's text of the *[Sutra of the Buddha's] Emission of Rays of Light (Fangguang [jing]* 放光[經]) was the result.[77]

Shixing died at seventy-nine. He was cremated according to *duwei* 闍維 [rites].[78] His corpse burned an entire day but was still intact. People of the country there were amazed and considered it strange, saying, "If he really attained the Dharmic path, he should disintegrate." Immediately his body shattered into tiny pieces. His bones were collected, and a stupa was erected over them. The former master of the monk Huizhi 慧志 told of this. Shigong 釋公 also reported it in detail.

Comments

Here already is our third story on the theme of how Buddhist sutras were transmitted to China. We have seen imperially commissioned importation (item 1) and a kind of mediumistic revelation (2). Here we have the more standard monk's pilgrimage and translation. Also, what is being imagined and argued about here is, in part, China's place in the history of the Buddhist tradition. The urgent question addressed in this narrative does not concern the doctrinal content of Greater Vehicle sutras but rather their

---

75. That is, if they truly record words spoken by the Buddha.

76. The involvement of Zhu Shulan in the transmission and translation of early sutras is described in *Chu sanzang jiji* 7.47c and 8.98b–c. See also Zürcher, *The Buddhist Conquest of China*, 23, 63–64 (these last pages on his involvement in the translation of the *Fangguang jing* 放光經), 78.

77. This is almost certainly the text now known as *Fangguang banruo jing* 放光般若經, a version of *The Sutra of the Perfection of Wisdom in Twenty-Five Thousand Lines*, translated by a team headed by Mokṣala in 291 (see Nattier, *Earliest Chinese Buddhist Translations*, 97) and preserved in the Taishō canon. See Zürcher, *The Buddhist Conquest of China*, 63–64, 339–340 n182, 341 n198, and Williams, *Mahāyāna Buddhism*, 45–62.

78. *Duwei* 闍維 was one transliteration of *jhāpeti*, which simply means cremation (see Mochizuki, *Bukkyō daijiten*, 3483c), so the text's wording is here redundant. Cremation was relatively unusual (though certainly not unheard of) in China prior to the ninth or tenth century (see Benn, *Burning for the Buddha*, 39). For a translation and discussion of Daoxuan's seventh-century treatise on Buddhist modes for disposing of the dead, see ibid., 100–101, 249–254.

authenticity as teachings of Gautama Buddha destined to travel east to China.

This is the only passage in our text that mentions the rift between the so-called Lesser and Greater Vehicles. It is also—more surprisingly—one of the few *Mingxiang ji* stories to mention the preservation of monks' bodily relics in stupas.[79]

The closing lines are our first example of an important feature of these tales: their mention of specific paths of their own transmission. Here, two monks are named as sources of the information conveyed in the story. Given the dates involved, they could not have been Wang Yan's own acquaintances. Rather, their names must have been attached to the story early on as authenticating devices, and they remained there right up until Wang gathered them, along with the rest of the narrative, into his compilation.

5[80]

During the Jin there lived one Zhao Tai 趙泰, styled Wenhe 文和, a native of Beiqiu in Qinghe.[81] His paternal grandfather had been governor of the capital. Tai was nominated from his commandery as a filial-and-incorrupt;[82] he was appointed to an office under a duke but did not report for duty. He had a local reputation for diligent study. Only later did he accept an official post. He died while holding the title of grand master of palace leisure.

When Tai was thirty-five, he one day felt a sudden pain in his heart. Moments later he was dead. His corpse was laid out on the ground, but his heart stayed warm and his body flexible. He had remained an uncoffined corpse for ten days when suddenly there was a gurgling noise in his throat. Shortly afterward he revived.

Tai said that when he first died, he dreamed that a person came and drew near[83] to the spot just below his heart. Two more men arrived, riding brown horses. Two of their attendants supported Tai under his arms, and

---

79. See part 1.

80. Source texts: *Fayuan zhulin* 7.330b–331a (section "the six paths [of rebirth]" [*liudao* 六道]); *Taiping guangji* 377.1; Lu, *Gu xiaoshuo gouchen*, 377; Wang Guoliang, *Mingxiang ji yanjiu*, 5; Wakatsuki, Hasegawa, and Inagaki, *Hōon jurin no sōgō teki kenkyū*, 56–67. Additional texts: *Fayuan zhulin* 6.316c–317a (citing *Zhao Tai zhuan* 趙泰傳); *Youming lu* 248 (as cited in *Bianzheng lun* 7.538b–539a; discussed in Takeda, *Chūgoku no setsuwa to kōshōsetsu*, 120–123); *Xuanyan ji* 27 (collected in Lu, *Gu xiaoshuo gouchen*, 369). Previously translated in Kao, *Classical Chinese Tales*, 166–171. Discussed: Mai, "Visualization Apocrypha," 116–117; Campany, "Return-from-Death Narratives," 120 n64.

81. Beiqiu was a district near what is now Qinghe district, Hebei province.

82. On this system for official promotion in the Jin period, a carryover from the Han, see Dien, "Civil Service Examinations," 102–104. For a recent discussion of the system during the Later Han, see de Crespigny, "Recruitment Revisited."

83. In both *Fayuan zhulin* and *Taiping guangji*, the verb used is *jin* 近.

they proceeded eastward for he knew not how many *li*.[84] They reached a great city wall of imposing height, bluish-black in color, like tin.

They took Tai in through the gate. Having passed through a double gate, they came among several thousand tile-roofed buildings. There were also several thousand people, men and women of all ages, standing in line. Five or six officers in black were going through a list of names, saying that these persons were to be presented before the magistrate.[85] Tai's name was thirtieth on the list.

A short time later, Tai, along with several thousand men and women, was led within. The magistrate sat facing west. After glancing briefly at the list of names, he sent Tai through a black door to the south. A man in scarlet sat in a great room calling out names one by one and asking what each person had done during his or her lifetime: "What sins did you commit? What meritorious and good works did you perform? Take care to reply truthfully, for we constantly dispatch from here six ranks of officers who are always among humans recording their good and evil deeds piecemeal. It is all set forth in detail. You will not be able to pass off fabrications." Tai, for his part, replied, "My father and elder brother are both officials, each with a salary of two thousand *tan* [of grain].[86] When I was a youth and was still at home, I studied, and that is all. I have no profession, and I have not committed any transgressions or evil deeds."

Tai was assigned to serve as director of waterworks. He was to take over two thousand people and transport sand to shore up riverbanks. He worked hard day and night. Later he was moved up to be supervisor of waterworks. In this position he came to be informed about all the purgatories.[87] He was given horses and troops and ordered to travel through and inspect the purgatories. In each purgatory he passed through, the tortuous punishments differed. In one, people had their tongues pierced with needles; their flowing blood covering their entire bodies. In another, people were bareheaded with loosened hair, naked, barefoot, being pulled along from the front and shoved from behind by men wielding large staffs. Iron couches and bronze pillars were heated through, and then these peo-

---

84. One *li* 里 is usually taken to have been equivalent to 0.576 kilometers, or roughly one-third of an English mile, though the precise distance varied by region and period. Some translators therefore render *li* as "third-miles." Below I leave it untranslated.

85. Here and in most cases below, "magistrate" renders *fujun* 府君, a somewhat vague designation of office that was also used as a generalized term of respect for those who were elder or of higher rank than the speaker.

86. One *tan* 石 as a unit of weight in this period was equivalent to about 26.4 kilograms.

87. "Purgatories" here renders *diyu* 地獄, literally "earth prisons," a translation I sometimes also use. *Diyu* was the most common Chinese term (in Buddhist, Daoist, and other contexts) for purgatories where souls of the dead were punished for their sins before being reborn. Convenient discussions include Sawada, *Jigoku hen*; Wang-Toutain, *Le Bodhisattva Kṣitigarbha en Chine*; Hou Xudong, *Wu liu shiji beifang minzhong Fojiao xinyang*, 66–84; Zhiru, *The Making of a Savior Bodhisattva*; Bokenkamp, *Ancestors and Anxiety*; Teiser, *The Ghost Festival*; Teiser, "Ghosts and Ancestors"; and Teiser, *The Scripture on the Ten Kings*.

ple were forced to embrace or lie down on them. They were burned on contact but were then at once brought back to life [for more of the same]. In another purgatory, sinners were cooked in giant cauldrons over hot stoves. Their heads and bodies would disintegrate, bobbing and floating in the oil. Demons with pitchforks stood nearby. Off to one side stood several hundred persons waiting to enter the cauldrons, embracing each other and sobbing sorrowfully. In yet another purgatory, there were numberless tall, broad sword trees; their roots, trunks, branches, and leaves were all made of swords. Crowds of people were arguing with each other. Some would then begin climbing up, as if happy to compete with the others, and once they did so their heads were severed and their bodies sliced apart into small pieces. Tai caught sight of his paternal grandfather and grandmother, as well as two younger brothers, in this purgatory. When they saw one another, they broke into tears.

As Tai was exiting through the gates of the purgatories, he saw two men approach, carrying documents. They said to some jailers, "There are three people on whose behalf their families have hung banners[88] and burned incense at stupas and monasteries to release them from punishment for their sins. Bring them out to the lodges of the fortunate."[89] Short-

---

88. "Banners" (or sometimes "streamers" or "pennants") here and throughout translates *fan* 幡, devotional items (that are sometimes also represented in Buddhist iconography) hung to adorn images and stupas, the donation of which generated merit for the living and fortune for the dead. See Hureau, "Buddhist Rituals," 1238. A sense of their importance is conveyed in a sutra passage preserved in *Fayuan zhulin* 36.568b: King Aśoka, the great royal patron of early Buddhism, falls ill, despite having sponsored the erection of twelve hundred stupas. When he asks why, he is told that his illness is due to his having failed to adorn the stupas with banners. Once he rectifies this situation, his illness is healed, and twenty-five years are added to his life span. In a larger sense, such banners were a subset of the sort of ornamentation (*zhuangyan* 莊嚴) that was central to Buddhist devotion in almost all its forms and that was also an activity and aspect of Buddhas and their realms. On this, see Teiser, "Ornamenting the Departed."

89. "Lodges of the fortunate" translates *fushe* 福舍. The sense of *she* 舍 is a small, temporary dwelling used by travelers, mourners, or those undergoing penitence or abstinence (compare *jingshe* 精舍, discussed in a note to item 11 below). *Fu* 福 is sometimes—quite justifiably—translated as "merit," but in other contexts, particularly as the term is usually used in this text, it is useful to distinguish between "merit" (here usually *gong* 功 or *gongde* 功德) and "fortune" or "the fortunate" (here usually *fu*), although our text is not rigorous in this distinction. As Teiser explains the related term *futian* 福田, or "field of fortune," "The whole concept is based on an agricultural metaphor. The lay person is like a farmer, his or her act is like a seed, the [monastic] Order or immediate recipient of the offering is like the field in which a seed is planted, the resulting merit is like the crop, and the deceased is like the person who benefits from or harvests the crop" (*The Scripture on the Ten Kings*, 103 n5; cf. Tsukamoto, *A History of Early Chinese Buddhism*, 1063, and Collins, *Selfless Persons*, 218–224). "Fortune" or (when it refers to groups of people) "the fortunate" below generally renders *fu*. As for the referents of the compound *fushe*, in vinaya texts (e.g., *Sifen lü* 四分律 742c, 754a; *Shisong lü* 十誦律 784c–785a) this term clearly refers to structures used for devotional activity in this world and might even be synonymous with "monastery"; in this sense it would be better translated as "lodges for [the cultivation of] fortune." In a related but not identical usage, in the travel narrative *Da Tang xiyu ji* 大唐西域記, at 937c (and

ly he saw three persons emerge from the purgatories. They were already dressed in ordinary clothing covering their entire bodies. They proceeded south to a gate labeled "The Great Lodge for the Opening of Light" (*kai-guang dashe* 開光大舍);[90] it was a triple gate made of luminescent vermillion. Seeing the three enter through the gate, Tai followed them.

The first thing he saw was a great palace everywhere encrusted with jewels, giving off dazzling light, its couches fashioned of gold and jade. He saw a divine person of extraordinary countenance and distinguished appearance seated on one of these seats. A large number of monks stood by his side in attendance. Then he saw the magistrate enter and pay respectful obeisance. Tai asked, "Who is this person, that even the magistrate pays him such homage?" The jailer said, "He is known as the World-Honored One, the Master Who Delivers Beings." In a moment, a command was given to all the beings in evil paths of rebirth to go out and hear a sutra preached. It was said that one million and ninety thousand persons left the purgatories at that moment and entered the One Hundred Li City.[91] All who made it to this point were beings who had observed Dharma. Although their conduct had been deficient, they were still fit to obtain salvation, and thus it was that the Dharma of sutras was opened to them. Within seven days, depending on the amount of good and evil they had done, they would be re-

---

other passages) *fushe* clearly refers to structures built by kings and wealthy donors (as acts of merit) to distribute food, lodging, and medicine—fortune—to the indigent. On such structures in China see Gernet, *Buddhism in Chinese Society*, 223–227, and Liu Shufen, "Art, Ritual, and Society," 35–36 (on related aid for travelers—charitable donations of bridges, wells, and groves of trees). (Compare the *yishe* 義舍, or "charity lodges," built and serviced by early Celestial Master Daoist communities: see Kleeman, *Great Perfection*, 69; Bokenkamp, *Early Daoist Scriptures*, 36–37; and Ōfuchi, *Shoki no dōkyō*, 163–169, where the Buddho-Daoist parallel is briefly noted. Kleeman and Ōfuchi both also note the similarity in function and nomenclature to government-administered hostels in the Han period.) But in *Chengju guangming dingyi jing* 成具光明定意經, a sutra mentioned in our text and which might well be a fourth-century apocryphon (see Nattier, *Earliest Chinese Buddhist Translations*, 94–102), at 455c *fushe* designates an area or type of structure in the heavens that can be visited in the course of a tour of the other world designed to demonstrate the reality of karmic recompense—a tour the Buddha vows to conduct himself in transformed form in future times when there is otherwise no Buddha active in the world. It is in this sense that *fushe* is also used—at least twice—in *Youming lu* 幽明錄, a compilation of anomaly accounts assembled fifty or so years before our text. One of these stories (that of Kang Ade) is anthologized in *Bianzheng lun* 7.538a, the other (a version of this story of Zhao Tai) in *Fayuan zhulin* 62.756a. In the former story, the protagonist, who has died but will shortly return to life, is shown an array of impressive tiled buildings termed "the *fushe*" and told, "All Buddha's disciples reside there. If one's fortune is great, one rises to be reborn in the heavens; if one's fortune is slight, one resides in these lodges" 云名 福舍，諸佛弟子住中，福多者上生天，福少者住此舍. A closely related term, *futang* 福堂, or "hall of the fortunate," again denoting a place in the unseen world, appears below in item 26.

90. This is the only occurrence of this term in the canon; it likely does not, therefore, reflect any standard usage.

91. *Baili cheng* 百里城, a name for this area of the purgatories that appears only in this story (and in later works that cite this story).

leased [to their next rebirth]. Before Tai had left the area he saw ten persons rise up into the void and depart.

Upon leaving this lodge, Tai saw another city, more than two hundred *li* square, called the City of Those Receiving Transformation of Bodily Form.[92] Those who had completed their examination and processing in the purgatories received in this city their recompense by transformation.[93] Tai entered the city and saw that there were thousands of earthenware-tiled buildings divided into quarters and lanes. In the center was a tall, impressive tile-roofed building with brightly colored railings and lattice-work. Several hundred bureau officials were busy collating documents, saying things like, "Those who killed living beings are to become mayflies that are born in the morning and die in the evening. Those who stole and robbed are to become pigs and sheep, to be butchered by others. Those who engaged in debauchery are to become cranes, ducks, and deer. Those who went back on their word[94] are to become owls. Those who did not repay their debts are to become donkeys, mules, oxen, and horses."

When Tai had finished his tour of inspection, he returned to the wa-terworks office. A supervisor there said to him, "Whose son are you?[95] What sin resulted in your being sent here?" Tai answered, "My paternal grandfather and my brothers all had salaries of two thousand *tan*. I was nominated as a filial-and-incorrupt and was appointed to an office under a duke but did not report for duty. I nursed my resolve and concentrated on goodness and was not tainted by evil." The supervisor said, "You have com-mitted no sins, and that is why you were made supervisor of waterworks. Otherwise there would be no difference between you and those people in the purgatories." Tai asked the supervisor, "How should a person conduct himself to receive a happy recompense after death?" The supervisor said only this: "Disciples who observe the Dharma with vigor[96] and adhere to

---

92. *Shoubianxing cheng* 受變形城, another name that appears only in this story (and in later works that cite it).

93. *Bianbao* 變報, that is, their rebirth.

94. Literally "those who were of two tongues" (*liang she* 兩舌). On this term see Zhou Junxun, *Wei Jin nanbeichao zhiguai xiaoshuo cihui*, 407.

95. Here following the text in *Taiping guangji*, not *Fayuan zhulin*.

96. This is the first occurrence in our text of *jingjin* 精進, the most common Chinese rendition of the Sanskrit *vīrya* (energy, vigor), the energetic, dedicated, intensive practice of activities bringing merit or insight. I have almost always included the word "vigor" in my otherwise slightly varying translations of this term in various contexts. *Jingjin* appears in many lists of qualities necessary to advance on the path, e.g., "the thirty-seven qualities of [those on] the path" or *sanshiqi daopin* 三十七道品, often used to render the Sanskrit *bodhipakṣa-dharma* (on which see Nattier, *Earliest Chinese Buddhist Translations*, 98 n244, and Gethin, *The Buddhist Path to Awakening*, 22–25, 284–302 and passim—in a sense Gethin's en-tire book is an explication of this set of categories). But it is also one of the six perfections, or *pāramitā*, in texts prescribing the bodhisattva path. See Mochizuki, *Bukkyō daijiten*, 2629b–2632a; the many discussions of "energy" in Pagel, *The Bodhisattvapiṭaka*; and, on narrative and visual embodiments of the idea, Bell, *Didactic Narration*, 70–72. On the general preva-lence of lists in Buddhism, see Gethin, "The *Mātikās*."

the precepts receive happy recompense without the slightest degree of punishment." Tai asked further, "As for the sins a person commits before he has begun to observe the Dharma, are these expunged after he begins to serve the Dharma?"[97] The reply was, "They are all expunged."

When they had finished talking, the supervisor opened a box and looked up Tai's allotted life span.[98] He saw that Tai had another twenty years to live. With this he sent Tai back home. As Tai was about to depart, the supervisor said, "Having seen what the retribution for sins in the purgatories is like, you should inform the people of the world, causing them to do good. The [effects of] good and evil deeds follow people like shadows and echoes. Can one afford not to be vigilant?"

At the time, the friends and relatives listening to Tai's account numbered fifty or sixty. Tai himself wrote an account to show to people of his day. This occurred on the thirteenth day of the seventh month of the fifth year of the Taishi period [269]. Tai thereupon, on behalf of his grandfather, grandmother, and two younger brothers, invited members of the sangha[99] and hosted great gatherings for [the bestowal of] fortune.[100] He commanded that all his sons and grandsons mend their ways and observe the Dharma, and he encouraged them to practice with vigor.

When his contemporaries heard that Tai had died and revived, and had seen in detail [the results of] sin and merit, they came in succession to ask him about it. At the time, some ten people, including the Superior Grand Master of the Palace Sun Feng 孫豐, a native of Wucheng,[101] and Marquis within the Passes Hao Boping 郝伯平 of Changshan,[102] gathered at Tai's home and asked in great detail about what he had seen. All went away fearful, and all became observant of the Dharma.

---

97. This question must have been asked often in the early centuries of Buddhist practice in China.

98. By the time Wang Yan compiled his *Mingxiang ji*, the idea that people from conception have a predetermined time to live (a *ming* 命)—a time that may be adjusted upward or downward for various reasons and by various means—was at least eight centuries old in China. Life span records were imagined to be kept by bureaucrats in the unseen world, adjusted periodically according to the reports made on people's sins by unseen spirit-monitors. See Bokenkamp, "Simple Twists of Fate"; Mollier, *Buddhism and Taoism Face to Face*, 100–113; Schafer, "The Stove God and the Alchemists"; Chard, "Rituals and Scriptures of the Stove Cult"; Chard, "The Stove God"; Kohn, "Counting Good Deeds"; Campany, "Living Off the Books"; and Campany, *To Live as Long as Heaven and Earth*.

99. Technically this term refers to the entire fourfold Buddhist community comprising monks, nuns, laymen, and laywomen. It is often used, however, as here, to refer to the assembly of monks and nuns.

100. *Fuhui* 福會; the idea, as explained in note 89 above, is that this devotional activity generates *merit*, which is then converted into *fortune* bestowed on another party—very often, as here, on the dead.

101. In today's Wucheng district, Shandong province.

102. Changshan was a commandery in what is now Zhengding district, Hebei province.

Comments

This story provides our first glimpse in *Signs of the Unseen Realm* of how utterly bureaucratic the afterlife was imagined to be. To die was to undergo processing by an enormous, usually inexorable administrative system. Here we find the first mention, too, of the notion of "allotted life span," or *ming* 命. These elements of the story were already quite old in China and would have seemed familiar to most readers.

But on the scaffolding of these indigenously familiar elements, the story (and many others like it) constructs specifically Buddhist arguments about how the afterlife works—about its courts, about the meting out of rebirth as various categories of animal in recompense for certain categories of sins. These elements were relatively new to some readers and hearers in Zhao Tai's day. We sense that the details of this hybridized afterlife are still being worked out here, and some of them—such as the unique nomenclature of the "One Hundred Li City"—would remain, as far as we know from extant texts, descriptive dead ends not taken up elsewhere. The most important thing the story shows about this hybridized afterlife is the efficacy of temple donations and the feeding of monks—rather than any of the standard indigenous options (notably including direct offerings and petitions)—for rescuing those suffering under its fearsome regime. When the protagonist asks his two key questions of the supervisor—"How should a person conduct himself to receive a happy recompense after death?" and "As for the sins a person commits before he has begun to observe the Dharma, are these expunged after he begins to serve the Dharma?"—the text, in answer, shifts to direct didactic mode, providing explicit instruction on how, in effect, to care for oneself in advance of one's own future death. We also learn of a way for the living to help those who, already dead, are caught in the throes of this baleful, dark penal system: they are to host monks at "fortune gatherings" to generate merit on behalf of the dead. This is the most important message this story has to deliver.

That Gautama Buddha himself is portrayed as actively preaching to the dead is, in the light of many other texts, decidedly odd. This role would eventually be assumed by the Bodhisattva Dizang 地藏, or Kṣitigarbha.[103]

For anyone wishing to understand how stories such as these came to be written, talked about, remembered, passed down through generations, and eventually included in a collection such as *Mingxiang ji*, the last two paragraphs make for fascinating reading. The protagonist is portrayed as "himself writing an account to show people of his day" (*zi shu ji yi shi shiren* 自書記以示時人). Many of the stories in this text must have similarly origi-

---

103. On whom see Zhiru, *The Making of a Savior Bodhisattva*; Wang-Toutain, *Le bodhisattva Kṣitigarbha en Chine*; Soymié, "Les dix jours de jeûne de Kṣitigarbha"; Sawada, *Jigoku hen*, 113–115; and de Visser, *The Bodhisattva Ti-tsang*.

nated as first-person accounts, some of them oral, others preserved in letters, jottings, testimonials, even stele inscriptions. We also see depicted
—within the very frame of the story of Zhao Tai's remarkable adventure—
its reception by others and its impact on them: people are described as
gathering at Zhao's home to hear his tale and as leaving with renewed ded-
ication to Buddhist practice.

6[104]

The monk Zhi Faheng 支法衡 lived in the early Jin period. He fell ill and
within ten days had died. Three days later he revived. He said that when he
died, he was taken away by someone. He saw what seemed to be offices in
several locations, but none were willing to take him. In a little while he saw
that there was an iron wheel with iron nails on it rolling toward them from
the west. No one was pulling it: it simply rolled along as if propelled by the
wind. There was a functionary[105] who shouted for sinners to come and
stand before the wheel. The wheel rolled forward and crushed them, then
backed up, repeating this cycle several times until the people were completely obliterated. The functionary then shouted to Heng, "Monk, come
and stand before the wheel!" Terrified, Heng reproached himself, saying,
"If I repent of not exerting myself with full vigor, must I stand before this
wheel now?" When he had finished speaking, the functionary said to him,
"Monk, you may go!"[106]

At this he raised his head and saw a hole in the sky above. Without
knowing how, he was raised upward toward it. His head protruded up
through the hole, and he held on to the rim with both hands. Looking
around, he saw palaces [ornamented with] the seven types of jewels[107] and

---

104. Source texts: *Fayuan zhulin* 7.331b (section "the six paths [of rebirth]" [*liudao* 六
道]); *Taiping guangji* 382.1; Lu, *Gu xiaoshuo gouchen* 379; Wang Guoliang, *Mingxiang ji yanjiu*,
6; Wakatsuki, Hasegawa, and Inagaki, *Hōon jurin no sōgō teki kenkyū*, 67–70. Additional texts:
Shimen zijing lu 1.810b; *Liudao ji* 4.157a.

105. Translating *li* 吏, in the this-world Chinese bureaucracy denoting a very low-rank-
ing official appointed at the local level (and not by a court commission) and evidently bearing a rank roughly parallel in the bureaucracy of the unseen world.

106. This detail underlines the power of confession and repentance, central components of the mode of Buddhist practice the text models for readers.

107. *Qibao* 七寶, seven types of precious gems decorating temples, images and the pinions and canopies offered to them, and Pure Lands, ubiquitous in Buddhist (especially
Mahāyāna) texts. The lists vary. One passage in Kumārajīva's translation of the *Lotus Sutra*
(*Miaofa lianhua jing* 妙法蓮華經, 32b17), for example, mentions gold, silver, colored glass or
lapis lazuli (*liuli* 琉璃 designating both, depending on context), agate (*cheju* 硨磲), carnelian
(*manao* 馬腦), pearls, and black mica (*meigui* 玫瑰), while a passage in the *Sutra on the Buddha
of Limitless Life Span* (*Wuliangshou jing* 無量壽經, 269c) lists gold, silver, colored glass, coral
(*shanhu* 珊瑚), amber (*hubo* 琥珀, or "tiger's soul"), agate, and carnelian. My identifications
rely on the work of Edward Schafer, particularly *The Golden Peaches of Samarkand*, 222–249.
See also Liu Xinru, *Ancient India and Ancient China*, 92–102.

celestial persons everywhere. Heng was overjoyed, but he was unable to ascend any further; he grew tired from the effort and returned to where he had been before. The person who had taken Heng away laughed and said, "What things did you see, such that you were unable to get up there?" He then turned Heng over to a boatman. The boatman launched his boat, designating Heng as the helmsman. Heng said, "I cannot take the helm," but the boatman compelled him. Several hundred boats were following Heng's. Heng did not know how to steer and ran the boat aground on an island shore. A functionary accused Heng, saying, "You are on the path yet have strayed away. By law you should be executed." He led Heng up the embankment. Drums rolled, and the execution was about to be carried out when suddenly two multicolored dragons pushed the boat back out into the water. The functionary only then pardoned Heng for his offense.

Heng was next transported thirty-odd *li* north, where he saw a riverside town with several myriad homes. Their occupants were said to be people in transit.[108] Heng snuck up the embankment. A pack of stray dogs of the village started after him to bite him, and Heng was terrified. Looking toward the northwest, he saw a lecture hall some distance away[109] filled with a large number of monks. He could hear the sound of sutra and hymn [recitation]. Heng ran toward them. The hall had twelve steps. When Heng had climbed the first step he saw his deceased master Fazhu 法柱 sitting on a Western seat.[110] When the master saw Heng, he said, "My disciple, why have you come?" He stood up, descended the stairs, and struck Heng in the face with his handkerchief, saying, "Do not come here!" Heng very much wanted to ascend to the hall and climbed several more steps upward. Fazhu again pushed him down. Only after a third attempt [by Heng] did his master desist. Heng [from the hall] saw a level expanse of ground and a well, thirty or forty feet deep, with no railing. Heng thought to himself, "This must be a natural well." Beside the well there was someone who said, "If it weren't natural, how could such a well have been formed?" Then Heng saw Fazhu [again] and started toward him, but he told Heng, "You should return by the way you came. The dogs will not bite you."

So Heng returned to the riverbank. He did not see his former boat

---

108. *Liuren* 流人—people on the move or displaced persons, perhaps migrants or, more likely in this context, people between death and rebirth. The term recurs in a similar context in item 59 below. Buddhist authorities had differed since early times on whether rebirth was immediate upon death or whether there was an intermediate period, with most Chinese Buddhist representations tending to the latter view. See Harvey, "The Between-Lives State," and Teiser, *The Scripture on the Ten Kings*, 1–15, 23.

109. *Taiping guangji* omits the previous four sentences.

110. "Western seat" translates *huchuang* 胡床, synonym *jiaochuang* 交床. For a Chinese description, see *Pinimu jing* 毘尼母經 845a3. Kieschnick, *The Impact of Buddhism*, 237, calls the *huchuang* a "foldable stool" and discusses its introduction from India; see also Zhou Junxun, *Wei Jin nanbeichao zhiguai xiaoshuo cihui*, 425, and Liu Yuanru, "Cong Xianbei," 233–234.

there any longer. He was thirsty and wanted to drink some of the water, and in doing so he fell into the river, and that is how he was able to revive.

After this in his comportment as a monk he upheld the precepts [more strictly] and kept to a vegetarian diet, his thoughts focused day and night on being a monk of exemplary conduct.[111] The monk Faqiao 法橋 later became his disciple.

Comments

Here we have, already, another of many glimpses of the afterlife afforded in the stories collected here. Each of these narratives contributes a brick, as it were, to the edifice that would become the medieval Chinese system of purgatories. The fact that the protagonist is here a monk and is repeatedly threatened during his brief stay in the purgatories (to the point of almost being executed for straying from the path) is clearly a warning against monastic laxity, a theme we will see elsewhere in the text.

The last paragraph demonstrates the dispositional impact of the experience on the tale's protagonist—an impact the text is meant to reproduce in its readers.

7[112]

In the An district near the Luo river,[113] there is Mount Huo 霍山,[114] so tall it blocks out the sun. Atop it is a stone basin several dozen feet in diameter. The springwater in the basin is five or six feet deep, and the basin is always full. An ancient legend says that it is a place where noted transcendents come to dine.

During the Jin there was a monk, Shi Sengqun 釋僧群, who dwelled as a hermit on the mountain. He often drank from this spring, with the result that he was never hungry. He thus cut off food intake.[115] The governor of An during the Jin, Tao Kui 陶夔,[116] heard of him and sought some of [the

---

111. *Fayuan zhulin* here has 於是出家持戒菜食，晝夜精思為至行沙門, which if read straightforwardly would indicate that Faheng only now became a monk when the whole story clearly assumes he already is one. In translating I therefore take the phrase *chujia* 出家 adverbially. This reading is supported by the two other versions. *Shimen zijing lu* has: 於是晝夜精思為至行沙門. Compare *Liudao ji*: 於是終身持戒菜食，晝夜精思為至行沙門.

112. Source texts: *Fayuan zhulin* 63.764c (section "praying for rain" [*qiyu* 祈雨]); Lu, *Gu xiaoshuo gouchen*, 381; Wang Guoliang, *Mingxiang ji yanjiu*, 7. Additional texts: *Gaoseng zhuan* 12.404a; *Yiyuan* 5.38; *Shenseng zhuan* 3.969a; *Shimen zijing lu* 2.813c.

113. An was the name of an administrative unit during the Jin, and the Luo river ran through it.

114. As Wang Guoliang points out, no Mount Huo is known from historical sources in this area. What might be meant is Huotong shan 霍童山.

115. Literally, "he cut off grains." See comments.

116. Tao Yuanming's great-uncle; he authored a work on the area (see Wang Guoliang, *Mingxiang ji yanjiu*, 7 n4).

water]. Qun sent some to him, but each time water was taken off the mountain, it soured. Tao therefore crossed the water to come to the mountain personally. At the time the skies were completely clear, but the moment Tao began climbing up the foot of the mountain a wind and rain rose up, and the skies darkened. This happened three times. In the end Tao never managed to reach the spring.

Qun's hermitage was separated from the spring by a mountain stream. Each morning and evening he came and went using a log as a bridge. One morning he was about to cross when he suddenly saw a duck with a broken wing. Its wings were spread across the log, and its head was turned, so that Sengqun could not get across again. He thought of using his monastic staff[117] to move the duck but feared he would cause it to fall and die. Because of this he cut off his consumption of the water, and soon he died of starvation. At the time it was said that he was 140 years old. When Qun was about to die, he told those assembled there: "In my youth I once struck a duck on its wing. Is this duck now the karmic retribution for my act?"

Comments

This story is a clear instance of ideological and religious contestation. Sengqun is on his way to transcendence. He is shown "cutting off grains" while living on a mountaintop associated with past transcendents; he is even reputed to be 140 years old. We see an official seeking access to the adept's secret longevity arts but not being admitted to the inner circle of knowledge—a motif ubiquitous in accounts of transcendents.[118] Everything about the narrative fits the pattern of the successful seeker of transcendence—that is, until karma trips Sengqun up. The message is clear: karma trumps transcendence-style longevity arts. Those arts may allow adepts to circumvent their allotted life span, but they do not allow karma to be circumvented: karma will play itself out, in this life or another.

Sengqun's case was taken up by other early medieval Chinese Buddhist writers. We find Huijiao, for example, mentioning him in his discussion of auto-cremation: "Only for a duck did Sengqun abstain from water and give up his body."[119] For Huijiao, Sengqun's was one of a number of recorded cases in which monks sacrificed themselves to benefit other creatures—a motivation that he regarded as permissible, unlike cases of auto-cremation, which he saw as of no benefit to other beings.[120]

---

117. The staff, or walking stick, with metal rings attached so that it jingled when shaken, was a standard component of a monk's equipment and as such became symbolic of monks, as can be seen in the several other mentions of it in our text. See also Beal, *Si-yu-ki*, 1.96 (on the staff of Gautama Buddha preserved as a relic), and Kieschnick, *The Impact of Buddhism*, 113–115.

118. See Campany, *Making Transcendents*, 88–129.

119. *Gaoseng zhuan* 12.406a.

120. See Benn, *Burning for the Buddha*, 49–52, 247–249.

8[121]

During the Jin there lived the monk Qi Yu 耆域, a native of India. He arrived from the Western regions by sea. He was on his way inland to Luoyang when he reached the old city of Xiangyang. He wished to hire a ferryman to take him across to the northern shore of the river, but the ferryman, seeing that he was a Western monk with tattered clothing, treated him rudely and would not take him. But when the boat reached the northern shore, Yu was found to be among the passengers. All who were aboard were stunned. As Yu proceeded ashore, two tigers arrived to meet him, laying back their ears submissively and flicking their tails. Yu stroked them on their heads with his hand, and with that they went off into the brush. At this, everyone on both riverbanks rushed up to try to make inquiries of him, but Yu never once replied the entire day. He then set off on his way. Several hundred people followed after him. At all times they could see him ahead of them but could not catch up.[122]

It was at the end of the reign of Emperor Hui 惠帝[123] that Yu reached Luoyang. The masters of the path[124] in Luoyang all went to pay their respects to him. Yu did not rise to receive them. Through an interpreter[125] he pointed to his clothing and said, "You are spreading the Dharma of Buddha. But you are not doing so with sincerity. All you do is sport fancy, ornamented attire and seek donations." Upon seeing the Luoyang palace, he said, "The palaces of the *trāyastriṃśa* heaven[126] resemble this. It would nor-

---

121. Source texts: *Fayuan zhulin* 28.491b–c (section "numinous anomalies" [*shenyi* 神異]); Lu, *Gu xiaoshuo gouchen*, 381; Wang Guoliang, *Mingxiang ji yanjiu*, 8; Wakatsuki, Hasegawa, and Inagaki, *Hōon jurin no sōgō teki kenkyū*, 188–192. Additional texts: *Gaoseng zhuan* 9.388a–c; *Ji shenzhou sanbao gantong lu* 3.431c; *Shenseng zhuan* 1.950c. Qi Yu is mentioned in many other sources.

122. Precisely parallel feats are attributed to transcendents in narratives of the same and earlier periods. For an example, see Campany, *To Live as Long as Heaven and Earth*, 170.

123. This was Sima Zhong 司馬衷, who reigned from 290 to 306. The end of his reign saw massive invasions by multiple non-Han forces from the north and west and the impending collapse of Chinese government in the north.

124. *Daoshi* 道士, here meaning monastic Buddhist practitioners.

125. Translating *yi yu* 譯語, a term that during the Tang and Song periods was used to designate interpreters assigned to the imperial bureau of foreign relations; see *Hanyu dacidian*, 11.448a.

126. *Daoli tian* 忉利天 (sometimes differently transliterated), the heaven of the thirty-three *devas*, or gods, ruled by Indra from his palace atop the cosmic Mount Meru; one of the multiple levels of the heavens that are comprised in the world of desire. The term can also refer to the gods dwelling in this level of the heavens. In the cycle of stories concerning Gautama Buddha, it is this level of the heavens to which he ascends to preach to his mother, Māyā; his redescent to this world down a celestial staircase was often depicted in Buddhist art. See Kloetzli, *Buddhist Cosmology*, 29; Lamotte, *History of Indian Buddhism*, 20, 32, 182, 686; Collins, *Nirvana and Other Buddhist Felicities*, 297–304, 311–316; Eugene Wang, *Shaping the Lotus Sutra*, 318–320; Eugene Wang, "Pictorial Program," 89 and fig. 3.11; and Strong, *Relics of the Buddha*, 139–141.

mally require the powers of the Dharma to make this, but for it to have been produced by the powers of the realm of birth and death, it must have required such arduous labors."

The monks Zhi Fayuan 支法淵 and Zhu Faxing 竺法興,[127] both young men, later came to see him. Yu rose to greet them. When Fayuan had finished paying his respects, Yu rubbed his head with his hand and said, "What an excellent bodhisattva has come from among sheep!" When he saw Faxing come through the door, he rushed over to greet him and paid his respects, then grasped Faxing's hand, placed it on his own head, and said, "What an excellent bodhisattva has come from among celestial beings!"

In the palace armory there was a man who had been ill for several years and was near death. Yu went to see him. He said to him, "How did you fall so low as to create this misfortune?"[128] He had the sick man laid on the ground on a bare mat, placed his alms bowl over the man's belly, and covered it with a cloth. After he had sung three stanzas of hymns in Sanskrit, he uttered an Indic spell[129] of perhaps a few thousand syllables. Soon a stench filled the room. The sick man said, "I will live!" Yu instructed someone to lift the cloth. In the bowl could be seen something resembling a foul mass of mud. The sick man soon recovered fully.

The governor of Changsha, Teng Yongwen 滕永文,[130] had previously been rather vigorous in his practice. At the time he was in Luoyang, and he had suffered from wind-induced spasms in his feet[131] for several years. Yu said a spell for him, and he immediately recovered. After several days he was able to get up and walk.

On the grounds of Manshui monastery 滿水寺[132] there was a bodhi tree[133] that had earlier withered and died. Yu spoke a spell toward it. Within in a week, the tree had produced new sprouts. At that time Zhu Faxing 竺法行 resided in this monastery. He was skilled at disputation and often sparred verbally with Director of the Imperial Secretariat Le Guang 樂

---

127. Both are mentioned, always together, in *Gaoseng zhuan* (4.350a and 9.388a, the latter being Qi Yu's hagiography, the former that of Yu Falan).

128. In other words, what deeds did you commit in the past to create the karma responsible for this illness?

129. Translating *fan zhou* 梵呪.

130. He is briefly mentioned in *Jin shu* 100.2622. The *Gaoseng zhuan* narrative of Qi Yu says Teng was a native of Nanyang.

131. Translating *liang jiao feng luan* 兩腳風攣; for comments on "wind" (*feng*) as a pathogen in medieval medical theory, see the note in item 3 above.

132. Its name is variantly given as Yu 雨 shui si. It is mentioned (as Manshui si) in the *Gaoseng zhuan* hagiography of Qi Yu (at 9.388a) and at the parallel point in the narrative in *Shenseng zhuan*. The monastery also appears in the list given in *Meisōden shō* 名僧傳抄, where it is once again connected with Qi Yu (and where it is not mentioned in any other connection).

133. The species of tree under which Gautama was said to have achieved his final enlightenment.

廣.[134] On seeing Yu he nodded his head and said, "We have already seen proof of your attainments on the path. We hope you will instruct us in the Dharma." Yu said, "To guard the mouth, control the thoughts, and commit no offense in the body: in this fashion the practitioner will surpass the world and depart."[135] Faxing said, "One who has attainments in the path should bestow that which has not already been heard. These are words recited by a seven-year-old novice, not what we hope to hear from an attainer in the path." Yu laughed and replied, "Yes, as you say, a seven-year-old can recite these words perfectly, but a hundred-year-old cannot put them into practice. Everyone knows to respect an attainer in the path, but they do not know how to practice it themselves and thus attain it for themselves. From my point of view it's very simple. The wonder is that you, sir, are fixated on 'that which has not already been heard!'"

People in the capital, both high-ranking and low, brought him gifts of clothing and other articles, amounting to hundreds of millions [in cash value]. He accepted all of them. When he was about to depart, he left them behind intact. All he took was eight hundred banners, which he loaded onto the backs of camels and sent ahead with a merchant[136] to return west to India, and one robe given to him by Faxing, which he carried personally. He said to Faxing, "In this place there will soon be new masses of sins committed. Why should I regret leaving?"

When Yu set out on his journey, several thousand people sent him off. After the noon meal at the Luoyang monastery [where he was staying] he hit the road. People who had set out that same day from Chang'an said later that they saw Yu that day in a Chang'an monastery. Also, the merchant whom Yu had sent ahead with the camels reached the river at Dunhuang, where he met his own younger brother, who was coming in from India. The younger brother said that Yu had recently been seen in the monastery at Dunhuang. A disciple of Yu, Ta Deng 濕登,[137] said that they had run into each other north of the Flowing Sands [Liusha 流沙][138] and had had a cordial conversation. When the days were counted up, the day of

---

134. An official biography of Le Guang appears in *Jin shu* 43.1243–1246.

135. In the Chinese, this is two lines of seven characters each—an easily remembered slogan. The *Gaoseng zhuan* version gives four lines of five characters each.

136. Here and throughout the rest of the story, the term I render as "merchant" is *guke* 估客, perhaps, given the context, a Chinese equivalent to the various Sogdian and other non-Chinese titles for caravan leaders or merchant chiefs in Central and Western Asia (although *Hanyu dacidian*, 1.1224b, simply defines the term as "traveling merchant"). See Dien, "Caravans and Caravan Leaders"; Rong, "*Sabao or Sabo*"; and de la Vaissière, *Histoire des marchands sogdiens*, 135–139.

137. In the *Gaoseng zhuan* story his name is Hu Tadeng, and he is not a disciple but a merchant.

138. An ancient and medieval name for a large and rather indeterminately defined Central Asian desert area, partly comprised in what is now Xinjiang province. See *Hanyu dacidian*, 5.1262b.

this meeting was the day on which Yu had left Luoyang. But for this to be possible he would have to have traveled ten thousand *li* in one day.

Comments

Another sort of contestation is evidenced in this tale. If one were to make a list of all the sorts of wondrous feats attributed in early medieval literature to seekers of transcendence, and if one were to imagine these as constituting a sort of repertoire,[139] and then if one were to compare that repertoire of feats to those attributed to wonder-working Buddhist monks (as I have in fact done), one would find overlap so thorough that it can only have been deliberately crafted. Here, for example, we see the ability to discern the hidden qualities of others (here with the Buddhist twist of including past lives—a narrative device that also serves as a sort of back-confirmation of rebirth), which I will refer to below as the "motif of recognition"; the use of spells;[140] rapid long-distance travel; healing; and mastery of animals—all of them previously associated with seekers of transcendence and now credited as well to Buddhist monks, particularly those classified as workers of wonders.[141]

9[142]

During the Jin there lived the monk Zhu Fodiao 竺佛調.[143] His country of origin is unknown. He came and went from Mount Chang[144] over many years. In his practice he stressed purity and simplicity and was not given to displays of verbal ornamentation. For this he was widely admired by his contemporaries.

On Mount Chang there were two brothers, both observers of the Dharma, who lived a hundred *li* away from the monastery. The wife of the older brother fell gravely ill. They transported her to a place beside the monas-

---

139. As is attempted in Campany, *Making Transcendents*, 39–61.

140. This story is our text's first mention of spells, which figured importantly in the repertoire of techniques mastered by practitioners of the Buddhist path, as well as by seekers of transcendence, shamans, and others. See Strickmann, "The Consecration Sūtra"; Strickmann, *Chinese Magical Medicine*; Strickman, *Mantras et mandarins*; Mollier, *Buddhism and Taoism Face to Face*; Copp, "Voice, Dust, Shadow, Stone"; and Copp, "Notes on the Term *Dhāraṇī*."

141. Both Huijiao's *Traditions of Eminent Monks* (*Gaoseng zhuan*) and Daoshi's *Fayuan zhulin* have discrete sections devoted to wonder-working monastics, and in both cases the rubric under which the notices are grouped is *shenyi* 神異, or "divine wonders."

142. Source texts: *Fayuan zhulin* 28.491c–492a (section "numinous anomalies" [*shenyi* 神異]); Lu, *Gu xiaoshuo gouchen*, 383; Wang Guoliang, *Mingxiang ji yanjiu*, 9; Wakatsuki, Hasegawa, and Inagaki, *Hōon jurin no sōgō teki kenkyū*, 192–195. Additional texts: *Gaoseng zhuan* 9.387c–388a; *Ji shenzhou sanbao gantong lu* 3.431c; *Shenseng zhuan* 1.954a–b. Previously translated in Kao, *Classical Chinese Tales*, 164–166.

143. The last syllable of his name may also be read as Diao.

144. *Gaoseng zhuan* mentions Changshan *monastery* here. It was located in what is now Shangqiu district, Henan province.

tery so that she could be near doctors and medicines. The older brother thus came to take Fodiao as his teacher, and he was often in the monastery, seeking instruction and practicing the path.

One day Fodiao unexpectedly went to their home. The younger brother asked about his sister-in-law's condition and how his older brother was doing. Fodiao said, "The patient will make it, and your brother is as usual." After Fodiao had left, the younger brother mounted his horse and went [to the monastery] as well. When he mentioned that Fodiao had come that morning, the older brother was startled and said, "The monk has not left the monastery since first thing this morning. How can you have seen him?" The brothers hastened to ask Fodiao about it, but he only smiled and made no answer. Both thought it strange.

Fodiao would sometimes go alone deep into the mountain for a year or half a year with several measures of dry cooked rice. Each time he returned there would be some rice left over. Someone once followed him into the mountain for several dozen *li*. That night there was a heavy snowfall. Fodiao entered a tiger's den in a rock niche to spend the night. When the tiger returned it lay down in front of the niche. Fodiao said, "I have taken your dwelling place here. I feel so ashamed!" But the tiger lowered its ears and went down the mountain. The person who had followed him was terrified.

Fodiao predicted the time of his death. People came from near and far. Fodiao instructed them: "Heaven and earth last long, but even they will eventually be destroyed. How much more is this the case for people and other creatures—and yet we wish to go on existing forever? If one can eliminate the three defilements[145] and concentrate the mind solely on perfection and purity, then although in bodily form we may differ, in spiritual attainment we will be the same." All who were present wept. Fodiao then returned to his chamber, sat down in the correct posture, covered his head with a fold of his robe, and shortly expired.

Several years later, eight of Fodiao's lay disciples[146] had gone into the western mountains [nearby] to collect wood when they suddenly saw Fodiao high on a cliff, his robe sparkling clean, giving the impression of one happy and at ease. Stunned, they all paid obeisance and asked, "Master, are you still here?" He said, "I am always here." He asked for news of acquaintances, then after a while departed. The eight disciples dropped what they were doing and hurried home to tell their comrades in the Dharma what had happened. But there was no way for the group to verify it. So they went together and opened up Fodiao's tomb and looked inside the coffin. There was no corpse within.

---

145. *Sangou* 三垢, sometimes known as the three poisons (*sandu* 三毒): concupiscence, anger or resentment, and ignorance. Compare the "five hindrances" (see Gethin, *The Buddhist Path to Awakening*, 173–174).

146. *Baiyi dizi* 白衣弟子.

Comments

This story's second paragraph seems to imply that the two brothers wanted proximity to the monastery's doctors and medicines. If so, this tells us something significant about how laypersons related to local monasteries: that they repaired there not simply for religious instruction and merit-making ritual but also for medical care, perhaps in exchange for significant merit-making donations of wealth. I know of no detailed study of this topic for medieval China.[147] But the translated vinaya texts clearly assume that monasteries provided care for the infirm and aged, primarily monks but also laypersons (at least those able to make significant donations).[148]

The monk Fodiao here performs more feats from the repertoire of transcendence seekers: simultaneous multilocality, mastery of wild animals, and accurate prediction of the timing of his own death. This surely self-conscious overlap with the cultural repertoire of transcendents is upended, on the other hand, and the story taken in a characteristically Buddhist direction, by the vivid lesson on impermanence delivered in the deathbed scene in the penultimate paragraph. But then comes a final twist: the story's conclusion is strongly reminiscent of transcendence lore after all, and the teaching of impermanence—at least when it comes to holy, wonder-working monks—is trumped. Based on this narrative, proponents of the quest for transcendence could have claimed Fodiao as one of their own.

10[149]

During the Jin there lived Jiantuole 犍陀勒. It is not known which country he came from.[150] He once traveled to Luoyang and passed several years there. Although all respected his comportment, none could fathom him. Later he said, "On Mount Panchi 盤鴟山[151] there is an ancient stupa and temple. If it could be reconstructed, the merit from this act would be limitless." A group of people agreed to do this and went with him to the

---

147. Gernet makes a few germane remarks in *Buddhism in Chinese Society*, 219–223.

148. *Pace* Silk, *Managing Monks*, 8, see Schopen, *Buddhist Monks and Business Matters*, 7–12, 104; Zysk, *Asceticism and Healing in Ancient India*, 44–52; and now Salguero, "Buddhist Medicine in Medieval China," 40–41, of which I only learned as this manuscript was going to press. Birnbaum, *The Healing Buddha*, collects some sutra material on healing in the Buddhist tradition.

149. Source texts: *Fayuan zhulin* 28.492a (section "numinous anomalies" [*shenyi* 神異]); Lu, *Gu xiaoshuo gouchen*, 384; Wang Guoliang, *Mingxiang ji yanjiu*, 10; Wakatsuki, Hasegawa, and Inagaki, *Hōon jurin no sōgō teki kenkyū*, 195–197. Additional texts: *Gaoseng zhuan* 10.388c–389a; *Ji shenzhou sanbao gantong lu* 3.431c–432a.

150. *Gaoseng zhuan* says he was "a Westerner."

151. Other than the geographic location given in this story, nothing else is known of the location of this mountain.

mountain. When they arrived, they saw only forest and dense underbrush, with no sign of foundations. Le pointed and said, "This is the foundation of the temple." Those in the group tried digging there and indeed found the stone base of the stupa. Later [Le] pointed out to them the locations of the lecture hall, the monks' sleeping quarters, the well, and the kitchen. Each time the group started digging they found just what Le had said would be there. After this they began to think there was something strange about him.

Once the temple was refurbished, Le became its abbot. The place was a hundred *li* from Luoyang. Each morning [Le] would arrive in Luoyang. After he had attended the assembly and heard the lecture he would always beg for a jar of oil and then carry it back to his temple. Although sometimes he would come early and sometimes late, he never broke the midday rule.[152] There was a man who could walk several hundred *li* in a day. He wanted to follow and thus test Le, so he once accompanied him. This man walked as fast as he could but could not keep up. Le looked back at him, laughed, and said, "Hold on to my robe and you won't get tired." Once the man took hold of his robe, seemingly without moving at all they had already arrived at the temple. This man then rested and only after several days returned. Only then did everyone realize Le was a divine man.

It is not known what happened to him after that.

Comments

This story is our first instance of the motif of ancient stupas, monasteries, bells, or images recovered from beneath the surface of the ground by a monk with the spiritual vision (or in some cases perhaps past-life recollection?) required to pinpoint their underground locations. This motif, which recurs in items 45 (Huida) and 55 (Fa'an) below, is, in part, a by-product of the pro-Buddhist argument (designed to counter calls for Buddhism's prohibition in China due to its foreign origin) that China, under the Indian emperor Aśoka or in still more ancient times, was once already a Buddhist kingdom.[153] The pseudo-Sanskrit name of the mountain in this narrative also invites readers to view it as the Chinese localization of an originally Indian holy place.[154]

The feat of preternaturally fast locomotion, often attributed to transcendents, is here credited to a Buddhist monk—yet another case of monks matching transcendence seekers in the extraordinary abilities attributed to them.

---

152. Those who had taken monastic vows were forbidden from eating meals after midday.

153. See Faure, "Les cloches de la terre"; Durt, "The Meaning of Archaeology in Ancient Buddhism"; Zürcher, *The Buddhist Conquest of China*, 277–280; and Campany, "À la recherche de la religion perdue."

154. My thanks to Stephen Teiser for pointing this out.

11[155]

Di Shichang 抵世常 of the Jin period was a native of Zhongshan 中山.[156] His family was greatly wealthy. During the Taikang period [280–289] people under the Jin regime were forbidden to become monks.[157] Shichang observed the Dharma with vigor. He secretly constructed an oratory[158] in his home and made offerings in support of monks, Yu Falan 于法蘭 among them.[159] No one from the sangha who came to his home [for food offerings] was refused or turned away.

---

155. Source texts: *Fayuan zhulin* 28.492a–b (section "numinous anomalies" [*shenyi* 神異]); Lu, *Gu xiaoshuo gouchen*, 384; Wang Guoliang, *Mingxiang ji yanjiu*, 11; Wakatsuki, Hasegawa, and Inagaki, *Hōon jurin no sōgō teki kenkyū*, 197–198. Additional texts: *Ji shenzhou sanbao gantong lu* 3.432a; *Fayuan zhulin* 54.694c (section "indolence and slackness" [*duoman* 惰慢]). Discussed in Pan Guiming, *Zhongguo jushi fojiao shi*, 78, who cites this story to suggest that, despite the prohibition on Chinese persons' becoming monks or nuns, the number of monastics continued to grow thanks to the sort of home oratories seen here.

156. A commandery in what is now Ding district, Hebei province.

157. What was the case, according to the histories, was that *Han Chinese* people were forbidden at this time—as they had been under the Eastern Han dynasty—to become monks. Foreigners were permitted to do so. See Li Gang, "State Religious Policy," 207–208.

158. Here and throughout, I render the Chinese expression *jingshe* 精舍 thus. In many early medieval contexts *jingshe* was the term chosen to render the Sanskrit *vihāra* (see Zhou Junxun, *Wei Jin nanbeichao zhiguai xiaoshuo cihui*, 432). This Sanskrit word was as multireferential as its Chinese counterpart. (See Schopen, "The Buddhist 'Monastery' and the Indian Garden," and Robson, "Introduction," 13.) I do not simply render *jingshe* as *vihāra* for three main reasons. First, many Anglophone readers are as unlikely to be familiar with the Indic term as with the Chinese. Second, whereas to most scholars of Indian Buddhism *vihāra* connotes a monastery, in many places in our text (as here) it can mean no such thing. Finally, unlike *vihāra* and associated Indic terms, *jingshe* does not connote "garden" or "pleasure-ground" (see Schopen, "The Buddhist 'Monastery' and the Indian Garden"). The Chinese term instead connotes a chamber or free-standing hut for religious practice; it is rather indeterminate as to size, but both terms in the compound connote simplicity—a space devoted only to the essentials. One might assume that such spaces were used primarily for meditation, but this assumption is probably mistaken: when they are mentioned, it is usually in connection with some sort of ritual performance (chanting sutras, circumambulation, confession), and there was another term, *chanfang* 禪房, that more specifically designated a space used for meditation. *Jingshe* is thus related to terms such as *fatang* 法堂, or "Dharma hall," and *zhaitang* 齋堂, or "abstinence hall." For Chinese readers it would surely have called to mind such indigenous, cognate, and homophonic or nearly homophonic terms as *jingshe* 靜舍 and *jingshi* 靜室, "cells/chambers of quietude," as well as the less frequently attested *jingshe* 淨舍, "cell of purity" (as seen for example in *Zhengyi fawen taishang wailu yi* 4b, a text probably predating the end of the Liang [see Schipper and Verellen, *The Taoist Canon*, 132–133]). For Buddhist-inclined readers it might also have conjured an association with *jingjin* 精進, *vīrya* (on which see the note to item 5 above). On Daoist analogues, including floor plans, see Yoshikawa Tadao, "'Seishitu' ko"; Strickmann, *Le taoïsme du Mao Chan*, 149–152; Pregadio, *The Encyclopedia of Taoism*, 573–575, s.v. *jingshi*; Kleeman, *Great Perfection*, 70; and Bokenkamp, "The Yao Boduo Stele," 64 (citing a passage from Lu Xiujing 陸修靜 that clearly shows that some Daoist families were outfitting their *jingshi* in the style of Buddhist *jingshe*, with altars, images, banners, canopies, and other ornamentations).

159. Yu Falan, as noted later in this tale, reappears in item 15 below. He is also the subject of a hagiography in *Gaoseng zhuan* 4.349c–350a.

Once a monk came to call who was dull and vile in appearance, his robe dirty and worn out, muddy from having traveled far. Shichang came out and paid obeisance to him, then ordered a servant to fetch water and wash the monk's feet. The monk said, "Shichang, you should wash my feet yourself." Shichang replied, "I am old and weary. I will have the servant replace me in this task." But the monk would not permit it. Shichang cursed under his breath and left. At this the monk displayed his power of divine feet:[160] his body transformed to become eight feet in length, his face became surpassingly strange, and he took off in flight and departed. Shichang beat his breast with regret and threw himself down in the mud.

At that time, between the monks and nuns at Di's home and those on the road toward it, there were fifty or sixty persons who looked and, from afar, were able to see very distinctly [the divine monk] in the air several hundred feet high. There was also a strange fragrance in the air that persisted for a month. [Yu] Falan was a noted Dharma master. There is a record concerning him later in this scroll.[161] Falan spoke of these events to his disciple Fajie 法階, and Fajie spoke of it often, so that there were many religious and lay who heard about it.

Comments

Lay donors were expected to be generous and to serve their monastic guests at communal meals without regard to status. This story makes that point by recounting a case where a donor's generosity was tested and found wanting. Here, as in other tales, the test is conducted by a mysterious divine monk of unkempt appearance, a stranger who appears during a hosted meal (often in conjunction with the abstinence ceremony, or *zhai* 齋), behaves oddly—sometimes breaking the monks' strict seating order by seniority—and then departs just as suddenly. This figure of the spirit-monk recurs multiple times in the stories below.[162]

This is the first, but not the last, instance in our text of the motif of a mysterious, pleasant, long-lasting fragrance that appears in conjunction with a Buddhist miracle and seems to function to announce the fact that a local site has been touched auspiciously by beings from the unseen world. Hagiographies of noted monks and of transcendents occasionally recount similar phenomena, and it may be that the makers of the Buddhist tales were using an indigenous trope.[163]

---

160. Translating *shenzu* 神足, a standard way of rendering the Sanskrit *ṛddhi pāda*, one of the "divine powers" (*shentong* 神通) said to result from ascetic, meditative practice. See Mochizuki, *Bukkyō daijiten*, 1794.

161. This refers to the story about Yu Falan given below, item 15.

162. This mysterious spirit-monk at the abstinence meal is also sometimes linked, implicitly or else explicitly (as in item 95), with the figure of Piṇḍola. See part 1 and the comments to item 95 for further discussion.

163. See items 11, 25, 34, 82, 87, and 94 in *Mingxiang ji* (and note the counterinstance, the stench of a deceased wicked person, in item 116). The fragrance motif appears in the *Shenxian zhuan* hagiographies of Ge Xuan, Ji Zixun, Wang Yuan, and Wang Lie, for transla-

The final paragraph is another clue to the paths of narrative transmission by which the stories in this and similar collections were formed. A certain monk who was present at some of the narrated events spoke of them to a named monastic disciple; that disciple spoke of it often to many other people, both monastics and laypersons; thus many came to hear about it.

12[164]

During the Jin the monk Kang Falang 康法朗 trained in Zhongshan. During the Yongjia period [307–312] he went west with another monk to India. They traveled past the Flowing Sands, over a thousand *li* in distance. At one point they saw by the side of the way a ruined Buddhist temple,[165] its halls no longer standing, overgrown and no longer maintained. Falang and the other monk performed reverent obeisance. They [then] noticed that there were two monks living there, one on each side of the place. One of them chanted sutras, while the other suffered from dysentery, his cell covered in filth. The sutra-chanter did nothing at all to care for the other monk. Falang and the other [pilgrim] monk worried greatly about the sick monk and stayed on to prepare rice gruel for him and clean his cell. On the sixth day, the sick monk's condition worsened, his diseased bowels flowing like a spring. Falang and the other [pilgrim] monk together cared for him. That night they said to each other that the sick man would certainly not live until daybreak. At dawn when they went to see about him, his face was radiant and pleased, and he did not seem ill at all. What had been filth in his cell was now flowers and pleasant aromas. Falang and the other monk then realized that these were disguised spiritual achievers[166] who

---

tions of which see Campany, *To Live as Long as Heaven and Earth*. It also figures in Huijiao's *Traditions of Eminent Monks* and other Buddhist monastic biographies.

164. Source texts: *Fayuan zhulin* 95.988a (section "illness and pain" [*bingku* 病苦]—an interesting classification, since the "illness" in this case is a conjured illusion designed as a test); *Taiping guangji* 89.3; Lu, *Gu xiaoshuo gouchen* 385; Wang Guoliang, *Mingxiang ji yanjiu*, 12. Additional texts: *Gaoseng zhuan* 4.347a–b; *Shenseng zhuan* 1.951a.

165. Often this term, *fotu* 佛圖 (given in both textual witnesses), would designate specifically a stupa. But in *Mingxiang ji* it usually (and quite clearly) designates a monastery or temple (terms that, in this study, I use interchangeably when it comes to Buddhist institutions)—perhaps a temple that housed a relic of the Buddha, but in any case a structure in which monks resided.

166. "Disguised spiritual achievers" is a somewhat loose translation of an otherwise unattested term, *dedao mingshi* 得道冥士—persons who have achieved enlightenment or great progress on the path (*dedao*) but normally do not reveal this to others (the sense of *mingshi*, literally "masters operating in concealment"). (*Taiping guangji* has *dedao zhi shi* 得道之士.) It is also possible that this *hapax legomenon* is simply due to a scribal error, *mingshi* 冥士 for *mingshi* 明士, a term used in some early texts (including, interestingly, *Chengju guangming jing* [see Nattier, *Earliest Chinese Buddhist Translations*, 99, and cf. Pu Chenzhong, "Notes on the *Chengju guangming jing*," 37], which is mentioned elsewhere in our text, is directed toward lay readers, and seems to have been particularly popular in the decades when Wang Yan was active) to render "bodhisattva" in Chinese.

tested people. The one who [had seemed] sick said, "The monk in the neighboring cell is my senior.[167] He long ago attained wisdom on the Path. You should go and pay him a reverential visit." Falang and the other monk had earlier looked down on the chanting monk for his apparent lack of compassion. But when they heard this they paid their respects [to the monk] and confessed their sins. The sutra-chanter said, "Both of you came here with sincere intentions. You will both alike enter the Path. Master Falang, your merit from your practice in former lives is meager; you will not fulfill your vow in this lifetime." To Falang's companion he said, "Your wisdom has deep roots; you will fulfill your vow in this lifetime." He then left them.

Falang later returned to Zhongshan and became a great Dharma master, venerated by[168] monks and laity alike.

Comments

In the scene recounting the master's ability to discern latent qualities in others we have another example of the motif of recognition, already glimpsed above (item 8) and a capacity highly prized in adepts and others in early medieval China.[169] Stories of advanced spiritual practitioners who appear in disguise to test the virtues and abilities of others would have been familiar, as well, to readers of the hagiographies of transcendents.[170]

13[171]

During the Jin there lived Zhu Changshu 竺長舒. His ancestors were Westerners who for generations had amassed property, and he was wealthy. During the Jin Yuankang period [290s] he lived in Luoyang. He upheld the Dharma energetically and was especially fond of chanting the *Sound Observer Sutra* [*Guanshiyin jing* 觀世音經].[172] Later, a fire broke out in his

167. The expression is *heshang* 和尚, a general term of respect for monks, here more specifically a monk's respectful way of referring to another monk who is senior to him in a monastic lineage.

168. Or, more literally, "taken as lineage elder by"; the phrase is *zong zhi* 宗之.

169. See Campany, *Making Transcendents*, 95, 101, 233.

170. For an example, see Campany, *To Live as Long as Heaven and Earth*, 161–168.

171. Source texts: *Fayuan zhulin* 23.459a–b (section "exhortation and guidance" [*jiangdao* 獎導]); *Bianzheng lun* 7.537c; Lu, *Gu xiaoshuo gouchen*, 385; Wang Guoliang, *Mingxiang ji yanjiu*, 13. Additional texts: *Guangshiyin yingyanji* 1 (Makita, *Rikuchō kōitsu Kanzeon ōkenki no kenkyū*, 14, translated in Campany, "The Earliest Tales of the Bodhisattva Guanshiyin," 91–92). Also, *Fayuan zhulin* 40.601a and *Ji shenzhou sanbao gantong lu* 1.410c record versions of another story about Zhu Changshu, quite different from this one and involving his devotion to a relic of the Buddha. *Fayuan zhulin* 95.988b refers to this Guanshiyin-related story as a marker in a list of stories acknowledged as having been drawn from the collection of Guanshiyin miracles by Fu Liang.

172. There were a number of sutras in circulation at the time—some of them composed in China—devoted to the Bodhisattva Guanshiyin (see Chün-fang Yü, *Kuan-yin*, 31–149), but usually the one titled simply *Guanshiyin jing* 觀世音經 was the chapter of the *Lotus Sutra*

neighborhood and was burning its way through homes. Changshu's family's home was made of thatch and stood directly downwind. Figuring that the fire was about to engulf their home, he and his family began removing belongings, but some could not be carried, and it looked as if there would not be time to remove them all. No firefighters were at hand. So they simply chanted the sutra with their whole minds. Soon the fire burned the house next to theirs and their own fence, but then the wind suddenly shifted, and the fire, just when approaching their house, died out. At the time everyone thought it was a numinous response.

In the village were four or five ruffians who poked fun, saying, "The wind just happened to turn. What is there of the divine in this? Let's wait for a very dry evening and then torch their house. If it doesn't burn, then we'll believe [divine intervention] is possible." Afterward, on a hot, dry day, with a strong wind kicking up, the young toughs prepared torches and stealthily threw them onto the roof. Three times they threw them, and three times they were extinguished. Frightened, they ran to their homes. The next morning they went severally to Changshu's home, told of what they had done the previous day, and apologized. Changshu responded, "I have no divine power. I only chanted the *Guanshiyin [Sutra]* to the utmost. This must have been a bit of good fortune sent by its awesome spiritual power. You all should cleanse your minds and become believers." From this point on, everyone in the village became respectful of such anomalies.

Comments

We see here the motif of striking, irrefutable confirmatory responses to devotion—in this case, devotion to Bodhisattva Guanshiyin. Here the motif is deployed, in part, to refute naysayers explicitly.

14[173]

During the Jin, on the west side of Mount Lu in Xunyang, there was the oratory known as Dragon Spring.[174] It was founded by the monk Huiyuan 慧遠. When Huiyuan first went to the south, he loved the foothills of this

---

devoted to this bodhisattva, which was often copied and circulated as an independent sutra (and may well have started its life that way in India).

173. Source texts: *Fayuan zhulin* 63.764c (section "praying for rain" [*qiyu* 祈雨]); Lu, *Gu xiaoshuo gouchen*, 386; Wang Guoliang, *Mingxiang ji yanjiu*, 14; Wakatsuki, Hasegawa, and Inagaki, *Hōon jurin no sōgō teki kenkyū*, 220–222. Additional texts: *Gaoseng zhuan* 6.357c (translated in Zürcher, *The Buddhist Conquest of China*, 240–253 [with the spring and dragon incidents reported at 241]); *Yiyuan* 5.31; *Shenseng zhuan* 2.957a; *Lushan ji* 1.1026b–c, 3.1039a; *Jingtu wangsheng zhuan* 1.109c. Discussed: Campany, "Notes on Sutra Texts," 62 n34. Capitanio, "Dragon Kings and Thunder Gods," 93–94, offers a translation of the story; mine differs only slightly.

174. Longquan 龍泉.

area and wanted to establish a monastery there but had not yet decided on the site for it. He and his disciples carefully combed the hills and streams of the area, and when they had grown tired they stopped to rest at this spot. The monks were thirsty. Together they stood and vowed, "If this is the place where we should erect the oratory, then we express the hope that by divine power a good spring will well up here." [Huiyuan] then stuck his staff into the ground. Clear springwater welled up, then spread to form a pool. They therefore built the hall behind it.

Once when there was an extreme drought, Huiyuan led the monks in reciting the *Sutra of the Oceanic Dragon King* [*Hailong wang jing* 海龍王經] to request rain on behalf of the people.[175] Before they had finished the recitation, a creature shaped like a giant snake appeared in the spring, rose up into the air, and flew off. Shortly afterward a heavy rain fell, inundating the land everywhere. Because of this miraculous appearance of a dragon, the retreat was named accordingly.

Comments

Rainmaking (along with other modes of weather control) was another feat that had been associated with religious adepts—especially shamans and transcendents—before Buddhism's arrival in China.[176] The ability to locate underground water sources, and the motif of the drawing forth of such sources by plunging a sword or staff into the ground, are rather widely distributed in the religious literature (both Buddhist and otherwise) of the period.[177]

This story (along with items 7 and 39) is one of the best examples in *Mingxiang ji* of what James Robson has termed "the power of place"—that is, the auspiciousness and sacred power of the locales of certain mountain temples, often captured in stories of the origins of such structures or of later miracles associated with them. Such stories were sometimes preserved

---

175. This same sutra, again in the context of a ceremony for summoning rain, is mentioned in item 56 below. The sutra as it exists today (Taishō 598) extends to four scrolls comprising twenty sections and was translated by Dharmarakṣa in 285 (see *Chu sanzang jiji* 2.7b). See also Boucher, "Dharmarakṣa and the Transmission of Buddhism," 24. (Another translation of the sutra was done by Dharmakṣema in 418 [see Chen Jinhua, "The Indian Buddhist Missionary Dharmakṣema"]; it was lost by the mid-Tang.) On rainmaking rituals in medieval China, see now Capitanio, "Dragon Kings and Thunder Gods." Ruppert, "Buddhist Rainmaking in Early Japan," discusses a few dragon narratives in the Chinese pilgrimage accounts of Faxian and Xuanzang, but he mentions the sutra literature only in passing (148). Orzech, *Politics and Transcendent Wisdom*, discusses only esoteric Buddhist rainmaking, which postdates our text. Chinese pilgrims to India, including Faxian and Xuanzang, reported on numerous temples to these dragon kings, or *nagārāja*, in South Asia.

176. See Capitanio, "Dragon Kings and Thunder Gods," the best recent Western-language study of the topic, and Campany, *Making Transcendents*, 168, 235, 242, 250.

177. For a study of these themes, see Soymié, "Sources et sourciers en Chine." For a study of this and other narratives that accumulated around Huiyuan on Mount Lu Xun, see Liu Yuanru, *Chaoxiang shenghuo shijie*, 29–80.

on stele inscriptions erected at the sites in question or alluded to in carvings made directly into mountain rocks.[178]

Huiyuan (334?–417?) is one of the most famous Buddhist leaders in China of this period. He is best known for having been a disciple of Daoan; for having spent many years at a retreat on Mount Lu frequented by both monks and laity; for his activities promoting a collective meditation fellowship focused on Amitābha known as the White Lotus Society; for his correspondence in his late years with Kumārajīva on meditation and points of Greater Vehicle doctrine, and for bringing that master's translations and teachings to the south; for having introduced preaching or lecturing as an important part of Buddhist assemblies; and for having successfully defended the right of Buddhist clergy not to bow before emperors against the ruler Huan Xuan's attempt to compel clerical obeisance.[179]

15[180]

During the Jin there lived the monk Yu Falan 于法蘭, a native of Gaoyang.[181] At fourteen he left the household [for the monastic life]. His talent and knowledge were deeply refined, his conduct impeccable. The monastery stood on a steep cliff. He was once sitting in meditation at night when a tiger entered his cell. It crouched before his mat. Falan patted its head with his hand. The tiger lowered its ears submissively and lay down. Only after several days did it depart.

Zhu Fahu 竺法護[182] was a native of Dunhuang. He too had impressive qualities, but was second to Falan. At that time the scriptures had been

---

178. See Robson, *Power of Place*; Robson, "Monastic Spaces and Sacred Traces"; Robson, "Buddhist Sacred Geography"; Stevenson, "Visions of Mañjusrī on Mount Wutai"; Birnbaum, "The Manifestation of a Monastery"; Faure, "Space and Place in Chinese Religious Traditions"; and, on the interface between Sound Observer miracle tales and particular sacred places in Japan, MacWilliams, "Kannon *Engi*." On stele inscriptions (and other rock inscriptions) as memory sites, see also Ch'en, "Inscribed Stelae"; Liu Shufen, "Art, Ritual, and Society"; Brashier, "Text and Ritual in Early Chinese Stelae"; Wong, *Chinese Steles*; Harrist, *The Landscape of Words*; and Campany, *Making Transcendents*, 222–225.

179. Among the many noted treatments of Huiyuan are Tang Yongtong, *Han Wei liang Jin nanbeichao fojiao shi*, 239–262; Zürcher, *The Buddhist Conquest of China*, 204–253; and Tsukamoto, *A History of Early Chinese Buddhism*, 757–888.

180. Source texts: *Fayuan zhulin* 63.764c–765a (section "praying for rain" [*qiyu* 祈雨]); Lu, *Gu xiaoshuo gouchen*, 386; Wang Guoliang, *Mingxiang ji yanjiu*, 15; Wakatsuki, Hasegawa, and Inagaki, *Hōon jurin no sōgō teki kenkyū*, 222–224. Additional texts: *Chu sanzang jiji* 13.97c; *Gaoseng zhuan* 4.349c; *Hongming ji* 2.14b24, 3.18c27, 3.20a–b; *Ji shenzhou sanbao gantong lu* 3.432a; *Beishan lu* 4; *Fayuan zhulin* 28.492a, 54.694c.

181. A commandery in what is now near Boye district, Hebei province. Yu Falan was seen above in item 10.

182. *Fayuan zhulin* gives Zhu Hu, but *Chu sanzang jiji* 13 and *Gaoseng zhuan* 1 give Zhu Fahu. I emend accordingly. This is the well-known and important translator Dharmarakṣa (active ca. 266–308), on whom see Boucher, "Dharmarakṣa and the Transmission of Buddhism," and Zürcher, *The Buddhist Conquest of China*, 65–70.

newly translated and contained many Indic words,[183] the words and phrases were confused and disorderly, and the sections and *gāthas*[184] were in disarray. [Fahu] grasped their essentials and prepared editions of them in fluent literary form. He also fed a band of disciples on the [same] mountain. On the mountain there ran a clear stream that was used for drinking and bathing. A woodcutter once muddied up the stream, which caused it to be blocked and thus soon to dry up [downstream]. Fahu approached the stream, hesitated, and then sighed, "If the stream is dry, how will we provide for ourselves?" The moment he had finished speaking, a large flow of clear water came pouring down, and soon the stream was running full again.

Both of these events happened during the reigns of [Jin] emperors Wu and Hui [265–307]. Zhi Daolin 支道林 [314–366][185] described them in a eulogy[186] that reads:

> Master Yu surpassed the world,
> Fully embodying the ultimate teaching;
> So well did he keep to his practice in the mountains and marshes
> That his kindness moved even tigers and rhinoceroses.
> Master Hu was pure and solitary
> Of such profound and perfect virtue
> That even a whisper in an empty creek bed
> Caused a dried-up spring to flow again.

Comments

We see more matching of Buddhist adepts' abilities to those of transcendence seekers—specifically, in this case, mastery of animals and of water flow.

16[187]

Jin-era Minister of Works He Chong 何充 (292–346), styled Cidao 次道, was a native of Lujiang. From his youth he believed in the Dharma and was

---

183. "Many Indic words" translates *fanyu shuduo* 梵語數多.

184. *Gāthas*, or *jie* 偈—a word probably pronounced "giat" in our period (see Pulleyblank, *Lexicon of Reconstructed Pronunciation*, 154)—are the verse portions of sutras that often summarize, restate, or elaborate upon the messages contained in preceding prose portions.

185. This is Zhi Dun 支遁, a well-known and highly literate monk who took up residence in the vicinity of the southern capital and consorted with a great many talented and powerful men of the day, from whose midst he attracted many followers and hangers-on. See Tang Yongtong, *Han Wei liang Jin nanbeichao fojiao shi*, 125–128; Zürcher, *The Buddhist Conquest of China*, 116–130; and Tsukamoto, *A History of Early Chinese Buddhism*, 338–361.

186. Or, just possibly, "made an image of and a eulogy about them," if one takes the *xiang* in *wei zhi xiang zan* 為之像贊 as referring to sponsoring the production of a devotional image.

187. Source texts: *Fayuan zhulin* 42.616a–b (section "[monks] receiving invitations [from laity]" [*shouqing* 受請—the Taishō edition has 愛請, but 愛 is clearly an error for 受, as

very disciplined in his practice of mental cultivation. He habitually placed in his abstinence hall[188] an empty seat covered by a mat and a floral canopy[189] decorated with jewels. He kept it set up for many years, and several spirit-anomalies occurred. On one occasion there was [in this hall] a large gathering of monks and laypersons, very crowded. Among the monks sitting in order [of seniority] was one whose face and robe were filthy, his apparent level of spiritual attainment very base. This monk emerged from the assembly, climbed up onto the seat, joined his palms together, and simply remained silent. He said nothing. The entire hall full of people were shocked and thought he must be deranged. Chong, too, was uneasy, his embarrassment showing in his face. When the midday meal was taken, this monk ate on the high seat.[190] When the meal was concluded, he picked up his alms bowl and left the hall. On his way out he looked at Chong and said, "To what end have you been exerting yourself so vigorously in the practice?"[191] He then tossed his bowl into the air, and he and it rose up and away into the sky.[192] Chong and the other laypersons and monastics present hurried behind to look at him. He gave off a beautiful, bright radiance that dazzled the eyes, then disappeared from view. Those chasing after the strange monk were all regretful, and for days afterward they prostrated themselves and made confession.

Comments

We have here another example of the motif of the strange monk at a ceremonial gathering. The last paragraph supplies another instance of the dis-

---

can be confirmed by checking this heading against the parallel one in *Zhujing yaoji* (also a Daoshi work) 1.1b1]); Lu, *Gu xiaoshuo gouchen*, 387; Wang Guoliang, *Mingxiang ji yanjiu*, 16; Wakatsuki, Hasegawa, and Inagaki, *Hōon jurin no sōgō teki kenkyū*, 211–212. Additional texts: *Gaoseng zhuan*, as quoted in *Fayuan zhulin* 19.428b; *Ji shenzhou sanbao gantong lu* 3.433a.

188. "Abstinence hall" translates *zhaitang* 齋堂. On the *zhai*, or "abstinence ceremony," see part 1.

189. Here "canopy" renders *zhang* 帳, a term sometimes more suggestive of "curtains"; elsewhere (as in item 76 below) it sometimes also renders *gai* 蓋. Both terms refer to tentlike suspensions of fabric over a seat or couch to mark it as an opulent place of honor (as well as to perform more utilitarian functions, such as keeping out insects and heat). See Dien, *Six Dynasties Civilization*, 301–303, and Angela Sheng, "From Stone to Silk."

190. "High seat" translates *gaozuo* 高座. The term was used to denote a range of ritual structures, from an elevated seat or platform to an altar on which images and sutras were placed (see Mochizuki, *Bukkyō daijiten*, 1043b–c). Modeled on the jeweled seat from which the Buddha is said in many sutras to have discoursed, in monastic or monastic-lay assemblies this elevated seat was reserved for the monk who was expounding the Dharma, pronouncing the precepts, or lecturing to the assembly of monks or monks, nuns, and laity combined. Salient passages describing these structures may be found (to cite a few examples) in *Renwang banruo poluomi jing* 825b, 829c–830a; *Fanwang jing* 1008a; and *Gaoseng zhuan* 353b24. It would be useful to have a good study of the *gaozuo* in Buddhist literature and ritual practice.

191. In other words, although your practice is "by the book," you have failed to recognize the presence of an august personage in humble guise. You follow the rules but lack discernment.

192. See comments.

positional impact of miraculous events on protagonists, witnesses, and hearers: in this case, we see that an encounter with a spirit-monk might induce an intensified bout of confession rituals.

This is one of two instances in our text in which a mysterious visiting spirit monk throws his alms bowl into the air and then flies off in its wake; the other episode occurs in item 19. This association of the alms bowl with paranormal flight is also evidenced in several transformation texts (*bian-wen* 變文) found at Dunhuang in which the monk Maudgalyāyana, known in Chinese texts as Mulian 目蓮, flies off after his bowl in exactly the same fashion.[193] Whether this association originated in China or had its roots elsewhere has yet to be researched. But what is clear is that the monk's alms bowl, like his metal-ringed staff and robe, was a potent synecdochal symbol of spiritual power. In item 8, a monk's bowl figures importantly in a curative procedure. In stories 18 and 19, food from a mysterious alms bowl suffices to feed the entire assembly gathered for an abstinence ceremony. Stories 17, 45 (where it is a case of the Buddha's own alms bowl), and (by implication) 18 speak of alms bowls in terms that imply their status as sacred relics once their owners have passed on. And in item 129 a monk donates his bowl and robe as an act of merit.

He Chong was a major figure in the early-fourth-century network of official-class Buddhist laymen so often mentioned in written sources from the period, men for whom an allegiance to Buddhist teaching and discipline was inseparable from their political, social, and familial ties. He is on record as having participated in a 340 debate on whether monks should be required to bow before rulers. He donated a residence to the sangha, and the structure became the first convent on record in China. The monk Zhi Dun (on whom more below), in his preface to a collection of poems about the abstinence ceremony, mentions him as having taken part in such gatherings.[194]

17[195]

During the Jin there lived the nun Zhu Daorong 竺道容. Her native place is unknown. She resided in Wujiang monastery 烏江寺.[196] She was very

---

193. See Mair, *Tun-huang Popular Narratives*, 90–91, 104, 112, 114, and Teiser, *The Ghost Festival*, 160.

194. See Pan Guiming, *Zhongguo jushi fojiao shi*, 87–88; Zürcher, *The Buddhist Conquest of China*, 106–110, 116–117, 160–163; and Hureau, "Réseaux de bouddhistes des Six Dynasties," 48–49, 51–52.

195. Source texts: *Fayuan zhulin* 42.616b (section "[monks] receiving invitations [from laity]" [*shouqing* 受請]); Lu, *Gu xiaoshuo gouchen*, 387; Wang Guoliang, *Mingxiang ji yanjiu*, 17; Wakatsuki, Hasegawa, and Inagaki, *Hōon jurin no sōgō teki kenkyū*, 213–215. Additional texts: *Biqiuni zhuan* 1.936b; *Fayuan zhulin* 31.526b; *Fozu tongji* 36.340b, 52.455c, 53.463c; *Baguan zhai fa*, scroll 1. Discussed: Zürcher, *The Buddhist Conquest of China*, 105; Lo, "Recovering a Buddhist Voice on Daughters-in-Law," 329–330.

196. This monastery was located in Wujiang district of Liyang commandery (in what is

strict in her observance of the monastic precepts and often experienced confirmatory responses to her devotions.[197] During the reign of Jin emperor Ming 明 [r. 323–325] she was served with particular reverence [by the emperor].[198] Flowers were placed on her mat to verify her attainments; they did not wither.[199] Jin emperor Jian 簡,[200] [by contrast,] during his reign [371–372] served the Way of Pure Water;[201] the master he served was a man known in the capital as Wang Puyang 王濮陽.[202] Inside the imperial residence he set up a Dao chamber.[203] Daorong tried hard to convert him, but the emperor could never be persuaded. Afterward, whenever the emperor entered the Dao chamber, he would see divine personages in the form of monks filling up the whole room. The emperor suspected it was something Daorong had done, so he [finally] served her as his master and upheld the correct Dharma. That the Jin imperial clan gave priority to the path of Buddha was due to the power of this nun. At the time she was revered and considered extraordinary; people called

---

now He district, Anhui province). It is mentioned in the *Biqiuni zhuan* account of Daorong; in a passage from *Jin Nanjing si ji* 晉南京寺記, as quoted in *Fayuan zhulin* 31.526b; twice in *Fozu tongji* (36.340b–c, 53.467b, both passages again mentioning Daorong); and in some much later, clearly derivative texts. All of these brief passages on the monastery also mention Daorong.

197. "Confirmatory responses to her devotions" somewhat clumsily translates *zhenggan* 徵感. *Zheng* 徵 connotes "proof," "evidence," "verification" (nominal or adjectival); *gan* 感, as discussed in part 1, connotes the "stimulus" of human action or intention that triggers a "response" (*ying* 應) from a divine being or the cosmos.

198. Zürcher (*The Buddhist Conquest of China*, 97) says that Emperor Ming "appears to have been the first Chinese monarch with outspoken Buddhist sympathies and interests."

199. A practice mentioned elsewhere in our text; see item 64 below.

200. More usually titled Emperor Jianwen 簡文.

201. The Way of Pure Water, or *Qingshui dao* 清水道, seems to have been a once-flourishing religious path that later died out. The most detailed record we have of its practices is found in *Inner Explanations of the Three Heavens* (*Santian neijie jing* 三天內解經, 4b), an early Celestial Master scripture that understands itself to be in competition with this alternate path; see Bokenkamp, *Early Daoist Scriptures*, 218–219. As Bokenkamp notes, this Way—from the *Inner Explanations* description, apparently a cult of water—is also mentioned in the *Lives of Nuns* version of Zhu Daorong's story; see *Biqiuni zhuan* 1.936b and Tsai, *Lives of the Nuns*, 30–31. (An alternate translation of this text is available: Li Jung-shi, *Biographies of Buddhist Nuns*. The standard attribution of this work to the monk Baochang 寶唱 has recently been questioned, though certainly not disproved: see De Rauw, "Baochang.") However, *Fayuan zhulin* (36.573a11–13) also quotes a text titled *Shuzheng ji* 述征記 concerning the origins of the cult (or perhaps of another cult with the same name?): In the northern barrens, the text says, the wife of a man surnamed Wang—her natal surname being Zhang—died and was buried; several years later her tomb was opened and incense was found to be still burning inside. Her family thus began worshiping her, and the cult was named the Way of Pure Water.

202. There is a brief notice on a certain [Wang?] Puyang in *Sandong zhunang* 1.5b3–8. It makes no mention of the Way of Pure Water, but, significantly, it does recount a miracle involving water. It also mentions the involvement of Emperor Jianwen.

203. Here, the term translated thus is *daoshe* 道舍; two sentences down, the expression used is *daowu* 道屋.

her "the Sage."[204] Xinlin monastery 新林寺 was built by the emperor for Daorong.[205]

At the outset of Jin emperor Xiaowu's reign [373] Daorong suddenly went into reclusion; no one knew where she was to be found. Her robe and alms bowl were accordingly given a burial. Beside the old monastery the tomb still exists.

Comments

We have here a striking instance of contestation between Buddhism and a particular, relatively obscure style of Daoism. Here the stakes of the contest are an emperor's patronage.

Funerary treatment of a holy person's belongings, especially when her body was no longer to be found, as in this instance, was known in both non-Buddhist and Buddhist contexts. The last sentence hints that Daorong's tomb beside her monastery was perhaps a pilgrimage site, or that sponsors of her memory and reputation hoped it might be.

18[206]

During the Jin there lived one Que Gongze 闕公則, a native of Zhao.[207] He lived quietly and undisturbed, devoting himself only to the service of the Dharma. During the time of Jin emperor Wu, he died in Luoyang. Monks and laity with one accord hosted a gathering for him at the White Horse monastery. That night they chanted sutras. At midnight they heard in the air overhead the sound of someone singing hymns.[208] Looking up, they saw a person of imposing and dignified appearance, smartly attired, who said: "I am Que Gongze. I have now been reborn in the realm of peace and bliss in the West.[209] In the company of several bodhisattvas I have come to listen

---

204. "The Sage" translates *shengren* 聖人; *Fayuan zhulin* 31, in citing *Jin nanjing si ji* 晉南京寺記, gives at this point *shengma* 聖嬭, or "holy mother" (?).

205. This monastery was located in Moling (in today's Jiangning district, Jiangsu province) and was built in 372 according to *Jin nanjing si ji* 晉南京寺記, as quoted in *Fayuan zhulin* 31.526b.

206. Source texts: *Fayuan zhulin* 42.616b–c (section "[monks] receiving invitations [from laity]" [*shouqing* 受請]); *Ji shenzhou sanbao gantong lu* 3.432a; Lu, *Gu xiaoshuo gouchen*, 388; Wang Guoliang, *Mingxiang ji yanjiu*, 18; Wakatsuki, Hasegawa, and Inagaki, *Hōon jurin no sōgō teki kenkyū*, 215–218. Additional texts: *Yiyuan* 5.36; *Wangsheng ji* 2.142c; *Hongming ji* 3.19a. Partially translated in Palumbo, "Dharmarakṣa and Kaṇṭhaka," 176; I did not locate this translation until after having prepared my own. Discussed: Pan Guiming, *Zhongguo jushi fojiao shi*, 77, who uses this story to argue for the early-attested establishment of Pure Land Buddhism in China and its appeal to laity; Mai, "Visualization Apocrypha," 30–31; Campany, "Notes on Sutra Texts," 62 n35.

207. A commandery located in today's Gaoyi district, Hebei province.

208. Translating *chang zan* 唱讚. Hymn singing was an important aspect of Chinese Buddhist devotional practice. See, for example, Lin Renyu, *Dunhuang fojiao gequ yanjiu*.

209. Translating *xifang anle shijie* 西方安樂世界, a common appellation for the Western Pure Land.

to the sutras." Everyone in the hall was stunned and leapt for joy; all were able to see him.

Around the same time there was also one Wei Shidu 衛士度, a native of Ji commandery.[210] He, too, was a zealous lay practitioner, and was Gongze's teacher. His mother also was deeply pious; she recited sutras and performed the long periods of abstinence,[211] and she often fed monks at her home. Once it was approaching midday when his mother went out of the abstinence hall along with a group of nuns and monks and looked off in the distance. Suddenly she saw something fall from the sky and land directly in front of her. It was an alms bowl full of rice, the fragrance filling the surrounding air. Everyone from the hall was filled with reverential awe and simultaneously performed respectful obeisance. The mother decided to circulate the bowl among those present for the abstinence ceremony to feed them. None of them were hungry again for the next seven days. It is said that this alms bowl still exists somewhere in the north.

Shidu was highly literate.[212] He composed a confession text for the ceremony of the eightfold abstinence.[213] Toward the end of the Jin, those observing the abstinences still used it. When he died during the Yongchang period [322] there were also numinous anomalies. Hao Xiang 浩像 in his *Traditions of Sages and Worthies* records them in detail.[214] That text says that Shidu, too, was reborn in the western land.

It was to these two figures that Wang Gai 王該 of Wuxing in his "Candles in Daylight"[215] was referring when he wrote:

---

210. Now Ji district, Henan province.

211. "Long periods of abstinence" translates *changzhai* 長齋; although this term was used to denote a great many specific practices (see Forte and May, "Chōsai"), here it probably simply means that Wei Shidu's mother faithfully participated in the thrice-annual long periods of abstinence for laity (carried out in the first fortnight of the first, fifth, and ninth months), an indication of unusually pious practice. See further Hureau, "Buddhist Rituals," 1215–1216.

212. The *Ji shenzhou sanbao gantong lu* witness breaks off at this point with the words "See *Mingxiang zhuan* [*sic*] 見冥祥傳."

213. *Guang hongming ji* 30 collects several such texts (*chan wen* 懺文) dating as early as the Jin. The phrase "the ceremony of the eightfold abstinence" (*baguan zhai* 八關齋), which recurs several times below, is simply another way of referring to the standard abstinence ceremony for laypersons, in which, for one day and night six times per month (and perhaps in some cases for longer periods three times per year), participating laymen and women refrained from killing, stealing, having sex, lying, drinking alcohol, sitting on high seats, using adornments and perfumes, and eating after noon. For an overview of ways in which it is mentioned in early medieval *zhiguai* texts, see Chen Hong, "Fojiao baguanzhai yu zhonggu xiaoshuo." Wang Sanqing (*Cong Dunhuang*, 8–9) points to this story as one of the earliest bits of evidence of the use of written documents during abstinence observances in China.

214. This text, *Shengxian zhuan* 聖賢傳, is not only lost; no other mention of it or of its author seems to have survived.

215. No other mention of this author or quotation of this work, *Rizhu* 日燭, appears to have survived. There was another Wang Gai in the Jin period, mentioned at several points in the *Jin shu*, but he was a native of Xindu.

Que, peerless, surmounted the empyrean;
Weidu followed in his tracks.
Both are now carefree in the state of no rebirth,
Both sloughed off their skeletons and achieved deathlessness.[216]

Comments

This story provides a clear depiction—pegged to a particular time and place in China—of the sort of celestial audience for sutra recital that is also depicted in some Mahāyāna sutras themselves.

The final verses equate *nirvāṇa* with transcendent-like nondying. This represents, I suspect, not a layman's failure to grasp the profound difference between these two religious goals but rather something more complex. We may read it as an appropriation of the language of "sloughing off the skeleton" and "deathlessness"—which, with an ancient non-Buddhist pedigree, carried prestige in the eyes of some readers—for the purposes of making clear the august achievements of Que and Weidu. Or we may read it as an attempt by a pro-transcendence author to co-opt these two Buddhist achievers into the ranks of those who had transcended in the indigenous way. Without more information on Wang Gai or his work, there is no good way to decide between these readings.

19[217]

During the Jin there lived one Teng Bing 滕並, a native of Nanyang.[218] His family had been pious believers for generations. His wife was of the Quan 全 clan of Wu commandery and was particularly capable of arduous discipline. Each time she hosted an abstinence assembly, she would not refuse to invite any [monks]; whoever came, she would host and make offerings to them all. One day the number of monks who showed up was too small, so she sent someone out into the streets nearby to look for others to invite. This person saw a monk sitting under the shade of a willow, so he invited the monk to accompany him back. When a temple worker[219] was serving

---

216. The line reads *ju tuihai yi busi* 俱蛻骸以不死.

217. Source texts: *Fayuan zhulin* 42.616c (section "[monks] receiving invitations [from laity]" [*shouqing* 受請]); Lu, *Gu xiaoshuo gouchen*, 388; Wang Guoliang, *Mingxiang ji yanjiu*, 19. Additional texts: *Ji shenzhou sanbao gantong lu* 3.432a.

218. Today's Nanyang district, Henan province. Teng Bing's father, Teng Xiu 脩, has a biography in *Jin shu* 57.1553.

219. *Jingren* 淨人, or "purifier," denoting nonmonastic temple workers who, because they had not taken the monastic vows, were permitted to carry out tasks prohibited as impurifying to monks, including agriculture, animal rearing, commerce, the handling of money, and kitchen work. See Gernet, *Buddhism in Chinese Society*, 70, 78, 336 n26, 356 n4; Silk, *Managing Monks*, 43 n18, 45 n29, 167; and Ch'en, *The Chinese Transformation of Buddhism*, 144. It is not surprising to see these workers portrayed as accompanying monks to lay homes, since monks could not accept certain donated items directly from laity. I thank Karashima Seishi for this observation.

the food, he[220] spilled it on the floor, leaving no other food available and no evident solution to the problem. The invited monk said, "There is enough food in my alms bowl to offer to everyone." He had Bing divide it up and distribute it. All present, men and women, monks and laity, had enough to eat. After the washing was done, he threw his alms bowl into the air and quickly ascended upward after it until he was out of sight.

Bing thereafter carved an image of the monk from wood and paid obeisance to it each morning and evening. Each time some misfortune was about to strike Bing's family, this image would be found to have fallen over....[221]

Bing's son Han 含, because of his meritorious service [in attacking] Su Jun 蘇峻, was [later] invested with an office in Dongxing.[222]

Comments

Not only do we have here another instance of a strange monk attending a meal at a lay household, but in this case the host also makes an image of the spirit-monk after his departure and offers devotion to it. The image performs a premonitory function for the family.

20[223]

Zhu Fajin 竺法進 was abbot of Kaidu monastery 開度浮圖. He was clever and widely learned and understood many diverse dialects.

When the capital was about to fall, he wished to hide out in the mountains and marshes. A large number of people urged him to stay, but Jin would not listen to them. A great assembly was held at which incense was burned to say farewell to him. Just as the incense was about to be distributed, a monk suddenly came and positioned himself on the high seat, his robe dirty, his face dark and swollen. Fajin considered him base and dragged him down to a lower-ranked position, but the monk climbed back up again. After Fajin had dragged him down a third time, he was no more to be seen. Once everyone's seats had been determined and they had sat down to eat, a sudden violent wind stirred up dust everywhere and overturned the tables. Fajin regretted and repented his error, blaming himself. In the end he desisted and did not head to the mountains.

At the time, people evaluated these events as follows. The age was about to fall into great disorder; it was thus unfitting that Fajin should have [planned to] head for the mountains. Also, both clerics and laity were of

---

220. Or she.

221. Ellipsis (*yun* 云) in the original.

222. Dongxing was a district in today's Xincheng district, Jiangxi province.

223. Source texts: *Fayuan zhulin* 42.616c (section "[monks] receiving invitations [from laity]" [*shouqing* 受請]); *Ji shenzhou sanbao gantong lu* 3.432b2; Lu, *Gu xiaoshuo gouchen*, 389; Wang Guoliang, *Mingxiang ji yanjiu*, 20; Wakatsuki, Hasegawa, and Inagaki, *Hōon jurin no sōgō teki kenkyū*, 218–220.

the utmost mind to have him stay with them, and this is why this divine anomaly appeared, to put a stop to his intention to depart.

Comments

Here once again we see the motif of the strange, often uncouth monk who appears unexpectedly at a merit assembly and breaks the order of seniority. In this case, the story reports a theory to explain this appearance, a theory developed in the social network of conversation about the reported anomalies. This last paragraph affords us a valuable glimpse of the activity of a community of people in developing a specific sort of reception of anomaly reports. It was in such communities that the stories collected in our text originated.

21[224]

During the Jin, Zhou Min 周閔,[225] a native of Runan, served as an officer of the guard. His family had venerated the Dharma for generations. During Sun Jun's 蘇峻 rebellion [328] people of the capital were hurriedly fleeing in all directions.[226] Min's family had a copy of the *Larger Perfection of Wisdom Sutra*[227] written on the front and back of an eighteen-foot-long expanse of silk. In addition they had several other book bags full of sutras, and this copy of the *Larger Perfection of Wisdom* was intermixed with them. At the moment when they had to flee, they traveled alone and could not carry everything; although they especially regretted leaving behind their prized sutra copy, they did not know which bag it was in. Time had run out, and they had to leave: there was no more time to look for it. Min paced anxiously. Suddenly, without their knowing how, the *Larger Perfection of Wisdom* emerged from a bag on its own power. Amazed and pleased, Min grabbed it and fled. The Zhou family has treasured it for generations, and it is said to be still extant.

Another story goes as follows.[228] The wife of Zhou Song 周嵩[229] was of

---

224. Source texts: *Fayuan zhulin* 18.417b (section "honoring the Dharma" [*jingfa* 敬法]); *Taiping guangji* 113.3; Lu, *Gu xiaoshuo gouchen*, 389; Wang Guoliang, *Mingxiang ji yanjiu*, 21; Wakatsuki, Hasegawa, and Inagaki, *Hōon jurin no sōgō teki kenkyū*, 123–126. Additional texts: *Gaoseng zhuan* 10.389b; *Mingbao ji*, as quoted in *Sanbao ganying yaolue lu* 2.845b; *Beishan lu* 7. Discussed: Campany, "Notes on Sutra Texts," 34–35.

225. It seems to be this same figure who is mentioned in passing at *Jin shu* 8.200; his official biography is attached to that of his father in *Jin shu* 69.1853–54.

226. The rebel Sun Jun is mentioned in *Gaoseng zhuan* (1.326a26) as having burned down a monstery built by the translator Kang Senghui 康僧會. On the quasi-oral-style wording of this sentence, see Zhou Junxun, *Wei Jin nanbeichao zhiguai xiaoshuo cihui*, 336.

227. Here and throughout, our text (like many others in this era) simply terms this famous sutra "the *Dapin* 大品," that is, the sutra in larger chapters or sections.

228. The content of this paragraph is paralleled by a passage in *Gaoseng zhuan* 10.389b; probably either the latter was based on our text or both were based on a common source.

229. He is mentioned in *Jin shu* 69.1837 and elsewhere in the histories.

the Humu 胡母 clan. They owned a copy of the *Larger Perfection of Wisdom* written on pure silk. Although the strip of silk was only five *cun*[230] wide, the entire sutra fit on it. The family also owned a relic, which they safeguarded in a silver vase. Both sutra and relic were kept stored in a deep chest. During the disorder of the Yongjia period, when the Humu clan was about to leave hastily to flee south to avoid the advancing enemy troops, the sutra and the relic both emerged of themselves from the chest. The family thus carried them on their persons when they fled and crossed the river to the southeast. They also once had an outbreak of fire. There was no time to retrieve the sutra. But although the entire household was consumed in flames, they later found the sutra completely intact beneath the ashes. [Sima] Daozi 道子, Prince of Kuaiji,[231] once approached Song's great-grandson Yun 雲 asking to make offerings to the sutra. Later it was housed for a short time in Xinzhu monastery 新渚寺. Liu Jingshu 劉敬叔 once remarked, "I once saw this sutra copy for myself. Its characters were each no bigger than a sesame seed. [The calligraphy] was skillfully done and very clear."[232] Xinzhu monastery is the one today known as Tian'an monastery 天安寺.[233] This sutra copy must have been written by the path-attaining monk Shi Huize 釋慧則. Some say that it was once recited at Jianjing monastery 簡靖寺[234] by the abbess there.

Comments

Mahāyāna sutras typically give specific instructions on how they are to be treated as cultic objects—handled with care as to ritual purity, presented with offerings and incense, kept in elevated places of honor in households and temples.[235] This story is an excellent example of how such sutras' prescriptions for their own veneration were taken up and put into practice in

---

230. A *cun* 寸 was equivalent to around 2.3 centimeters.

231. Remembered largely for drunkenness and misrule, Sima Daozi was the son of Jin emperor Jianwen and was killed by Huan Xuan in 402 at the age of thirty-nine. See Holcombe, *In the Shadow of the Han*, 32. In *Gaoseng zhuan* (12.406c) he is credited with having sponsored the construction of a certain Zhicheng monastery 治城寺 for the monk Shi Faxiang 釋法相. Cao Daoheng ("Lun Wang Yan," 28) has argued that this story's representation of Sima Daozi's meeting with Zhou Song's *great-grandson* is anachronistic.

232. Liu Jingshu, who flourished in the early fifth century and may have lived past the middle of it, was himself the compiler of a large collection of anomaly accounts, titled *Yiyuan* 異苑, or *Garden of Marvels*, a text that contains a few tales overlapping in content with ones in our text. For more, see Li Jianguo, *Tang qian zhiguai xiaoshuo shi*, 372–382; Liu Yuanru, *Shenti, xingbie, jieji*, 133–185; and Campany, *Strange Writing*, 78–79. He is also mentioned in item 56 below, again as an eyewitness to phenomena featured in a *Mingxiang ji* tale.

233. This monastery is mentioned in *Gaoseng zhuan* 7.372c (in the hagiography of Daowen), in *Xu gaoseng zhuan* 5.465c, twice in *Chu sanzang jiji* (2.12c, 9.67c), and in later sources. It also figures importantly in item 109 below.

234. This monastery is mentioned in *Gaoseng zhuan* 10.389b and in *Fayuan zhulin* 95.988a–b (but the latter passage is simply a quotation of the former).

235. The classic essay on this topic is now reprinted, with updated addenda, in Schopen, *Figments and Fragments of Mahāyāna Buddhism*, 25–62.

China.[236] Two particular, unusual, skillfully executed copies of a single especially prestigious sutra were important enough to people to have this story preserved about them. Explicit mention is made of the making of offerings to them; careful attention is paid to recording the names of individuals who copied them and their spiritual attainments. Families treasure them. Their miraculous feats are narrated—feats that demonstrate that these sutra copies are seen as agents, not inert objects.

Note that the family is mentioned as treasuring a relic as well as a sutra, storing them side by side in a chest, the relic also contained in a reliquary vase. This is one of the relatively few glimpses in our text of devotion to relics of the Buddha and of monastic achievers.

22[237]

Shi Shiguang 史世光, who lived during the Jin period, was a native of Xiangyang. In the eighth year of the Xianhe period [333] he died in Wuchang. On the seventh day,[238] the monk Zhi Fashan 支法山[239] was reciting the *Smaller Perfection of Wisdom Sutra*[240] when he grew tired and dozed off. He seemed to hear a human voice coming from atop the altar.[241] The Shi family had a maidservant named Zhang Xin 張信 who saw Shiguang on the altar wearing clothes and a cap just as he did in life. He told Xin: "I was supposed to fall into the purgatories, but because the Reverend Zhi recited the sutra for me, Tanhu 曇護 and Tanjian 曇堅 welcomed me to ascend to the paradise of the seventh Brahma heaven."[242] Tanhu and Tanjian were the deceased *śrāmaṇera*[243] of Fashan.

Later, when Fashan returned [to the Shi household] to recite the *Larger Perfection of Wisdom Sutra* for him, [Shiguang] returned to the altar. While

---

236. For more on this theme, see Campany, "Notes on Sutra Texts."

237. Source texts: *Fayuan zhulin* 5.303c–304a (section "the six paths [of rebirth]" [*liudao* 六道]); *Taiping guangji* 112.1; Lu, *Gu xiaoshuo gouchen*, 390; Wang Guoliang, *Mingxiang ji yanjiu*, 22; Wakatsuki, Hasegawa, and Inagaki, *Hōon jurin no sōgō teki kenkyū*, 39–42. Additional text: *Liudao ji* 1.113b. Discussed: Mai, "Visualization Apocrypha," 118–119.

238. Buddhist funeral observances, a subcategory of abstinence ceremonies sometimes termed *yingzhai* 營齋 (literally "protective *zhai*"; the scope of the medieval usage may have ranged more broadly—as does the modern scholarly category of *yingjian zhai* 營建齋—to include any *zhai* performed for protection, as for example on the occasion of the construction of a new home or temple or a wedding; see Wang Sanqing, *Cong Dunhuang*, 127–214), were often performed at seven-day intervals over a period of forty-nine days. See Teiser, *The Scripture on the Ten Kings*, 24–25, and item 68 (the story of Huichi) below.

239. He is mentioned again in item 59 below.

240. Here, as often in our text, referred to simply as the *Xiaopin* 小品, "the sutra in smaller chapters."

241. "Altar" here translates *lingzuo* 靈座, literally "seat for spirits." Elsewhere in the text such small domestic structures are simply termed *zuo*, or "seat."

242. Translating *shang di qi fantian kuaile chu* 上第七梵天快樂處; this is another of the multiple levels of heaven in the realm of desire (on which see the note to item 8 above).

243. Meaning novice disciples who have just taken monastic vows; the Chinese term *shami* 沙彌 is a partial transliteration.

he had been alive he had donated[244] two banners. Now they were in the temple, so Shiguang called out, "Zhang Xin, get the banners and send them to me!" Xin replied, "I will." At once she died. Xin took the banners, and they both flew northwest till they surmounted a blue mountain, its top the color of lapis lazuli.[245] On reaching the summit they could see in the distance the gates to the heavens. Shiguang took the banners and then escorted her toward the way back. He gave her a bit of blue incense resembling a croton bean and said, "Present this to Reverend Zhi." Before starting back she watched from afar as Shiguang passed through the gates to the heavens. Then she set out on the path back, and suddenly she revived. She no longer saw the incense in her hand, and the banners were still hanging in the temple. When Shiguang and Xin had been leaving the house, his five-year-old son had seen them, pointed to them, and said to his grandmother, "Father is flying up to the heavens. Do you see, Grandma?"

Later, Shiguan would sometimes return to his family home with a dozen or more celestial persons, lingering for a while and then going back. Each time he came, his hair would be pinned up and covered with a woolen bonnet,[246] and on departure it would be uncovered and loose. Xin [once] asked about it, and he replied, "In the heavens there are hats, but we don't wear them here. Later I will put back on my celestial hat." Together with the other celestial persons, he would perform songs on drums and lutes in a procession into his mother's ancestral hall. Xin asked, "Why do you repeatedly come here?" He said, "I come in order that you will all recognize merit and sin, as well as to amuse Mother." The tone of the lutes was clear and marvelous, of a different caliber than the sounds of this world. Everyone in the family, young and old, was able to hear it. But when they heard the sound it was as if from the next room over; they were not able to hear it directly. Only Xin could hear it clearly.

After a while they would depart. Xin would go alone to send them off. [On one occasion] she saw Shiguang enter through a black doorway and then reemerge after a short while. He told her, "My father-in-law is in there. Every day he is given the bastinado, and the pain of it is hard for him to bear. I just went in to check on him. He is guilty of taking life, so this is the recompense he receives. You should tell my mother-in-law to assemble monks to recite sutras: this will enable his release." His father-in-law was the General of Light Chariots Bao Zhong 報終.[247]

---

244. Here and throughout, "donate" renders *gongyang*供養, the standard Chinese Buddhist term for any act of prestation that generates merit, and perhaps the single most potent type of devotional act recommended to laypersons in our text.

245. Or perhaps "colored glass"; the term *liuli* 琉璃 can refer to either.

246. "Woolen bonnet" translates *qia* 帢, a headcloth or soft head covering without a brim; for a recent discussion of Chinese headgear in this period (though not specifically of the *qia*, unfortunately) with illustrations, see Dien, *Six Dynasties Civilization*, 312–326.

247. *Taiping guangji* drops the father-in-law's name. (Wang Guoliang, as well as Wakatsuki, Hasegawa, and Inagaki, agree in taking the characters *bao zhong* 報終 as the father-in-law's name, though it strikes me as a very odd name, and there is no other record of him.)

Comments

This story imparts a great deal of detailed information on the workings of the Buddhist heavens. The story's placement in Daoshi's *Fayuan zhulin*—in the section on the heavens—indicates that it was received as a source of reliable insight into the celestial realms.

Generally speaking, the unexpected, frequent, or otherwise out-of-season return of the dead to the realm of the living was seen as a problem in early medieval China.[248] This story seems, in part, to constitute a response to this concern about the returning dead. Here the visitation of the dead is recast not as a threatening expression of a spirit's discontent, a menacing demand for more offerings, but as an occasion for religious instruction and even the continued performance by the dead—in the realm of the living—of rites of hospitality for other dead family members. It has a dual purpose, one specifically Buddhist ("in order that you will all recognize merit and sin") and one much older in China ("to amuse Mother"). And the most important lesson imparted here, other than that the dead suffer punishment for their sins in the afterlife, is that their living family members have the opportunity to help them by sponsoring ritual assemblies of monks and laity (with meals for the monks) and the recitation of sutras.

23[249]

Zhang Ying 張應, who lived during the Jin, was a native of Liyang.[250] He habitually served the profane gods with drumming, dancing, and impure sacrifices. In the eighth year of the Xianhe period [333] he moved his family to Wuhu.[251] His wife fell ill. Ying made sacrifices until his resources were almost exhausted. His wife, who was from a Buddhist family, told him, "Beseeching ghosts will be of no benefit against this illness of mine. I ask that you perform a Buddhist service." Ying agreed. He went to an oratory[252] and met Zhu Tankai 竺曇鎧. Tankai told him: "The Buddha is like a healing medicine. If you find medicine but do not take it, it will be of no benefit, even though you look at it." Ying agreed that he would serve the Buddha. Tankai then agreed to come to [Ying's house for] an abstinence assembly the next day. Ying returned home. That night he dreamed of a man more

---

248. See Bokenkamp, *Ancestors and Anxiety*; Nickerson, "The Great Petition for Sepulchral Plaints"; and Nickerson, "Taoism, Death, and Bureaucracy."

249. Source texts: *Fayuan zhulin* 62.756b–c (section "offerings" [*jici* 祭祠]); Lu, *Gu xiaoshuo gouchen*, 391; Wang Guoliang, *Mingxiang ji yanjiu*, 23. Additional texts: *Linggui zhi* 24 (cited in *Bianzheng lun* 7.538a, partial overlap; see Campany, *Strange Writing*, 94); *Fayuan zhulin*, as cited in *Taiping guangji* 113.1; *Liudao ji* 1.113a.

250. A commandery located in what is now He district, Anhui province.

251. An important port on the Jiang river, located in what is now Anhui province.

252. The term here is not *si* 寺 but *jingshe* 精舍; a small monastery is likely meant.

than eight feet tall coming from the south. He came through the door and said, "Your home is disorderly. It is thus impure." He then saw Tankai coming up behind, who said, "He has only just expressed his intent. You cannot blame him yet."

Ying was good with his hands, so when he awoke he lit candles and built a high seat and an altar to the Mother of Demons [Guizimu 鬼子母].[253] The next day, when Tankai arrived, Ying told him of the dream. With this he received the five lay precepts, destroyed and discarded his images of gods, and set out a great [feast as] offerings [to create] fortune.[254] His wife's illness at once improved, and soon she was completely cured.

In the second year of the Xiankang period [336] Ying went to a depot to buy salt. On his way back by boat to Wuhu he came ashore for the night. He dreamed he saw three persons hooking him with steel hooks. Ying said, "I am a disciple of Buddha." They continued pulling him, saying, "You were a sinner[255] for a long time." Frightened, Ying said, "Let me go and I'll give you a *sheng* 升[256] of wine."[257] Only then did they release him. They told him, "Just watch out, lest someone come for you later on." Upon waking, his bowels hurt, and he had severe dysentery; upon reaching home he was suffering greatly. Ying had long since lost touch with Tankai. He was ex-

---

253. The phrase is *zuo gaozuo ji Guizimu zuo* 作高座及鬼子母座. Guizimu, the Mother of Demons, known in Indic sources as Hāritī, is mentioned in many texts translated into Chinese from the third century onward. The basic outlines of her story are as follows: She had been a demon who bore one thousand demon children and stole and ate the offspring of others until she was converted by the Buddha into a protectress of children and of women and a giver of children to women who desire them. Another anomaly-account story involving her may be found in *Yiyuan* 5.15. The classic study of the textual sources is Peri, "Hāritī, la Mère-de-démons"; see also Dhirasekera, "Hāritī and Pāñcika." She was a popular subject of iconography; studies include Bivar, "Hāritī and the Chronology of the Kuṣāṇas"; Lesbre, "La conversion de Hariti au Buddha"; and Murray, "Representations of Hariti."

254. *Dashe fugong* 大設福供.

255. Both *Fayuan zhulin* and *Liudao ji* have *panzou* 叛走, "rebel," "deserter," or "fugitive." I translate the term as "sinner" because, in the context, I assume these otherworld enforcers are referring to Ying's way of life prior to taking the Buddhist precepts. I also wonder whether perhaps the term is being used here as a functional equivalent (or else simply a scribal error) for the terms *fanfu* 凡夫, *fanren* 凡人, or in particular the phonetically and graphically similar *fantu* 凡徒, used in many Buddhist texts to render the Indic *pṛthajana*, indicating benighted persons outside the Buddhist fold—persons who have not taken the triple refuge or the five lay precepts (see Mochizuki, *Bukkyō daijiten*, 120b–c and 4706b–c). The enforcers use the derogatory pronoun *nu* 奴, literally "slave," in addressing Ying; on this usage, relatively recent at the time, see Zhou Junxun, *Wei Jin nanbeichao zhiguai xiaoshuo cihui*, 241.

256. A *sheng* 升 during this period was equivalent to about three hundred milliliters.

257. The "wine" (*jiu* 酒) in question here and throughout was not made from fermented grapes but from fermented grains. "Wine" is not a perfect translation, since Anglophone readers normally assume such a drink is made from grapes, but there seems to be no better single-word alternative. On the rationale for the translation and the nature of the ancient and medieval Chinese beverages denoted by this term, see H. T. Huang, *Fermentations and Food Science*, 149–281 (esp. 149–150 on the translation choices and 272–278 for a comparative discussion of Western and Chinese alcoholic beverages).

tremely ill. He sent for [Tankai], but the monk was not present at the moment. Soon thereafter Ying expired. After a day had passed he revived. He said that several men with hooks had come and taken him away toward the north. They descended an embankment, and he saw at the bottom a boiling cauldron, knives, swords, and other implements of torture. Ying then realized that this was an earth prison.[258] He wanted to call on his master, but he had forgotten Tankai's name, so he merely yelled, "Master, save me!" At the same time he called on the Buddha. In a few minutes, a person came from the west; he stood over eight feet tall and wielded a metal baton. He drove back the men with the hooks, saying, "He's a disciple of Buddha! What are you doing here?" The men with the hooks grew frightened and dispersed. The tall man led Ying away, saying, "Your allotted life span is exhausted; you do not have long to live. You may return home only temporarily. Sing three stanzas of hymns, find out the name of your master, and three days from now, when your allotted life span again expires, you will cross over and be reborn in the heavens." Ying then revived. He was now even more terrified. For the next three days he maintained abstinence,[259] chanted hymns, and sent someone to find out Tankai's name. At midday, when he had taken his last meal, Ying paid obeisance to Buddha and recited a hymn. Then one by one he bade farewell to all his family members. He bathed, put on fresh clothes, and died as if falling asleep.

Comments

The contestational nature of this story could not be clearer. It argues for the replacement of the indigenous cult to local gods with Buddhist practice, which, for many reasons—not least among them the Buddhist prohibition against killing—is presented as incompatible with the sacrifice-based cult of the gods. The afterlife scene, where the punishment for sacrifice is made clear, acts as a confirmation of the teaching of non-killing. Here, as in some other narratives, we see that the monastic master of a layperson was thought capable of acting as his advocate before the purgatorial courts.

The closing emphasizes the events' dispositional impact on the protagonist in a scene depicting his "good death" in accordance with Buddhist norms. Such deathbed scenes in *Mingxiang ji* are reminiscent of narratives of the deaths of devotees of the Pure Lands, many of which were collected in texts specifically reflecting (and designed to promote) devotional practices focused on Amitābha.[260]

---

258. "Earth prison" translates *diyu* 地獄, a term I sometimes render as "purgatories." See item 5 above for further discussion.

259. *Chi zhai* 持齋.

260. See Stevenson, "Death-Bed Testimonials of the Pure Land Faithful," and Mai, "Visualization Apocrypha." Cf. Stone, "By the Power of One's Last Nenbutsu," for Japanese analogues.

24²⁶¹

During the Jin there lived one Dong Ji 董吉, a native of Yuqian.²⁶² His family had observed the Dharma for three generations, and Ji himself was an especially vigorous practitioner. He always observed the abstinence regulations and [at such times] recited the *Śūraṃgama Sutra*. Whenever there was an illness in his hamlet, people would invite Ji to recite the sutra. Of those he succored in this way, many recovered.

He Huang 何晃 of the same hamlet was also a layman who observed the Dharma. During the Xianhe period [327–334] he suddenly contracted an illness due to a mountain miasma and was quarantined. Huang's older brother worriedly sped to request Ji's help. The residences of the Dong and He families were some sixty or seventy *li* apart and separated by a wide stream. It was the fifth month, and there was heavy rain. When Huang's brother had crossed the stream, the floodwaters had not yet arrived. But when, after finishing his noon meal, Ji set out for the He family home, the floodwaters had rushed down from the mountain, and the stream was no longer fordable. Nor could Ji swim. He paced back and forth, sighing, then sat on the bank for a long while, wanting to descend to the water but not daring to try to cross. Ji was a reliable person and was determined to keep his appointment, so he sorrowfully roused his mind and vowed, "In saving others from distress, I take no account of my own safety. I place myself under the protection of the Tathāgata Mahāsattva, that he may watch over me in response to my sincerity." He then took off his clothes and used them to secure the sutra and its book bag to the top of his head, then ventured into the water. The water was neck high, but when Ji went across it came up only to his knees. When he had reached the opposite bank, he was dismayed to find that he had lost the book bag and sutra. On reaching Huang's home he apologized profusely, weeping and blaming himself. Then, glancing upward, he saw the sutra and bag on the high seat. Joyfully he took it down and examined it. The book bag was moist as if it had been dropped in water, but when he opened it and looked at the sutra inside, it was dry and intact. At this, everyone in the hamlet began to observe the Dharma.

To the northwest of Ji's home there was a tall, steep mountain. It harbored many demons that often attacked nearby residents. Ji planned to use the power of the sutras and precepts²⁶³ to subdue them. To this end he cleared timber from a perimeter four or five *mou* around the mountain

---

261. Source texts: *Fayuan zhulin* 18.417b–c (section "honoring the Dharma" [*jingfa* 敬法]); *Taiping guangji* 112.2; Lu, *Gu xiaoshuo gouchen*, 392; Wang Guoliang, *Mingxiang ji yanjiu*, 24. Previously partially translated in Campany, "Notes on Sutra Texts," 48–49.

262. Located in what is today still known as Yuqian district, Zhejiang province.

263. Translating *jing jie zhi li* 經戒之力. (The same phrase appears in both *Fayuan zhulin* and *Taiping guangji*.)

and built a small hut, inside of which he set up a high seat[264] and recited the *Śūraṃgama Sutra*. After a hundred-odd days, it grew very still; no sounds were heard on the mountain, and demonic attacks on the people ceased. Afterward several persons arrived at Ji's hut and talked with him for a long time. Ji thought to himself: judging from these guests' speech, they are not from Yuqian; furthermore, the mountain is extremely isolated and out of the way. Why have they come here? Suspecting they were demons, he said to them, "Might you gentlemen be the demons of this area?" They replied, "Yes. Hearing of your pure and virtuous conduct, we came to see you. Furthermore we would like to ask you one favor, which we think you will grant us. For generations we have held this mountain; it has been left under our control by travelers and residents alike. Since you have arrived here, we have been disturbed and uneasy. We wish now to establish a new boundary line. We will mark the line by killing trees." Ji said, "It is my hope that this quietude can be preserved. I intend no disturbance by reciting the sutra. I would be delighted to accept your offer and look forward to receiving fortune and assistance from you." The demons said, "And we will rely on you, sir, not to attack us any further." After they had said this, they departed. By the next day, the trees around the perimeter that Ji had cleared all had withered and died. They looked as if they had been burned.[265]

Ji died at age eighty-seven.

Comments

It is not entirely clear why the *Śūraṃgama Sutra* (*Shoulengyan jing* 首楞嚴經), of which several early translators had produced versions (most of which are no longer extant),[266] was so especially valued in early medieval China, but valued it certainly was. Its key teaching might be described as a blending together of a Mahāyānist doctrine of emptiness with the affirmation of the virtually limitless saving, form-shifting powers of bodhisattvas, and it is probably this latter emphasis—shared by some other sutras frequently mentioned in our text, most especially the *Lotus* (though the latter has very little to say on emptiness)—along with its promise that its recitation has the power to suppress demons, that accounts for its popularity in these early centuries in China. This sutra is mentioned again in items 36, 45, and 81 below.[267]

---

264. Here the phrase "high seat" (*gaozuo* 高座) probably designates an altar or elevated table or platform on which the sutra is placed while being recited, not a seat on which Ji himself sits during recitation.

265. The *Taiping guangji* text breaks off here.

266. See Nattier, *Earliest Chinese Buddhist Translations*, 75, 88, 116, 123. This early-translated sutra is not to be confused with a later, indigenous Chinese composition by the same title, on which see Benn, "Pseudo-*Śūraṃgama Sūtra*."

267. In Kumārajīva's translation (*Shoulengyan sanmei jing*, 2.641a10–13), for example, the scripture explicitly promotes its demon-quelling powers among its many other benefits. Ji Zhichang, "Dong Jin jushi Xie Fu kao," 76–78, points out the importance of this sutra in early medieval Buddhist miracle tales in China.

We see here another tale of miracles attributed to an individual's copy of a powerful sutra. Two uses of sutra recitation are suggested: healing and protection from demonic attack.

Note that the demons retain a certain domain of their own; they are domesticated but not annihilated. They are not, in any one-dimensional sense, "evil." This is rather typical of the Buddhist tradition, which, likewise in the cases of *nāgas*, *yakṣas*, and other such beings, has often retained a place for them: they have their proper jobs to do.[268] The problem is not their existence per se but the fact that they sometimes end up out of place.

25^{269}

During the Jin there lived one Zhou Dang 周璫, a native of Shan district in Kuaiji.[270] His family had observed the Dharma for generations. When Dang was sixteen, he began observing a vegetarian diet, adhering to the abstinence regulations, chanting the *[Sutra on] Achieving the [Bright Light Concentration] (Chengju guangming dingyi jing* 成具光明定意經), and sometimes reciting [other] sutras.[271] [That year] when the long abstinence period of the first month had ended, he went to invite monks to an eightfold abstinence assembly that he intended to host. When he reached Xiangshi monastery 鄉市寺, he invited his master,[272] Zhu Sengmi 竺僧密, along with Zhi Fajie 支法階 and Zhu Fomi 竺佛密, asking them to bring with them the *Smaller Perfection of Wisdom [Sutra]* so that it could be chanted on the day of abstinence. On the day in question, when the three monks arrived for the abstinence ceremony, they realized they had forgotten to bring the *Smaller Perfection of Wisdom Sutra*; they did not discover this until the midday meal

268. See Bloss, "Ancient Indian Folk Religion"; Bloss, "The Buddha and the Nāga"; and Sutherland, *The Disguises of the Demon.*

269. Source texts: *Fayuan zhulin* 18.417c–418a (section "honoring the Dharma" [*jingfa* 敬法]) (Zhonghua dazang jing ed. 71.468c–469a); *Taiping guangji* 110.2; Lu, *Gu xiaoshuo gouchen*, 393; Wang Guoliang, *Mingxiang ji yanjiu*, 25; Wakatsuki, Hasegawa, and Inagaki, *Hōon jurin no sōgō teki kenkyū*, 126–129.

270. Located in what is now Sheng district, Zhejiang province.

271. *Chengju guangming jing* (preserved in the canon as Taishō 630, *Chengju guangming dingyi jing* 成具光明定意經, or *Sutra on Achieving the Bright Light Samādhi*, attributed to Zhi Yao 支曜) was definitely early enough to be the one mentioned here, but it might be apocryphal, "an indigenous composition combining bits and pieces of Buddhist lore with ideas and terminology from other sources" (Nattier, *Earliest Chinese Buddhist Translations*, 100). On the question of the authenticity and overall nature of this sutra, which to my knowledge has yet to be studied in depth by modern scholars, see ibid., 94–102; Nattier, "Zhu Fonian's *Shizhu duanjie jing*," 247; Pu Chengzhong, "Notes on the *Chengju guangming jing*" (responded to by Nattier in the article just cited); and Zürcher, "Earliest Chinese Buddhist Texts," 284, 290. On the general phenomenon of indigenously composed or "apocryphal" Buddhist sutras, see Makita, *Gikyō kenkyū*; Kuo, "Sur les apocryphes bouddhiques chinois"; and Tokuno, "The Evaluation of Indigenous Scriptures."

272. Or possibly this phrase *qi shi* 其師 indicates the head monk of the just-mentioned monastery.

was finished and it was time to begin the recitation. They were very regretful. Dang's home was in Banyi hamlet, thirty *li* from the monastery, and there was no one to send to get the sutra. Right up to the moment for people to light incense, the family regretted not having the sutra available, and Fomi paced about nervously.[273] After a short while, someone was heard knocking on the door, saying they were bringing the *Smaller Perfection of Wisdom Sutra.* Astonished, Dang was secretly overjoyed. On opening the door, he saw a youth in a single-layer gown[274] and a cap. He had never seen the youth before, nor was it an hour when people would normally be out and about. Dang suspected it must be a divine anomaly, so he prostrated himself, accepted the sutra, and invited the youth to be seated. The youth declined but said he would return that night to hear the sutra. When the guest monks went out to see him, he suddenly vanished. A fragrance filled the house.

When they examined the sutra, it turned out to be Fomi's copy. The monks and laypersons in attendance were stunned and delighted. The sutra had been locked securely inside a chest in a storeroom. When Fomi returned later and examined the lock, it was undisturbed.

After this, all of the dozen or so families in the hamlet became Buddhist devotees, and their respect and affection for Dang deepened. Later Dang left the household, taking the Dharma name Tanyi 曇嶷.[275] He recited a great many sutras totalling two hundred thousand words. And so on.[276]

26[277]

During the Jin there lived one Sun Zhi 孫稚, styled Fahui 法暉, who was a native of Banyang district in the territory of Qi.[278] His father, Sun Zuo 祚, was a superior grand master of the palace under the Jin. Zhi took up Buddhism when he was still young. In the eighth month of the first year of the

---

273. As will be seen below, the forgotten sutra copy belonged to Fomi.

274. Here and throughout, "single-layer gown" translates *danyi* 單衣. The question, as so often when reading old texts, is why this type of garment is so frequently mentioned. The answer seems to be that it was synonymous, for contemporary readers, with court attire (see *Hanyu dacidian*, 3.420). Whenever we see an otherworld figure described as wearing a *danyi*, we, it seems, are to understand that the personage in question is a member of the unseen bureaucracy (and not, for example, a demon or sprite).

275. According to *Meisōden shō* 名僧傳抄, a selective summary of the now-lost *Mingseng zhuan* 名僧傳 (see De Rauw, "Baochang," 203 n1), this monk was once the subject of a biography in that text. To my knowledge, no further information on him survives.

276. Ellipsis in the original, although several editions of the Taishō canon (but not the Zhonghua canon), as well as the *Taiping guangji* version, omit the final *yun* 云.

277. Source texts: *Fayuan zhulin* 91.958a (section "breaking the abstinence [regulations]" [*po zhai* 破齋]); Lu, *Gu xiaoshuo gouchen*, 394; Wang Guoliang, *Mingxiang ji yanjiu*, 26. Additional texts: *Xuanyan ji* 20, as cited in *Bianzheng lun* 7.537c and collected in Lu, *Gu xiaoshuo gouchen*, 368; *Fayuan zhulin*, as cited in *Taiping guangji* 320.4; *Liudao ji* 88.112b.

278. Today's Zichuan district, Shandong province.

Xiankang period [September 335], when he was eighteen, he died of illness.

Later his father, Zuo, moved to Wuchang. On the eighth day of the fourth month[279] of the third year [of the Xiankang period, 337], the monk Yu Fajie 于法階 was carrying an image of the Venerable One in procession[280] and passed by the family's doorway. All the family members went out to watch, and when they did so they saw Zhi there among the crowd moving along in the procession. When he saw his parents, he knelt before them and asked after their health; then they returned home together. Zuo had been ill, and Zhi told him, "There is no cause for this other than that you didn't take sufficient care of yourself. You will feel better in the fifth month." When he had finished speaking he took his leave and departed.

On the fifteenth day of the seventh month[281] of the same year he returned, again kneeling and asking after their welfare just as he had done when alive. He said that his maternal grandfather was serving as magistrate of Taishan[282] and that, on seeing Zhi, had mentioned Zhi's mother's byname[283] in asking, "You are her son! You should not have come yet! What are you doing here?" Zhi had answered, "My paternal uncle had me sent here to be punished as a replacement[284] for him." The magistrate gave an order for this to be looked into, and he intended to have [the uncle] punished; Zhi was released and pardoned. Zhi's older brother Rong 容, byname Siyuan 思淵, was by his side at the time. Zhi told him, "Even though [when you die] you leave behind your former body, you are in a happy, pleasant place, and all you must do is read books, nothing else. I hope you will have no difficulties later. [To this end,] I would urge you to practice [Buddhism] with vigor, cultivating goodness in all your thoughts, and

---

279. The day on which the Buddha's birthday was most often celebrated in China. The procession mentioned here formed part of the festivities on this day in the ritual calendar.

280. *Xing zun xiang* 行尊像; "the Venerable One" is a common epithet of the Buddha. The bathing and carrying in procession of Buddha images were important devotional activities, particularly as part of the festival activities surrounding the Buddha's birthday (whether celebrated on the eighth day of the fourth month or the eighth day of the second month). See *Luoyang qielan ji* 1010b8–15, translated in Wang Yi-t'ung, *A Record of Buddhist Monasteries*, 126–127; Hureau, "Buddhist Rituals," 1235–1237; Boucher, "Sutra on Bathing the Buddha"; and Ch'en, *The Chinese Transformation of Buddhism*, 263–265. On the complexities of the Buddhist festival year and the variance in the dates of celebration of the Buddha's birth, see Chapman, "Carnival Canons," 255–285.

281. This, in turn, was the date of the Buddhist festival for the dead, on which see Teiser, *The Ghost Festival.*

282. The otherworld official known as Taishan fujun 太山府君 (a title, not a person's name—the office was filled by successive appointees, here including an ancestor of the story's protagonist!) had long been indigenously conceived of as overseeing the summoning and registration of the newly dead. See Campany, "Return-from-Death Narratives," 106–109 and passim.

283. Elsewhere I translate this term *zi* 字 as "style(d)," but in this context that would lead to confusion.

284. "Replacement" translates *dai* 代. See comments.

good fortune will naturally follow. When my two years of study are completed, I am to be born next into a royal family. I had five hundred classmates who are still now in the halls of the fortunate;[285] when their study is completed they will all be reborn upward into the sixth heaven. Originally I was to be reborn up there as well, but due to my attempt to save and gain release for an ancestor, a karmic fetter was created, thanks to which I alone will merely be born in a royal household."

Come the seventh day of the seventh month[286] of the fifth year [339] Zhi returned again. He said that in the city of Zhu 邾[287] there would be an outbreak of banditry. He mentioned many particulars, and they all turned out just as he had said they would. His family kept these things quiet and did not spread them about. He also said, "Many of our ancestors are being punished for their sins.[288] You should create fortune for them.[289] I am now receiving embodiment as a human,[290] so you need not make any more ef-

---

285. "Halls of the fortunate" translates *futang* 福堂, which, like the term *fushe* 福舍 seen in item 5 above (as well as the term *fudi* 福地 that occurs in item 67 below), in such contexts denotes an afterlife domain reserved for those who have cultivated merit while alive—or those who have had merit transferred to them for their benefit. For example, the *Consecration Sutra* (*Guanding jing* 11.530c25) tells the story of a man who died, returned to life a week later, and told his family of having been taken by the "spirits of goodness," or *shanshen* 善神, to be shown the halls of the fortunate in the heavens, as well as the purgatories below the earth. *Hongming ji* 1.3b–c quotes *Mouzi lihuo lun*: "Though they die, the spirits of those who have attained the Path return to the halls of the fortunate [*futang*], while, when doers of evil die, their spirits meet with misery" (cf. the translation and discussion in Keenan, *How Master Mou Removes Our Doubts*, 94–96 [but 188 n148 is, I believe, in error: *futang* refers here neither to the Pure Lands nor to the fortunate paths of rebirth]). *Fu* is used as a verb, with its object being the person to whom fortune is intended to be conveyed by one's meritorious acts, in a passage quoted from *Mohe jiaye dubinmu jing* (attributed in the Taishō to Guṇabhadra, active in Jiankang 443–468, but listed in Sengyou's catalog [*Chu sanzang jiji* 4.23b6] among "texts whose translators' names are lost") in *Fayuan zhulin* (716b14) and *Zhujing yaoji* (6.57a) concerning Mulian's concern for his mother's suffering in the afterlife: "I should bestow fortune on her" (*wu dang fu zhi* 吾當福之), he thinks. *Chu sanzang jiji* 9.68c quotes a preface to the *Piyu jing* 譬喻經 (trans. Yijing [635–713]) in which the hope is expressed that, by means of the sutra, beings on earth "might forever ascend to the halls of the fortunate." *Jinglü yixiang* 17.94a quotes *Chu lieshi shejia xuedao jing* 出獵師捨家學道經 thus regarding the benefits of the Buddha's preaching to a group of hunters: "that they might forever leave the condition of birth-and-death and dwell everlastingly in the halls of the fortunate" (*yong li shengsi chang chu futang* 永離生死常處福堂). This same phrase appears in a similar context (a discourse to hunters) in *Chu yao jing* 5.636a.
    286. In item 102 below, a dead person also tells his living family that he will return to visit them on 7/7. See the comments to that item for reasons why this is so.
    287. In what is today Huanggang district, Hubei province.
    288. It is possible that Zhi is talking here not about the family ancestors in general but about his paternal uncle, who was mentioned above. It depends on what one takes the scope of the word *duo* 多 to be here: "many ancestors" or "many sins."
    289. "Create fortune" translates *zuo fu* 作福.
    290. *Wo jin shou shen renzhong* 我今受身人中, meaning that he is due to be reborn as a human being. The passage is a bit confusing, in that it seems to suggest he is *now* a human being, yet he is currently a ghost (understood in most Buddhist texts as a separate path of rebirth), not a living person.

forts on my behalf; just focus on saving the ancestors. I desire that my father and elder brother apply themselves diligently to earning merit so as to produce fortune. During meals[291] they should see to it that everything is fresh and clean.[292] If every last detail is in accord with Dharma, they will receive the highest merit; if less so, less merit; and if they cannot do at least this much then they are simply wasting their expenditure for no reason. They should see to it that all are [served] equally, that in their minds there is no sense of other versus self. The merit will then be greatest."

Zuo at the time had a maidservant. Before Zhi had returned this time, the maidservant had suddenly grown ill and seemed on the verge of dying, her entire body afflicted. Zhi said, "This maidservant had been about to try to escape, so I simply gave her a whipping to prevent her from leaving." When they inquired of the maidservant she said, "Earlier I did in fact intend to flee and had agreed on a date for it with others. But when the day arrived I stayed here." And so on.[293]

Comments

This story is yet another case of a periodically returning deceased member of a Buddhist family. Note the points at which he appears—nodes in the Buddhist as well as the indigenous festival calendar, times (like the times when the abstinence ceremony was performed) when the boundaries between the seen and unseen worlds were especially porous. The mention of the magistrate of Taishan is another example of the blending of indigenous and Buddhist facets. But with the line "My paternal uncle had me sent here to be punished as a replacement [*dai* 代] for him," and the shape the ensuing story takes, we again see this text contesting the indigenous culture of plaints and replacements in the afterlife.[294] In the penultimate paragraph we see norms for ritual practice being authenticated by providing them with a source in the unseen world—a dynamic also at work in other stories of this and similar genres.[295] Such details function to instruct the living on proper practice and to provide warrants from the unseen realm for such practice.

---

291. The implication—as made clear by the different wording of the version of the story given in *Liudao ji* (88.112b)—is that these are meals *served to monks and nuns* for the creation of merit.

292. This passage as given in *Liudao ji* is punctuated differently, so as to read: "I desire that my father and elder brother apply themselves diligently to earning merit, producing fortune, and feeding monks. During meals they should see to it that everything is fresh and clean." "Earning merit" here translates *wei gongde* 為功德, and "producing fortune" translates *zuo fu* 作福.

293. Ellipsis (*yun yun* 云云) in the original.

294. Compare items 11 and 119 in this respect, and see the further comments in part 1.

295. For examples from the old, indigenous "common religion," Buddhism, and Daoism, involving norms for praxis as well as iconography, see Harper, "Resurrection in Warring States Popular Religion"; Teiser, "Having Once Died"; Teiser, *Reinventing the Wheel*, 125 n12; and Verellen, "Evidential Miracles in Support of Taoism," 256–257.

The penultimate paragraph stresses not only the importance of strict adherence to ritual regulations but also—a theme not often sounded in our text—the importance of purity of intention. In the latter respect it may be compared to item 65.

27[296]

Li Heng 李恆,[297] styled Yuanwen 元文, who lived during the Jin, was a native of the territory of Qiao 譙.[298] When he was young, a monk called on him and said, "Your karmic reward is about to arrive, but the opposite will follow after. If you can maintain frugality and cultivate [yourself on] the Path rather than serving in office, your merit will increase, and its opposite will decrease. I urge you to do this!" But Heng was by nature ambitious, and moreover came from a low-status family.[299] He only asked about how he could obtain office and showed not a bit of interest in understanding how to cultivate himself on the Path. [The monk] gave him a copy of a sutra, but Heng was unwilling to accept it. He merely persisted in asking how to attain honor, rank, and wealth. The monk said, "If you are to wear the insignia of office, then you will at most serve over three commanderies. If you can stop at serving over only one, it would be better." Heng replied, "As long as I am to come into wealth and status, why should I worry about later suffering?"

The monk spent the night at Heng's home. Heng got up during the night and saw that the monk's body filled up the entire bed. He went in to summon his family, and everyone came to peek at the monk. He then transformed into a huge bird and perched on a rafter above. At dawn he returned to his earlier form and departed. Heng saw him out the door, and then the monk suddenly was no more to be seen. Heng thus knew the monk was a divine personage.

Because of this Heng began to serve Buddha, but even so he could not

---

296. Source texts: *Fayuan zhulin* 56.712c (section "riches and honor" [*fugui* 富貴]); Lu, *Gu xiaoshuo gouchen*, 395; Wang Guoliang, *Mingxiang ji yanjiu*, 27. Additional texts: *Fayuan zhulin*, as cited in *Taiping guangji* 89.4.

297. Some sources, including *Fayuan zhulin*, write his given name as Chang 常.

298. Today's city of Haozhou in Anhui province.

299. "Low-status family" translates *hanmen* 寒門, a term denoting families not poor or of commoner status but rather of undistinguished lineage, in contrast to elite families with nobler pedigrees. For discussions of the term in this period, see Jansen, *Höfische Öffentlichkeit im frühmittelalterlichen China*, 49–53; Pearce, Spiro, and Ebrey, introduction to *Culture and Power*, 25–26, 29–31; Grafflin, "Reinventing China," 162; Dien, "Civil Service Examinations," 102–103; and Chittick, *Patronage and Community in Medieval China*, 3. For treatments of social class and particularly the patron-client relationship, a defining type of social relationship during this and preceding periods, see Ebrey, "Later Han Upper Class"; Ebrey, "Patron-Client Relations"; Tang Changru, "Clients and Bound Retainers"; Mather, "Intermarriage as a Gauge of Family Status"; and now especially Chittick, *Patronage and Community in Medieval China*.

exert himself with full vigor. Later he served as governor at Xiyang, Jingxia, and Lujiang, and as a general. During the Taixing period [318–321] he was involved in planning for the Qian Feng 錢鳳 rebellion,[300] and so was executed.

Comments

This story is an excellent example of the theme of the appearance of mysterious spirit-monks and their relationships with lay hosts.

28[301]

During the Jin there lived one Dou Chuan 竇傳,[302] a native of Henei.[303] During the Yonghe period [345–356], Gao Chang 高昌, regional inspector of Bingzhou, and Lü Hu 呂護, regional inspector of Jizhou, each had command of a private military force[304] and did not get along with each other. Chuan worked under Chang's supervision and served as chief of staff. Hu sent cavalry to attack, and Chuan was taken prisoner. Along with six or seven others he was jailed and placed under heavy fetters and locks. A date was set for their execution. The monk Zhi Daoshan 支道山 was in Hu's encampment at the time. He and Chuan had earlier been acquainted. Hearing of Chuan's dire predicament, Daoshan went to see him in jail. They conversed through the bars of the door. Chuan told him, "In this perilous situation, I have only hours to live. Is there any way in which I might be saved?" Daoshan answered, "If you can apply your whole mind to taking refuge and making a request, there will certainly a response to this stimulus."[305]

Now Chuan had some prior awareness of Guanshiyin. So, at Daoshan's suggestion, he focused his mind and concentrated his thought. Day and

---

300. Qian Feng was in the service of Wang Dun, a major figure in the late Western and early Eastern Jin societies. On these events, see Graff, *Medieval Chinese Warfare*, 80–82; Holcombe, *In the Shadow of the Han*, 29–30; Lewis, *China Between Empires*, 63–64; Mather, *Shih-shuo Hsin-yü*, 596; and *Jin shu* 98.2553–2568.

301. Source texts: *Fayuan zhulin* 17.410b–c (section "honoring Buddhas" [*jing Fo* 敬佛]); *Taiping guangji* 110.1; Lu, *Gu xiaoshuo gouchen*, 395; Wang Guoliang, *Mingxiang ji yanjiu*, 28; Wakatsuki, Hasegawa, and Inagaki, *Hōon jurin no sōgō teki kenkyū*, 111–114. Additional texts: *Guangshiyin yingyanji* 4 (Makita, *Rikuchō kōitsu Kanzeon ōkenki no kenkyū*, 16–17, translated in Campany, "The Earliest Tales of the Bodhisattva Guanshiyin," 94–95); *Guanshiyin chiyan ji* 78.94a, citing *Zhenzhuan shiyi* 真傳拾遺.

302. Instead of Chuan 傳 as Dou's *ming*, some versions, including *Taiping guangji*, have Fu 傅—a common variation in texts from this period. In this case there is no knowing which version of the name is correct.

303. Henei was a commandery in what is now Qin district, Henan province.

304. For literati to have private military forces at their disposal was not uncommon at the time; see Tian, *Beacon Fire and Shooting Star*, 68–75.

305. "There will certainly be a response to this stimulus" translates *bi you ganying* 必有感應. This is a succinct statement of the notion of stimulus-and-response that is implicit throughout the text.

night for three days he gave himself over [to the bodhisattva's protection] with utmost sincerity. Then, looking at his fetters, he noticed they seemed looser than before. He tried putting pressure on them, and they fell away from his body. He then concentrated his mind again and said, "I have now received divine fortune in having my fetters and locks opened. But I still have several companions here, and I am of no mind to flee without them. Since Guanshiyin's divine power to save works everywhere, all of us should be freed." The moment he finished speaking, the fetters fell off of all the others as if someone had cut through them. So they opened the door and ran out before anyone noticed them. They scaled the city wall and fled. At the time it was almost dawn; they traveled four or five *li*, but then, once the sky lightened, they dared not proceed farther. They hid in a grove of trees. Soon, once their escape had been discovered, horsemen fanned out in all directions to find and recapture them. They set fire to underbrush and climbed trees, searching everywhere. It was only the small area surrounding Chuan's hiding place that the search party failed to cover. So Chuan and the others managed to escape.

Everyone in his village was moved to deeper reverence and faith by this miracle: all became faithful upholders of the Buddha's Dharma. As for Daoshan, he later crossed the Jiang river and told of this incident in detail to the layman Xie Fu 謝敷.[306]

Comments

This story's closing passage is an example of the networks of social relationship and narrative exchange that are both represented in, and gave rise to, our text. After pointing out the impact of the narrated events on "everyone" in the village in question, the text goes on to say that an eyewitness to the reported events, the monk Daoshan, personally related the tale to another named individual, Xie Fu. Xie Fu (fl. late fourth to early fifth century) was an associate of the famous monk Zhi Dun, a key propagator of Buddhism among well-placed scholar-officials in the southern capital, Jiankang, and Xie himself also compiled one of the earliest collections of pro-Buddhist miracle tales—a dozen or so stories of miraculous interventions by the Bodhisattva Guanshiyin.[307] In item 32 below, it is the same Xie Fu who is recorded as having heard another tale of miraculous response, not in that case from an acquaintance of the protagonist but from the protagonist himself. And it is once again Xie Fu who is the protagonist of yet another tale (item 36 below), this time involving not an intervention by Guanshiyin but the miraculous powers of the *Śūraṃgama Sutra*.

---

306. See comments.

307. That is, the *Guangshiyin yingyan ji*. See Wang Guoliang, *Wei Jin nanbeichao zhiguai xiaoshuo yanjiu*, 302–303; Campany, "The Earliest Tales of the Bodhisattva Guanshiyin"; Campany, "The Real Presence"; and Campany, *Strange Writing*, 68–69. On Xie Fu, see also Ji Zhichang, "Dong Jin jushi Xie Fu kao," and Zürcher, *The Buddhist Conquest of China*, 136–137, 139, 145.

29[308]

During the Jin, Commander-in-Chief Huan Wen 桓溫 [312–373][309] in his later years to some extent observed the Dharma of Buddha and fed monks and nuns. There was a certain nun, her name now lost, who came from a distant place and sought Wen out as her *dānapati*.[310] The nun's sources of support were variable, and Wen held her in the utmost regard, so he installed her in a residence in his home. Each time the nun bathed, she took an unusually long while at it. Wen wondered why, so [one day] he spied on her. He saw her strip off her clothes; wielding a knife, she proceeded to cut open her belly, spill out her guts, sever her head from her body, sever her four limbs, and strip the flesh from them. Wen marveled and was terrified, then withdrew. When the nun left the bath chamber her body was back to normal. Wen asked her about it frankly, and she replied, "If you rise to become ruler, your punishment will resemble this." At the time Wen had just begun plotting to become emperor, and on hearing this he was disappointed. But he took the warning seriously and to the end behaved appropriately as a subject. The nun then said farewell and suddenly vanished.

Comments

This is one of those stories where a prediction is made, and the reader, coming later in time, knows of outcomes that characters in the story cannot know; such stories depend for their impact on readers' assumed knowledge of how things turned out. Therein lies a puzzle in this case, however, since every early medieval reader would have known of Huan Wen's attempted usurpation of power and ultimate defeat. (He was defeated by the Murongs in 369.) Perhaps we may read this account, especially its closing lines, as a southern author's futile attempt to salvage Huan's reputation. On the other hand, it is true that Huan Wen never attempted to declare himself emperor outright: he died before he had a chance to do so. This story could thus be read as an explanation of why he never took the step of launching a new dynasty.

---

308. Source texts: *Fayuan zhulin* 33.545a (section "promoting fortune" [*xing fu* 興福]); Lu, *Gu xiaoshuo gouchen*, 396; Wang Guoliang, *Mingxiang ji yanjiu*, 29; Wakatsuki, Hasegawa, and Inagaki, *Hōon jurin no sōgō teki kenkyū*, 206–207. Additional texts: *Youming lu* 108 (Lu, *Gu xiaoshuo gouchen* 228, based on *Taiping yulan* 395.5b); *Jin shu* 98.2576; *Ji shenzhou sanbao gantong lu* 3.433a; *Jiankang shilu* 9. Note: Some traditional editions of *Soushen houji* include a version of this story as item 2.5, but I concur with Li Jianguo's reasons for rejecting its attribution to that text (see *Xinji Soushen ji, Xinji Soushen houji*, 706–707).

309. On Huan Wen, a major figure of his era (and one who had a deep impact on Buddhist monasticism, first by questioning monks' right not to bow to rulers and then by accepting it after a debate), see Zürcher, *The Buddhist Conquest of China*, 110–112; Graff, *Medieval Chinese Warfare*, 122–126; Mather, *Shih-shuo Hsin-yü*, 536–537; Grafflin, "Reinventing China," 163–168; and Lewis, *China Between Empires*, 64–66.

310. That is, a generous lay donor; the term *tanyue* 檀越 was a transliteration.

The nun's special ability to know the future, as well as her symbolic acting out of it, again parallels a motif found in hagiographies of seekers of
transcendence.[311] The motif of a Buddhist monastic opening the torso to
clean out impurities recurs in other narratives.[312]

<h1 style="text-align:center">30[313]</h1>

During the Jin[314] there lived one Li Qing 李清, a native of Yuqian in Wuxing. He served under Huan Wen 桓溫 [at various times] as commander-
in-chief, adjutant, and protector-general. While working at headquarters
he contracted an illness, then returned home and died. After one night he
revived. He gave the following account. At first he saw message-bearers arrive with a written message and flags;[315] they summoned him with the
words, "The lord[316] wishes to see you." Qing assumed it was Huan Wen who
was summoning him, so he got up, fastened his belt, and departed. Outside he saw a bamboo carriage, which he was ordered to enter. The two
messengers pushed it along swiftly, at the pace of a gallop. They arrived at
a crimson gate. There he saw Ruan Jing 阮敬, who had been dead for over
thirty years. Jing asked Qing, "When did you arrive? Do you know how my
family is doing?" Qing said, "Your family is extraordinarily wicked." Jing
wept and asked, "Do you know how my sons and grandsons are doing?"
Qing replied, "They're doing all right." Jing then asked, "If I now arrange
for your release, can you look after my family?" Qing said, "Yes. If you could
do this, it would be a great favor to me." Jing explained, "The monk Sengda
僧達 is the official in charge here. He has shown me much kindness. I will
plead our case to him."

He returned inside the gate. After a long time he sent someone out to
announce, "The four-story temple opposite was built by this department.
Sengda often enters the temple at sunrise to perform obeisance. You may
go there to seek help." Qing entered the temple and saw a monk, who said
to him, "You were my disciple during your seven previous lifetimes. You
have received fortune for seven lifetimes, but you have become mired in
the pleasures of the world and have thus forgotten and lost your original

---

311. See Campany, *Making Transcendents*, 163–165, and Campany, *To Live as Long as
Heaven and Earth*, 212–215, 228–229, 336.

312. As, for instance, in the hagiography of the wonder-working monk Fotucheng 佛圖
澄; see *Gaoseng zhuan* 9.386c–387a. Compare item 33 below.

313. Source texts: *Fayuan zhulin* 95.988c–989a (section "illness and pain" [*bingku* 病苦]);
Taiping guangji 379.2; Lu, *Gu xiaoshuo gouchen*, 396; Wang Guoliang, *Mingxiang ji yanjiu*, 30.

314. *Fayuan zhulin* lists Song, not Jin, as the relevant dynasty, but based on the story's
content this is clearly erroneous.

315. The envoys arrive bearing *xin* 信 and *fan* 幡 (the wording is the same in *Fayuan
zhulin* and *Taiping guangji*), as they do below in item 77, the story of Li Dan.

316. Here translating *gong* 公.

fund of karma. For having abandoned what is upright and sought what is deviant, you are headed for a harsh punishment. But now you should correct your ways and confess. Your master will emerge [from the gate] tomorrow. You should seek his help."

Qing returned to the carriage, where he passed a bitterly cold night. At dawn the gate opened, and Sengda emerged to walk to the temple. Qing followed after him and knelt in homage. Sengda told him, "You must reform your heart and entrust your life to the Buddha, Dharma, and sangha. By taking this triple refuge you can avoid an untimely death.[317] If you follow [the precepts] diligently, you can also prevent yourself from undergoing suffering." Qing then took refuge and received [the precepts]. Qing then also saw the monk he had met the previous day. The monk prostrated himself and pleaded, "This man was my disciple in previous lives. He has ignored what is right and neglected the Dharma, and he is about to be punished as a consequence. But he has only now taken refuge, so I hope he may be treated with compassion." The reply was, "In previous lives he was someone who [established] fortune,[318] so it should be easy for him to be rescued." They then turned about to face the crimson gate again.

Soon a messenger emerged to say, "Commander-in-Chief Li may depart!" Ruan Jing also came out through the gate at this moment. He gave Qing a green bamboo staff and instructed him to close his eyes and sit astride it. Qing did as he was told. Suddenly he arrived at his home. In the house there was much weeping and wailing. Neighbors and relatives crowded so tightly into the hall that, though he tried to enter, he could not. It then happened that a man who had been sent to buy wood [for the coffin] was returning; family members and guests all followed him in to observe the procedure. There was only Qing's corpse on the floor. Qing entered the room and stood before his corpse. Upon smelling its stench, he thought to himself that he regretted having returned. But guests pressed in on him from behind, and before he knew it he was back in his corpse, and he revived.

He thereupon looked after Ruan Jing's family, dividing his own dwelling so that they could live there. From then on he entrusted his heart to the three treasures[319] and was diligent in his belief in the teachings of the Dharma. He became a most outstanding disciple.

---

317. "Untimely death" translates *hengsi* 橫死. To suffer an untimely death was often (and sometimes still is, in contemporary Chinese communities) to become a vengeful spirit liable to prey upon living persons as substitute victims; see Cohen, *Tales of Vengeful Souls*.

318. Translating *xian shi furen* 先是福人 (the wording is the same in *Fayuan zhulin* and *Taiping guangji*); that previous lives are in question is implied but not stated explicitly.

319. The Buddha, the Dharma (the Buddha's teachings), and the sangha (the fourfold assembly of those who practice his teachings).

Comments

Here we visit the purgatories again. This return-from-death story is unusual in its protagonist's promise to reform the wicked living family of a dead acquaintance encountered in the afterlife. We see here again the figure of the monk pleading on behalf of his lay disciple before the earth-prison courts. The story echoes non-Buddhist return-from-death tales too, however, in details such as the negotiation and the use of a bamboo staff for rapid long-distance or interworld travel.[320]

31[321]

Lü Song 呂竦, styled Maogao 茂高, who lived during the Jin, was a native of Yan province.[322] For a while he lived in Shifeng.[323] The river in the south of this district rushes over cliffs and falls, winding its way through many twists and turns; it is also full of boulders. To negotiate it even in broad daylight inspired great fear. Song told the following story. His father had once been traveling on this river and was still over ten *li* from home when the sun began to set and a severe storm blew in, making it so dark that one could no longer tell east from west. Resigning himself to drowning otherwise, he simply gave over his whole mind to Guanshiyin, at times chanting, at times calling him to mind. In a little while, he saw firelight on the shore, as if someone were carrying a torch. The light illuminated every detail of the river. Eventually he was able to get home, the fire always leading him at a distance of ten or so paces in front of the boat.

Later, Song traveled extensively with Xi Jiabin 郗嘉賓,[324] and it was Chi who passed this story down.

---

320. For two cases of very similar use of bamboo staves for magical travel in *Traditions of Divine Transcendents*, see Campany, *To Live as Long as Heaven and Earth*, 163 (Hu gong sends his disciple Fei Changfang home on a bamboo staff; while traveling, Fei feels as if he is asleep; the same detail is mentioned in *Hou Han shu* 82B.2743–2745) and 191 (Jie Xiang sends a messenger on a bamboo staff to buy goods at a distant market; the messenger is instructed to close his eyes while en route).

321. Source texts: *Fayuan zhulin* 65.785a (section "saving from danger" [*jiuwei* 救厄]); Lu, *Gu xiaoshuo gouchen*, 398; Wang Guoliang, *Mingxiang ji yanjiu*, 31. Additional texts: *Guangshiyin yingyanji* 5 (Makita, *Rikuchō kōitsu Kanzeon ōkenki no kenkyū*, 17); *Fayuan zhulin*, as cited in *Taiping guangji* 110.13.

322. In today's Fan district, Shandong province.

323. A district located in what is now Tiantai district, Zhejiang province.

324. This is Xi Chao 超 (336–377), byname Jingxing 景興, alternate byname Jiabin. An official biography is preserved in *Jin shu* 67.1802–1805; he is also mentioned at 75.1964 and in *Nan shi* 22.604. Xi authored the lay-targeted Buddhist treatise *Essentials in Upholding the Dharma (Fengfa yao* 奉法要), on which see Zürcher, *The Buddhist Conquest of China*, 164–176.

32[325]

Xu Rong 徐榮, who lived during the Jin, was a native of Langye.[326] He once went to Dongyang[327] and on his way back was passing through Dingshan[328] when the boatman, not paying attention, steered the boat into a whirlpool. The boat spun around and was about to be capsized. Rong, with no other options, concentrated on summoning Guanshiyin. In a moment, it was as if several dozen men combined their strength and pulled the boat so that it leapt out of the whirlpool and returned to the steady current. They drifted downstream. It was already late in the day, the sky was darkening, and wind and rain were coming up. They did not know where to head next, but the waves were picking up. Rong kept reciting the *[Guanshiyin] Sutra*[329] without cease. In a short while, they saw a bright firelight on top of a mountain, and they headed in its direction and thus were able to find a safe shore. But once they had docked safely in the darkness, they no longer saw the light. All the travelers thought it strange and suspected it was not a fire made by humans.

The next morning they asked people on the shore, "Last night, what was that firelight on the mountain?" Everyone there was startled, asking, "With a storm like that, how could there have been a fire? Furthermore, we saw nothing." Only then did they realize that it had been a divine light.

Rong later served as protector-general in Kuaiji, where Xie Fu 謝敷[330] heard him speak of this. Traveling on the same boat with Rong at the time were the monk Zhi Daoyun 支道蘊 and Jin Dushi 謹篤士, and they both saw this. Later they spoke of it to Fu Liang 傅亮,[331] and what they said matched what Rong had said.

Comments

The last paragraph again bears striking witness to the social and narrative processes by which our text was formed. Both eyewitnesses and interlocutors are mentioned. Xie Fu was seen above. Fu Liang (374–426), mentioned again in the next item, was the son of a friend of Xie Fu's and himself the

---

325. Source texts: *Fayuan zhulin* 65.785a–b (section "saving from danger" [*jiuwei* 救厄]); Lu, *Gu xiaoshuo gouchen* 398; Wang Guoliang, *Minxiang ji yanjiu*, 32. Additional sources: *Guangshiyin yingyanji* 6 (Makita, *Rikuchō kōitsu Kanzeon ōkenki no kenkyū*, 17–18); *Guanyin cilin ji* 2.88b; *Fayuan zhulin*, as cited in *Taiping guangji* 110.14.

326. A commandery located near what is now Linzhe district, Shandong province.

327. Located in what is now Jinhua district, Zhejiang province.

328. Located in what is now Qiantang district, Zhejiang province.

329. Or perhaps simply "reciting sutras"; no title is given, but in many other stories of this type it is specifically the *Lotus Sutra* chapter devoted to the bodhisattva—often simply termed the *Guanshiyin Sutra*—that is recited in such circumstances.

330. See comments.

331. See comments.

compiler of another group of miracle tales.[332] He was very highly placed, second in command in the central government as director of the imperial secretariat, or *shang shu ling* 尚書令.

33[333]

During the Jin Xingning period [363–365] there lived the monk Zhu Fayi 竺法義. He dwelled in the mountains and was an avid practitioner. He resided on Mount Bao in Shining.[334] He was well versed in numerous scriptures and had especially good command of the *Lotus Sutra*. He took in and trained disciples, of whom he often had more than one hundred.

In the second year of the Xian'an period [372], he suddenly felt a strange sensation in his heart. Afterward he was acutely ill for a protracted time. He tried various cures, but none helped. His days were numbered.[335] He gave up trying to effect a cure but instead entrusted himself with utmost sincerity to Guanshiyin. He kept it up for several days. One day he fell asleep and dreamed he saw a monk arrive to see about his illness, then set out to cure it: the monk cut him open and pulled out his bowels and liver, then washed them clean of filth. He saw that many impure things had collected and concentrated in them. Once the washing was complete, the monk returned the organs to Fayi's body and said to him, "Your illness is now cured." When he awoke, his ailments had dissipated, and soon he had recovered fully. Considering that the *Lotus Sutra* says that "sometimes [the bodhisattva Guanshiyin] appears in the image of a monk or brahman,"[336] one suspects that the monk seen in Fayi's dream may have been such an instance. Fayi died in the seventh year of Taiyuan [382].

The six items from the story of Zhu Changshu to this one concerning Fayi were compiled by Director of the Imperial Secretariat Fu Liang 傅亮.

---

332. See Campany, *Strange Writing*, 68–69.

333. Source texts: *Fayuan zhulin* 95.988b (section "illness and pain" [*bingku* 病苦]), 17.409b (section "honoring Buddhas" [*jing Fo* 敬佛]) (translation is based on the former version, the latter being only an apparent summary of the healing episode, although the story is attributed in *Fayuan zhulin* 95, as in *Taiping guangji* 110.3, to *Shuyi ji*); Lu, *Gu xiaoshuo gouchen*, 398; Wang Guoliang, *Mingxiang ji yanjiu*, 34. Additional texts: *Guangshiyin yingyanji* 7 (Makita, *Rikuchō kōitsu Kanzeon ōkenki no kenkyū*, 18); *Gaoseng zhuan* 4.350c; *Beishan lu* 4.594b; *Guanyin cilin ji* 2.87a.

334. Shining was a district in what is now Shangyu district, Zhejiang province.

335. Literally, "his days were reaching the point at which [his family would place before his face] a linen cloth" to detect cessation of breathing.

336. This phrase, in precisely the same wording, appears in Dharmarakṣa's translation of the *Lotus Sutra* (*Zheng fahua jing*, 10.129c) in the chapter devoted to the Bodhisattva Guangshiyin 光世音 (as he is here named). For translations of Kumārajīva's version of the same passage, see Hurvitz, *Scripture of the Lotus Blossom*, 314–315, and Robert, *Le sûtra du Lotus*, 366–367.

Liang said that his own father[337] had once traveled to see Fayi and that whenever Fayi spoke of this incident he wore a look of reverential awe.

Comments

This story's comments on the *Lotus Sutra* are a fascinatingly explicit attempt to match up reported experiences on Chinese soil to the many promises of imported Buddhist scriptures. As mentioned in part 1, the last paragraph imparts to us valuable information on how *Signs from the Unseen Realm* and similar works came to be assembled.

34[338]

Du Yuan 杜願, styled Yongping 永平, who lived during the Jin, was a native of Fu in Zitong.[339] His family was very wealthy. There was a son named Tianbao 天保 whom Yuan adored. When the child was nine, in the third year of the Taiyuan period [378], he contracted a sudden illness and died. Several months later, a sow the family was raising gave birth to five piglets. One of them was noticeably plumper than the others. Later, when a new supervisor arrived, Yuan selected and slaughtered this piglet for the ceremony. Suddenly there was a monk who appeared before Yuan and said to him, "This piglet was your son. How can you have forgotten him after only a hundred-odd days?" As soon as he had spoken these words, he just as suddenly vanished. Looking about in all directions, Yuan saw him in the western sky, rising up through the air and flying away. A fragrance filled the air everywhere about and did not disperse for the rest of the day.

Comments

This story deals vividly with the implications of the doctrine of rebirth for the indigenous practice of sacrifice and attendant consumption of meat. It is as blunt and concise an argument for vegetarianism as one is likely to find anywhere—an argument in narrative form, driven home by the piercing words of the suddenly appearing spirit-monk. Valérie Lavoix has shown that it was not primarily monks in China but laymen—very much the sort of men (and some women) portrayed in our text, even including some of the same individuals—who advocated vegetarianism most stridently.[340]

---

337. This was Fu Yuan 瑗, on whom see the Fu Liang biographies in *Song shu* 43.1335–36 (and cf. 94.2306) and *Nan shi* 15.441–442.

338. Source texts: *Fayuan zhulin* 52.677b (section "family" [*juanshu* 眷屬]); Lu, *Gu xiaoshuo gouchen*, 399; Wang Guoliang, *Mingxiang ji yanjiu*, 35. Additional texts: *Ji shenzhou sanbao gantong lu* 3.433a; *Fayuan zhulin*, as cited in *Taiping guangji* 439.2.

339. Near today's Mianyang district in Sichuan province.

340. For more, see part 1; Lavoix, "La contribution des laïcs au végétarisme"; Kieschnick, "Buddhist Vegetarianism in China"; and Gjertson, "Rebirth as an Animal."

35³⁴¹

During the Jin there was one Tang Zun 唐遵, styled Baodao 保道, a native of Shangyu.[342] In the eighth year of the Jin Taiyuan period [383–384] he died of a sudden illness. The next day he revived. He said: Someone had summoned him to go. They arrived at a walled city. Before they had entered it, he saw his father's cousin emerge from the city and ask him in amazement, "Why have you come?" Zun replied, "It has been years since I was separated from my aunt and sister. I wanted to go and ask after their welfare. I was supposed to set out this morning, but during the night I was urgently summoned here by several people. I am permitted to return soon, but I don't know the way back."[343]

His father's cousin said, "Your aunt died two years ago. Your older sister's son, Daowen, was recently brought here. He was fortunate enough to be released, but he delayed his departure so as to watch a performance and did not leave immediately. Only after several days did he return, but his family had already sealed his body up in its coffin. When he reentered [his body] in the coffin, he shook and moved the coffin about, hoping family members would notice and open the lid. But the coffin was already on its way [in a funeral procession] on the road. It tumbled off the carriage. Some in the family wanted to open it, but when a diviner was consulted, he said to do so would be inauspicious, so they didn't dare. And so he was unable to return to life. Now he is a corvée laborer shoveling sand,[344] undergoing great suffering. So you should leave quickly rather than staying here any longer. As for your other older sister,[345] she has also died and is now with your aunt together here in the earth prisons, suffering both day and night.[346] I don't know when she might be released.[347] When you go back today, you should urge her children[348] to make merit so as to help expedite her release."

---

341. Source texts: *Fayuan zhulin* 97.1003a23ff. (section "mortuary practices" [*song zhong* 送終]); Lu, *Gu xiaoshuo gouchen*, 399; Wang Guoliang, *Mingxiang ji yanjiu*, 36. Additional texts: *Liudao ji* 4.158a–b.

342. A district located in what is now Zhejiang province.

343. This return-from-death story is unusual in that the apparent reason for the protagonist's untimely death was his desire to visit distant relatives he had not realized were already dead. This desire opens the door to a didactic experience for him—and for readers of the tale.

344. Translating *jin wei ba sha zhi yi* 今為把沙之役. The commentary to the story given in *Liudao ji* reads: "The sutras say that on the path of ghosts and spirits, shoveling sand, carrying rocks, and building waterworks are retributions for sins. This is what is meant here."

345. The term used is *xiaojie* 小姊, in contrast to the term *dajie* 大姊 above, implying that the second older sister mentioned is younger than the first one mentioned, yet older than Tang Zun.

346. It is not entirely clear whether her detention owes to her own sins or to the fact that she is caught in a liminal situation vis-à-vis the otherworld bureaucracy.

347. Released, that is, to be reborn into the next path of rebirth.

348. Or her son.

He then pointed out the way home to Zun. When they were about to part, he again instructed Zun: "You are able to return to life. It is a rare felicity. We are in the world but a moment, as briefly as dust on the wind. The heavens and hells, suffering and joy, are our karmic recompense. Before, I had heard these words; now I look upon the reality. You should devote yourself totally to meritorious deeds and serve [your elders] with filial respect. When you receive the Dharma and are observing the precepts, take care not to violate them lest, once you have left human form, you enter this place of punishment. Once you are suffering here, what use will it be to have regrets? Devotion requires constant mindfulness; it is not something that can be done suddenly. My relatives did not believe in punishment and fortune while they were alive. Now they have fallen into degradation, subject to suffering for a lengthy period, in unbearable pain with no respite. They wish they could have just one day to convert their wickedness to goodness, but how could they obtain this now? This is what I have realized, so I am instructing you accordingly. I exhort you to transform those in your household so that you can all exert yourselves together!" When he had finished speaking, he wept, and so they parted.

Zun followed the route and soon arrived at his home. His family's preparations of the coffin were almost complete, and the funeral had already been held. Zun returned to his corpse, which soon started to breathe again. After several days he had recovered. He exhorted and instructed his family and acquaintances. All of them became upholders of the great Dharma.

Zun's aunt had married Xu Han 徐漢 of Nanjun, the older of his two older sisters had married Le Yu 樂瑜 of Jiangxia, and the younger had married into the Yan 嚴 family of Wuxing. All of them had been far away and had not been heard from for a long time. Once Zun had recovered, he traveled to the three commanderies to inquire about his aunt and the younger of his two older sisters. He learned that his younger older sister and her son had indeed died. The older sister confirmed that when Daowen had been encoffined, the coffin had shaken and fallen off the carriage, just as his uncle had said. When the older sister heard what Zun had to say about how Daowen had died before his time,[349] she suffered great remorse and donned mourning garments for him once again.

Comments

A critique of indigenous notions of death pollution seems to be implied by the passages about the protagonist's nephew, Daowen.[350]

---

349. Translating *heng si* 橫死, implying an unjustly early death—a death that occurred before the deceased's proper allotted life span was used up.

350. On similarly themed Buddhist narratives in medieval Japan, see Stone, "Do *Kami* Ever Overlook Pollution?"

36[351]

Xie Fu 謝敷, styled Qingxu 慶緒, who lived during the Jin, was a native of Shanyin in Kuaiji.[352] He was the son of the elder brother of Xie You 輶, a general of the Defense Command. In his youth he had much talent, but he remained a recluse in Dongshan,[353] a pious Buddhist who never flagged in his vigorous practice. He made a copy of the *Śūraṃgama Sutra* by hand. [This copy] was once in the White Horse monastery in the [southern] capital[354] when a fire broke out. Various objects, including all the other sutras, were consumed in the flames; but in the case of this scripture alone, only part of the outside paper wrapper was burned away. All the characters were intact; not one was lost. At the time when Fu died, his friends suspected he might have been a Path-attainer.[355] When they heard about this sutra copy, all of them were even more astonished.

In the eighth year of the Yuanjia period [431], there was a great fire in the city of Puban.[356] The fire even crossed the river; nothing could be saved from it. Everything, from the garrison to the people's residences, was totally destroyed. Only the oratories, stupas, and monasteries were spared. Among the small homes in the neighborhoods, many of those containing sutras and images were not burned, either. Often it was the case that, although a dwelling was completely destroyed, among the ashes would be recovered an intact sutra, its paper as immaculate as it had been before. The entire city sighed in wonder, and many experienced a deepening of reverence and faith.

Comments

Xie Fu was commented on above (items 28, 32); he was important in the early-fifth-century circles that generated some of the stories compiled here. Here we see the power of sutra copying as a devotional act, and of sutras as numinous agents in the world. The second substory has nothing to do with Xie Fu but seems to have ended up attached to the first substory because they shared the theme of the sutra copy that is impervious to

---

351. Source texts: *Fayuan zhulin* 18.418a (section "honoring the Dharma" [*jing fa* 敬法]); Lu, *Gu xiaoshuo gouchen*, 400; Wang Guoliang, *Mingxiang ji yanjiu*, 37; Wakatsuki, Hasegawa, and Inagaki, *Hōon jurin no sōgō teki kenkyū*, 129–131. Additional texts: *Fayuan zhulin*, as cited in *Taiping guangji* 113.5. Discussed: Ji Zhichang, "Dong Jin jushi Xie Fu kao"; Campany, "Notes on Sutra Texts," 63 n44.

352. Shanyin was a district located in what is still called Shanyin district, Zhejiang province.

353. In today's Shangyu district, Zhejiang province.

354. There was apparently a monastery by this name in Jiankang as well as in Luoyang; the latter was renowned as the oldest recorded Buddhist monastery in China (see item 1).

355. "Path-attainer" here translates *de dao* 得道. Roughly speaking, the meaning is that his associates thought that perhaps he had entered into the levels of spiritual attainment normally credited only to advanced monastic practitioners.

356. Puban was a district in what is now Yongji district, Shanxi province.

fire—as if someone, on hearing or reading the first substory, said, "I know of a similar case. Let me add it."

37³⁵⁷

During the Jin, the wife of Wang Ningzhi 王凝之, who served the Jin as left general, was the daughter of Xie Yi 謝奕.[358] She lost both her sons in succession. She mourned them incessantly, weeping and wailing for several years, as one would mourn one's parents. Later, she suddenly one day saw her two sons both arrive before her, bound in shackles and fetters. They comforted and encouraged her with these words: "You should not be so hard on yourself. We ourselves committed sins. If you wish to extend compassion and mercy to us, you can perform acts for [the generation of] fortune."[359] With this, her grief and pain subsided, and she diligently set about earning merit.

Comments

It is poignant to see here that a mother's grief subsides even though she learns her sons are suffering in the unseen world—because she now at least has a viable way to help them. This simple story, in a way a role-reversed version of the famous story of Mulian and his mother,[360] takes its place in a body of instructional narrative inculcating new ways to help the dead. Acts of merit create fortune transferable to the dead; one can now help the dead more powerfully, but only indirectly.

38³⁶¹

Zhi Dun 支遁, styled Daolin 道林, was a native of Chenliu[362] and lived during the Jin. He was possessed of an extraordinary appearance and was, of

---

357. Source texts: *Fayuan zhulin* 33.545b (section "promoting fortune" [*xing fu* 興福]); Lu, *Gu xiaoshuo gouchen*, 401; Wang Guoliang, *Mingxiang ji yanjiu*, 38; Wakatsuki, Hasegawa, and Inagaki, *Hōon jurin no sōgō teki kenkyū*, 208–209. Additional texts: *Youming lu*, as cited in *Taiping guangji* 320.10 (Lu, *Gu xiaoshuo gouchen*, 226); *Yiyuan* 6.25 (6.7b); *Jin lu* 晉錄, as cited in *Bianzheng lun* 7.537c4–5.

358. Both men appear in the official histories. *Jin shu* 80.2102–2103 indicates Wang Ningzhi was the second son of Wang Xizhi, the famous painter and calligrapher, and even Wang Ningzhi's wife is the subject of a brief story in *Jin shu* 96.2516. Xie Yi is mentioned at *Jin shu* 8.202–203, 13.376, 75.1964, and 83.2176.

359. Translating *zuo fu* 作福.

360. See Teiser, *The Ghost Festival*.

361. Source texts: *Fayuan zhulin* 72.833c (section "the four modes of birth" [*sisheng* 四生]); Lu, *Gu xiaoshuo gouchen*, 402; Wang Guoliang, *Mingxiang ji yanjiu*, 39. Additional texts: *Gaoseng zhuan* 4.348b; *Shimen zijing lu* 2.813c–814a.

362. A commandery located in what is now Chenliu district, Henan province. *Gaoseng zhuan* 4 says that Zhi Dun was a native of Linyu district, also located in today's Henan province.

all the old monks of his time, among the most elegant. He often debated with his teacher concerning the categories of creatures. He maintained that chicken eggs did not have enough life function to make killing them a sin as severely punishable as that for [killing] motive beings. Soon afterward his teacher died. Dun suddenly saw his teacher's form appear before him, holding a chicken egg in his hand. He broke the egg open and showed Dun the chick inside. It emerged from the shell and walked about. Dun then realized [his error] and repented of what he had earlier said. A moment later, the teacher and the chick both vanished.

Comments

The monk Zhi Dun (314–366) was a towering figure in Buddhist circles in the southeast from 340 to his death in 366. Deeply learned, he gathered many prominent associates around him, including He Chong (featured in item 16). He is known for these connections, which produced many anecdotes about him (preserved not only in *Traditions of Eminent Monks* but also in *Recent Anecdotes from the Talk of the Age*, or *Shishuo xinyu* 世說新語), as well as for his scriptural exegeses, only fragments of which survive.[363] Here, however, he is presented in a way that is out of sync with, and perhaps intentionally contests, these other portrayals: a vision of his dead friend silences the eloquent debater, trumping his fancy scholastic moves—a narrative pattern structurally similar to stories from this period in which a ghost appears and definitively defeats the debater who argues, with all the rhetorical skill in the world, that ghosts do not exist.[364]

The content of the debate mentioned here is also worth pausing over. We glimpse the sorts of conversations that must have taken place among thoughtful people trying to work out the consequences of the teaching of rebirth and the rule against taking life in such areas as the taxonomy of beings and the food supply. Like items 34 above and 92 below, this story wades into these debates.[365]

39[366]

The seven ridges that make up Mount Lu 廬山 join on the eastern side, forming a sharp peak. Its face is sheer, and no one has ever climbed it. During the Taiyuan period of the Jin, the governor of Yuzhang, Fan Ning 范寧

---

363. The best treatment is still to be found in Zürcher, *The Buddhist Conquest of China*, 116–136.

364. On this trope of "the ghostly apologue," see Campany, "Ghosts Matter," 23–25.

365. For a study of Daoxuan's (first half of seventh c.) implicit taxonomic system, see Chen Huaiyu, "A Buddhist Classification of Animals and Plants."

366. Source texts: *Fayuan zhulin* 19.428b (section "honoring the order of monks" [*jing seng* 敬僧]); Lu, *Gu xiaoshuo gouchen*, 402; Wang Guoliang, *Mingxiang ji yanjiu*, 40; Wakatsuki, Hasegawa, and Inagaki, *Hōon jurin no sōgō teki kenkyū*, 135–136. Additional texts: *Ji shenzhou sanbao gantong lu* 3.433a–b; *Lushan ji* 1.

[339–401],[367] was launching the building of a school and sent men to cut timber on the mountain. They saw a person in a monk's robe flying toward them in the air. When he had drawn near, he spun around and crouched on the peak. After a long while, he vanished into the clouds and mist. There were several persons picking medicinal herbs nearby at the time, and they all saw this as well. One of them who was able to write circulated an account of the whole matter.[368] This was the basis for the remark by the monk Shi Tandi 釋曇諦 in his "Rhapsody on Mount Lu" ("Lushan fu" 廬山賦):[369]

> Responding to perfected ones, he traverses clouds to crouch on mountain peaks;
> Receding into the distance, concealed by light, he enters the darkness.

Comments

This story affords us another glimpse of the dense social and intertextual matrices in which the narratives collected by Wang Yan were formed and transmitted. An anomaly involving a spirit-monk is observed by a group of people, a literate man among them writes and distributes a record of the event, this record is then alluded to in a monk's rhapsody, and all of this is in turn gathered up in the story preserved here.

As Wang Qing has pointed out, Fan Ning was an ancestor of Fan Zhen 縝, Wang Yan's bitter opponent in the debate over the soul's survival after death that may have helped move Wang Yan to compile this text. Wang's inclusion of this story is a none-too-subtle critique of Fan Zhen for having abandoned his own ancestor's clear Buddhist convictions.[370]

---

367. Fan Ning has a biography in *Jin shu* 75.1984–1989. He was a man of locative tendencies like Gan Bao, Ge Hong, and Wang Yan. He was the father of the Buddhist apologist Fan Tai 泰; he also donated a garden park to become part of the grounds of Anle monastery 安樂寺 in Jiankang (Zürcher, *The Buddhist Conquest of China*, 150). Mather (*Shih-shuo Hsin-yü*, 518–519) writes of him: "[His] family was devoutly Buddhist, but like many other Buddhists in public life Fan Ning favored the Ru-ist 'Teaching of Names' (*mingjiao*) and passionately opposed the 'frivolity and libertinism' of the philosophical Daoists. His diatribe against Wang Bi and He Yan is included in his biography in *Jin shu*" (see *Jin shu* 95.1984–1985; Fan also wrote commentaries on the *Analects* and on the Guliang commentary to the *Spring and Autumn Annals*). Here I pause to interject that this is in fact not surprising at all, since *mingjiao* 名教 was not a branch of Confucianism but an intellectual and religious mode that spanned multiple religious and ideological traditions, as mentioned elsewhere above and below. Mather continues: "In both his early posts as magistrate of Yuhang and Yuzhang (Jiangxi) he worked tirelessly to build schools and promote promising scholars. At court, as clerk in the Central Secretariat, he pushed for measures to restore the old rituals but became so unpopular he asked to leave to return to the provinces." See also Zürcher, *The Buddhist Conquest of China*, 403 n6.

368. Translating *neng wen zhi shi xian wei zhi xing* 能文之士咸為之興.

369. Huijiao included a biography of Tandi in *Gaoseng zhuan* 7.370c–371a; Tandi died in 411 at age sixty. This rhapsody is at least partially anthologized in *Yiwen leiju* 7.134.

370. See Wang Qing, "Jinyang Wangshi de jiashi menfeng," 145.

40[371]

During the Jin there lived the monk Shi Senglang 釋僧朗. His practice of the [monastic] precepts was clear and strict; both foreigners and Chinese respected and marveled at him. On one occasion he had, together with several other monks, received a Dharma invitation.[372] When they were half-way there Senglang suddenly told his companions, "The robes and other articles you left at the temple seem to have been stolen." They went back at once and found that the items had indeed been pilfered.

During the Taiyuan period he was in a valley on Mount Jinyu in Fenggao district[373] building a stupa and temple and making images. It was toward the end of Fu Jian's 苻堅 regime [351–384], and Buddhist monks had been declared illegal;[374] only Senglang and his group were spared, due to the respect in which he was held. Both religious and lay believers often came to visit him. No matter how many people ended up coming on any given day, Senglang always knew in advance how many to expect. He had his disciples gather provisions accordingly, and his predictions were never off.

There had long been tigers in his valley, and they had many times attacked people. Once the temple was built, however, they acted like domes-

---

371. Source texts: *Fayuan zhulin* 19.428b (section "honoring the order of monks" [*jing seng* 敬僧]); Lu, *Gu xiaoshuo gouchen*, 402; Wang Guoliang, *Mingxiang ji yanjiu*, 41; Wakatsuki, Hasegawa, and Inagaki, *Hōon jurin no sōgō teki kenkyū*, 137–140. Additional texts: *Gaoseng zhuan* 5.354b; *Ji shenzhou sanbao gantong lu* 2.433b, 3.433b; *Shi Lao zhi* 釋老志 (trans. Hurvitz, *Scripture of the Lotus Blossom*, 51); *Shenseng zhuan* 2.959a; *Shuijing zhu* 8.106 (Jishui 濟水 chapter). Note: This story is not equivalent to *Xi Guanshiyin yingyanji* 59 (Makita, *Rikuchō kōitsu Kanzeon ōkenki no kenkyū*, 51–52).

372. *Shou fa qing* 受法請, that is, received an invitation to a lay family's home for a Buddhist observance and (probably) a pre-midday meal.

373. Fenggao district was in what is now the northeast sector of Taishan district, Shandong province. Mount Jinyu lies northwest of the great Mount Tai.

374. Fu Jian, who by 370 had conquered much of northern China, attempted and failed in 383 to annex the south and reunify China; he was defeated at the battle of Fei river and died two years later (see Mather, *Shih-shuo Hsin-yü*, 520; Graff, *Medieval Chinese Warfare*, 67–69; and Rogers, *The Chronicle of Fu Chien*). Like several other rulers and officials of the era, Fu Jian ordered a "selection" (*shatai* 沙汰; see *Hanyu dacidian*, 5.952) from among the sangha, and what this meant was "wholesale examination and compulsory secularization of those [monks and nuns] who in knowledge or personal conduct fell short of the required standards" (Zürcher, *The Buddhist Conquest of China*, 259; on Fu Jian's order, see *Gaoseng zhuan* 5.354b14; Zürcher, *The Buddhist Conquest of China*, 414 n27; and Li Gang, "State Religious Policy," 216)—a process obviously motivated not by concern for monastic purity but rather to minimize the loss of the government's tax and corvée labor base due to large numbers of ordinations. But Fu Jian is also on record as having employed monks such as Daoan as advisors at his court (see Zürcher, *The Buddhist Conquest of China*, 200–201, and Li Gang, "State Religious Policy," 215–216). This is not the first time we have seen *Mingxiang ji* seemingly overstate the degree of opposition to Buddhism by a ruler. For a discussion and translation of the major narrative on Fu Jian and his military and political exploits, see Rogers, *The Chronicle of Fu Chien*.

tic animals. The Xianbei Murong De 慕容德[375] used the revenues from these two districts to provision his court. Down to today the valley is still called Master Lang Valley.

Comments

We see here an example of how the collective memory of wonder-working monks, like that of ancient sages, mythical figures, rulers, and seekers of transcendence, was sometimes tied to particular localities and geographic features, either by the work of narrative exchange in local communities or by the efforts of authors of translocal texts to construct "an empire of memory"[376]—or both.

41[377]

During the Jin there lived the monk Shi Faxiang 釋法相, a native of Hedong.[378] He often dwelled alone in the mountains and practiced with extreme austerity. Birds and wild beasts gathered around him and became as tame as domestic animals.[379] At the Mount Tai shrine 太山祠[380] there was a large stone chest filled with treasure. Faxiang was once walking on the mountain and stayed in the temple overnight. He saw a man in a black robe and martial cap[381] who commanded him to open the chest, then vanished. The stone lid on the chest must have weighed over thirty thousand catties, but when Faxiang tried it, it slid open easily. He then took the treasure from inside and distributed it to the poor.

Later he crossed over to Jiangnan and resided at Yuecheng monastery 越城寺.[382] He suddenly began wandering about and living a dissolute life,

---

375. Murong De (336–405), a Xianbei leader, founded the short-lived Southern Yan regime (400–410) in the north. See *Jin shu* 127.3161–3173; *Wei shu* 95; and, for a summary of the confusing military and political picture at his historical juncture, Graff, *Medieval Chinese Warfare*, 69–73. Liu Yuanru, "Cong Xianbei," 253, cites this story in passing as an instance of Xianbei and other northern regimes' rulers' tendency to respect monks.

376. Nylan, "Wandering in the Ruins," the best available interpretive essay on early medieval topographic texts.

377. Source texts: *Fayuan zhulin* 19.428c (section "honoring the order of monks" [*jing seng* 敬僧]); Lu, *Gu xiaoshuo gouchen*, 403; Wang Guoliang, *Mingxiang ji yanjiu*, 42; Wakatsuki, Hasegawa, and Inagaki, *Hōon jurin no sōgō teki kenkyū*, 140–142. Additional texts: *Gaoseng zhuan* 12.406c; *Ji shenzhou sanbao gantong lu* 3.433b; *Liudao ji* 3.138c.

378. Hedong was a commandery located in today's northern Xia district, Shanxi province.

379. Once again we see here, as at several points above, the attribution to spiritually advanced monks of the mastery of wild animals—an ability also often credited to transcendents in this period.

380. This is likely the temple mentioned in *Fengsu tongyi* 10.366–367 and in the "Treatise on the Forms of the Earth" (*Dixing zhi*) in *Wei shu* 106B.2522.

381. This is presumably either the god himself or his spirit-envoy.

382. To my knowledge, the only early mentions of this monastery that survive occur in the iterations of this story listed above.

clowning and behaving ridiculously, sometimes appearing naked, sometimes robed and capped as if for court. Defending-the-North General Sima Tian 司馬恬,[383] despising his uncouth conduct, summoned him and gave him poisoned ale. Although Tian plied him with three beakers of the ale, Faxiang's faculties remained completely intact, and he sat perfectly at ease.[384]

He died at the age of eighty-nine, at the end of the Yuanxing period [404].

Comments

Especially in the penultimate paragraph, we see a trope very common in this period: the cultural or religious figure who is "beyond the realm" (*fangwai* 方外) and demonstrates, by his indifference to mere convention, his superior wisdom and cultivational attainment.[385]

The sacred mountain Taishan in Shandong had for many centuries been associated with the legitimation of dynasties and rulers by means of the mysterious *feng* and *shan* sacrifices.[386] Read in this light, the story of Faxiang clearly appears to be an instance of ideological contestation—specifically, an attempt to insert the Buddhist monastic community into this old, indigenous imperial cult: it is a monk, not a minister or ruler, to whom the powerful god of the mountain redirects his treasure, and the monk uses it to succor the poor, not to fill imperial coffers.

42[387]

During the Jin there lived one Zhang Chong 張崇, a native of Duling in the area of the capital. From his youth he observed the Dharma. During the Jin Taiyuan period [376–397], after Fu Jian had been defeated

---

383. A few biographical details on him are found in *Jin shu* 37.1107. He is also mentioned in a few other anomaly accounts, including *Youming lu* 61 (Lu, *Gu xiaoshuo gouchen*, 255) and *Yiyuan* 7.16. He died in 390.

384. Poisoning and other sorts of malicious sorcery were a source of frequent worry for many in China at the time. The best recent discussion may be found in Mollier, *Buddhism and Taoism Face to Face*, 55–99.

385. This theme is ubiquitous in works from the period (but is unusual in this collection, with rare exceptions, such as item 64), so much so that it has, if anything, perhaps been overemphasized in recent scholarship. For brief further discussion see Campany, "Two Religious Thinkers," 185–188.

386. See Lewis, "Sacrifices of Emperor Wu of the Han." On the inscriptions carved on the mountain over many centuries, many of them commemorating ritual occasions, see Harrist, *The Landscape of Words*, 219–270.

387. Source texts: *Fayuan zhulin* 65.785b (section "saving from danger" [*jiuwei* 救厄]); Lu, *Gu xiaoshuo gouchen*, 403; Wang Guoliang, *Mingxiang ji yanjiu*, 43. Additional texts: *Xi Guanshiyin yingyanji* 49 (Makita, *Rikuchō kōitsu Kanzeon ōkenki no kenkyū*, 47); *Fayuan zhulin*, as cited in *Taiping guangji* 110.8; *Guanyin cilin ji* 2.88c. Discussed: Campany, "The Real Presence," 246.

[383],[388] among the commoners of Chang'an there were over a thousand households fleeing south to take refuge with the Jin regime. If they were caught by border guard units they were deemed itinerant bandits; their eldest male would be killed and the remaining sons and women taken prisoner. Chong and a group of four others were shackled by their hands and feet and buried up to the waist, each twenty paces distant from the next. The next day they were to be shot by mounted archers for sport. Bereft of any other hope, Chong focused his mind entirely on Guanshiyin. That night, his shackles suddenly broke open of themselves, and he was able to work his body free. So he ran away and was able to escape. But he was pained to think of his comrades. Passing by a Buddhist temple, he again called the name of Guanshiyin and made obeisance with his utmost mind. He placed a stone in front of himself and made a vow, saying, "I intend now to cross the Jiang to the south and complain of this disorder to the Jin emperor so that he may seek justice for their wronged cloudsouls[389] and save their wives and children. If my heart's wish is to be granted, may this stone break in two." After he had done obeisance, the stone broke. When Chong reached the [southern] capital he thus set forth a white tiger beaker[390] and detailed his grievance. The emperor was merciful; estimating what each of them was likely to bring on the market, he offered this amount for each.[391] The monk Zhisheng 智生 witnessed this with his own eyes.

Comments

Zhang Chong's "vow" and declaration fit an indigenous pattern; they also fit the Buddhist "act of truth": both exist somewhere on the conceptually complex spectrum that includes wish and vow.[392]

---

388. See Graff, *Medieval Chinese Warfare*, 66–68.

389. Belief in the dangerous power of "wronged cloudsouls" (*yuanhun* 冤魂), who were liable to file plaints in the unseen world and thus bring trouble on the living, was of long standing in China (and is still quite important today). For a translation and study of a sixth-century collection of stories of such cases (a collection that was a source for Daoshi's *Fayuan zhulin*), see Cohen, *Tales of Vengeful Souls*. See also Campany, *Strange Writing*, 377–379.

390. The phrase is *fa baihu zun* 發白虎樽. This refers to a supposedly ancient (or at least late classical) practice that is surprisingly little documented in early texts, according to which the setting forth of such a vessel (a wine vessel in the shape of the white tiger, an animal emblematic of the west) permitted a person to speak freely and without fear of reprisal even in the presence of social superiors—perhaps under the divine protection of the tiger. See *Song shu* 14.345 for a rather unsatisfactory explanation. Other mentions may be found at *Taiping yulan* 761.3510; *Nan Qi shu* 19.381, 23.434; and *Nan shi* 22.593.

391. I take this as meaning that he ordered the money to be used to buy the family members from their captors for what they would have brought on the slave market.

392. This terrain has barely begun to be explored adequately. See Rao, "Tan fojiao de fayuan wen"; Bokenkamp, "The Silkworm and the Bodhi Tree," 326–331; Tai, "Shilun zhaiwen"; Tai, "Wei wangzhe yuan"; Teiser, "Ornamenting the Departed"; and Mai, "Visualization Apocrypha," 66–72.

43[393]

During the Jin there lived one Wang Yi 王懿, styled Zhongde 仲德,[394] a native of Taiyuan.[395] He once served as probationary chariot and horse general. His family had observed Dharma for generations. His father, Miao 苗, served as governor of Zhongshan during the time of Fu Jian and was killed by Dingling tribesmen.[396] Zhongde and his older brother Yuande 元德[397] fled south carrying their mother in their arms. Scaling precipitous heights, hungry, exhausted, and out of provisions, they had run out of other possibilities and gave their minds over to the three treasures. They suddenly saw a youth leading a green bullock. When he saw that Yi and the others were hungry, he gave each of them a meal, then suddenly vanished.

At the time there had been incessant rains, and the water was high. Yi, looking out over the floodwaters, could not tell where the water might be shallow enough to be fordable. In a moment there came a white wolf. It circled about ahead of them, crossed the river, and then returned, as if meaning to lead them across. This happened three times. So they followed the wolf and forded the river. The water came up only to their knees. Soon they were on dry land again and proceeded south to take refuge at the Jin court.

Later he went from being a minister in the Ministry of War to serving as regional inspector of Xuzhou. Once, he was about to host an abstinence ceremony. On the night in question he sprinkled and swept, set out flowers and incense, and arranged a number of sutras and images. Suddenly he heard the sound of the recitation of sutras and hymns coming from the Dharma hall;[398] the sound was pure and melodious. When Yi went to look he saw five monks before the Buddha seat, of dignified and unusual appearance, radiating an air of spiritual attainment. Yi knew they were no ordinary monks, and his heart was full of joy and respect. The monks turned around, continued chanting, but then, before [Yi] had made sense

393. Source texts: *Fayuan zhulin* 65.785b–c (section "saving from danger" [*jiuwei* 救厄]); Lu, *Gu xiaoshuo gouchen*, 404; Wang Guoliang, *Mingxiang ji yanjiu*, 44. Additional texts: *Fayuan zhulin*, as cited in *Taiping guangji* 113.4. Previously partially translated in Campany, "Notes on Sutra Texts," 36.

394. Official biographies of Wang Yi may be found in *Song shu* 46.1390–1393 and *Nan shi* 25.671–674.

395. Taiyuan was a commandery located in the northwest part of what is now Taiyuan district, Shanxi province. The Taiyuan Wangs were an important and powerful aristocratic clan in these centuries, and Wang Yan himself may have been descended from them. For an excellent study of an important cultic site in the area (although later than the period treated here), see Miller, *The Divine Nature of Power*.

396. The Dingling were yet another northern nomadic people who became involved in military struggles in northern China in this era. Sometimes this appellation seems to be used to denote their leader, as in *Xuanyan ji* 35 (collected from *Taiping guangji* 116 in Lu, *Gu xiaoshuo gouchen*, 445).

397. He is mentioned in *Song shu* and *Nan shi*.

398. *Fatang* 法堂.

of the words, the monks suddenly flew up into the sky and departed. Between the friends, relatives, and guests who were present, there were many who saw this. They all leapt for joy and redoubled their efforts toward faith and enlightenment.

Comments

This story resembles a typical tale of Guanshiyin's saving intervention, but, surprisingly, that bodhisattva and his scripture are never mentioned.

Note that the protagonist is depicted as having an abstinence hall in his home, and that it is on the evening of an abstinence ceremony (for which he is depicted personally cleaning the ritual space) that spirit-monks appear. We are thus given to understand that pious performance of the abstinence ceremony is a "stimulus" that elicits a divine "response" in the form of spirit-monks and associated anomalies.

It is possible that this Wang Yi from Taiyuan was an ancestor of Wang Yan.

44[399]

During the Jin there lived Cheng Daohui 程道惠,[400] styled Wenhe 文和, a native of Wuchang. Throughout his life he upheld the Way of the Five Pecks of Rice and did not believe that there was such a person as the Buddha. He often said, "Of the correct ways that have come down from ancient times, none surpasses that of Laozi.[401] Why would anyone believe the deluded words of Western barbarians and take them as a superior teaching?"

In the fifteenth year of Taiyuan [390–391] he died of illness. A place beneath his heart[402] remained warm, so his family did not encoffin him. After several days he revived. He said that when he first died, he saw a dozen or so persons tie him up and take him away. They encountered a monk who said, "This person has fortune from former lives.[403] He may not be tied up." So he was untied, and they urged him along at a more relaxed pace.

---

399. Source texts: *Fayuan zhulin* 55.709a–b (section "destroying what is deviant" [*po xie* 破邪]); Lu, *Gu xiaoshuo gouchen*, 404; Wang Guoliang, *Mingxiang ji yanjiu*, 45. Additional texts: *Xuanyan ji* 27, as cited in *Bianzheng lun* 7.539a–b and collected in Lu, *Gu xiaoshuo gouchen*, 443; *Guangyi ji* (cited in *Taiping guangji* 382.2); *Liudao ji* 4.158b–c. Previously translated in Kao, *Classical Chinese Tales*, 172–175, and Gjertson, *Ghosts, Gods, and Retribution*, 10–13. Discussed: Mai, "Visualization Apocrypha," 122; Campany, *Strange Writing*, 334; Campany, "Return-from-Death Narratives," 118–119. Cheng Daohui is mentioned numerous times in *Song shu*, e.g., at 5.77, 43.1331–1335, and 44.1349.

400. Some versions write Hui as 慧.

401. He is here called Li Lao 李老, "Li the Aged One."

402. On the anatomically rather loose sense of this term, *xinxia* 心下, in this and similar texts—often occurring in tales of this type as a somatic explanation (frequently supplemented by a bureaucratic explanation) of why the protagonist is able to return from death to life—see Zhou Junxun, *Wei Jin nanbeichao zhiguai xiaoshuo cihui*, 215–216.

403. *Ci ren su fu* 此人宿福.

The road was level and even, but on both sides were thickets of thorns so dense that one could not have inserted a foot within. Groups of sinners were driven into the brambles; their agonized cries as their flesh was lanced pierced the ear. Seeing Hui walking on the road, they sighed in envy, "The disciples of Buddha get to walk on the road; they are persons who have cultivated fortune."[404] Hui replied, "I do not uphold the Dharma." The others laughed and said, "It's just that you have forgotten." Hui then recollected that in a former life he had honored the Buddha; since then he had undergone five births and deaths during which he had forgotten his original aim. In his present life he had fallen in with evil persons in his youth, so that, before coming to understand deviant and correct paths, he had been deluded into a deviant one.

They then arrived at a great city. He was taken straight into an office.[405] He saw a man of perhaps forty or fifty years of age, seated facing south. The man was startled on seeing Hui and said, "You should not have come here." Another man, wearing a single-layer gown and a turban[406] and holding a ledger book, responded, "This man has destroyed earth-god shrines[407] and killed people. Because of these sins he should indeed have come here." The monk whom he had encountered earlier had followed him in and now went all out to plead his case, saying, "Destroying earth-god shrines is no sin. This person's fortune from former lives is great. Although killing others is a grave sin, the retribution for this act has not yet arrived." The one seated facing south said, "The ones who arrested him should be punished." He then ordered Hui to be seated and apologized, saying, "The petty demons were mistaken and indiscriminate. You were wrongly arrested and brought here. But this was also caused by your having forgotten your former lives and not knowing enough to uphold the great Dharma." On the verge of sending Hui back, the official temporarily made him a general in charge of review and inspection and sent him on a tour of the earth prisons. Happily he took his leave and went out.

He was led along, passing many walled cities, each of which was an earth prison where many millions of people were receiving retribution for their sins. He saw one [earth prison] where dogs ripped people into pieces, so that their flesh fell off and their blood covered the ground. In another, flocks of birds with beaks like spears flew in with great speed and fell on

---

404. Some other versions of the story have a textual variant that would mean: "Even the road that the disciples of Buddha get to walk is better than others!"

405. *Tingshi* 聽事; on the contemporary sense of this relatively new compound term, see Zhou Junxun, *Wei Jin nanbeichao zhiguai xiaoshuo cihui*, 367–369.

406. On "single-layer gown" (for *danyi* 單衣), see the note to item 25 above. "Turban" translates *ze* 幘, but *ze* here and in similar contexts may be short for *pingshangze* 平上幘, a sort of tight-fitting pillbox cap, or some similar tight-fitting, head-hugging cap. See Dien, *Six Dynasties Civilization*, 313. For a quick sense of the varieties of headgear in the period, though unfortunately not including the nomenclature for all of the types, see ibid., 321.

407. *Fa she* 伐社.

sinners suddenly, entering their mouths and piercing holes through them from within, the victims writhing, screaming as their sinews were broken and their bones scattered. The rest of what he saw more or less resembled what was seen by Zhao Tai 趙泰 and Xiehe 屑荷,[408] so I do not record them in any further detail here. Only these two bits [of description] are different, so I have recorded them here in detail.[409]

When he had completed his tour, Hui was sent back. Again he saw the monk he had encountered earlier. The monk gave him a bronze object shaped like a small bell and said, "When you reach your home, leave this outside the gate; do not take it inside. On such-and-such year, month, and day you will be in peril, so be very careful. If you pass through this, you will live to ninety."

At that time, Hui's home was south of the grand boulevard in the capital. As he returned across the Acacia Bridge he saw three relatives speaking with one another in a carriage and grieving over his death. Arriving at his gate, he saw a maidservant weeping as she went off to market. None of them had seen him. Before entering through the gate he put the bronze object in a tree outside it. Light rays shot out from it and shone into the sky, diminishing and finally going out only after a long while. Upon reaching the door he could smell the stench of his corpse, and this filled him with disgust and loathing. By then the guests and relatives were hurrying through the mourning rites, and many of them were bumping into Hui, so he could not linger any longer. He approached and entered his corpse and suddenly revived. When he spoke of seeing the relatives in the carriage and the maidservant going off to market, it all tallied.[410]

Hui later became a chamberlain for law enforcement. Once as he prepared to hear a case in the western hall he was suddenly struck dumb before taking his position, and he could recognize no one. Half a day later he recovered. When he calculated the date he realized that it was the precise time the monk had warned him about. Soon afterward he was transferred to the post of inspector-general of Guangzhou. He died in Yuanjia 6 [429] at the age of sixty-nine.

Comments

We have here another story that foregrounds Buddhist-Daoist contestation—in this case, within the context of demonstrating the lingering soteriological power of one's Buddhist devotion in past lives. Even though in this life the protagonist has routinely dismissed Buddhism and touted the superiority of Daoism, he is saved from afterlife punishment and sent back

---

408. The story of Zhao Tai appears as item 5 above, and that of "Xiehe," or Liu Sahe, appears as item 45 just below. The latter's name is similarly given as Xiehe in *Ji shenzhou sanbao gantong lu* 1.405b.

409. As mentioned in part 1, this is a revealing bit of self-reference in our text.

410. That is, they confirmed his account of what he had seen.

to life on account of his fortune accumulated from previous lives of practice that he himself has forgotten (but of which others remind him).[411] Here again we see a monk acting as a layman's advocate before the purgatorial courts, in this case bearing witness to merit he had earned in previous lives.

45[412]

During the Jin there lived the monk Huida 慧達, surnamed Liu 劉, named Sahe 薩荷.[413] He was a native of Lishi in Xihe.[414] Before he left the household he was skilled in soldiering and had not heard the teaching of Buddha. He was martial by nature and loved to hunt. At thirty he died of a sudden illness. Because his body remained warm and supple, his family had not yet buried him. On the seventh day he revived and gave the following account.

Just after he died, he saw two men seize him, tie him up, and lead him away. They traveled northwest. The road climbed uphill, then leveled off; trees were arrayed on either side. He saw a man standing in the road, holding a bow and wearing a sword. He told the two men to take Sahe toward the west. He saw many buildings with white walls and red columns. Entering one of the homes, Sahe found an attractive woman. He approached her and asked for food. A voice came from midair: "Do not give him any." A man wielding an iron club emerged from the ground and made as if to strike him. Sahe fled. He entered a dozen or so homes in succession, each time with the same result.

He headed northwest again. He saw a woman riding in a carriage. She handed him a scroll, which he accepted. Continuing west, he arrived at an

---

411. At the level of the family, rather than of the isolated individual, this is an idea that is not entirely without indigenous precedent—as seen in the *Scripture of Great Peace*, for example. See Hendrischke, "The Concept of Inherited Evil." On the relations and slippages between family and individual karma in this period, see Maeda, "Between Karmic Retribution and Entwining Infusion." See also Zürcher, "Buddhist Influence on Early Taoism," 135–141.

412. Source texts: *Fayuan zhulin* 86.919b–920b (section "confession and repentance" [*chan hui* 懺悔]); Lu, *Gu xiaoshuo gouchen*, 406; Wang Guoliang, *Mingxiang ji yanjiu*, 46. Additional texts: *Gaoseng zhuan* 13.409b; *Fayuan zhulin* 31.516c, 38.585a; *Shenseng zhuan* 3.965b; *Liang shu* 54; *Nan shi* 78; *Ji shenzhou sanbao gantong lu* 1.404b, 1.405b, 1.406a, 3.434c; *Shimen zijing lu* 1.803c–804a; *Fahua zhuanji* 6.76b; *Guang hongming ji* 15.201b. Discussed: Campany, "Buddhist Revelation and Taoist Translation," 5 n15; Shinohara, "Two Sources of Chinese Buddhist Biographies," 148–160; Vetch, "Liu Sahe"; Vetch, "Lieou Sa-ho et les grottes de Mokao"; Martin, "Buddhism and Literature," 910; Whitfield, "The Monk Liu Sahe"; Wu, "Rethinking Liu Sahe"; Mai, "Visualization Apocrypha," 118 n51, 123; and in many other studies (see comments for two of these).

413. Other texts have several variants on his name, including the Xie He 屑荷, seen in item 44.

414. Lishi district was located in a district today known by the same name in Shanxi province.

ornate home where a woman with tiger teeth sat in the doorway. Inside were beautiful couches, curtains, mats, and tables.[415] A young woman was within. She asked Sahe, "Did you bring the scroll?" He gave it to her. She compared it to another text that she already had. Shortly he saw two monks, who asked him, "Do you recognize us?" Sahe said, "No." The monks said, "You should now entrust your life to Śākyamuni Buddha." He resolved[416] to do as they said, and so he followed the monks and set out again.

From a distance he caught sight of a city wall, similar to the wall of Chang'an but black. This must have been the Iron Wall.[417] He saw an enormous man, his skin black, his hair hanging to the ground. The monks said, "That is an earth-prison demon." It was very cold there. There were ice formations like rocks. They would fly apart, and if they landed on someone's head, the head would be severed; if they landed on someone's feet, the feet would likewise be severed. The monks said, "This is the prison of cold and ice."

Sahe then recollected his former lives. He realized that long ago, during the era of the Buddha Vispaśyin,[418] the two monks had been his masters. While he was a *śrāmaṇera*,[419] he committed a crime and therefore was unable to receive the precepts. Although there had been other Buddhas in the intervening world eras, he had not been able to become the follower of any of them. Twice he had attained rebirth as a human—once as a Qiang, and this time in the territory of Jin.

He also saw his great-uncle inside this prison. His uncle told him, "When I was in Ye, I did not realize I should serve Buddha. When I saw others bathing his image, I tried imitating them, but I was unwilling to affix coins [to the image].[420] For this reason I am now receiving punishment. But

---

415. The northwesterly direction and the tiger teeth mentioned here are unmistakable yet surprising allusions to the Queen Mother of the West, or Xiwangmu 西王母, goddess of techniques and drugs of transcendence, long the subject of legend. See Loewe, *Ways to Paradise*, 90; Cahill, *Transcendence and Divine Passion*, 80–81.

416. Translating *fanian* 發念.

417. *Tiecheng* 鐵城, a name for the wall surrounding the purgatories. A *Tiecheng nili jing* 鐵城泥犁經 survives (Taishō 42). Sengyou lists it and says that a copy was extant in his day (*Chu sanzang jiji* 4.27c16), so it existed by the end of the fifth century, but he places it in his long list of works by "unknown translators" in the fourth chapter of his catalogue, so it is likely to have been indigenously composed.

418. The Buddha Vipaśyin 維衛佛, one of a standard series of Buddhas believed to have preceded Śākyamuni, was the most ancient of them all, often reckoned to have lived some ninety-one kalpas ago (each kalpa itself being an almost unimaginably long span of time). See Nattier, *Once Upon a Future Time*, 20–21; Vogel, "The Past Buddhas"; von Hinüber, "Three New Bronzes from Gilgit," 40–41; Durt, "The Meaning of Archaeology in Ancient Buddhism"; and Vetch, "Liu Sahe," 65. This is, then, a feat of almost unimaginably extreme recall, of a sort usually attributed only to Buddhas.

419. That is, a monastic novice.

420. The bathing of Buddha images, particularly on the day marking the anniversary of Siddhartha's birth, was an important ritual. See Boucher, "Sutra on Bathing the Buddha"; and Liu Shufen, "Art, Ritual, and Society," 37–38.

I also have some residual fortune from having bathed [the image], so I am fortunate to be able to attain rebirth in the heavens [soon]."

Next Sahe saw the earth prison of the mountain of swords. And he passed through all the other [purgatories] in succession, seeing a great many things. Each prison had its own walls; they were not in the same enclosure. People were as numerous as grains of sand, incalculably many. The punishments, sufferings, and regulations there more or less matched what is said in scriptures.

Ever since Sahe had set foot in the earth prisons, a certain light had been noticeable. But now suddenly a brilliant golden radiance appeared before him. He saw a man perhaps twenty feet tall, of beautiful shape and appearance, his body a golden hue. Those nearby said, "The Bodhisattva Guanshiyin!" All rose to pay obeisance. Two monks of identical appearance headed off toward the east.[421] When Sahe had finished paying obeisance, the bodhisattva expounded on the Dharma for him, perhaps a thousand or more words. He concluded by saying: "Whenever one acts so as to establish fortune for the departed, whether they be one's parents, siblings, relatives of up to seven generations ago, relatives by marriage, friends, or passersby, whether done in an oratory or in the home, whoever among those departed may be suffering will be released. On the fifteenth day of the seventh month, monks receive end-of-retreat offerings;[422] to present offerings at this time is most effective. If one provides vessels and fills them with offering foods, with each dish labeled "such-and-such a person personally presents this to the three treasures," the fortune dispensed thereby will be especially great, and the recipients' felicity will be greater and faster.[423] If monastics and laity can confess their sins and wicked deeds from this and previous lifetimes, and make a full rendition of them publicly in the assembly, leaving out no instances, and do this confession with utmost sincerity, their sins will be expunged. If those who are too weak or modest and are ashamed to confess their sins before the assembly are able to recall and say them silently in a private place, without missing an instance, their sins too will be expunged. If there remain sins that one omits from confession but without intentionally concealing them, although one will not escape punishment, the retribution will be relatively light. But if one cannot repent, cannot have a remorseful heart, this is called holding

---

421. Judging from subsequent lines of the story, the eastward heading probably is meant to suggest that these beings are now headed to China, here understood as located east and south of the earth prisons.

422. "End-of-retreat offerings" indirectly renders *la* 臘, in Buddhist contexts denoting the ceremonies attending the end of the monastic summer retreat, which traditionally lasted ninety days. See Kuo, *Confession et contrition*, 19; *Hōbōgirin*, s.v. *ango* 安居 (unsigned article); and, on the pre-Buddhist, indigenous festival also known as *la*, see Bodde, *Festivals in Classical China*; and *Taiping yulan* 33.

423. Presumably because this assists the keepers of tallies of meritorious acts, who might otherwise at times be prone not to credit the merit to its proper agent.

fast to one's sins and not turning back. When such a one's life span is used up, he will fall into the earth prisons. Additionally, if one builds stupas or temples, or even just adds earth or wood to the materials for their construction, whether painted or bejeweled, and offers these with sincerity, the fortune one obtains thereby will be great. If [however] one sees a stupa or temple that is overgrown with brush, and does not clear the brush away but passes on by, even if one performs obeisance the merit will be exhausted immediately." He said further, "The sutras are venerable texts, fords of transformative instruction. The merit attached to the *[Prajñā]pāramitā sutra* is foremost; that of the *Śūraṃgama [sutra]* is next. For persons of goodness, the place where [these] sutras are recited and chanted will become a [space of] diamonds, but the many beings who have only eyes of flesh cannot perceive this. If you can recite [them] diligently, you will not fall into the earth prisons. The final version[424] of the *Prajñā[pāramitā sutra]* and the alms bowl of the Tathāgata will later reach the Han land in the east. If you can establish one act of merit with respect to this sutra or this bowl, you will receive rebirth in the heavens as recompense and will obtain manifold quantities of merit." What he said was very copious; this is merely a digest.

As Sahe was about to take his leave, the bodhisattva told him: "You would otherwise have received retribution for your sins through successive eras. But because you have now heard the teaching of the sutras, let your heart be joyful: you will now receive only a lightened retribution, after which you will have escaped [any further punishment] and will be able to return to life. You should become a monk. At five places, in Luoyang, Linzi, Jianye, Maoyin, and Chengdu, there are stupas [commissioned by] King Aśoka. Also, in Wu there are two stone images made by spirits sent by King Aśoka; they quite faithfully reproduce [the Buddha's] bodily marks.[425] If you can go to these places and pay obeisance, you will not fall into the earth prisons." When he had finished speaking, he set off eastward. Sahe paid obeisance and took his leave.

He set out on a great road toward the south. It was over a hundred paces wide. Those walking on it were too many to count. Along the roadside were high seats, dozens of feet tall, with monks sitting on them and many other monks arrayed around them. There was a man wielding a brush, standing and facing north, who said to Sahe: "When you were in Xiangyang, why did you kill a deer?" Sahe knelt down and replied, "Someone else shot the deer; I only helped carve it up. Also, I ate no meat from it. Why should I receive retribution for this?" At once the spot in Xiangyang where the deer had been killed became visible; the brush, trees, hills, and rivers suddenly filled the eyes. The black horses that [the hunting party] had ridden could all speak, and they all gave witness that Sahe had killed the deer at a certain time of a certain day, month, and year. Terrified, Sahe

---

424. Translating *ding ben* 定本.
425. On "bodily marks" (*xiang* 相 or *lakṣaṇa*), see the note to Wang Yan's preface above.

had no response to make. In a moment a man with a pitchfork forked him and threw him into a boiling cauldron. Sahe watched as his own limbs burned away. He then felt a breeze from the embankment nearby, and when he no longer felt it, his body was whole again. The man wielding the brush again spoke: "You also shot a pheasant, and on one occasion you killed a goose." At this Sahe was again pitchforked into the cauldron and burned as before.

After he had received this retribution, Sahe was sent away. He entered a large walled city, where a resident said to him, "You received only light punishment for your sins, and furthermore are allowed to return to life. This is due to the power of your fortune. Now, from this point on, will you continue sinning or not?" He then dispatched someone to escort Sahe back. From a distance Sahe saw his former body, and in his mind he did not want to return to it. But the man escorting him pushed and pulled him so that, after a long time, he finally reattached himself to his form[426] and thus was able to revive. He upheld the Dharma with vigor and diligence, at once leaving the household and taking the [Dharma] name Huida. At the end of the Taiyuan period he was still residing in the capital. Later he departed for Xuchang. It is not known how he ended up.

Comments

Liu Sahe (Huida) was the subject of many stories in which he is shown "discovering" ancient Aśokan stupas and images in the soil of China. Those exploits are mentioned here, but this story in effect supplies the karmic background for them. With the line "The punishments, sufferings, and regulations there more or less matched what is said in scriptures" (*lue yu jing shuo xiang fu* 略與經說相符), we see another kind of grounding of Buddhism in Chinese soil: the "matching" shows that Buddhism is being authentically practiced and experienced in China, just as it also authenticates the truth and efficacy of the imported scriptures. This Chinese individual's reported vision "tallies with" what the imported texts say one should see when one has died.

This story contains one of the longest "historical" visionary discourses by the Bodhisattva Guanshiyin on record. The discourse imparts a wealth of detailed instruction, much of it on the practice of confession (but also mentioning cultic devotion to sutras and stupas and temple building), none of it however very novel. Note the prediction about two kinds of cultic objects making their way to China—a particular version of the *Prajñāpāramitā sutra* and Gautama Buddha's alms bowl. An otherworldly warrant is here being provided for those sacred objects.

---

426. *Jiujiu fu xing* 久久乃附形; this phrasing recalls the terms in which "possession" of living persons by spirits was described. For a brief discussion, see Li Jianmin, "They Shall Expel Demons," 1141–1142.

Liu Yuanru has recently offered a detailed comparison between the story of Liu Sahe incorporated into *Mingxiang ji* and the narratives about him found in Daoxuan's *Ji shenzhou sanbao gantong lu* (which gives the most comprehensive account of his life, pilgrimage, and cultic reception after his death) and Huijiao's *Gaoseng zhuan* (which focuses on his "discoveries" of Aśokan artifacts in China).[427] Her study provides a good example of how much it is true that the divergent interests of multiple compilers and texts—even when, as in this case, all the compilers and texts in question "are Buddhist"—can yield very different accounts of the same figure.[428] (Earlier, Wu Hung's excellent article on the various narratives of Liu Sahe had made the same point, but had gone further to incorporate visual works as well.)[429] But I find her discussion problematic in several ways. She imagines that only a comparison among the different accounts of Liu Sahe will allow for a "complete map of his life,"[430] whereas I doubt that such texts as these give us any access to such a thing.[431] She also asserts repeatedly that each of these authors, based on their respective rhetorical interests and abilities, "selected" (*caiyong* 採用) elements of a shared story (she does not go so far as to claim a shared urtext) about Liu Sahe, whereas there is no evidence for such a shared narrative, and in a manuscript culture such as that of early medieval China we must assume that there existed many competing accounts and sources concerning any given figure or event.[432] In other words, absent further evidence, the differences among these three

427. *Chaoxiang shenghuo shijie*, 129–194. She largely repeats herself on the same topic on pp. 230–239.

428. This is the main point argued (regarding a different religious tradition) in Campany, *Making Transcendents*, 216–258.

429. See "Rethinking Liu Sahe."

430. *Chaoxiang shenghuo shijie*, 137.

431. On the hazards—and possibilities—inherent in using hagiographical material as evidence, see Campany, *Making Transcendents*.

432. A similar problem crops up in the same work, p. 258, where Liu assumes that Wang Yan "rewrote" (*gaixie* 改寫) an account found in an earlier collection of miracle tales (i.e., Liu Yiqing's *Xuanyan ji*). It is theoretically possible (1) that Wang did indeed have a copy of the earlier account, (2) that Wang Yan's copy of that account matched the one we now have, and (3) that the differences between Wang Yan's "version" and the earlier one were the direct and sole result of Wang's rewriting. But given that early medieval China was a manuscript culture (and all that that entails, as discussed in part 1), and given the ways in which those manuscripts have been preserved, none of these points should simply be assumed without evidence or argumentation. (It is also worth noting that, regarding the overlaps between stories in these two works, Wang Qing finds that, other than two stories that are identical in both—suggesting either that Wang Yan copied material from Liu Yiqing's text or that they shared a common source for these two items—the two texts seem to belong to different "textual traditions" rather than Wang's stories being "rewritings" of Liu's, probably derived from differing oral or written sources; see his "Jinyang Wang shi de jiashi menfeng," 151.) Another problematic feature of Liu's discussion is that she opens it by briefly citing a few (to some extent mutually incompatible) Western models for the study of hagiographic texts but then does not use these models to inform her own inquiry.

accounts of Liu Sahe are just as likely to reflect differences in the many
sources on him that no doubt circulated—sources which were probably
not equally available to the three compilers—as they are to have resulted
from the compilers' work of "selection" from a larger, common "original"
narrative to which they all somehow enjoyed equal access.[433] Finally, she
reads the *Mingxiang ji* narrative of Liu's purgatorial journey through the
lens of the Buddhist doctrines of emptiness and the illusoriness of sensory
perception,[434] but there is no evidence that Wang Yan intended the account
to be taken that way and much evidence suggesting that he meant this and
the many similar accounts in his text to be taken as true recountings of individuals' actual experiences—decidedly nonempty reports of the nonil-
lusory realities awaiting his readers in the unseen world, in light of which
he called upon them to adopt and intensify Buddhist practice. Her interpretive move here seems to result from seeing "Buddhism" as a single, uniform, essentialized set of teachings that uniformly applied in all Buddhist
texts. This is a view to which I have provided an alternative in part 1.

46[435]

During the Jin the monk Zhu Fatun 竺法純 served for a time as the abbot
of Xianyi monastery 顯義寺 in Shanyin.[436] During the Yuanxing period, as
the monastery was being built, he went to Lanzhu[437] to buy lumber, traveling by boat on the lake. The owner of the timber was a woman. They needed to go to the timber-cutting site together to agree on a price, so they set
out along with others on boats. As soon as they were under way on the
great lake, a violent storm arose, creating waves the size of hills. Fatun's
boat was small, and water was coming in. His life hung in the balance. He
thought that perhaps his conduct had not been correct, to have suddenly

---

433. This is not at all to negate the importance of compilers' own interests in their selection and shaping of narrative material. It is simply to reject the assumption that what they
had to select from was a single commonly shared and available text.

434. *Chaoxiang shenghuo shijie*, 178–179.

435. Source texts: *Fayuan zhulin* 17.409c (section "honoring Buddhas" [*jing Fo* 敬佛]);
Lu, *Gu xiaoshuo gouchen*, 409; Wang Guoliang, *Mingxiang ji yanjiu*, 47; Wakatsuki, Hasegawa,
and Inagaki, *Hōon jurin no sōgō teki kenkyū*, 96–97. Additional texts: *Xi Guanshiyin yingyanji* 8
(Makita, *Rikuchō kōitsu Kanzeon ōkenki no kenkyū*, 29); *Gaoseng zhuan* 12.406c (where Zhu
Fatun is given a brief biography, grouped under "reciters of sutras," and is also said to have
been the abbot of Xianyi monastery); *Fayuan zhulin*, as cited in *Taiping guangji* 110.10; *Guanyin cilin ji* 2.86c; *Fahua zhuanji* 4.62b.

436. Shanyin was a district in what is now Shaoxing district, Zhejiang province. This
monastery is mentioned in Zhu Fatun's *Gaoseng zhuan* biography (see above) and in *Xu
gaoseng zhuan* 8.483c.

437. Twenty-five *li* southwest of Shanyin, Lanzhu was the site of the Orchid Pavilion im-
mortalized by the great painter and calligrapher Wang Xizhi 王羲之 in his preface to the
"Rhapsody on Winding Water" (*Qushui fu* 曲水賦).

met with this misfortune, and he feared that it had been inappropriate for him to travel together with the woman. So he began chanting the *Guanshiyin Sutra* with his whole mind. Soon a large boat floated up behind and came alongside Fatun's boat. It was already night at the time, and travel on the lake had ceased. Fatun thought to himself: this large boat should not be here at this hour; it must be by divine power. So Fatun and the others were able to climb aboard the large boat, and just as they did so, the small boats sank. The large boat drifted along, pounded by the waves, and soon they were able to climb ashore.

47[438]

During the Jin there lived the monk Shi Kaida 釋開達. In the second year of the Long'an period [398] he climbed to a high spot to gather licorice[439] and was seized by Qiang tribesmen. It was a famine year, and the Qiang and Hu people were eating each other. So they placed Kaida inside a fenced enclosure, intending to eat him. There were already a dozen or so people within. As the days went on, the Qiang would remove them one by one, cooking and eating them, until only Kaida remained. Ever since his capture he had been reciting the *Guanshiyin Sutra* continuously, not flagging in his mindfulness. The next day he was due to be eaten. As day broke, suddenly a large tiger appeared and began chasing off the Qiang, roaring angrily. The terrified Qiang scattered in all directions. The tiger then advanced toward the stockade and chewed through the fencing until there was a gap big enough for a person to pass through. As soon as it had completed this, it walked away. At first, when Kaida watched the tiger gnaw through the fence, he thought he would certainly perish. But when the hole was opened and the tiger did not enter, he wondered to himself at the oddity of this and decided it must be due to the power of Guanshiyin. Since the Qiang had not yet returned, he was able to slip out through the fence and flee. Traveling by night and hiding during the daytime, he managed to make his escape.

---

438. Source texts: *Fayuan zhulin* 17.409c (section "honoring Buddhas" [*jing Fo* 敬佛]); Lu, *Gu xiaoshuo gouchen*, 409; Wang Guoliang, *Mingxiang ji yanjiu*, 48; Wakatsuki, Hasegawa, and Inagaki, *Hōon jurin no sōgō teki kenkyū*, 98–99. Additional texts: *Xi Guanshiyin yingyanji* 46 (Makita, *Rikuchō kōitsu Kanzeon ōkenki no kenkyū*, 45–46); *Fayuan zhulin*, as quoted in *Taiping guangji* 110.9; *Guanshiyin chiyan ji* 1.93a; *Guanyin cilin ji* 2.87a. Discussed: Campany, "The Real Presence," 254 n59.

439. *Gancao* 甘草, or licorice, was an important herbal element of the indigenous Chinese pharmacopeia; see Unschuld, *History of Pharmaceutics*, 33, 111–112, 120, 240. It is mentioned quite a few times in the Sino-Japanese canon, but—at least in early works—usually in discussions of the categories of flavor, where it is given as a paradigmatic case of sweetness. In one instance a root ingredient of incense is compared in shape to *gancao* (see *Fayuan zhulin* 36.573b).

48[440]

During the Jin there lived Pan Daoxiu 潘道秀, a native of Wu command-ery.[441] When he was twenty-odd years of age he served as a military supervisor. He participated in a northern campaign that ended in failure. Daoxiu hid out but was captured by the enemy and taken from place to place as a slave. Whenever the enemy soldiers were absent he looked for an opportunity to escape south, but the right moment proved elusive.

From his youth he had believed in the Dharma of Buddha, so now he continuously with utmost mind focused his thoughts on Guanshiyin. Each time he dreamed, he saw [Guanshiyin's] image. Later he managed to flee south but had lost his way when, deep in the mountains, he suddenly saw [the bodhisattva's] true form, similar to the ones now used in processions. So he made obeisance. The moment he finished, the figure suddenly disappeared. Only then did he manage to find his way back south and return to his native land. Afterward he practiced with vigor and redoubled his effort. He died at age sixty.

Comments

The similarity of the bodhisattva's "true form" (*zhenxing* 真形) to images "now used in processions" functions to validate the iconography for Guanshiyin current in China at the time—another sort of matching of Chinese practice to canonical norms.

49[442]

During the Jin there lived one Luan Gou 欒苟;[443] his family's place of origin is not known. From his youth he observed the Dharma. He once served as magistrate of Fuping.[444] Before that, he once was involved in the north-

---

440. Source texts: *Fayuan zhulin* 17.410a (section "honoring Buddhas" [*jing Fo* 敬佛]); *Taiping guangji* 110.6; Lu, *Gu xiaoshuo gouchen*, 409; Wang Guoliang, *Mingxiang ji yanjiu*, 49; Wakatsuki, Hasegawa, and Inagaki, *Hōon jurin no sōgō teki kenkyū*, 101–102. Additional texts: *Xi Guanshiyin yingyanji* 61 (Makita, *Rikuchō kōitsu Kanzeon ōkenki no kenkyū*, 53); *Guanshiyin chiyan ji* 1.94a; *Guanyin cilin ji* 2.87b. Discussed: Campany, "The Real Presence," 254 n57.

441. Today's Wu district, Jiangsu province.

442. Source texts: *Fayuan zhulin* 17.410a (section "honoring Buddhas" [*jing Fo* 敬佛]); *Taiping guangji* 110.7; Lu, *Gu xiaoshuo gouchen*, 410; Wang Guoliang, *Mingxiang ji yanjiu*, 50; Wakatsuki, Hasegawa, and Inagaki, *Hōon jurin no sōgō teki kenkyū*, 102–104. Additional texts: *Xi Guanshiyin yingyanji* 45 (Makita, *Rikuchō kōitsu Kanzeon ōkenki no kenkyū*, 45, trans. in Campany, "The Earliest Tales of the Bodhisattva Guanshiyin," 89); *Guanyin cilin ji* 2.87b. Discussed: Campany, "The Real Presence," 247.

443. In some texts his name is given as Luan Xun 欒苟.

444. Fuping was a district near what is now still known as Fuping district, Shaanxi province.

ern campaign against Lu Xun 盧循[445] when his unit met with misfortune. His convoy of lashed-together boats was hit with fire bolts, and the rebels were drawing near. They were in midriver, the wind was whipping the waves ever higher, and Gou feared for his life, but he nonetheless chanted "Guanshiyin" and focused his thoughts on the bodhisattva. Shortly thereafter he saw a person in the river, standing alone, the water coming only to his waist. Gou knew in his mind that it was a response elicited by his prayerful concentration, so, with the enemy closing, he leapt into the water toward the man. His body floated easily, and it felt as though his feet were touching land. Soon a large transport ship arrived to rescue the troops from the defeated unit. Gou thus escaped harm.

50[446]

The monk Shi Fazhi 釋法智, who lived during the Jin, while he was still a layman often traveled alone. He once was passing through a great marsh when he suddenly encountered a wildfire rising up on all sides around him. All escape routes were already blocked. He therefore began with utmost mind and reverence to chant [the name or sutra of] Guanshiyin. Soon the fire passed him by. In the entire marsh there was not a single stalk of vegetation remaining unburned except in the small area around Fazhi. From this point on he began to observe the great Dharma reverentially.

Later he served as a general under Yao Xing 姚興 [366–416][447] and participated in the northern campaign against the caitiffs.[448] During the

---

445. Lu Xun was married to the younger sister of Sun En (d. 402), who launched a partially Daoism-inspired rebellion with his uncle and others in 398. After Sun's suicide, Lu Xun continued the rebellion until he was defeated by forces under the command of Eastern Jin general Liu Yu, who, some twenty years later, would found the Song dynasty. For more details see *Jin shu* 100.2631–2636; Pregadio, *Encyclopedia of Taoism*, s.v. "Sun En," 924–925; Miyakawa, "Local Cults around Mount Lu"; Zürcher, *The Buddhist Conquest of China*, 154–155; and Eichhorn, "Description of the Rebellion of Sun En."

446. Source texts: *Fayuan zhulin* 17.410a (section "honoring Buddhas" [*jing Fo* 敬佛]); *Taiping guangji* 110.19; Lu, *Gu xiaoshuo gouchen*, 410; Wang Guoliang, *Mingxiang ji yanjiu*, 51; Wakatsuki, Hasegawa, and Inagaki, *Hōon jurin no sōgō teki kenkyū*, 104–106. Additional texts: *Xi Guanshiyin yingyanji* 2 (Makita, *Rikuchō kōitsu Kanzeon ōkenki no kenkyū*, 26); *Guanyin cilin ji* 2.87b; *Guanshiyin chiyan ji* 1.93b; *Xu gaoseng zhuan* 25.645c; *Meisōden shō.*

447. On the sinicized Qiang military leader Yao Xing, ruler of the Former Qin regime (on which see Lewis, *China Between Empires*, 74–79) after his father, Yao Chang, see Kanno, "Yōshi to Bukkyō"; Wang Guoliang, *Mingxiang ji yanjiu*, 144 n2; *Jin shu* 10; *Wei shu* 3; Graff, *Medieval Chinese Warfare*, 69; and Li Gang, "State Religious Policy," 216–219. For an Indo-European hypothesis about the etymology of the ethnonym Qiang 羌, see Beckwith, *Empires of the Silk Road*, 375–376.

448. This campaign occurred in the winter of 401; Yao Xing attacked the Wei forces and was routed. Here and throughout, "caitiffs" (cowards; despicable persons) translates *lu* 虜, *suolu* 索虜, or *suotoulu* 索頭虜, all of which were pejorative terms used by southern writers

army's retreat, he lost his horse and was encircled [by the enemy]. So he hid in a thicket beside a gully, but there was only enough cover to hide his head. Once again he concentrated on Guanshiyin, his mind intently focused. Across the gully he could hear the opposing troops being issued commands to find and kill him, but the troops passed him by, and no one saw him. He was thus able to escape to safety.

Later he left the household [to become a monk].

51⁴⁴⁹

During the Jin there lived Nangong Ziao 南公子敖,⁴⁵⁰ a native of Shiping.⁴⁵¹ He was serving in the defensive force at Xinpingcheng⁴⁵² when it was sacked by Changle Gong 長樂公, son of the caitiff Fofo 佛佛虜.⁴⁵³ The several

---

to refer to the conquering rulers of much of northern China at the time, otherwise known as the Tuoba 拓跋 (both syllables sometimes written with other graphs), a Mongolic (Beckwith, *Empires of the Silk Road*, 103, 113) tribe within the Xianbei 鮮卑 confederation and founders of the Northern Wei dynasty (so called to distinguish it from the Wei regime founded by Cao Cao and his sons at the end of the Han) unifying the north in 386 and perduring until the mid-sixth century. These pejorative terms combined an adjectival reference, fictive or not, to the northerners' hairstyle (braided) and a noun meaning "captive"; in the latter respect "caitiff" is therefore a good match etymologically. See further Rogers, *The Chronicle of Fu Chien*, 214 n161, and *Hanyu dacidian*, 9.750. For convenient overviews of these northern peoples and their military and political vicissitudes during the period, see Dien, *Six Dynasties Civilization*, 1–14; Lewis, *China Between Empires*, 73–85, 145–151; Graff, *Medieval Chinese Warfare*, 54–75, 97–137; and, for a distinctly non-Sinocentric view, Beckwith, *Empires of the Silk Road*, 90, 103, 113–114. For a medieval Chinese treatise on the Tuoba, focusing (like most modern treatments, in fact) not on their culture but on their political and military exploits, see *Song shu* 95.2321–2367. For an overview of treatments of these northern conquerers in works of the *zhiguai* genre during the period, but one that has little to say about *Mingxiang ji* and nothing on the term *suo*, see Liu Yuanru, "Cong Xianbei."

449. Source texts: *Fayuan zhulin* 17.410a–b (section "honoring Buddhas" [*jing Fo* 敬佛]); *Taiping guangji* 110.16; Lu, *Gu xiaoshuo gouchen*, 410; Wang Guoliang, *Mingxiang ji yanjiu*, 52; Wakatsuki, Hasegawa, and Inagaki, *Hōon jurin no sōgō teki kenkyū*, 106–108. Additional texts: *Xi Guanshiyin yingyanji* 17 (Makita, *Rikuchō kōitsu Kanzeon ōkenki no kenkyū*, 33); *Guanyin cilin ji* 2.87c; *Guanshiyin chiyan ji* 1.94b.

450. Some texts, including *Taiping guangji*, write the surname as 南宮.

451. Shiping was a commandery headquartered in what is now southeastern Xingping district, Shaanxi province.

452. A Xianbei settlement located in today's Shanxi province.

453. Little more is known of Changle Gong, who may not have actually been a son of Helian Bobo but rather a member of his comitatus (see Beckwith, *Empires of the Silk Road*, 12ff.). "The caitiff Fofo" is an alternate and pejorative designation for Helian Bobo 赫連勃勃, Xiongnu founder of the short-lived Xia 夏 regime (407–431) centered in the great northern bend of the Yellow River before its conquest by the Northern Wei. (He is also mentioned—extremely pejoratively, showing him punished for his desecration of the image of Buddha—in *Xuanyan ji* 34, collected from *Bianzheng lun* 7.540a in Lu, *Gu xiaoshuo gouchen*, 444–445.) Its capital, Tongwancheng 統萬城, a grand and extremely well-built city by the standards of the time, which fell in 427, has been excavated in recent decades; see Dien, *Six Dynasties Civilization*, 17–18, 257. On the Xia see also Graff, *Medieval Chinese Warfare*, 72.

thousand souls caught in the city were all executed. Ziao, although re-signed to his imminent death, still concentrated his mind to the utmost on Guanshiyin. When it came his turn to be executed, as the blades were about to fall, some remained suspended, and some broke apart. Those wielding the weapons suddenly lost all their strength; they no longer had control of their four limbs. At that time Changle Gong was personally at-tending the executions. Shocked, he asked what was happening. Ziao blurted out, "I can make saddles." At this, he was pardoned. Ziao himself was unaware of having said these words. Later on he was able to flee to safety.

He made a small image [of Guanshiyin]. He kept it in a box of fragrant wood, and whenever he traveled he wore it on the top of his head.[454]

Comments

The variety of Guanshiyin's means of saving devotees from peril is well il-lustrated by this case, where it seems to be the bodhisattva who puts into the protagonist's mouth precisely the words that will save his life.

52[455]

During the Jin there lived one Liu Du 劉度, a native of Qing city in Ping-yuan district.[456] In his hamlet there were a thousand or so families, all ob-servers of the great Dharma. They fashioned and erected images and made donations to monks and nuns. During the period of the caitiff overlord Mumo 木末,[457] this district often harbored refugees. This angered Mumo, and he intended to slaughter the entire city. The people were terrified and had resigned themselves to dying. But Du uprightly and sincerely led them to turn their lives over to Guanshiyin. Soon Mumo saw an object fall from

---

454. Like sutras, small images were apparently sometimes worn on the head, both as an act of devotion and as a measure of talismanic protection. For discussion of some instances involving sutras, see Campany, "Notes on Sutra Texts."

455. Source texts: *Fayuan zhulin* 17.410b (section "honoring Buddhas" [*jing Fo* 敬佛]); *Taiping guangji* 110.15; Lu, *Gu xiaoshuo gouchen*, 411; Wang Guoliang, *Mingxiang ji yanjiu*, 53; Wakatsuki, Hasegawa, and Inagaki, *Hōon jurin no sōgō teki kenkyū*, 109–111. Additional texts: *Xi Guanshiyin yingyanji* 43 (Makita, *Rikuchō kōitsu Kanzeon ōkenki no kenkyū*, 44); *Sanbao gan-ying yaolue lu* 3.852b; *Guanshiyin chiyan ji* 1.94a; *Guanyin cilin ji* 2.87c. Discussed: Campany, "Notes on Sutra Texts," 47.

456. Following the city name as given in *Taiping guangji*, not *Fayuan zhulin*. Pingyuan was a commandery located in what is now southeastern Pingyuan district, Shandong province.

457. The identity of this figure is unclear, in part because only an abbreviated name is given for him here. It may be the military commander Xu Mumo 許木末, who is recorded as having killed his general Murong Chong 慕容沖, a governor who rebelled against Fu Jian (*Jin shu* 9.233), in Chang'an in 386 (*Jin shu* 9.235). At this writing I do not know what the re-lationship was between Murong Chong and the better-known military and dynastic figure Murong Chui (of whom Graff, *Medieval Chinese Warfare*, has many mentions).

the sky and wrap itself around a column in his palace. Shocked, he examined it, and it turned out to be a copy of the *Guanshiyin Sutra*. He had someone read it. Mumo was delighted and thus halted the executions. In this way the city avoided harm.

53[458]

During the Jin there lived one Guo Xuanzhi 郭宣之, a native of Taiyuan. In the fourth year of the Yixi period [408–409] he was appointed by Yang Siping 楊思平[459] to command the garrison at Liangzhou.[460] Because of having killed Fan Yuanzhi 范元之 and others, Yang was brought up on charges, and Xuanzhi was also imprisoned along with him. Xuanzhi simply focused his mind utterly on the Bodhisattva Guanshiyin. The next night, as he was falling asleep, he suddenly saw the bodhisattva's radiant light filling his cell. Looking up reverentially, Xuanzhi pleaded for an official pardon. After a while the figure vanished. Soon thereafter, Xuanzhi was the only one of the group to be pardoned.

After his release, Xuanzhi fashioned an image based on the form he had seen and set it up in his oratory.[461] Later he served successively in Lingling[462] and Hengyang, and he died in office.

54[463]

During the Jin, Yu Shaozhi 庾紹之, a native of Xinye, when young was styled Daofu 道覆. He served as governor of Xiangdong. He was a cousin of Zong Xie 宗協[464] of Nanyang, and the two were close friends. At the end of the Yuanxing period [404] he died of illness. During the Yixi period [405–

458. Source texts: *Fayuan zhulin* 17.409c–410a (section "honoring Buddhas" [*jing Fo* 敬佛]); Lu, *Gu xiaoshuo gouchen*, 411; Wang Guoliang, *Mingxiang ji yanjiu*, 54; Wakatsuki, Hasegawa, and Inagaki, *Hōon jurin no sōgō teki kenkyū*, 99–100. Additional texts: *Xuanyan ji* 23 (collected in Lu, *Gu xiaoshuo gouchen*, 369); *Xi Guanshiyin yingyanji* 24 (Makita, *Rikuchō kōitsu Kanzeon ōkenki no kenkyū*, 36–37); *Bianzheng lun* 7.537c–538a, and as cited in *Taiping guangji* 110.12; *Guanshiyin chiyan ji* 1.94c; *Guanyin cilin ji* 2.87b.

459. He is mentioned in *Jin shu* 10.260.

460. Liangzhou was an administrative unit established by the Jin and centered in what is now Zhaohua district, Sichuan province.

461. It is telling that, here as elsewhere, sufficiently well-to-do laypersons are mentioned as having had such a structure in their homes.

462. A commandery in what is now Lingling district, Hunan province.

463. Source texts: *Fayuan zhulin* 94.978a–b (section "wine and meat" [*jiu rou* 酒肉]); *Taiping guangji* 321.10; Lu, *Gu xiaoshuo gouchen*, 411; Wang Guoliang, *Mingxiang ji yanjiu*, 55. Additional texts: *Yiyuan* 6.12 (6.4a–b), also anthologized in *Taiping yulan* 644.3b.

464. Emending *Fayuan zhulin*'s Song 宋 to Zong 宗 in accordance with *Taiping guangji* 321. It must be a different Zong Xie who is mentioned in passing (in *Song shu* 66.1729–1730 and *Nan shi* 24.650) as having held the office of garrison recorder (*fu zhubu* 府主簿), since the Zong Xie discussed in this story is said here to have died in 407 or 408, years before the establishment of the Song dynasty.

419] his form[465] suddenly appeared to call on Xie. His body, face, and clothing were all as they had been when he was alive, but both his feet were in shackles. Upon arriving he removed the shackles and sat down. Xie asked him, "How is it that I am able to see you?" He replied, "I was fortunate to be allowed a temporary return, and since you and I were always close, I came here." Xie asked about various matters regarding ghosts and spirits; Shaozhi answered quite vaguely and was not very forthcoming. He said only: "You should exert yourself in [Buddhist] practice. Do not kill living beings. If you cannot stop entirely, do not, at least, sacrifice bulls, and when eating meat, never eat the hearts of creatures." Xie said, "Between the organs and the flesh, is there really such a difference?" The response was, "The heart is the residence of the spirits of goodness.[466] The sin in that case is especially grave." Shaozhi went on to ask in detail about his relatives; then they discussed the affairs of the day. Shaozhi had not yet asked for any wine. Xie often drank dogwood wine, so he called for some.[467] When the wine arrived, his partner toasted but did not drink, saying that the beverage smelled like dogwood. Xie asked, "Do you dislike it?" Shaozhi replied, "All the lesser officials [of the other world] fear it, not only me."[468] Shaozhi as a person had had a strong, clear speaking voice, and during this dialogue he was no different.

After a while, Xie's son came to summon him away. When Shaozhi heard the approaching footsteps, he suddenly had a frightened look, and he told Xie, "The *qi* of life will be encroached upon! I cannot linger here. We will see each other again in three years!" With that he reattached his shackles, stood, shuffled out the door, and then vanished.

---

465. That is, his *xing* 形, or "bodily form," which I often render in these pages simply as "form." The term is not completely synonymous with *ti* 體, "body"; on the other hand, its usage varied from tradition to tradition, text to text, and context to context, though a fixation on the purportedly univocal "doctrine" of an essentialized "Daoism" might lead one to think otherwise (*pace* Pregadio, "The Notion of 'Form' ").

466. See comments.

467. Here dogwood has been used to flavor the wine; elsewhere we have record of dogwood seeds being used to flavor tea and preserves (see Huang, *Fermentations and Food Science*, 385, 555).

468. Other woods were more commonly reputed to have apotropaic powers to ward off unwelcome spirits—most commonly peachwood, but also mulberry, jujube, cinnamon, and paolownia. All these are mentioned in the third century BCE demonography translated and studied in Harper, "Spellbinding." Mentions of dogwood as a type of wood, seed, or blossom that spirits fear are relatively scarce. Story 9 in *Xu Qi Xie ji* 續齊諧記 (cited in *Taiping yulan* 32.2b–3a, and cf. the modern annotated edition in Wang Guoliang, *Xu Qi Xie ji yanjiu*, 39–40; translated in Campany, *To Live as Long as Heaven and Earth*, 168), however, purports to explain the origins of a custom in which women wore pouches of dogwood at their waists on the ninth day of the ninth month. And *Records of Local Customs* (*Fengtu ji* 風土記), quoted in that same *Taiping yulan* section (32.3b), says that the use of dogwood on this festival day "is said to ward off noxious *qi*" (*yan bi e qi* 言辟惡氣). Other texts quoted in the section credit such use of dogwood (along with the consumption of chrysanthemum-blossom wine) on Double Nine as being conducive to longevity.

Xie afterward won an official appointment. He did indeed die three years later.

Comments

This is the first mention in our text of the "spirits of goodness," or "beneficent spirits" (*shanshen* 善神), and one of the pieces of information this story wants to convey about them—information that may have been news to many readers—is (in addition to the fact that they reside in the heart) that they are present even in animals, not just human beings. Quite a few Buddhist texts translated into or else originally composed in Chinese in the centuries before our text was compiled speak of these "spirits of goodness."[469] Usually they were said to be sent from the heavens to protect those who do good[470] and to abandon those who do evil deeds.[471] In particular, they encircle and protect those who obey the precepts[472] or who, even when sleeping, think on them;[473] the *Sutra of the Four Celestial Kings*[474] imagines five of them per precept encircling and protecting the lay practitioner, for a possible total of twenty-five. Item 71 below again mentions these spirits.

The special prohibition on killing bovines here is significant in light of the "beef taboo" that later became a prominent feature of Chinese Buddhism.[475] This passage is, in fact, one of the earliest extant indications in Chinese literature of the particular gravity attached to killing bovines.

55[476]

During the Jin, the monk Shi Fa'an 釋法安 was a disciple of the Dharma master [Hui]yuan on Mount Lu. In the last year of the Yixi period [418–419], tiger attacks in Yangxin district[477] were extremely numerous. In the district there was a great old tree at an earth-god shrine, beneath which a temple had been built. Several hundred people lived near it, and each night there were one or two fatalities from tiger attacks. Fa'an was once

---

469. For a recent study, see Ikehira, "Butsu Dō ni okeru gokai."

470. As in *Zuochan sanmei jing* 282a–b; *Pusa chutai jing* (as it is known for short) 1058a; *Shizhu duanjie jing* (as it is known for short) 1032b; and *Chu yao jing* 751b.

471. As in *Wuliangshou jing* 276c and *Jinguang ming jing* 343a–b.

472. As in *Yu ye jing* 867a.

473. As in *Shisong lü*, the earliest-translated vinaya text, 130a.

474. *Si tianwang jing* 118b; for more on this sutra, see comments to item 124 below.

475. On which see Goossaert, "The Beef Taboo."

476. Source texts: *Fayuan zhulin* 19.428c–429a (section "honoring the order of monks" [*jing seng* 敬(僧)]); Lu, *Gu xiaoshuo gouchen*, 412; Wang Guoliang, *Mingxiang ji yanjiu*, 56; Wakatsuki, Hasegawa, and Inagaki, *Hōon jurin no sōgō teki kenkyū*, 142–144. Additional texts: *Gaoseng zhuan* 6.362b–c; *Shenseng zhuan* 2.958b; *Fayuan zhulin* 89.945b. Discussed: Lo, "Recovering a Buddhist Voice on Daughters-in-Law," 330–331.

477. Today's Yangxin district, Hubei province. Some versions invert the name to Xinyang district, which was also located in today's Hubei.

traveling through this district. Dusk was approaching, so he headed to this hamlet, but, because of their fear of tigers, the people had long since closed up their gates; furthermore, they did not know Fa'an, so they were not willing to take him in. Passing beneath the tree, Fa'an sat down there to meditate throughout the night. Toward dawn, a tiger arrived, carrying a person in its mouth, passing north of the tree. When it saw Fa'an, it seemed at once happy and startled, and it crouched down before him. Fa'an expounded the Dharma for it and bestowed the precepts on it. The tiger simply lay on the ground without moving; then, after a while, it departed.

At dawn, villagers searching for the victim's remains arrived below the tree. On seeing Fa'an they were stunned. They said he must be a divine person not to have been killed by the tiger. From then on, the tiger attacks subsided. At this the people of the area were even more reverential and awed, and almost the entire district's population, nobles and commoners, began observing the Dharma.

Later, Fa'an wanted to paint a [Buddha] image on a mountain cliff, but he could not find any malachite. He then intended to use verdigris but could find none of it either. One night he dreamed that a person approached his bed and said, "There are two bronze bells here. You may take them." Next morning Fa'an dug at the spot and found them, and thus was able to use them to make [two] images. Later, when Dharma master Huiyuan[478] wanted to make an image, Fa'an donated one of his as a contribution. As for the other, the governor of Wuchang, Xiong Wuhuan 熊無患, once borrowed it so that he might contemplate it, so Fa'an simply left it with him and did not seek its return.[479]

56[480]

During the Jin[481] there lived the monk Zhu Tangai 竺曇蓋, a native of Qin commandery.[482] He was truly a strict practitioner; lifting his alms bowl and shaking his staff, he converted numerous monks, nuns, laymen, and lay-

---

478. I assume this is Lushan Huiyuan, on whom see the comments to item 14.

479. The passage is somewhat confusing, since it opens by clearly saying that Fa'an "wanted to paint an image on a mountain cliff" (*yu huaxiang shanbi* 欲畫像山壁)—a common enough devotional practice, as many extant sites attest—but concludes by speaking of two images that he gave to others. One possible explanation—supported by the wording in the *Shenseng zhuan* version—is that, having retrieved the bells, he decided to cast free-standing bronze images with them instead of painting a two-dimensional image on a cliff face.

480. Source texts: *Fayuan zhulin* 63.764b–c (section "praying for rain" [*qiyu* 祈雨]); Lu, *Gu xiaoshuo gouchen*, 412; Wang Guoliang, *Mingxiang ji yanjiu*, 57. Additional texts: *Gaoseng zhuan* 12.406c. Discussed: Lo, "Recovering a Buddhist Voice on Daughters-in-Law," 331–332; Capitanio, "Dragon Kings and Thunder Gods," 92–93 (Capitanio offers a partial translation of the story, from which mine differs at points); Campany, "Notes on Sutra Texts," 62 n34.

481. *Fayuan zhulin* places him in the Han, but this is clearly impossible given the people and events mentioned in the story, so Wang Guoliang emends the text, as do I.

482. Located in today's Liuhe district, Jiangsu province.

women.[483] He lived on Mount Jiang,[484] where he often practiced *pratyutpan-na.*[485] He especially excelled at the use of divine spells[486] and often obtained responsive manifestations. Sima Yuanxian 司馬元顯 deeply revered and supported him. General of the Guards Liu Yi 劉毅, on hearing of his strict practice, summoned him to Gushu,[487] where he grew very fond of him.[488]

In the fifth year of the Yixi period [409–410][489] there was a great drought. Lakes and streams dried up, and trees and vegetation withered. The people sacrificed repeatedly over many weeks to the [gods of] the mountains and rivers, but there was no [divine] response. Liu Yi then invited monks and sponsored an abstinence ceremony; Tangai was among the invitees. When the abstinence ceremony was concluded, they personally boarded skiffs and floated along on the rivers and streams—civil and martial officials, nobles and commoners, the entire province[490] making a procession. In midstream, Tangai lit incense, made obeisance, and with utmost sincerity and ardor recited the *Sutra of the Oceanic Dragon King* [*Hailong wang jing* 海龍王經].[491] With the first syllable of the recitation, clouds started forming overhead; when he had recited half the sutra, the clouds were gathering from all sides; just as he was finishing reciting the scroll, a torrential rain began pouring down, enough so that the year's harvest was a success.[492] Liu Jingshu 劉敬叔 was serving on the staff of Liu Yi

---

483. The term used is *sibei* 四輩, meaning the four branches of the Buddhist community indicated in the translation.

484. Also known as Mount Zhong, northeast of Nanjing in Jiangsu province.

485. *Banzhou* 般舟. This transliteration of a Sanskrit word meaning "present [time]" is often joined with *sanmei* 三昧 / *samādhi* / "meditation" and sometimes refers to any number of techniques of meditation and/or visualization of Buddhas. One important scripture on such visualizations, translated by 179, was the *Banzhou sanmei jing* 般舟三昧經, on which see Harrison, *The Pratyutpanna Samādhi Sūtra*, and Harrison, "*Buddhānusmṛti.*" Daniel Stevenson (personal communication) is of the view that the term *banzhou* was used at the time specifically to denote practices that were based on this text, which was well-known among fifth-century monastics, and not to denote other forms of "meditation" or visualization more generally.

486. For more on spells, see the note to item 8 above.

487. A city in what is now Dangtu district, Anhui province.

488. Both of these figures are known from the official histories and other documents. Liu Yi, known for a military success against Huan Xuan, is the subject of a biography in *Jin shu* 85.2205–2211; see also Graff, *Medieval Chinese Warfare*, 87. Sima Yuanxian was the son of Sima Daozi; both were dominant figures on the late Eastern Jin political scene until they were executed by Huan Xuan in 402. See Zürcher, *The Buddhist Conquest of China*, 113, 155; Graff, *Medieval Chinese Warfare*, 85–87; and Holcombe, *In the Shadow of the Han*, 32.

489. The text has *yixing* 義興; Lu Xun and Wang Guoliang suggest emending to *yixi* 義熙, and I follow suit.

490. "The entire province" translates *qing zhou* 傾州.

491. See the note on this sutra in item 14 above.

492. This incident is also mentioned in *Gaoseng zhuan* 12.406c, where Tangai is again linked with Sima Yuanxian and in this case also his father, Sima Daozi.

and was personally present at this gathering. He witnessed this event with his own eyes.[493]

Comments

This story's portrayal of the monk Tangai's activities is a good example of how spells (here termed *shenzhou* 神咒) and meditation, two different idioms of action, were wielded—sometimes by the same practitioner—as parallel modes of protection. We see contestation over the power to make rain between sacrifice-based models, ancient and indigenous in China, and the imported technique of sutra recitation. Note the cooperation portrayed here between the monk and the local official in the quest for rain. Note also that the rainmaking event is a communal enterprise, not a monk's solitary endeavor: there is a participating crowd, who are also there to bear witness to the miraculous response. In that crowd is a named individual, Liu Jingshu (mentioned elsewhere in our text), who made his own compilation of anomaly accounts, *Garden of Marvels* (*Yiyuan* 異苑).[494]

57[495]

During the Jin there lived one Xiang Jing 向靖, styled Fengren, a native of Henei. While in Wuxing commandery he buried his young daughter. At the time when she first became ill, she had been playing with a small knife; when the girl's mother tried to take it away, the girl refused to give it up, and the mother's hand was cut. A year after the funeral, the mother again gave birth to a girl. When she was three years old, she asked her mother, "Where is the knife from before?" The mother said, "There is none." The girl said, "Formerly we struggled over the knife, injuring your hand. What do you mean there is none?" The mother was struck with amazement and spoke of it to Jing, who asked, "Do we still have that knife?" The mother answered, "Because I missed our former daughter too much, I don't use it." Jing said, "Find several knives and collect them in one place. We will have our daughter choose one." When the girl saw them she was very pleased. She immediately picked up the knife from before, saying, "This is mine." The parents and everyone else present thus confirmed that their former daughter was the previous rebirth of their current daughter.

---

493. On Liu Jingshu, see the note in item 21 above.

494. On which see Li Jianguo, *Tang qian zhiguai xiaoshuo shi*, 372–381; Wang Guoliang, *Wei Jin nanbeichao zhiguai xiaoshuo yanjiu*, 322–323; Liu Yuanru, *Shenti, xingbie, jieji*, 133–186; and Campany, *Strange Writing*, 78–80, 85, 343–362.

495. Source texts: *Fayuan zhulin* 26.479c–480a (section "[Karmic effects from] past lives" [*su ming* 宿命]); Lu, *Gu xiaoshuo gouchen* 413; Wang Guoliang, *Mingxiang ji yanjiu*, 58; Wakatsuki, Hasegawa, and Inagaki, *Hōon jurin no sōgō teki kenkyū*, 167–169. Additional texts: *Guiyuan zhizhi ji* 2.464a; *Liudao ji* 2.126c.

Comments

It is unusual in rebirth stories to see a child reborn in the same family to the same parents. Above we saw a story (item 3) exploring the implications of a person's rebirth into different families.

58[496]

During the Jin, the monk Senghong 僧洪 resided at Waguan monastery 瓦官寺 in the capital.[497] In the twelfth year of the Yixi period [416–417], there was a government prohibition on founding with metals. Senghong set his mind on casting a fourteen-foot metal image, with the thought: "As long as the image is completed, I will die with no regrets." So he secretly cast it. When the casting was finished and the image was still in the mold, Senghong was arrested and imprisoned in the local garrison under tight locks and fetters. In his mind he concentrated on Guanshiyin, and he recited [the *Guanshiyin Sutra*] one hundred times each day. Later he dreamed that the metal image he had cast came to his prison cell, rubbed his head with its hand, and said, "Do not worry." The image had a small square hole in its chest where the coloration of the bronze showed signs of scorching.

On the day Senghong was to be executed, the government horses and bulls refused to enter the enclosure. People at the time wondered at this. A week later an announcement of amnesty arrived from Pengcheng.[498] So Senghong was released. [He then discovered that] the image had broken out of its mold.

Comments

Wang Yan, in his preface, mentions rampant theft of metal Buddhist images due to the general scarcity of metal. The central government often sought to control the use of metal, a phenomenon central to this story.[499]

---

496. Source texts: *Bianzheng lun* 7.537c; Lu, *Gu xiaoshuo gouchen*, 533–534; Wang Guoliang, *Mingxiang ji yanjiu*, 59. Additional texts: *Xi Guanshiyin yingyanji* 22 (Makita, *Rikuchō kōitsu Kanzeon ōkenki no kenkyū*, 35); *Gaoseng zhuan* 13.410c; *Fahua zhuanji* 5.71c; *Guanyin cilin ji* 2.89c. Discussed: Campany, "Notes on Sutra Texts," 59 n10.

497. Judging from its numerous mentions in *Gaoseng zhuan* (1.324a, 5.354c–355a, 5.355b, 5.357a, 6.363a, 6.365b, etc.), *Fozu tongji*, *Lidai sanbao ji*, and other works, this important temple was located in or near the southern capital. There may, however, have been more than one monastery by this name.

498. The "from" does not appear in *Bianzheng lun* 7, making it seem as if Senghong is imprisoned in Pengcheng, but the versions of the story given in *Xi Guanshiyin yingyan ji*, *Gaoseng zhuan*, and *Fahua zhuanji* all have the imperial pardon arriving *from* Pengcheng, and I follow those readings here.

499. See Gernet, *Buddhism in Chinese Society*, 17–25; at 23–24 he mentions this case of Senghong in passing.

59[500]

Shi Changhe 石長和 lived during the [Later] Zhao period and was a native of Gaoyi in the state of Zhao.[501] When he was nineteen, he fell ill for a period of a month or more and then died. His family being poor, they had not yet acquired the necessary funeral provisions when, four days later, he revived. He said that when he first died, he headed southeast. He saw two people on the road about fifty paces ahead of him. He walked more quickly, but the two persons ahead of him also began walking more quickly, so that he remained fifty paces behind. On either side of the road there was thick underbrush with thorns like falcon talons. He saw huge throngs of people walking through the underbrush, their bodies cut open by the thorns so that the ground flowed with blood. When they saw Changhe walking along on the level road, they sighed and said, "Only disciples of Buddha get to walk on the great road."

Proceeding ahead, he saw several thousand tiled buildings and imposing towers. One building was extremely tall, and near its top was a large man wearing a long-sleeved gown sitting in a window. Changhe bowed to him, and the man in the tower said, "Lord Shi, you have come? We parted over twenty years ago." At that moment Changhe seemed to recall the earlier parting. He had known a horseman named Meng Cheng 孟承 and his wife who had died some years earlier. The man in the tower said, "Did you know Meng Cheng?" Changhe said, "Yes, I knew him." The man said, "When Meng Cheng was alive, he was unable to maintain rigorous practice; now he is a servant who does my cleaning for me. Meng Cheng's wife, on the other hand, practiced rigorously; the place where she resides is delightful." He pointed to a building to the southwest and said, "Meng's wife is there." Meng's wife then opened a window and saw Changhe. She warmly asked how he was doing, then asked by turn about each member of her family. She said, "When you return, Lord Shi, I hope you will go and see them and carry my letter to them." In a few moments Changhe saw Meng Cheng carrying a broom and pail as he passed to the west of the tower. He, too, asked how his family was faring. The man in the tower then said, "I hear that Yu Longchao 魚龍超 is vigorous in his faith. As for you, how do you practice?" Changhe answered, "I do not eat fish or meat, I drink no alcohol, I regularly recite sutras, and I succor those who are sick and in distress." The man said, "Ah, so what was said about you [by others] was not wrong."

---

500. Source texts: *Fayuan zhulin* 7.331c (section "the six paths [of rebirth]" [*liudao* 六 道]); *Taiping guangji* 383.13; Lu, *Gu xiaoshuo gouchen*, 413; Wang Guoliang, *Mingxiang ji yanjiu*, 60; Wakatsuki, Hasegawa, and Inagaki, *Hōon jurin no sōgō teki kenkyū*, 71–74. Additional texts: *Youming lu* 266 (Lu, *Gu xiaoshuo gouchen* 279–280, based on *Bianzheng lun* 7.358b).

501. Gaoyi was a district in what is now northwestern Boxiang district, Hebei province.

The two of them talked for a long time. The man in the tower then said to the official record keeper, "Check what the name register says about Lord Shi, to be sure there was no mistake." The record keeper checked the ledger and said, "He has thirty years of allotted life span remaining." The man in the tower asked, "Do you wish to return, sir, or not?" Changhe replied, "Yes, I would like to return." The man then ordered the record keeper to secure a carriage, horses, and two functionaries to escort Changhe back. Changhe bowed, took his leave, mounted the carriage, and started back. The way that he had taken earlier was now stocked with vessels and provisions used by functionaries and people in transit.[502] Suddenly they reached his home. He disliked the stench of his own corpse and did not want to reattach himself to it.[503] He was standing beside the head of his corpse when a deceased younger sister of his came and pushed him from behind, so that he fell onto his corpse's face, and thus he was able to revive.

The future monk Zhi Fashan 支法山 had at that time not yet left the household. It was because he heard what Changhe recounted that he formed the resolve to enter the path. Fashan lived during the Xianhe period [326–334].

Comments

Among this story's rhetorical argumentative devices is the emphasis on visible karmic effects: the visitor to the unseen realm *has only to look* to discern whose karma warranted favorable afterlife placement and whose did not.

Zhi Fashan is mentioned above (item 22). This is a major example of the dispositional impact of a miracle story: here we have direct testimony to the fact that Fashan became a monk because of hearing Changhe's narrative of his return-from-death experience.

60[504]

During the Zhao 趙 there lived Dan 單 (some sources give Shan 善)[505] Daokai 道開, whose place of origin is unknown. The text recording his story[506]

---

502. The parallel passage in the version attributed by *Bianzheng lun* to *Youming lu* also mentions roadside lodges (*ting* 亭). The idea seems to be that what had earlier been scenes of punishment on either side of the road were now transformed into comfort stations for more fortunate otherworld travelers.

503. *Bu yu fu zhi* 不欲附之. Compare the note on a similar phrase in item 45 above.

504. Source texts: *Fayuan zhulin* 27.485a (section "utmost sincerity" [*zhicheng* 至誠]); Lu, *Gu xiaoshuo gouchen*, 415; Wang Guoliang, *Mingxiang ji yanjiu*, 61; Wakatsuki, Hasegawa, and Inagaki, *Hōon jurin no sōgō teki kenkyū*, 179–182. Additional texts: *Gaoseng zhuan* 10.387b (translated in Soymié, "Biographie de Chan Tao-k'ai"); *Jin shu* 95.2491–2492; *Ji shenzhou sanbao gantong lu* 3.433a.

505. This variant occurs in the original text.

506. Translating *biezhuan* 別傳, meaning a biographical or anecdotal account of an individual. The *Sui shu* bibliographic catalog (33.978) lists a *Daoren Shan Daokai zhuan* 道人善道開傳 in one scroll, by Kang Hong 康泓.

says he was a native of Dunhuang whose original surname was Meng 孟. He left the household as a youth. He wanted to live in poverty and seclusion in the mountains, so he first cut off grains and food. He began by denying himself[507] starches; after three years he subsisted on prepared pine needles; after thirty years he would only swallow a pebble from time to time; once the pebble went down[508] he would abstain from alcohol, meat, and fruits. To ward off colds he ate hot peppers and ginger. His energy and strength were thus vitiated, but his skin was glossy and moist, and he could walk as if flying. The mountain gods tested him several times but never managed to disturb him. Transcendents often came; he could not tolerate their company either, so each time he would chew garlic so as to cause them to withdraw.[509] He sat upright in quiet contemplation, sleeping neither day nor night.

For a long time Daokai dwelled in Gouhan.[510] In the twelfth[511] year of the Jianwu period [346], Shi Hu 石虎[512] invited him to come in to his capital at Ye from Xiping.[513] Daokai did not travel by boat or carriage but instead walked over seven hundred *li* per day. When he was passing through Nan'an,[514] he took on a youth of thirteen or fourteen as a *śrāmaṇera*;[515] he was able to keep up with Daokai's walking speed. Upon arriving [at Ye] they resided in the Zhaode monastery 昭德佛圖.[516] Daokai wore a robe so coarse and threadbare that his back and legs were often visible. Inside his chamber he set up an awning eight or nine feet high and wove thatch on top to make a tent, inside of which he would meditate. He cut off grains [there] for seven years [but] would often [instead] ingest a medicinal com-

---

507. Reading *jin* 禁 for *jin* 進.

508. The verb is *xia* 下, which in this context might perhaps be understood as "once he had passed the stone [through his digestive tract]."

509. See comments.

510. A district in what is now Linxia district, Gansu province.

511. Here following *Gaoseng zhuan*.

512. Shi Hu was a Xiongnu leader who, after killing off the son and heir of his uncle Shi Le 勒 (r. 319–333), succeeded Le as ruler of the Later Zhao regime, a position he retained from 335 until his death in 349. It was during his reign that the Zhao capital was transferred to Ye 鄴 in what is now northern Henan. He availed himself of several Buddhist modes of imperial legitimation. See Gu Zhengmei, *Cong tianwang chuantong dao Fowang chuantong*, 77–98; Mather, *Shih-shuo Hsin-yü*, 563; Lewis, *China Between Empires*, 74–76, 147; Graff, *Medieval Chinese Warfare*, 62, 64; Zürcher, *The Buddhist Conquest of China*, 181–184, 259–260, 265; Dien, *Six Dynasties Civilization*, 301–302; and Li Gang, "State Religious Policy," 214–215.

513. Xiping was a commandery in what is now Xining district, Gansu province. Ye was the capital adopted by Shi Hu, located in what is now Linzhang district, Henan province.

514. A commandery in what is now northeastern Longxi district, Gansu province.

515. A novice, *shami* 沙彌.

516. This monastery is known from other sources (including Daokai's *Gaoseng zhuan* hagiography, which similarly links the monastery to Daokai; *Xu gaoseng zhuan* 7.480b; and *Lushan ji*; cf. *Luoyang qielan ji* 2.1007a, where it is a matter of a village named Zhaode) and was located in or near Ye in Linzhang district, Henan province. Here again *fotu* 佛圖 can only mean a monastery, not (or not only) a stupa.

pound that smelled like pine needles and *fuling* fungus. He was skilled at curing eye diseases, and he would often travel from town to town, [using this skill to] succor the common people. Princes and gentlemen from near and far constantly sent him gifts. He accepted them all and then distributed them to others without the slightest remainder.

Toward the end of Shi Hu's reign, Daokai knew in advance of the coming disorder, so he went south with his disciple to Xuchang. In the third year of the Shengping period [359–360] he reached Jianye, then continued on to Panyu[517] and resided on Mount Luofu. There he lived at ease in seclusion until dying in the seventh month of the same year. He left instructions for his body to be exposed in the forest, and his disciple complied.[518] Yuan Yanbo 袁彥伯[519] of Chen commandery was serving as governor of Nanhai in the first year of the Xingning period [363–364]; he traveled to this peak and climbed it with his younger brother Yingshu 穎叔.[520] They reached and venerated Daokai's skeletal remains, burning incense and paying obeisance.[521]

Comments

Up until the last paragraph's report of Daokai's demise, and excluding the bit about his shunning of transcendents, this story could be taken as an account of a successful transcendence seeker: it has all the necessary earmarks. His use of garlic to ward off transcendents seeking his company is telling: garlic was an herb transcendence seekers were often instructed to avoid, as the shapers of this story obviously knew. So, like some other tales in *Signs from the Unseen Realm*, this one is clearly in contestation with the quest for transcendence. In pointed contrast to the values and goals of that

---

517. A district, still known by the same name, in Guangdong province.

518. The *Gaoseng zhuan* version here speaks more specifically of a cave, whereas *Fayuan zhulin* simply writes "in the forest."

519. This is Yuan Hong 宏 (328–376), remembered mostly for his literary talent; his official biography is grouped under the "literati" section of the *Jin shu* (92.2391–2399). He is not to be confused with the Yuan Hong 元宏 who reigned as Emperor Xiaowen of the Northern Wei dynasty from 471 to 499 (on whose military campaign in an area where Wang Yan was serving at the time see Chittick, *Patronage and Community in Medieval China*, 76–77).

520. Here following *Gaoseng zhuan*; *Fayuan zhulin* gives the younger brother's name simply as Ying 穎.

521. *Taiping yulan* 759.6a–b preserves a passage from a text titled *Luoshan shu* 羅山疏 by Yuan Hong, and the *Gaoseng zhuan* version of this story includes Yuan's encomium on the mountain. The former excerpt further associates Daokai with the lore of transcendence in the following terms: "Shan Daokai's remains were in a stone chamber beneath the north face. His body had decayed away; all that remained were white bones. Formerly I knew this practitioner of the path in the capital. To hear him was to sigh with feeling. His practice was extraordinary. He must have simply slipped out of his bones like a cicada exuviating [*dang chantuo jiegu er* 當蟬蛻解骨耳]. In the cave there was a basin filled with incense. Having reached the place, we swept and cleaned it and burned incense."

quest, it is here the practitioner's skeletal remains in a mountain cave that become a focal point for veneration.

61[522]

During the Qin[523] there lived one Xu Yi 徐義, a native of Gaolu.[524] From his youth he observed the Dharma. He served as imperial secretary under Fu Jian. Near the end of Fu Jian's reign, troops rebelled, captured Yi, and prepared to execute him, burying his feet in the ground and tying him by the hair to a tree. That night, he focused his thoughts completely on Guanshiyin. After a while he fell asleep. He dreamed of a man who said to him, "The situation is extremely urgent. Why are you sleeping?" Yi then woke with a start and saw that the guards were all exhausted and asleep. He tried moving, and, with his hands and hair loosened, he was able to work his feet free as well; thus he fled. A hundred paces away he hid in a small thicket. He could hear his pursuers galloping up and could see many torches. They circled right around the thicket in which he was hiding, but no one ever saw him. At daybreak the rebels dispersed. Yi took refuge in a monastery in Ye and thus escaped the situation.

62[525]

During the Qin there lived one Bi Lan 畢覽, a native of Dongping.[526] In his youth he was observant of the Dharma. He participated in Murong Chui's 慕容垂 [327–397] northern campaign.[527] When his force was defeated by the caitiffs, he fled alone on horseback. Caitiff cavalry gave chase and were closing in on him when he, with utmost mind, chanted the [name or sutra

---

522. Source texts: *Fayuan zhulin* 17.409b (section "honoring Buddhas" [*jing Fo* 敬佛]); *Taiping guangji* 110.14; Lu, *Gu xiaoshuo gouchen*, 415; Wang Guoliang, *Mingxiang ji yanjiu*, 63; Wakatsuki, Hasegawa, and Inagaki, *Hōon jurin no sōgō teki kenkyū*, 92–94. Additional texts: *Xu Guangshiyin yingyanji* 1 (Makita, *Rikuchō kōitsu Kanzeon ōkenki no kenkyū*, 19–20); *Jin shu* 115.2947; *Guanshiyin cilin ji* 2.89b.

523. This could refer to the so-called Former Qin (351–384) founded by Fu Jian, the Later Qin (384–417) founded by Yao Zhang, or the Western Qin (385–431) founded by Qifu Guoren. Given the later reference to Fu Jian, the Former Qin is probably meant.

524. A district near the Zhao capital city of Ye.

525. Source texts: *Fayuan zhulin* 17.409b (section "honoring Buddhas" [*jing Fo* 敬佛]); *Taiping guangji* 110.18; Lu, *Gu xiaoshuo gouchen*, 416; Wang Guoliang, *Mingxiang ji yanjiu*, 62; Wakatsuki, Hasegawa, and Inagaki, *Hōon jurin no sōgō teki kenkyū*, 94–95. Additional texts: *Xi Guanshiyin yingyanji* 56 (Makita, *Rikuchō kōitsu Kanzeon ōkenki no kenkyū*, 50); *Guanshiyin chiyan ji* 1.94c; *Guanyin cilin ji* 2.89b.

526. Located in what is now Dongping district, Shandong province.

527. See *Jin shu* 123, and Graff, *Medieval Chinese Warfare*, 70. This battle took place in December 395.

of] Guanshiyin. He was thus able to escape. He then entered deep into the mountain but lost his way. Again he gave over his thoughts entirely [to Guanshiyin]. That night he saw a monk, dressed in a monastic robe and holding a staff, pointing out a path to him. He thus found his way safely back home.

63[528]

During the Song there lived the monk Facheng 法稱.[529] As he was about to die he said, "The god of Mount Song has told me, 'General Liu in Jiang-dong[530] will receive Heaven's mandate. I have deposited thirty-two discs and one gold ingot as surety.'"[531] When the [future] founder of the Song [Liu Yu] heard of it, he ordered the monk Huiyi 惠義[532] to go to Mount Song. The monk traveled seven days and seven nights, then dreamed of an old man with long hair at the temples[533] who pointed out a location to him. On waking, he realized where the place was, went there, dug in the ground, and found the surety objects.

Comments

This is, in many ways, a typical story of miracles and signs of divine favor told to legitimate the founding of a new dynasty—in this case, the Liu Song (420–479).[534] The only Buddhist element in the tale is the monk. One might therefore be surprised to find the story here. But if it is accurately attributed to *Signs from the Unseen Realm*, it can be read as an instance of contestation, attempting to insert the sangha into this old pattern of dynasty legitimation: the monk here mediates between the mountain god and his legitimacy-conferring palladium, on the one hand, and the would-be ruler, on the other. In this respect it may be compared to item 41 above.

---

528. Source texts: *Taiping guangji* 276.35; Lu, *Gu xiaoshuo gouchen*, 416; Wang Guoliang, *Mingxiang ji yanjiu*, 64. Additional texts: *Song shu* 27.784, 786; *Gaoseng zhuan* 7.368c; *Nan shi* 1.23.

529. *Song shu* and *Gaoseng zhuan* both place him in Jizhou 冀州.

530. I.e., Liu Yu 劉裕, founder of the Song dynasty.

531. "Surety" translates *xin* 信, indicating authenticating seals.

532. The name of the monk differs in the various sources, some of which write the Hui differently and some of which give the monk's name as Fayi 法義. Huiyi and Fayi were both very common Dharma names.

533. Hairstyles deserve a discussion in their own right. See, for example, Harper, "A Chinese Demonography," 475–478; and Dien, *Six Dynasties Civilization*, 312–314, 322. Here, the long hair at the temples seems meant to signify that the figure in question is a local god.

534. On such legitimizing strategies, see Lipiello, *Auspicious Omens and Miracles in Ancient China*; Goodman, *Ts'ao P'i Transcendent*; Wechsler, *Offerings of Jade and Silk*; and Campany, *Strange Writing*, 92–94, 121–124, 309.

64[535]

During the Song there lived Guṇavarman,[536] which in Chinese is Gongde Kai 功德鎧; he hailed from a line of princes of Gandhāra.[537] He left the household while still young and was called the Master of the Three Baskets.[538] At the beginning of the Song he arrived in the Central Kingdom and traveled about, translating numerous sutras.[539] His practice of the monastic rules was spirited and eminent; no one was his peer. The monk Huiguan 慧觀, admiring his character, wanted him to come to the capital and reside at Zhihuan monastery 祇洹寺.[540] Many who came at the time to visit him there suspected he was not an ordinary fellow. He had a mysterious aura of the divine about him, such that none could fathom him. He once accepted an invitation to visit Dinglin monastery 定林寺 on Mount Zhong. On this occasion, monks and laypersons picked a mass of flowers and scattered them on the mats of monks as a test to see which ones were spiritual achievers.[541] The flowers wilted before all the monks but one: those before Guṇavarman remained as fresh as when they had been picked. After this everyone in the capital revered him even more.

Guṇavarman died on the eighteenth day of the ninth month of the eighth year of the Yuanjia period [8 November 431]. He had shown no sign of prior illness. He just sat down with his legs crossed, gathered in his robe, joined his palms together, and remained thus through the night; the expression on his face never changed. Some at the time said he must be in deep meditation. Then they found a note he had left under his mat, saying

---

535. Source texts: *Fayuan zhulin* 42.616c–617a (section "[monks] receiving invitations [from laity]" [*shouqing* 受請]); Lu, *Gu xiaoshuo gouchen*, 416; Wang Guoliang, *Mingxiang ji yanjiu*, 65. Additional texts: *Chu sanzang jiji* 14.104b; *Gaoseng zhuan* 3.340a (translated in Robert Shih, *Biographies des moines éminents*, 125–137); *Ji shenzhou sanbao gantong lu* 3.433c; *Shenseng zhuan* 3.963a–b. Discussed: Campany, "Notes on Sutra Texts," 62 n35.

536. Transliterated here as Qiunabamo 仇那跋摩, elsewhere often with the first syllable rendered as *qiu* 求.

537. The toponym Jibin 罽賓 was at the time mostly used to designate a region that included much of Gandhāra and adjacent areas of northwest India, not just Kashmir. See Kuwayama, "Pilgrimage Route Changes," 107–113; Boucher, *Bodhisattvas of the Forest*, 207 n37; and Nattier, "Zhu Fonian's *Shizhu duanjie jing*," 232 n5.

538. That is, the three categories of Buddhist scriptures: sutras, vinayas, and polemical and theoretical and other writings (*śāstras*).

539. *Chu sanzang jiji* 14.104b credits him with translations of several sutras, all having to do with monastic regulations.

540. This monastery is mentioned repeatedly in *Gaoseng zhuan* (e.g., at 3.340, 342, 344; 7.368c [on its founding], 369b; 8.379a; 13.414a, 415c). *Gaoseng zhuan* 14.419c likewise connects Qiunabamo with it. See also *Biqiuni zhuan* 2.938a; *Shenseng zhuan* 3.964c; and *Hongming ji* 12.78a.

541. Translating *yan qiu zhenren* 驗求真人. This same motif appears above in item 17.

he had attained the second fruit of a *śramaṇa*.[542] From this they realized he had expired. Disciples watching over him detected a whiff of fragrant smoke in the air. Over two hundred persons in the capital attended his funeral. During that occasion, scriptures were being chanted during the night, and a crowd was gathered on the steps outside the doors to listen. Just before dawn, a creature resembling a dragon descended from a cloud in the southwestern sky, wrapped itself around the corpse, and then flew off. All who were present saw it.

Before Guṇavarman died, he composed thirty *gāthas*[543] and consigned these to his disciples, saying, "You should show these to a monk from India."

65[544]

During the Song there lived one Chen Anju 陳安居, a native of Xiangyang.[545] His paternal uncle when young followed the customs of spirit-mediums.[546] Drumming, dancing, sacrifices, images of gods, and shrine spaces filled his residence. His father alone venerated and believed in the Dharma of Śākya[muni], observing the abstinence regulations each day and night. Later, his uncle died without any sons, so Anju's father arranged for him to be adopted into his brother's line.[547] Although Anju thus went to live in his uncle's family's home, he kept to his strict [Buddhist] practice, rejecting and not participating in the family's impure sacrifices. After this he suddenly fell ill. He sometimes lost his senses and began performing[548] songs for the gods; he became befuddled and lapsed into error. This went on for several years. But in his mind he managed to remain steadfast. He often vowed: "If I lose my determination not to take life, then may I have my own four limbs cut off to experience the same thing [that sacrificial victims do]."[549] Family members remonstrated with him, but Anju paid them no mind.

---

542. That is, on the path to arhatship he was claimed to have reached the second stage, or "fruit" (here *er guo* 二果; more commonly *er dao guo* 二道果), that of "once-returner," after which point he would be reborn only once more. See Gethin, *The Foundations of Buddhism*, 194; Buswell and Gimello, introduction to *Paths to Liberation*, 8. Cf. items 101 and 124 below.

543. *Sanshi jie* 三十偈. The verses are implied to have been written in an Indic script.

544. Source texts: *Fayuan zhulin* 62.756c–757c (section "offerings" [*jici* 祭祠]); Lu, *Gu xiaoshuo gouchen*, 417; Wang Guoliang, *Mingxiang ji yanjiu*, 66. Additional texts: *Fayuan zhulin*, as cited in *Taiping guangji* 113.9. This *Taiping guangji* version contains some significant variations from the *Fayuan zhulin* text, and in the translation I point out most of them.

545. What was then—and is still—known as Xiangyang district is located in Hubei province, at the confluence of the Mian/Han and Tang/Bai rivers.

546. Translating *shi wusu* 事巫俗 (the wording given in both versions).

547. This was—and in some Chinese contexts still is—a common practice.

548. Or perhaps composing, depending on how one understands *wei* 為 here. The phrase (in both versions) is *er fa ze wei ge shen zhi qu* 而發則為歌神之曲.

549. Here following the wording of the *Taiping guangji* version, which is a bit less laconic and therefore clearer.

Two years later, in the first year of the Yongchu period [420–421],[550] his illness worsened, and he died. However, a place beneath his heart remained faintly warm, so the family did not prepare his body for burial. On the night of the seventh day, those who were watching over his corpse felt something like a wind come up from between his feet and cause his garments to rustle. At this he revived and made sounds. At first his family members thought it was a corpse zombie,[551] and so they all fled; but later he could move a bit and asked for juice. His family was then delighted. They asked, "Where did you return from?" Anju then told of all he had seen and experienced.

He said that at first several dozen men resembling envoys and wielding swords summoned him away.[552] The followers in the party wanted to tie him up, but the chief messenger said, "This man has fortune. You may not bind him." After they had traveled over three hundred *li*, they came to a walled city with a vast array of towers and buildings. The messenger took him into one of the headquarters.[553] It resembled a government office. At the back was a man who gave Anju a brush and a sheet of paper and said, "You should enter your name on the death [registers] twenty-four times."[554] Anju did as instructed, entering his name the indicated number of times. An official then emerged from within and called out in a loud voice, "Anju may enter!"

He went in and was told he would be subjected to a probe into his wickedness. There were two jailers. One said, "Apply the large shackles." The other said, "This man has accumulated some fortune. We should use only

---

550. The *Taiping guangji* version places this at three years later but omits mention of a date.

551. Translating *shijue* 屍蹶, apparently a variant of *shijue* 尸蹶, a term, attested as early as *Shi ji* 史記 and Liu Xiang's *Shuoyuan* 說苑, for a comalike state in which a person is as if dead or unconscious yet still living. See *Hanyu dacidian* 4.4a.

552. The *Taiping guangji* version does not mention weapons here.

553. Here preferring the *Taiping guangji* phrasing.

554. The line in both *Fayuan zhulin* and *Taiping guangji* reads: *ke shu ershisi tong siming* 可 疏二十四通死名. I know of no reference to new inductees into the afterlife making entries in multiple copies of ledgers. The number twenty-four can only be explained, I think, if we understand there to be twenty-four distinct zones or levels of purgatory envisioned in this story, with the new arrival required to register in all of them. I know of no system of twenty-four *diyu* in Buddhist texts in China, but such an enumeration appears in several Daoist texts from the early medieval period (as well as many more texts, particularly ritual compendia, from the Song, Yuan, and later periods). See, for example, *Taishang cibei jiuyou bazui chan* 8.9a (a text dated in to the Tang in Schipper and Verellen, *The Taoist Canon*, 567–568, but without any rationale provided for this dating); *Taishang dongshen dongyuan shenzhou zhibing kouzhang* 7a–b (dated to the Six Dynasties period in Schipper and Verellen, *The Taoist Canon*, 272–273); and *Sandong zhunang* 7.16b–22a (on this text, compiled ca. 680 from earlier materials, see Schipper and Verellen, *The Taoist Canon*, 440–441, and Campany, *To Live as Long as Heaven and Earth*, 378). See also Sawada, *Jigoku hen*, 18–19, and Xiao Dengfu, *Han Wei liuchao Fo*, 589–590, 596, 603. I am grateful to Terry Kleeman and Chang Chaojan for their suggestions regarding this passage.

the three-foot shackles." They debated back and forth and could come to no decision, so they inspected the records together. After a long while, the three-foot shackles were applied.

After a short time, Anju saw a nobleman followed by several dozen attendants, his form and face quite elegant. The man asked him, "How did you come to be here?" Anju told him in detail. The nobleman then said, "Your uncle is the one who sinned. It should have been only he who was arrested and processed here. Because he had earlier planted some small degree of merit, he has been granted a temporary bit of time at large. And yet he has dared to file a plaint?[555] Your father and I have known each other since we were young. Seeing you brings back memories.[556] Come and follow me on a tour of the place." The jailer was unwilling to release Anju's shackles, saying, "The magistrate gave no such order. I do not dare act on my own." The nobleman said, "He'll be under my care. I won't let him run away and escape." With that, the jailer freed him.

The nobleman then took Anju through all the various earth prisons, and they looked upon the many kinds of punishment, which roughly matched the descriptions given in scriptures.[557] They had not yet made a complete round when someone arrived with a summons: "The magistrate summons Anju!" Anju was terrified and begged the nobleman to save him, but the latter replied, "You yourself are without sin. Just answer truthfully, and you will have nothing to worry about."

Anju arrived at a chamber and saw several hundred people in fetters moving forward at once. Anju ended up third in line. When they reached the bottom step, a man wearing an official's cap stood before each prisoner and read aloud a ledger[558] of his or her sins. In the case of the first prisoner the man said that, when the prisoner was first married, he and his wife both swore an oath that, whether they had a son or not, they would never leave each other. But the man had been a libationer,[559] and his wife, too, had been an upholder of the Dao. Together they had converted and led many followers and taken male and female disciples[560] and corrupted them.[561] Then he had abandoned his first wife, and she had repeatedly filed plaints

---

555. *Gaosu* 告訴. The clear implication is that the uncle had filed an official complaint against Anju, causing his illness and eventual death. See comments below and part 1 above.

556. The line literally reads *jian ru yiran* 見汝依然, "seeing you, it is as before."

557. *Lue yu jingwen xiang fu* 略與經文相符 (in both versions). See comments.

558. "Ledger" here translates both versions' *bu* 簿.

559. Libationers (*jijiu* 祭酒) were ordained officers of local communities of the Celestial Master Daoist religion. See Stein, "Remarques sur les mouvements du taoïsme," 42–59; Kleeman, *Great Perfection*, 69–70, 72; and Bokenkamp, *Early Daoist Scriptures*, 36, 67 n15, 217.

560. *Taiping guangji* has "they obtained a female disciple and corrupted her."

561. The charge of licentiousness was so frequently lodged by pro-Buddhist writers against Daoist communities that it became a standard polemical trope. For an example, see *Guang hongming ji* 10.152a–b (citing the polemical treatise *Xiaodao lun* 笑道論, or *In Mockery of the Dao*, completed by Zhen Luan 甄鸞 in 570) and the translation in Kohn, *Laughing at the Tao*, 147–149.

alleging injustice. The magistrate then said, "Your having broken the oath of husband and wife is not the sin of both of you; it is the sin of only one of you. The position of teacher is one of the three key social roles,[562] and to have corrupted it is no different than a father defiling his son. You are hereby remanded to the Department of Law for full punishment!"

Next the man in the cap read the register[563] of the second person in line, a woman whose name Anju had forgotten. He said her home had been in Huangshui hamlet, Guanjun district, in Nanyang.[564] In her home the stove was situated at the kitchen doorway, and once when the woman fell asleep there, a child crawled up onto the stove and defecated and urinated into it.[565] When this woman woke up she begged the gods' forgiveness and washed the area clean. But her father-in-law cursed her, saying, "There must be no righteous gods and spirits[566] if this woman is allowed to perpetrate this impurity." When the Director of Allotted Life Spans[567] heard of the affair, he had her arrested and brought in. The magistrate said, "To fall asleep at the stove is not a misdeed. The child had no knowledge [and is therefore inculpable]. And she has already asked forgiveness of the gods, so there is no sin here. But the father-in-law's curse, saying there is no righteousness, is an act of slander against the spirit world. Arrest him and bring him in." In a little while the man arrived in the custody of red-clad officers.[568]

---

562. Lord, father, teacher.

563. "Register" here translates *cidie* 辭牒.

564. This district was located in what is now Deng district, Henan province.

565. Unsatisfyingly rendering *jia an cuanqi yu fuzao kou* 家安爨器於福竈口. (The phrase is the same in *Taiping guangji*, except that the word *fu* 福 does not appear.) The passage implies a distinction between the *cuanqi* 爨器 and the *zao* 竈 (further speaking of a "mouth" or "opening" of the "fortunate stove," or *fuzao kou* 福竈口, apparently a *hapax legomenon*), but I am unclear on the specific referents of these terms at the time. The latter term might perhaps designate an image of the stove god placed near the working stove. Dien, *Six Dynasties Civilization*, 307–309, discusses the design of household stoves in the period but offers no specifics that would help in sorting out this passage.

566. Literally, "no gods and spirits on the path of Heaven" or something similar. The sense of *tiandao guishen* 天道鬼神 here is difficult to capture in translation.

567. This important deity, Siming 司命 (a title, not a name), inspector and enforcer of people's life spans, was associated with the stove because he was reckoned to periodically receive reports on people in each household from the god of the stove. To create ritual impurity at the stove was to do something highly inauspicious. See Schafer, "The Stove God and the Alchemists"; Chard, "Rituals and Scriptures of the Stove Cult"; Chard, "The Stove God"; Campany, "Living Off the Books"; Campany, *To Live as Long as Heaven and Earth*, 47–60; and Harper, "Contracts with the Spirit World," 235 n22. The stove god had been the recipient of sacrifice since at least the late Warring States period; see *Fengsu tongyi jiaozhu* 8.

568. The term *chiguan* 赤官, which I here render as "red-clad officers," occurs only very seldom in pre-Tang texts. During the Tang and Song it sometimes referred to imperial-level officials. At *Song shu* 36.1080 it apparently designates a class of district-level officers. It is used (as here and elsewhere in this text—including the next item) in some Daoist texts for celestial officers of many types, but to the best of my knowledge all such usages fall later than this text, and most date from the Song or later.

Then it was Anju's turn. The man at the foot of the stairs read all the names and writs, setting forth the plaint filed by his uncle and so forth.[569] The magistrate said, "This man serves the Buddha. He is a man of great virtue! His uncle slaughtered innocents and misled the common people. The sin should rightfully be placed with him. But because he had earlier amassed a small quantity of merit, his [recent] sins have not yet been accounted for,[570] and yet now he has lodged this plaint against someone who is innocent?" He ordered the uncle's immediate arrest. Before he had been brought in, the magistrate sent Anju back, saying, "You may return. If you amass sufficient karmic merit, you will live to be ninety-three. Be as diligent as you can, so that you do not have to return here!"

When Anju left the chamber, an officer told him, "You may remove your name from among those who have died." Once Anju had erased his name [in each ledger] by turns, he wanted to return to where the nobleman had been, but the latter then arrived and told him, "I learned that you have no other reason to be here and may return. Excellent! Cultivate virtue with utter diligence! My own merit was only slight, so I was unable to be reborn in the heavens as my recompense but instead am assigned here to assist the magistrate. Still, my duties are slight and enjoyable. Such is the perfection of the way of spirits. My family home is in Wan,[571] and my family name is such and such, and my given name such and such. When you go back, please pass along for me this message: Observe the Dharma to the utmost degree, and do not transgress the Buddhist prohibitions! And tell them everything that you saw and heard here." He thereupon dispatched three guards to escort Anju back.

As soon as they had passed through the gate and gone several steps, a messenger handed Anju a talisman[572] and told him, "Hold on to this talisman. If you pass through any border checkpoints, show them this and do not try to sneak through. If you sneak through, punishment will follow. If you find your way blocked by water, throw this talisman into the water, and you will be able to cross."

Anju took the talisman and headed home. After going a long distance he found his way blocked by a great river; he had no way to cross it. Following the instructions he had been given, he threw the talisman. When he did so, the terrain before him mysteriously turned out to be the courtyard

---

569. *Fayuan zhulin* has *mingdie* 名牒, "names and writs," where *Taiping guangji* has *mingdie* 明牒, "bright writs." At the end of this sentence *Fayuan zhulin* has *yun yun* 云云, "and so forth," while *Taiping guangji* lacks these two graphs.

570. Following the variant reading in *Fayuan zhulin* (which corresponds to the wording in *Taiping guangji*).

571. A district located in what is now Nanyang district, Henan province.

572. *Fu* 符. On the nature and functions of these efficacious objects, see Strickmann, *Mantras et mandarins*; Strickmann, *Chinese Poetry and Prophecy*, 94, 97; Strickmann, *Chinese Magical Medicine*; Mollier, "Talismans"; Hsieh, "Writing from Heaven"; Robson, "Signs of Power"; and Campany, *To Live as Long as Heaven and Earth*, 61–69.

of his family home. Just then he could hear the sounds of weeping and wailing issuing from within the house. The three escorts urged him to return to his former body, but when Anju smelled the stench of decay that had already set in, he said, "I cannot go back in any longer." The escorts then pushed him forward, and he fell on the feet of the corpse.

Anju soon recovered. Wishing to verify[573] the case of the woman from Huangshui hamlet, he went to Guanjun district, made inquiries, and found that there was indeed such a woman. When they saw each other, it was just as before, and it seemed as if they were old acquaintances. She said, "I died and was able to return to life. My father-in-law died on the same day." When she told of what he had heard and seen, it matched exactly what Anju had said.

Anju then received the five precepts from a teacher with the Dharma name Senghao 僧昊, a native of Xiangyang who late in his life lived in Changsha. He had originally lived in the same hamlet as Anju and heard his story from Anju's own lips. He was also personally present when Anju died. Anju did indeed live to be ninety-three.

Comments

In this complex story we see not one, or even two, but four vectors of contestation. First, a stark opposition is established between Buddhist abstinences and the ritual service of local gods. Sacrifice is, as we have seen elsewhere in our text, the key issue: upholding Buddhism, even for laity, meant abandoning animal sacrifice. Being Buddhist was in this sense deeply countercultural. Second, there is a critique here of the culture of afterlife "plaints," similar to the critique elsewhere in our text of "replacements": both are opposed by the teaching of karma. Third, in the substory about the libationer and his wife, we see another critique of Celestial Master Daoism; in the afterlife, this story argues, it becomes very clear that Buddhism is a superior path and that Celestial Master adherents are misguided. And fourth, in the substory about the woman, the child, and the stove, we seem to have a critique (again not without parallel instances elsewhere in our text) of indigenous notions of ritual impurity.[574] In response to these notions, instruction is here offered in the principles of the Buddhist system, and those principles are karmic: things like knowledge, understanding, and intent come into play in the deliberations over right and wrong, sin and merit—not prohibitions against activities deemed automatically impurifying of the stove area[575] regardless of intent. This story takes its place alongside many others weighing in from all sides of the debates

---

573. See comments.

574. Compare item 35 above. On partially analogous narratives in medieval Japan, see Stone, "Do *Kami* Ever Overlook Pollution?"

575. On which see in particular Chard, "Rituals and Scriptures of the Stove Cult," 6, 39–41.

sparked by the differences between certain aspects of the Buddhist repertoire and certain aspects of other modes of religious culture in China.

Again we see in this story a statement to the effect that the content of a
protagonist's visionary experience matches Buddhist scriptures. Such passages testify to a persistent concern to show that visions undergone by people in China confirmed what the imported sutras said, just as, on the other
hand, sutras legitimized what would otherwise have been merely personal
and idiosyncratic visions.

The protagonist, having returned from the unseen world, "verifies"
(*yan* 驗) what he saw there by looking up the woman in the distant hamlet.
Such verification, in several senses and in several directions, is central to
Signs from the Unseen Realm and other texts like it.

66⁵⁷⁶

During the Song there lived the monk Senggui 僧規, who resided at a monastery in Wudang.⁵⁷⁷ At the time Zhang Yu 張瑜, a native of the capital, was
living in the district and often invited Senggui to his home to receive offered meals. On the fifth day of the twelfth month of Yongchu 1 [24 January 421], Senggui suddenly died without any signs of prior illness. Two days
later he revived and gave the following account.

During the second watch of the night of the fifth day, he heard an argument in the lane outside.⁵⁷⁸ In a moment he saw five men with torches
and banners come into his room and scold him. Terrified, he dropped to
the floor. They tied him up with red cords and led him away. They proceeded to a mountain that was devoid of vegetation and covered in black
soil like iron. Around the sides of the mountain white bones were piled.
Several dozen *li* further on they came to an intersection. There was an
enormous man there, wearing armor and brandishing a staff, who asked
the five men, "How many are coming?" They answered, "Only one." They
took Senggui onto one of the roads, and after a while they reached a city
wall. Within were several dozen tiled buildings. In front of the buildings
was a tree over a hundred feet tall. At its top were iron branches shaped
like a water-drawing mechanism.⁵⁷⁹ Around the tree were variously sized
containers holding different quantities of soil. There was a man wearing a

---

576. Source texts: *Fayuan zhulin* 83.900b–901a (section "the six perfections" [*liudu* 六
度]); *Shimen zijing lu* 1.810c; Lu, *Gu xiaoshuo gouchen*, 420; Wang Guoliang, *Mingxiang ji yanjiu*, 67. Additional relevant source: *Liudao ji* 4.161a.

577. Wudang was a district located in what is now Jun district, Hubei province.

578. This overheard argument is unusual in stories of this type. Normally, functionaries of the earth prisons simply show up and take the protagonist away—an act with sinister
overtones, resembling an arrest by unwelcome government agents.

579. The Chinese is *jiegao* 桔槔. There is no common English word for this device, a
mechanism for drawing water from a well; "shadoof," of Arabic origin, is a rarely used English term for it.

crimson robe and turban[580] who asked Senggui, "When you were alive in the world, what sins and meritorious acts did you amass? Answer truthfully and do not speak falsely." Senggui was terrified and did not yet make any reply. The crimson-robed man told another person who resembled a sub-official functionary, "Open the ledgers and look up his sins and merits." In a moment the functionary went to the tall tree and lifted a container of soil and hung it on the iron branch as if weighing it. The functionary said to Senggui, "This measures the balance of sin and merit. Your merit is slight and your sin great. You must first undergo punishment." Shortly there came another man in a long robe and cap who said to Senggui, "You are a monk. Why do you not think on the Buddha? I have heard that confessing one's sins can save one even from the eight difficult conditions."[581] At this Senggui with a unified mind called on the Buddha. The man in the cap and gown told the functionary, "You can weigh this man's [sin and merit] again. Since he is a disciple of Buddha, he can be freed." The functionary again hung up the container of soil, and this time it was perfectly balanced.[582]

Senggui was taken next before an inspector to be evaluated. The inspector looked over his ledger while holding a brush, lingering over it a long time. There was another person in a crimson robe and black hat,[583] wearing insignia of office and holding a jade tablet, who arrived and said, "The ledger of life span counts does not yet have this man's name entered into it." The overseer looked startled and gave orders to his attendants to go and arrest so-and-so. After a while, Senggui watched as the five men who had tied him up came in and the overseer said to them, "Killer demons,[584] why did you bring the wrong person in?" Then he whipped them.

---

580. *Yi ze bing chi* 衣幘並赤. On the sense of *ze* (here rendered "turban" but perhaps short for *pingshangze* 平上幘, a sort of tight-fitting pillbox cap), see the note to item 44 above. Note again the mention here of an afterlife official clothed in red. Elsewhere in this period we similarly see stories of tours of the afterlife in which the officials of the baleful realm are described as wearing "a crimson robe and a pillbox cap" (*zhuyi pingshangze* 朱衣平上幘), as, for example, in *Yiyuan* 5.20.

581. *Banan* 八難, the eight conditions in which it is difficult to see a Buddha or hear his teaching. One common list of these runs as follows: in the purgatories; as a hungry ghost; as an animal; in Uttarakuru (the northern continent where life is pleasant, on which see Collins, *Nirvana and Other Buddhist Felicities*, 319–324 [who notes that throughout Pali literature Uttarakuru is "the standard of comparison for wealthy cities everywhere," 320], and Kloetzli, *Buddhist Cosmology*, 25–26, 58); in the long-life heavens (where life is pleasant and long); as deaf, blind, and dumb; as a philosopher (!); and in a world-era between one Buddha and his successor. See Mochizuki, *Bukkyō daijiten*, 4221c–4222b.

582. This scene may be the earliest datable detailed depiction of a system for measuring karma by means of tree branches that act as scales. In later texts, however, it seems to be only clothes that, representing karma, are weighed in the balance, not buckets of soil. See Seidel, "Datsueba," and Teiser, *The Scripture on the Ten Kings*, 33.

583. Note that an afterlife official is here again described as wearing red garments.

584. "Killer demons" translates *shagui* 殺鬼, one of many terms for lower orders of malevolent spirit-beings.

Shortly thereafter a messenger said, "The Celestial Thearch has summoned the monk." He then arrived at the palace of the thearch. He passed through many halls decorated in gold and jewels so bright that he was unable to fix his gaze on them for long. The thearch's attendants were clad in crimson robes and jeweled caps and wore many fine ornaments. The thearch said, "You are a monk. Why did you not carefully maintain discipline, so that you allowed yourself to be wrongly apprehended by such petty killer demons?" Senggui bowed his head toward all the Buddhas, praying for favor and asking for their blessing. The thearch spoke again: "Your allotted life span is not yet exhausted. You will now be sent back. You should take care to practice with vigor. Do not loiter in the homes of laypersons! When the killer demons seize people, they often take the wrong one, as happened in your case."[585] Senggui said, "How may the danger of mistaken seizure best be avoided?" The thearch answered, "To broadly establish meritorious practices[586] is best. If you cannot manage this, the next best measure is to observe the eightfold abstinence. [By doing so] you will avoid mistakenly applied misfortune[587] while you are still alive, and you avoid the purgatories [earth prisons] after you die."

When he had finished speaking he sent Senggui away. He had not traveled far on the return route when he saw an oratory full of a large number of monks. He saw among them Dharma Master Bai 白法師, the [former?] abbot of the monastery at Wudang, as well as his disciple Huijin 慧進.[588] The living quarters were spacious and well ordered. Senggui requested to take up residence there, but a monk replied, "This is a domain of the fortunate;[589] it is not a place for which you are qualified." The messenger took Senggui back to Yu's home and then departed.

---

585. A significant remark for two reasons: it suggests that monks and nuns were sometimes prone to linger unwarrantedly in the homes of their well-to-do lay hosts, enjoying the hospitality and conversation, and it provides a rationale for avoiding this practice: the lifespan-limit-enforcing spirits of the unseen world were more likely to snatch people from such environments than (presumably) from monasteries.

586. Or more literally "practices leading to fortune," *fu ye* 福業.

587. *Henghuo* 橫禍, clearly referring here to unwarrantedly early death, an expression similar to (but less specific than) *wangsi* 枉死. The synonymous term *hengsi* 橫死 occurs elsewhere in our text.

588. A monk by this name is the subject of item 126 below, but they appear to be different persons. I add "former" in the text because it remains unclear (at least to me) whether we are to understand that the figures glimpsed here are once-living, now-deceased monks or are, on the other hand, living figures who are here also appearing as spirit-monks of the sort mentioned in many other stories.

589. "Domain of the fortunate" translates *fudi* 福地—from the context clearly meaning an afterlife area reserved for those with fortune to their credit, similar to the "lodges of the fortunate" and "halls of the fortunate" seen above. In some sorts of texts—such as those narrating the life of Gautama Buddha—this phrase is often used for places where Siddhartha meditates or preaches (or cultic sites where he is said to have meditated or preached in the past); in others—such as hagiographies and histories—it sometimes refers to monasteries.

Comments

Like some other stories in our text, this one seems designed in part as a critique of monks' lax observance of precepts.

67[590]

He Danzhi 何澹之,[591] a native of Donghai,[592] served as chamberlain of the National Treasury under the Song dynasty. He did not believe in the sutras or Dharma and often performed harmful acts. During the Yongchu period [420–423] he fell ill. He saw a demon, its form very tall and strong, with a bull's head and a human body, grasping an iron pitchfork in its hands, standing watch over him day and night. Worried and fearful, he commissioned a Daoist to make petitions, talismans, seals, and registers for him, but when they had all been prepared and submitted, he still saw the demon just as before.[593] A monk with whom he was acquainted, Huiyi 慧義,[594] heard of his illness and went to call on him. When Danzhi told him of what he saw, Huiyi replied, "This is Bull-Head Apang.[595] Punishment and fortune are not murky matters; people simply summon them themselves. If you can turn your mind toward Dharma, this demon will vanish." But Danzhi was deeply deluded and incorrigible. Soon thereafter he died.

Comments

Here the protagonist summons a Daoist priest (termed *daojia* 道家) to expel a demon in the ways standardly deployed by such specialists: "petitions, talismans, seals, and registers." These means will not work, the story insists (in another clear instance of interreligious contestation), because the demonic haunting is due to the protagonist's own karma. Having been

---

590. Source texts: *Fayuan zhulin* 83.901a4ff. (section "the six perfections" [*liudu* 六度]); Lu, *Gu xiaoshuo gouchen* 421; Wang Guoliang, *Mingxiang ji yanjiu*, 68. Additional texts: *Liudao ji* 3.140c.

591. An apparently different figure by this same name who lived during the Jin is mentioned in the preface to the *Wuliang yi jing* 無量義經 collected in *Chu sanzang jiji* (9.68b1–2), as well as in *Fahua zhuanji* 2.54c.

592. A commandery located in what is now Shandong province.

593. These are all standard Daoist responses to such situations. Put briefly, all of these ritual documents and gestures were designed to invoke the assistance of the appropriate higher divine authorities in quelling the demonic disturbance while at the same time reminding the demonic powers that they lacked divine authorization for their attack. On petitions (*zhang* 章), see most recently Verellen, "The Heavenly Master Liturgical Agenda."

594. He is the subject of a hagiography in the section on commentators and expounders of sutras (*yijie* 義解) in *Gaoseng zhuan* 7.368c–369a.

595. *Niutou Apang* 牛頭阿旁. A fixture of visual representations of the Buddhist purgatories, this fearsome creature is mentioned in a scripture anthologized in the late-sixth-century compendium *Jinglü yixiang* (50.268a) as installed in the fifty-second of sixty-four purgatories for the purpose of causing terrible fear in the beings reborn there—their karmic recompense for having frightened others while they lived in human form.

granted this warning sign, the benighted protagonist nonetheless fails to reform. His story in turn becomes a warning for readers of the text.

68[596]

During the Song, the monk Zhu Huichi 竺慧熾, a native of Xinye,[597] resided in the Four-Story monastery in Jiangling.[598] In Yongchu 2 [421–422 C.E.] he died. His disciples held a seven-day gathering[599] for him. On the first day, at dusk, just after the incense had been lit, the monk Daoxian 道賢 went to look in on Huichi's disciples. When he arrived at the door to the chamber, he suddenly saw something dimly resembling a human form. Looking more closely, he saw that it was Huichi. His visage and clothing were no different than when he was alive. Huichi said to Daoxian, "Was the meat you ate for your morning meal delicious?" Daoxian replied, "Yes, it was." Huichi said, "I too am guilty of having eaten meat. Now I have been reborn in the earth prison of hungry dogs."[600] Daoxian was speechless with fright. Before he could reply, Huichi spoke again: "If you do not believe me, have a look at my back." Then he turned around and showed Daoxian his back. Daoxian saw three yellow dogs, [the back] half of whose bodies resembled donkeys. Their eyes glowed a fierce red, illuminating the room.

---

596. Source texts: *Fayuan zhulin* 94.978b23ff. (section "wine and meat" [*jiu rou* 酒肉]); Lu, *Gu xiaoshuo gouchen* 421; Wang Guoliang, *Minxiang ji yanjiu*, 69. Additional texts: *Shimen zijing lu* 2.814a; *Yiyuan* 異苑 5.32 (5.9a–b, also anthologized in *Taiping guangji* 324.2).

597. A commandery located in present-day Xinye county, Henan province.

598. Jiangling was the seat of a commandery located in what is now Jiangling county, Hubei province. I have no further information on the monastery by this name.

599. One meaning of the phrase "seven-day gathering" (*qiri hui* 七日會) that fits this context is a Buddhist funerary observance, attested in Chinese sources from at least as early as the fifth century, involving seven gatherings of monks, nuns, and laypersons, held every seven days, who would observe extra precepts, recite sutras, and engage in other meritorious activities on behalf of the deceased while praying for his or her welfare. The forty-nine-day schedule corresponded to the length of time often reckoned to pass between a being's death and its rebirth. See Teiser, *The Scripture on the Ten Kings*, 24–25, and Mollier, *Buddhism and Taoism Face to Face*, 69; on the larger range of meanings (including this funerary one) see Mochizuki, *Bukkyō daijiten*, 2503a–c. Abstinence ceremonies were often performed as part of or in conjunction with the funerary rites, the merit from them converted into fortune for the deceased, and when *zhai* were so performed they were often termed *yingzhai* 營齋; cf., for example, the passage in the Song-period *Shishi yaolan*, 305b–c.

600. By some reckonings, this was the thirty-fifth in a series of sixty-four hells, each specializing in punishment for a class of sins. *Jinglü yixiang* (267c) quotes a passage from the *Sutra of Questions Concerning the Earth Prisons* (*Wen diyu jing* 問地獄經) that briefly describes this purgatory in which those who took life while in the human path of rebirth are attacked by vicious dogs. This sutra, also sometimes referred to under the title *Wen diyu shi jing* 問地獄事經, seems to have been translated rather early, despite not being mentioned in *Chu sanzang jiji*; see *Kaiyuan shijiao lu* 224c and *Gaoseng zhuan* 324c (the biography of Lokakṣema, where a monk named Kang Ju 康巨 is credited with its translation). The latter passage is the earliest extant datable mention of the text.

They made as if to bite Huichi, then stopped. Daoxian fainted with fear and came to only after a long time. He told of this in detail.

69[601]

During the Jin there lived one Wang Lian 王練, styled Xuanming 玄明, a native of Langye; he served the Song as palace attendant.[602] His father, Min 珉, styled Jiyan 季琰, served under the Jin as secretariat director. Among their acquaintances was a Western[603] monk who, each time he observed Min's style and ability, was filled with respect and delight and would say to his colleagues, "If in my next life I were able to be this man's son, then in this life I will wish for this!" Min, hearing of it, joked with the monk in return, "Given the Dharma master's talent and conduct, you certainly can be my son!"

Some time later, the monk died of illness. Slightly more than a year later, Lian was born. As soon as he began talking, he could understand foreign speech. As for rarities from distant lands, silver utensils, pearls and shells, things he had never seen since birth and things of which he had never heard the names, he proceeded to name them all and knew where they were produced. Furthermore, he was naturally drawn to Westerners more than to Han people. Everyone said he must have been the Western monk in his former life. Min therefore styled him Alian 阿練,[604] and when he was grown he called him...[605]

Comments

We catch a glimpse, at the end of this rebirth story, of a social matrix of opinion and conversation at work. A boy is born; members of the surrounding community, noting certain of his strange traits, conclude he must be

---

601. Source texts: *Fayuan zhulin* 26.479c (section "[Karmic effects from] past lives" [*su ming* 宿命]); *Taiping guangji* 387.2; *Bianzheng lun* 7.537c; Lu, *Gu xiaoshuo gouchen* 422; Wang Guoliang, *Mingxiang ji yanjiu*, 70; Wakatsuki, Hasegawa, and Inagaki, *Hōon jurin no sōgō teki kenkyū*, 165–167. Additional texts: *Liudao ji* 2.126b. *Chu sanzang jiji* 10.89b and *Gaoseng zhuan* 3.339a mention Wang Lian's status as *dānapati* and his role in preparing digests of *jiemo wen* 羯磨文.

602. He is mentioned in passing as having held this office in *Song shu* 58.1591. Wang Min (361–388) was a noted and highly placed Buddhist devotee; see *Gaoseng zhuan* 1.328a; Zürcher, *The Buddhist Conquest of China*, 104, 213; and Mather, *Shih-shuo Hsin-yü*, 592. It appears that some of his letters were collected by the great Daoist master Tao Hongjing 陶弘景; see the list in *Huayang Tao yinju ji* 1.15a–b. These were members of the famous Wang clan of Langye.

603. For "Western," some sources have *fan* 梵, others *hu* 胡.

604. Wang Guoliang (*Mingxiang ji yanjiu*, 172 n7) suggests this was perhaps an abbreviated form of *alianer* 阿練兒 and a transliteration of the Indic Arinya or something similar; in support he cites *Yiqie jing yinyi* 14.394b (and cf. 16.404b). This same name or term recurs in item 102 below. It is clearly a term of respectful address for monastics, as noted in Zhou Junxun, *Wei Jin nanbeichao zhiguai xiaoshuo cihui*, 187, 435–436.

605. Ellipsis in the original.

the late Western monk now reborn. It is because of this activity of theirs that we have this story.

70[606]

During the Song there lived one Sun Daode 孫道德, a native of Yizhou.[607] He observed the Dao and was a libationer. He had surpassed the age of fifty and still had no sons. He lived near a [Buddhist] monastery. In the Jingping period [423–424] a monk told Daode, "If you are determined to have a son, you should reverently and with utmost mind recite the *Guanshiyin Sutra*. You may thus hope for success."

Daode then gave up serving the Dao and, single-mindedly taking the monk's instructions to heart, took refuge in Guanshiyin. Within a few days he had a dream response.[608] His wife at once conceived and subsequently gave birth to a boy.

Comments

We see here another facet of the multifront interreligious contestation reflected in, and to some extent shaped by, our text: "serving the Dao" will not guarantee male offspring; reciting the *Guanshiyin Sutra* will. In later times the bodhisattva was well known, often supplicated, and sometimes iconographically represented as "giver of sons."[609] This story (along with item 103 below) is one of the earliest glimpses of that role in extant Chinese texts.

71[610]

During the Song, one Qi Sengqin 齊僧欽 was a native of Jiangling. His family upheld the Dharma. When he was around nine or ten years old, one who was skilled at divining by physiognomy[611] told him he would not live

---

606. Source texts: *Fayuan zhulin* 17.410b (section "honoring Buddhas" [*jing Fo* 敬佛]); *Taiping guangji* 110.20; Lu, *Gu xiaoshuo gouchen*, 422; Wang Guoliang, *Mingxiang ji yanjiu*, 71. Additional texts: *Guanshiyin chiyan ji* 1.95c; *Guanyin cilin ji* 2.87c. Previously translated in Campany, "The Earliest Tales of the Bodhisattva Guanshiyin," 88.

607. Yizhou was a commandery centered in what is now Jianning district, Sichuan province.

608. Translating *mengying* 夢應.

609. See Chün-fang Yü, *Kuan-yin*, 133–137 and *passim*.

610. Source texts: *Fayuan zhulin* 62.757c6ff. (section "offerings" [*jici* 祭祠]); Lu, *Gu xiaoshuo gouchen* 423; Wang Guoliang, *Mingxiang ji yanjiu*, 72. An alternate translation of this story appears in Fu-Shih Lin, "Chinese Shamans and Shamanism," 33–34.

611. *Shan xiang zhan* 善相占. On Chinese arts of physiognomy (or the divination of an individual's fate based on his or her bodily characteristics), see Despeux, "Physiognomie"; Lessa, *Chinese Body Divination*; Smith, *Fortune-tellers and Philosophers*; Zhu, *Handai di xiang-renshu*; Field, *Ancient Chinese Divination*; and Kohn, "Mirror of Auras." Buddhists in China developed their own methods for divining karma, though I am not yet aware of any that were based on physiognomy; see, for example, the late-sixth-century *Zhancha shan'e yebao jing*, studied in Kuo, "Divination, jeux de hazard et purification," and Lai, "The *Chan-ch'a ching*."

past the age of seventeen. His parents and siblings were very worried. Sengqin reapplied himself in strict observance of the abstinence regulations. At age sixteen, at the end of the Song Jingping period [ca. 424], he developed a serious illness. His family observed the abstinence regulations to the utmost. They also made profane sacrifices[612] to seek fortune. But his illness was still not cured. At the time there was a shamaness[613] who said, "This young man's strength of merit is formidable. Demons do not dare draw close to him.[614] He naturally has spirits of goodness protecting him.[615] But the illness still has not improved for a long time, which may indicate a natural limit in his life span. In the world there are methods for inquiring into people's life spans. In my youth I served the celestial gods, so I am somewhat familiar with these methods. I will try them for you." In an uncultivated place she set out a repast of wine and dried meats, and lit incense and lamps.[616] Sometimes it would be as if she were unconscious; at other times she would return to her senses. Over several nights this happened multiple times. After seven days and nights she said, "I begin to feel that I see something. I see the spirits of goodness praying and making requests on behalf of Sengqin. Because of this, two counts[617] will be added [to his allotted life span]. His illness will certainly be cured. There is no reason to worry." Sengqin then recovered. He redoubled his pious efforts. He died twenty-four years later, just as the spirit medium had said. Thus, a count must be twelve years in length.[618]

Perhaps the closest Buddhist analogue to physiognomy was the discourse on the distinctive bodily characteristics (*xiang* 相 or *lakṣaṇa*) of Buddhas.

612. I.e., meat offerings to gods in local temples.

613. "Shamaness" translates *nüwu* 女巫.

614. In other words, the sort of demonic attack that one might otherwise have suspected as the cause of illness is ruled out due to the effects—invisible to most, but visible to the shamaness—of the boy's Buddhist piety.

615. See comments below, as well as comments to item 54 above.

616. Offerings of wine and dried meats to spirits were (and still are today) a very common gesture. A textual variant has the shamaness burning paper money rather than lighting incense, but the use of paper money for this purpose is otherwise undocumented before the late Sui dynasty (seventh century), and so, unlike Wang Guoliang, I believe this variant was formed well after the fifth century, in an era when burning paper money to send it to spirits was common. See Hou Ching-lang, *Monnaies d'offrande*, 3–17.

617. *Suan* 算.

618. These "gods (or spirits) of goodness" (*shanshen* 善神) are mentioned in some scriptural sources as protectors of those Buddhists who keep the precepts and observe fasting restrictions, as discussed above. For examples, see Sørensen, "Divine Scrutiny of Human Morals." These lines refer to a system by which people's life spans were believed to be a function of periodic divine observing and reporting of their sins to celestial bureaus and consequent augmentation or reduction of their length of life. This was an old, indigenous system; it also had Buddhist parallels, as discussed in Sørensen, ibid. On the indigenous Chinese system, see Bokenkamp, "Simple Twists of Fate"; Chard, "Rituals and Scriptures of the Stove Cult"; Kohn, "Counting Good Deeds"; Mollier, *Taoism and Buddhism Face to Face*, 100–133; Schafer, "The Stove God and the Alchemists"; Campany, "Living Off the Books"; and Campany, *To Live as Long as Heaven and Earth*, 47–60.

Comments

Here we learn that the "spirits of goodness," or "beneficent spirits" (*shan-shen* 善神), mentioned in other tales and in some scriptures, as an added dimension of their usual protective function even add years to the life spans of the appropriately pious. We also see another case in which an indigenous type of religious specialist—a shamaness, or spirit-medium—is reported to see phenomena in the unseen world that confirm what Buddhist texts and teachings say about that world: here, specifically, the activities of the *shanshen*. This is an example of interreligious contestation via co-optation.

72 [619]

During the Song there was one Wei Shizi 魏世子, a native of Liang commandery.[620] He and his son and daughter upheld the Dharma and practiced the religion assiduously; only his wife remained deluded and refused to credit the Buddha's teachings. Early in the Yuanjia period, a daughter, aged thirteen, died of illness, then revived after seven days and said, "We should set up an altar and place a copy of the *Sutra of the Buddha of Limitless Lifespan*[621] on it." Shizi accordingly set up an altar with a copy of the sutra. Although before this the daughter had regularly practiced abstinence and observed prohibitions on the fast days[622] and had often paid obeisance, she had never once looked inside a sutra text. But now she ascended the altar and recited the text in clear, orderly tones. She also announced to her father, "I died and was reborn in the Realm of [the Buddha of] Limitless Lifespan. There I saw the pond and lotus blossoms where you, my brother,

---

619. Source texts: *Fayuan zhulin* 15.400b1ff. (section "honoring Buddhas" [*jing Fo* 敬佛]); *Taiping guangji* 114.2; Lu, *Gu xiaoshuo gouchen*, 423; Wang Guoliang, *Mingxiang ji yanjiu*, 74; Wakatsuki, Hasegawa, and Inagaki, *Hōon jurin no sōgō teki kenkyū*, 79–80. Additional texts: *Fozu tongji* 28.289c; *Wangsheng ji* 2.138b; *Wangsheng xifang ruiying zhuan* 1.107b; *Jingtu lun* 3.99a; *Jushi zhuan* 4.190a; *Jingtu shengxian lu* 8.293c. (These latter two texts cite *Mingxiang ji* by title.) Translated: Mai, "Visualization Apocrypha," 373; I have borrowed some phrasing from this translation.

620. Located in modern Henan province.

621. This sutra is more formally known as the *Sutra on Visualizing the Buddha of Limitless Life Span* (*Guan wuliangshoufo jing* 觀無量壽佛經), of which an edition is included in the Sino-Japanese Buddhist canon (Taishō 365). It is claimed to have been translated from Sanskrit in the early fifth century but now is generally regarded by scholars as having been composed in Chinese around this same time, either in China or in Central Asia. It later was seen as a foundational text of the Pure Land tradition. The sutra contains a detailed series of instructions on how to visualize being reborn in Buddha Amitābha's Pure Land. A translation is available in Inagaki and Stewart, *The Sutra on the Contemplation of Amitāyus*.

622. That is, had scrupulously observed the regulations of the periodic *zhaijie* ceremony, on which see above.

and myself will later be reborn by transformation.[623] Only there was none for mother. I could not overcome my sorrow and longing over this, so I returned here to bring this report." When she had finished speaking these words, she died again. From this point on, her mother became a pious believer in the teachings of Dharma.

Comments

This story is, among other things, a "confirmation" by visionary experience of Pure Land scriptural teaching. It is also another instance of narrative contestation—here, against the simple neglect of Buddhist practice and belief, with intrafamilial tension between practitioners and nonpractitioners. And it reflects the hope, seen in other stories in our text (for example, item 124) and in many votive inscriptions from this and later periods, that members of families might be reborn together in fortunate states in the future.

73[624]

During the Song there lived Zhang Xing 張興, a native of Xinxing.[625] He was something of a believer in the Dharma of Buddha and had previously received the eight precepts[626] from the monks Sengrong 僧融 and Tanyi 曇翼.[627]

Once he was seized by robbers. He managed to flee, but his wife was captured, held captive, and interrogated[628] over a period of several days. Then wildfires broke out in the district, and the cage in which she was being held was temporarily placed by the roadside when Sengrong and

---

623. One of the key visualizations enjoined in the *Sutra on Visualizing the Buddha of Limitless Life Span* involves seeing oneself reborn in the Western Land of Utmost Bliss sitting cross-legged on a lotus flower. See *Guan wuliangshoufo jing* 344b, and Inagaki and Stewart, *The Sutra on the Contemplation of Amitāyus*, 108–109.

624. Source texts: *Fayuan zhulin* 17.410c–411a (section "honoring Buddhas" [*jing Fo* 敬佛]); *Taiping guangji* 110.21; Lu, *Gu xiaoshuo gouchen*, 423; Wang Guoliang, *Mingxiang ji yanjiu*, 75; Wakatsuki, Hasegawa, and Inagaki, *Hōon jurin no sōgō teki kenkyū*, 114–116. Additional texts: *Gaoseng zhuan*, as cited in *Fayuan zhulin* 62.757; *Gaoseng zhuan* 13.410c; *Xu gaoseng zhuan* 25.645; *Guanyin cilin ji* 2.90a; *Guanshiyin chiyan ji* (citing *Guanyin ganying*) 1.95c.

625. A commandery located in what is now Jiangling district, Hubei province.

626. These are the eight abstinences observed by laypersons during the *zhai*: not to kill, steal, speak falsely, drink alcohol, or engage in sexual misconduct; not to wear cosmetics or jewelry, or dance or listen to music; not to sleep on elevated beds; and not to eat after noon.

627. Stories of a monk by the name Sengrong are preserved in *Gaoseng zhuan* 6.362b, *Xu gaoseng zhuan* 25.645b, and *Fahua zhuanji* 7.79a, but they all seem to concern a monk who lived later than the one mentioned in our story here. Likewise, a Shi Tanyi is the subject of a *Gaoseng zhuan* biography (5.355c), but he, too, appears to have lived after the events narrated here.

628. Here and elsewhere, "interrogate" translates an expression, *lüechi* 掠笞, that implies physical torture.

Tanyi came walking along and passed by her. Frightened, she called out to them, "*Ācārya*,[629] can you do anything to help me?" Sengrong answered, "We monks are weak and have no way to save you. But it is only necessary to think on Guanshiyin with diligence, and you will soon be freed." Xing's wife then began praying and thinking intently all day and night. After a dozen or so days, she dreamed one night of a monk who nudged her with his foot and said, "Psst! Get up!" Startled, the wife jumped up. The locks and fetters binding her had all been loosened. So she ran toward the door. It, however, was still shut, and she was under heavy guard. So there was no way out. Fearing she would be noticed, she returned to her pen and put the fetters back on. Soon she had fallen asleep again. Again she dreamed of the monk, who this time said, "The door has been opened!" She woke and ran out through the door. The guards were all asleep, so with quiet steps she fled the area.

It was a dark night. She had gone perhaps several *li* when she suddenly encountered someone. She dropped to the ground in fear, but when the two identified themselves she realized that the man was her husband. They embraced with mixed joy and sorrow. That same night they went to Senghong and Tanyi, who hid them, and so they escaped the situation.

This occurred early in the Yuanjia period.[630]

74[631]

At the beginning of the Song Yongchu period [420],[632] there lived the *śrāmaṇera* Tanwujie 曇無竭, a native of Huanglong.[633] He recited the *Guanshiyin Sutra* and earnestly cultivated himself in purity. Along with twenty-five compatriots he went off to visit Buddhist lands, firmly resolved to carry sutras back through the perilous wilderness. When they had reached Śrāvastī[634] in India they encountered on the road a herd of mountain elephants. Tanwujie entrusted his life to reciting the sutra and chanting the name [of the bodhisattva]. With that, a lion emerged from the forest near-

---

629. This renders *sheli* 闍梨, short for *asheli* 阿闍梨, a term created to transliterate the above Sanskrit term of respectful address for monks.

630. This long reign period during the Liu Song dynasty lasted from 424 to 454.

631. Source texts: *Fayuan zhulin* 65.786a (section "saving from danger" [*jiuwei* 救厄]); Lu, *Gu xiaoshuo gouchen*, 424; Wang Guoliang, *Mingxiang ji yanjiu*, 73. Additional texts: *Chu sanzang jiji* 15.113c; *Gaoseng zhuan* 3.338b–339c; *Ji shenzhou sanbao gantong lu* 3.426b; *Fayuan zhulin*, as cited in *Taiping guangji* 110.22; *Shenseng zhuan* 2.959c; *Fahua zhuanji* 4.66a; many other sources. Discussed: Campany, "Notes on Sutra Texts," 33.

632. *Fayuan zhulin* gives *yuanjia chu*, but I follow Wang Guoliang (*Mingxiang ji yanjiu*, 175 n1) in emending the reign period based on *Chu sanzang jiji* and *Gaoseng zhuan*.

633. Located in present-day Chaoyang district, Rehe province.

634. *Shewei* 舍衛, a medieval Chinese transliteration of the name of a city in northeastern India, famous in Buddhist lore for its park and *vihara*, where Gautama Buddha spent many rainy-season retreats and gave sermons.

by. The elephants fled quickly in alarm. Later the party encountered a herd of wild bovines advancing on them, snorting and bellowing and about to do them harm. Tanwujie entrusted his life as before, and a great eagle suddenly flew down and caused the animals to scatter. Thus they were saved.

75 [635]

During the Song there was one Tang Wenbo 唐文伯, a native of Ganyu[636] in Donghai. His younger brother loved to gamble, and the family's wealth was exhausted. In the village was a Buddhist temple. Passersby often placed coins on the image of the Buddha there. Wenbo's younger brother stole these coins.

Much later, he fell ill. A diviner said, "This calamity is due to having stolen the Buddha's money."[637] The father of the family angrily said, "What deity is Buddha, that he should cause this to happen to my son? I will try taking more things [from the temple] by force. If he can cause another illness, then I will believe it." The wife of the previous commandary prefect, He Xinzhi 何欣之, had donated four bejeweled brocade canopies to the temple.[638] The father stole these and used them as waist sashes. In less than a hundred days, the father had also fallen seriously ill; the sores started at the points on his waist where he had worn the sashes. This happened during the early years of the Yuanjia period.[639]

Comments

Note the use of divination in the action sequence and in the narrative. Here, divination provides another sort of confirmation of Buddhist teaching, functionally parallel to the visionary account in item 71, for example. Here, too, an indigenous technology for the production of divine knowledge "confirms" aspects of Buddhist religion. The location of the sores on the man's body is an added layer of confirmation of the source of his suffering.

---

635. Source texts: *Fayuan zhulin* 79.874c28ff. (section "the ten evil acts" [*shi e* 十惡]); Lu, *Gu xiaoshuo gouchen* 424; Wang Guoliang, *Mingxiang ji yanjiu*, 76.

636. A district that still bears this name is located in today's Jiangsu province.

637. On the regulations surrounding monastic ownership of property and the notion of the Buddha as owner and permanent resident of monastic properties, see Chen Huaiyu, *The Revival of Buddhist Monasticism*, 138ff.; Gernet, *Buddhism in Chinese Society*, 65–93; and, for Indian precedents, Schopen, "The Buddha as an Owner of Property."

638. Such donations were, again, a ubiquitous merit-making activity. See Gernet, *Buddhism in Chinese Society*, 195–228; Kieschnick, *The Impact of Buddhism*, 157–219; Wu, "What Is Bianxiang?" 135; Ho, "Building on Hope"; Abe, "Provenance, Patronage, and Desire"; Liu Shufen, *Ancient China and Ancient India*, 162–173; and McNair, *Donors of Longmen*. On canopies (here *gai* 蓋), see the note to item 16 above.

639. A long period that lasted from 424 to 454.

Like some other stories in our text, this one vividly illustrates the notion of the Buddha as an owner of monastic property.

76[640]

During the Song there lived the monk Shi Daojiong 釋道囧,[641] originally surnamed Ma 馬 and a native of Haozhi in Fufeng.[642] His practice and attainments were especially pure, and he had been known for this since his youth. In the ninth month of the second year of the Yuanjia period [October 425], Daojiong was performing a Samantabhadra abstinence ceremony[643] for someone. Forty-odd monks and laypersons were gathered. On the seventh day, just as the time for the midday meal arrived, there suddenly came a person wearing a linen shirt and trousers, riding horseback; he pulled up in front of the hall,[644] dismounted, and paid obeisance to Buddha. Daojiong, thinking he was an ordinary person, extended him no special courtesy. The man then remounted, lashed the horse, and suddenly disappeared. A red glow lit the sky, not dissipating for a long while.

---

640. Source texts: *Fayuan zhulin* 17.408c–409a (section "honoring Buddhas" [*jing Fo* 敬佛]); Lu, *Gu xiaoshuo gouchen*, 425; Wang Guoliang, *Mingxiang ji yanjiu*, 77; Wakatsuki, Hasegawa, and Inagaki, *Hōon jurin no sōgō teki kenkyū*, 89–92. Additional texts: *Fayuan zhulin* 65.784c–785a; *Gaoseng zhuan* 12.407a (a biography that mentions that Daojiong resided at a monastery in Jiankang to which Wang Yan later consigned his personal image of Sound Observer); *Ji shenzhou sanbao gantong lu* 3.426c; *Xi Guanshiyin yingyanji* 6 (Makita, *Rikuchō kōitsu Kanzeon okenki no kenkyū*, 28); *Fahua zhuanji* 4.62c; *Hongzan fahua zhuan* 1.14a; *Guanshiyin chiyan ji* 1.95b; *Guanyin cilin ji* 2.90a. Note: Item 98 below (based on the passage cited from *Mingxiang ji* in *Fayuan zhulin* 65) is another story about Shi Daojiong; both were clearly included—but separately—in Wang Yan's text (or at least in some early version of *Mingxiang ji*), and the second story alludes to the first. Here is a synopsis of the subnarratives involving Daojiong given in these sources: (1) Miracles during Samantabhadra abstinence ceremonies (*Fayuan zhulin* 17, *Gaoseng zhuan* 12, *Ji shenzhou sanbao gantong lu* 3); (2) Sound Observer miracle while gathering stalactites (*Gaoseng zhuan* 12, *Fayuan zhulin* 65, *Ji shenzhou sanbao gantong lu* 3, *Xi Guanshiyin yingyanji* 60); (3) vision of being transported by carriage into the presence of an august personage (*Fayuan zhulin* 17, *Gaoseng zhuan* 12, *Ji shenzhou sanbao gantong lu* 3—the first two of these, but not the last, locate this event at Nanjian monastery); (4) miracle while performing Sound Observer abstinence ceremony in the home of Liu Yiqing (*Fayuan zhulin* 65; *Gaoseng zhuan* 12 notes that he was invited by Liu Yiqing but does not narrate the story of the abstinence-ceremony miracle in Liu's home); (5) Sound Observer miracle in which Daojiong is saved while crossing a river (*Xi Guanshiyin yingyanji* 6, *Gaoseng zhuan* 12). On these various sources and their relationships, see the excellent discussion in Shinohara, "Two Sources of Chinese Buddhist Biographies," 136–139.

641. Some versions, including some editions of *Fayuan zhulin*, give Jing 璟 in place of Jiong 囧.

642. Haozhi was located in what is now an area near Qian district in Shaanxi province.

643. That is, a Puxian *zhai* 普賢齋, an abstinence ceremony centering on supplication of this bodhisattva, on whom see the comments.

644. *Tang* 堂; elsewhere in this and other texts we find the phrase *zhaitang* 齋堂 used to designate a special room in the homes of well-to-do lay families for the purpose of hosting abstinence ceremonies.

In the twelfth month of the third year [late January or early February 427], he was again performing a Samantabhadra abstinence ceremony in the home of a lay family. On the last day, two monks of ordinary appearance came in and paid obeisance to Buddha. Everyone in the assembly thought they were common monks and did not welcome them especially respectfully. Someone asked casually, "Where do you reside?" and the monks answered, "In the next hamlet over." In the assembly at the time was a layman named Zhang Dao 張道. He detected that there was something odd about the monks, so with his utmost mind he made obeisance to them. When the monks went out through the gate, they had walked several dozen steps when suddenly there was a swirl of dust and they rose straight up into the sky, ascending until the eye could no longer make them out.

In the seventh year [430–431], Daojiong traveled with several fellow disciples to the capital. The minister of works He Shangzhi 何尚之[645] had begun constructing the Nanjian monastery 南澗精舍, and Daojiong temporarily stayed there. One night he suddenly saw four men riding atop a new carriage followed by four attendants. The party arrived in his room and ordered him to accompany them. Suspicious because it was the middle of the night, Daojiong made no reply but simply shut his eyes; unawares, he was then conveyed up onto the carriage. In a while they reached Chenqiao, some distance away in the same commandery. There Daojiong saw a nobleman wearing a cloak and a single-layer gown of sheer cloth[646] sitting on a couch under an awning shaped like a floral canopy, attended by several hundred officers wearing yellow robes. When the man saw Daojiong he was startled and said, "I said I only wanted to know the location of a monk who practices *pratyutpanna*,[647] whose mental vigor has resulted in far-reaching attainments. Why have you brought him here with you?" With that, he sent people to escort Daojiong back. When they arrived outside the monastery gate, the escorts suddenly vanished. The gate was closed as it had been before. Only after Daojiong had knocked and yelled for a long time did the monks within, startled, report to one another that they heard someone outside and finally opened the gate to admit him. When they inspected the chamber where he had been staying, they found it, too, was still closed up as it had been earlier.

Comments

With the line "He detected that there was something odd about the monks, so with his utmost mind he made obeisance to them," we have an example of the motif of recognition, an important element in the cultural reper-

---

645. He Shangzhi (382–460) is mentioned many times in *Song shu* and has an official biography in that work (66.1732–1733).
646. "Sheer cloth" translates *jianbu* 箋布; compare Mather, *Shih-shuo Hsin-yü*, 182.
647. See note in item 56 above.

toire in this period.[648] Here, as elsewhere in *Mingxiang ji*, it is a matter of a layperson recognizing spirit-monks in his presence despite their seeming ordinariness.

The Bodhisattva Samantabhadra, mentioned twice in this story and also in items 108 and 109 below, was, as our text attests, along with Guanshiyin sometimes the focus of particular devotion during abstinence ceremonies.[649] He was the subject of a visualization sutra translated in the first half of the fifth century.[650] He was a favorite subject of iconography, at least in slightly later periods, often depicted astride a white elephant.[651] But I suspect the main impetus behind his importance in the social and religious circles that gave rise to our text was his depiction in the final chapter of the *Lotus Sutra*. That chapter tells of the vows Samantabhadra took in a previous era to protect from all harm all those who, in the latter days of the Dharma, devote themselves to the *Lotus Sutra*, in particular to its recitation over a continuous twenty-one-day period. The bodhisattva, this chapter promises, will assist their memory lest they forget any sutra verses and will ensure their rebirth in the *trāyastriṃśa* heaven,[652] where the devotee will consort with eighty-four thousand goddesses who will come to welcome him.[653]

77[654]

During the Song there lived Li Dan 李旦, styled Shize 世則, a native of Guangling. His filiality, strictness of practice, and purity of character were known throughout his area. On the fourteenth of the first month of the

---

648. On this motif see Henry, "The Motif of Recognition"; Shryock, *The Study of Human Abilities*; Mather, *Shih-shuo Hsin-yü*, xxii–xxiii and 248–273; and Company, *Making Transcendents*, 95, 101, 233.

649. Compare *Gaoseng zhuan* 7.369b14–19 and 8.379a26–28, among other texts. Both of those cases mention a *zhai* ceremony lasting twenty-one days, as prescribed in the *Lotus* as well as in the visualization sutra mentioned in the next note.

650. The sutra in question is *Guan Puxian pusa xingfa jing* 觀普賢菩薩行法經. See Kuo, *Confession et contrition*, 64–67, and Eugene Wang, *Shaping the Lotus Sutra*, 20–21.

651. Several examples are discussed in Eugene Wang, *Shaping the Lotus Sutra*, and Ning, *Art, Religion and Politics*.

652. See note to item 8 above.

653. In the third-century translation of Dharmarakṣa, *Zheng fahua jing* 正法華經, this chapter is titled "Rejoicing in Samantabhadra" (*Le Puxian* 樂普賢), while in the early-fifth-century translation of Kumārajīva (*Miaofa lianhua jing*) it is entitled "The Exhortation of the Bodhisattva Samantabhadra" (*Puxian pusa quan fa* 普賢菩薩勸發). Only in the latter translation is the bodhisattva described as riding a white elephant, a fact that attests to the special importance of Kumārajīva's version in the formation of Chinese iconography.

654. Source texts: *Fayuan zhulin* 6.315a–b (section "the six paths [of rebirth]" [*liudao* 六道]); *Taiping guangji* 382.4; Lu, *Gu xiaoshuo gouchen*, 425; Wang Guoliang, *Mingxiang ji yanjiu*, 78; Wakatsuki, Hasegawa, and Inagaki, *Hōon jurin no sōgō teki kenkyū*, 51–54. Additional texts: *Liudao ji* 4.160a. Note: Both *Fayuan zhulin* and *Taiping guangji* cite this item from *Mingbao ji*, but Lu Xun and Wang Guoliang treat it as a *Mingxiang ji* story, and I concur.

third year of Yuanjia [5 February 426], he died of illness, but the area below his heart did not grow cold, and after seven days he revived. He ate a bit of congee, and after a night of rest he recovered.

He said that when he died a man arrived at the head of his bed carrying a written message and a flag[655] and announced, "The magistrate[656] has summoned you." Dan followed him and departed. They proceeded due north. The road was very level and clean. They arrived at a city wall with imposing towers resembling the palace watchtowers of today. The messenger urged him, "Dan, proceed forward!" He reached a large courtroom where some thirty officers in single-layer gowns and blue turbans sat arrayed in rows. One man wearing an open gown sat on the eastern side behind a table; there were over a hundred attendants and guards standing nearby. Upon seeing Dan, someone said to the seated officers, "He should be shown the prisons, so that the world will know about them." As soon as Dan had heard these words, he raised his head and looked around in all directions; the former scene had completely vanished, and he was in the midst of the earth prisons. He saw crowds of sinners receiving painful retribution, moaning and crying out. He could not bear to look. Then another messenger arrived and announced: "Message from the magistrate: You may return, sir. We will be welcoming you here again." With this he returned.

In the first month of the sixth year [late February or March 429] he died again, then seven days later revived again and recounted what he had seen; it roughly resembled what he had seen previously. This time some of the imprisoned sinners sent word back to their families, saying that they had sinned while alive and asking that their families perform acts of fortune on their behalf. They gave their surnames and styles and said that they would be known to their acquaintances in their respective villages. Dan made inquiries according to what they had said and was able to locate all the families. He also said, "In the upcoming *jiashen* year[657] there will be a great pestilence that will wipe out all wicked people. Disciples of Buddha should perform the eightfold abstinence and cultivate their minds so as to do good deeds. In this way they can avoid the disaster."

Dan had originally been a Daoist libationer. He now intended to abandon his registers[658] and base himself solely on the Dharma. But the Dao-

---

655. Compare item 30 above, where envoys performing the same function arrive with the same accoutrements.

656. Here translating *fujun* 府君.

657. Corresponding to Yuanjia 21 (444–445).

658. Each libationer, and indeed by some accounts each member of a Celestial Master parish, had a register (*lu* 籙) listing the gods and spirits with whom he or she had a contractual relationship. See Kleeman, *Great Perfection*, 72; Kohn, *Laughing at the Tao*, 108; and, for an account of how this system is represented in Tang-era texts, Ren, *Zhongguo daojiao shi*, 340–390.

ists[659] took issue with this, so he ended up following both sets of practices. Even so, he constantly encouraged others to convert and to perform the eightfold abstinence.[660]

Comments

This story yet again engages in contestation with Daoism, here with an interesting twist: the protagonist does not completely abandon the Daoist community but remains within it, working to turn others toward Buddhism.

The warning about the coming year is one of the few apocalyptic-sounding passages in our text. Many religious writings from this era sound the apocalyptic note much more strongly than do the extant stories collected by Wang Yan.[661]

78[662]

Zheng Xianzhi 鄭鮮之,[663] a native of Yingyang,[664] who served as imperial secretary and chief administrator, in the fourth year of the Yuanjia period [427–428] was in the imperial cortege on a tour of inspection. The night they reached the capital he suddenly died. His spirit spoke through a medium[665] and said: "My allotted life span ended long ago; I should have de-

---

659. *Daomin* 道民.

660. *Er chang quan hua zuo baguan zhai* 而常勸化作八關齋. Chen Hong, "Fojiao baguan-zhai yu zhonggu xiaoshuo," 161–162, sees this story as evidence of a "blending" (*ronghe* 融合) of Buddhism and Daoism; I see it as indicating a strong tension between the two, albeit in the guise of narrating one man's way of negotiating that tension.

661. See, for example, Strickmann, "The Consecration Sūtra," 86–89; and Zürcher, "Prince Moonlight."

662. Source texts: *Fayuan zhulin* 6.315b (section "the six paths [of rebirth]" [*liudao* 六道]); Lu, *Gu xiaoshuo gouchen*, 426; Wang Guoliang, *Mingxiang ji yanjiu*, 79; Wakatsuki, Hasegawa, and Inagaki, *Hōon jurin no sōgō teki kenkyū*, 54–55. Additional texts: *Bianzheng lun* 7.539c gives what is obviously a related, but different, account of the same figure: "Zheng Xian, styled Daozi, was skilled at methods of physiognomy and thus knew that his own allotted life span was short. He was thinking that there was nothing he could do to lengthen it. Then in a dream he saw a monk and asked him what he must do to lengthen his life. [The monk answered] that on the six [monthly] abstinence days [*liu zhai ri* 六齋日] he should release living beings, fix his thoughts on goodness, keep to the abstinence restrictions and uphold the precepts. By this means he would be able to extend his years and obtain good fortune. So Xian upheld the Dharma and thereby lived a long life." Lu, *Gu xiaoshuo gouchen*, 444, collects this as item 31 of *Xuanyan ji*. See also *Liudao ji* 3.140c.

663. An official biography in appears in *Song shu* 64.1691–1698; according to it, Zheng lived from 364 to 427.

664. A commandery at the time, centered in what is now Yingyang county, Henan province.

665. The expression is *nai lingyu zhuren* 乃靈語著人; *ling* (which I render nominally as "his spirit") could instead be understood adverbially, yielding a translation along the lines of "he possessed someone in order to speak spiritually." Similar wording occurs in item 124 below.

parted this world much earlier. Since that year passed I have relied on respectful faith in the law of Buddha, releasing living beings and making donations, and simply by means of this merit I have extended my life by several years. Retribution in both the dark and light worlds follows [actions] as shadows [follow objects] or echoes [follow sounds]. You should leave behind vulgar practices and in your mind venerate the great teaching." At the time there were many people of high standing who heard him say this.

Comments

Here is another instance of the promise that Buddhist devotional acts (here, the releasing of living beings and the making of offerings) extends the life span of the devotee. We also see here another example of the use of information delivered via spirit possession to confirm Buddhist teachings.

79 [666]

During the Song there lived one Zhou Zong 周宗, a native of Guangling commandery. In the seventh year of the Yuanjia period [430–431], he followed Dao Yanzhi 到彦之 on a northern campaign.[667] The force was defeated. Zong, along with six others from his city, fled and traveled furtively. North of Pengcheng they came to an empty monastery with no monks residing in it. Within it was a [Buddha] image bearing bodily marks made from crystals. These they stole and took into town to exchange for food. One of the men was weakened by illness, and the others, slighting him, did not share any of the food with him. Three or four years after they had returned home, Zong and each of the other five by turn contracted leprosy and died. Only the man who had received none of the food escaped this fate and survived.

80 [668]

During the Song[669] there lived one Guo Quan 郭銓, styled Zhongheng 仲衡, a native of Shunyang. He served as regional inspector of Yizhou in the [late] Jin period. At the outset of Yixi [405] he was involved in the group

---

666. Source texts: *Fayuan zhulin* 79.875a (section "the ten evil acts" [*shi e* 十惡]); *Taiping guangji* 116.4; Lu, *Gu xiaoshuo gouchen*, 426; Wang Guoliang, *Mingxiang ji yanjiu*, 80.

667. Details on this campaign appear in *Nan shi* 25.674–676.

668. Source texts: *Fayuan zhulin* 91.956a4ff. (section "keeping the abstinence ceremony" [*shou zhai* 受齋]); *Taiping guangji* 324.3; Lu, *Gu xiaoshuo gouchen*, 427; Wang Guoliang, *Mingxiang ji yanjiu*, 81. Additional texts: *Xuanyan ji* 25 (as quoted in *Bianzheng lun* 7.539a, and collected in Lu, *Gu xiaoshuo gouchen*, 369).

669. There is some confusion about the dynasty in which this notice is set, not surprisingly since the events here narrated span the end of the Jin and beginning of the Song. The *Taiping guangji* quotation of this story does not open with "Song."

around Huan Xuan 桓玄 and was killed.[670] Some thirty years after his death, in the eighth year of Yuanjia [431–432] his form suddenly appeared[671] and paid a visit to the home of his son-in-law, Liu Ningzhi 劉凝之 of Nan commandery,[672] arriving via an impressive carriage and entourage. He said to Ningzhi: "I have been reproached for something.[673] If you host on my behalf an assembly of forty monks, I can be extricated from the situation." When he had finished speaking, he vanished. Liu thought that what he had seen was a *wangliang* demon,[674] so he gave the matter no further thought. The next night, Quan appeared in a dream to his daughter, saying, "I am being reproached and about to be punished. I already told your husband and asked him to host an assembly for me. How is it that he has still shown no compassion for me a day later?" Then, when she rose the next morning, she saw Quan going out through the door, saying angrily, "So you really won't help me? Today I am to be punished for my crime." His daughter jumped up and detained him, asking, "Where should we hold this abstinence ceremony?" He replied, "Have it at my home." In a moment he vanished.

Ningzhi anxiously set up and hosted the assembly. When it was over, a messenger arrived saying that he had been sent by Quan, and what Ningzhi heard was this: "Thanks to your kindness and sagacity, I am to be pardoned in that matter." When the messenger had finished speaking, he suddenly vanished. After this [Quan's ghostly appearances] stopped.

Comments

This story of the visitation of a living family by the dead again takes up the dreaded phenomenon of plaints. The deceased has been blamed for something; a grievance has been filed. His only recourse is to appeal to his living family members for help. Had the situation continued, the living family would doubtless have begun to suffer from sickness and other ills. But the story instructs as to the proper way to address such problems: the sponsor-

---

670. This sentence is based on the quotation of the story in *Taiping guangji*. The events in question are narrated in *Jin shu* 10. For modern treatments, see Graff, *Medieval Chinese Warfare*, 87–99, 90; Lewis, *China Between Empires*, 69; Grafflin, "Reinventing China," 167–168; and Zürcher, *The Buddhist Conquest of China*, 154–157. Huan Xuan is noted for his attempt, finally abandoned, to compel monks to bow to emperors; see Pan Guiming, *Zhongguo jushi fojiao shi*, 155–161; Zürcher, *The Buddhist Conquest of China*, 214–215, 231–239, 249–252; and Campany, "Chinese History and Writing about 'Religion(s).'"

671. Translating *hu xian xing* 忽見形.

672. Liu Ningzhi (390–448) is the subject of official biographies in *Song shu* 93.2284 and *Nan shi* 75.1868.

673. Translating *you zhe shi* 有謫事.

674. The *wangliang* 魍魎 demon (a binome also written with other graphs in other texts) had been known as a mischievous, vaguely malevolent, certainly predatory spirit since Warring States times. See Harper, "A Chinese Demonography," 481–483. For an excellent collection of recent studies of Chinese demon lore from this and earlier periods, see Pu Muzhou, *Guimei shenmo*.

ing of an abstinence ceremony and the making of donations to monks and nuns.

81[675]

Sima Wenxuan 司馬文宣 was a native of Henei.[676] He was a rather pious Buddhist. In the ninth year of Yuanjia [432–433] he lost both his mother and his younger brother. At dawn on the day of the full moon he suddenly saw his brother's form atop the household altar;[677] he looked no different than when alive. He seemed troubled, sighed, and pleaded for something to eat and drink. As a test, Wenxuan said in reply, "When you were alive, you cultivated the ten meritorious acts.[678] If what the scriptures say is correct, you should have attained rebirth in the heavens or as a human being. For what reason have you been reborn among ghosts?" But the form only sighed and looked up and down, saying nothing. That same night Wenxuan saw his brother in a dream, and he said, "Because I cultivated good deeds while I was alive, I received the favor of being reborn in the heavens as recompense. The ghost on the altar this morning was a demon; it was not I. I was afraid you would be doubtful or confused about it, so that is why I have come to tell you this."

Next morning Wenxuan invited a monk to recite the *Śūraṃgama Sutra* while he had someone else strike at the ghost. It fled under the bed and then ran outside the door, its form hideously ugly. The entire family was frightened and hurled curses after it. The ghost cried, "I'm hungry and was asking to eat, that's all!" After several days it left.

Several days later, at the head of his mother's altar there was a ghost, its body red in color and very tall and large. Wenxuan's eldest son, Xiaozu 孝祖, spoke with it at length and in detail. At first everyone was frightened of it, but later they grew accustomed to its presence, and the ghost for its part also grew close to them, coming and going from the house along with family members. When word of this spread through the capital, the people

---

675. Source texts: *Fayuan zhulin* 6.314b (section "the six paths [of rebirth]" [*liudao* 六道]); *Taiping guangji* 325.3 (both citing *Mingbao ji*); Lu, *Gu xiaoshuo gouchen*, 427; Wang Guoliang, *Mingxiang ji yanjiu*, 82; Wakatsuki, Hasegawa, and Inagaki, *Hōon jurin no sōgō teki kenkyū*, 45–48. Additional texts: *Liudao ji* 3.139c. Discussed: Campany, "Notes on Sutra Texts," 62 n36.

676. A commandery near what is now Xinyang district, Henan province.

677. *Lingzuo* 靈座.

678. *Shishan* 十善, consisting of the avoidance of committing any of the ten wicked acts: taking life, stealing, debauchery, lying, deceptive speech, coarse language, filthy language, covetousness, anger, and erroneous views (Mochizuki, *Bukkyō daijiten*, 2282b–2283c). These are outlined already in the *Sutra in Forty-Two Sections*, some version of which, though perhaps not as early as claimed in legend, was nonetheless extant before the end of the Eastern Han (220 CE). See Sharf, "The *Scripture in Forty-Two Sections*," 365, and Heng-ching Shih, *The Sutra of Forty-Two Sections*, 34. These ten categories of avoidances are also expounded upon at some length in Xi Chao's *Fengfa yao*; see Zürcher, *The Buddhist Conquest of China*, 165–166.

coming to have a look filled the lanes near the home. At that time a monk from Nanlin monastery 南林寺 along with the monk Senghan 僧含, who resided in Lingwei monastery 靈味寺,[679] both conversed with the ghost, also in great detail. The ghost said, "In my previous life[680] I was honored and of noble status, but because I committed numerous wicked deeds and had not yet received full retribution for them [when I died], I was reborn this way, as a ghost. In the next *yin* 寅 year,[681] four hundred ghosts[682] will set in motion a great plague. Those who will suffer from this calamity will not include monks,[683] but only those with especially large numbers of sins who have failed to perform acts of fortune and goodness. This is why I was sent here: to inspect people in this regard."

The monks proffered it some food, but the ghost replied, "I have my own supply. You needn't offer this food." Senghan said, "Ghosts know a lot![684] What were my previous births? For what reason did I come to be a monk in this life?" The ghost replied, "You were a human being. The cause of your having left the household [in this life] is a vow that you made [in a previous life]." He asked about many other matters concerning birth and death, and the ghost answered all his questions with uncanny accuracy. He spoke of a great many details that are not recorded here. Senghan then asked, "The paths of humans and ghosts are different. Since you are not seeking food, why are you remaining here so long?" The ghost answered, "There is a certain girl in these parts. She should have been among those rounded up, but because she is diligently upholding the precepts, this is hard to bring about. This is why I've been lingering here so many days. I am ashamed at having inconvenienced my host for so long."

From this time onward, the ghost did not often manifest its form. Those who went to see it could only hear its voice. The time was Yuanjia 10. On the twenty-eighth day of the third month [3 May 433] the ghost told Wenxuan, "I came temporarily to stay here, yet your family was in the midst of conducting [ceremonies of] fortune [for the dead].[685] Having caused you such a fright, how could I have dared to stay so long?" Xiaozu said, "If you are permitted to stay in any case, why must you ghosts appropriate the

679. This monastery's founding is mentioned in *Gaoseng zhuan* 7.370b, where it is likewise connected with the monk Senghan, and elsewhere in that work as well. Senghan reappears in item 82 below.

680. It is possible that more than one previous lifetime is intended here.

681. This presumably means the next year in which *yin* is one of the two conjoined terms used to designate it in the "stem and branch" system.

682. Or possibly "four hundred detachments of ghosts," if we understand the *bu* 部 in *sibai bu gui* 四百部鬼 not as a counter for ghosts but as meaning something like "units" or "departments."

683. This could equally well mean: "will not include *you two* monks."

684. Or possibly "You, ghost, know much." I punctuate the passage differently than does the Taishō edition.

685. *Yingfu* 營福; that is, ceremonies generating merit for the purpose of securing good fortune for the deceased.

altars of departed family members?" The ghost replied, "Your departed family members each have their proper assigned places. This altar was pointlessly set up,[686] so I took advantage of it and stayed here." With this the ghost said farewell and departed.

Comments

This unusual story dramatizes changes in the relations between the living and the dead in China—changes that represented, in part, adjustments to Buddhist understandings of the human dead. We are presented, in effect, with three models of "ghosthood" (all alike termed *gui* 鬼). First we have the spirit of unknown provenance who poses as a dead relative, seeking food. Then we have the actual deceased family member, who appears in a dream only to warn the living family but asks for nothing. Finally we have the ghost—who bears no other relation to the family—who takes up long-term residence in the home, and whose function seems to be to collect sinners and send them on their way to death. This ghost, whose function suggests he may be one of the "killing ghosts" or "killing demons" mentioned elsewhere in our text, is polite and forthcoming, and provides much information on the unseen world to its hosts as well as to visitors both lay and monastic. It is crucial to note that neither the second nor the third ghost seeks food; only the first one does. Indigenous models of food offerings to ancestors are here being challenged by a basic Buddhist system of merit making and merit transfer by means of sanctioned moral and ceremonial protocols.[687]

82[688]

During the Song there lived He Tanyuan 何曇遠, a native of Lujiang. His father, Wanshou 萬壽, served as palace aide to the censor-in-chief. Tanyuan upheld the Dharma vigorously and observed the bodhisattva precepts.[689] When he was eighteen, in the ninth year of Yuanjia [432–433], he was bereaved of his father. He grieved to the point of making himself ill and was on the verge of dying. [But] in addition to his weeping and throw-

---

686. *Ci zuo kong she* 此座空設; I understand *kong* to function adverbially here. In other words, although the family intends to render offerings to the dead at this ritual site, such observance is in fact not required by the dead, so the altar and its contents serve no useful function.

687. For reflections and sources on this tension, see Teiser, *The Ghost Festival*, 196–213.

688. Source texts: *Fayuan zhulin* 15.400b (section "honoring Buddhas" [*jing Fo* 敬佛]); *Taiping guangji* 114.3; Lu, *Gu xiaoshuo gouchen*, 429; Wang Guoliang, *Mingxiang ji yanjiu*, 83; Wakatsuki, Hasegawa, and Inagaki, *Hōon jurin no sōgō teki kenkyū*, 81–83. Additional texts: *Jushi zhuan* 4.189c; *Fozu tongji* 28.282a; *Wangsheng xifang jingtu yingrui zhuan* 1.107a.

689. On the range of disciplines and ordination ceremonies that may be referred to by this locution, mostly based (in China at least) on the indigenously composed *Fanwang jing*, see Hureau, "La cérémonie de réception"; Hureau, "Buddhist Rituals," 1227–1230; Funayama, "The Acceptance of Buddhist Precepts"; and *Hōbōgirin*, s.v. *bosatsukai* 菩薩戒.

ing himself about [with grief] he [also] fixed his mind entirely on the Pure Land and repeatedly prayed for a response.

At that time Tanyuan [frequently] invited monks [to his home], and there were often several of them there, including his master, Senghan 僧 含. Tanyuan often confessed to Senghan his karma[-generating] deeds from previous lives, fearing he had troublesome karmic conditions, but for a long time he had no responsive sign. Senghan would each time encourage him, urging him not to flag in his efforts. On the night of the sixteenth day of the second month of year ten [of Yuanjia, 22 March 433], he had finished reciting sutras, and the [visiting] monks had gone to sleep. In the middle of the fourth watch he suddenly began chanting and singing hymns.[690] Senghan, startled, asked him why, and Tanyuan said, "I saw the Buddha's body, the color of yellow gold, its size like that of the images current nowadays.[691] A golden light surrounded his body and rose up some eight feet over it. Banners, flowers, and pinions followed behind him, filling up all the surrounding space. It was simply beautiful beyond words." Tanyuan at the time was staying in the western wing [of his home]. He said further, "The Buddha came from the west, then turned to face west, stood in the doorway, and commanded [me] to depart quickly."

The entire next day Tanyuan was weak and at times seemed to stop breathing. That night his condition worsened greatly. But his face wore a delighted expression, and he got up to wash his hands. [The monk] Senghan put incense in his hands and picked flowers from the garden for Tanyuan to sprinkle before the Buddha on his behalf.[692] Tanyuan's mother said to him, "If you depart now, will you still think of us?"[693] Tanyuan made no reply, and soon afterward he collapsed. His family had already been [Buddhist] believers, and on hearing of these numinous anomalies they were both joyful and awed, not grieving much. At the fifth watch Tanyuan suddenly died. An intense fragrance filled the whole house and did not dissipate until several days later.

Comments

This story echoes the long-standing Chinese motif of the death summons[694]—the summons in this case being to the Western Pure Land, and

---

690. The day of the month and the nocturnal recitation alert us to the fact that the context here is an abstinence ceremony in Yuan's home.

691. Alternatively, "its size similar to that of the image carried in the procession today."

692. *Yao yi san Fo* 遙以散佛: I take the *yao* here to mean that Senghan intends Tanyuan to offer the incense and flowers on his behalf (literally "from afar") since Senghan cannot be there to do it personally. In the *Taiping guangji* version, the monk Senghan is not mentioned at this juncture, and Tanyuan picks flowers in order to "scatter them in the air" (*san kong* 散空).

693. Or, "In departing now, is it that you no longer think of us?"

694. For examples see Bokenkamp, "Answering a Summons," and Campany, "Return-from-Death Narratives."

delivered by the Buddha himself. The peaceful deathbed scene signifies that Tanyuan has succeeded in attaining the land of bliss.

83[695]

During the Song there lived the nun Shi Zhitong 釋智通; she resided in Jianjing 簡靜 [monastery] in the capital. She was of a lovely, youthful appearance, and her faith in the path was not steadfast. When her master died she left the path and married Liang Qunfu 梁群甫 of Wei commandery.[696] She gave birth to a son. When the child was six years old, the family was very poor and had insufficient means to buy material for clothing. When Zhitong had been a nun, she had had several scrolls of the *Sutra of the Buddha of Limitless Lifespan*, *Lotus*, and other sutras, all on undyed silk. She bleached the fabric and sewed it to make clothes for the boy. A year later she fell ill. She was confused and frightened, and her whole body was covered with wounds that resembled burns. Every day she pulled a liter's worth of thin white worms from her body. The pain was unbearable, and she screamed day and night. She often heard a voice in midair saying, "Because you destroyed sutras to make clothes, you are receiving this punitive retribution." In a little over a week she was dead.

Comments

Such stories as this one are the counterpart of tales of sutras as powerful agents: here it is the terrible consequences of destroying or desecrating sutras that are illustrated.

84[697]

During the Song, there were two sisters of the Lun 侖 clan who were natives of Zengcheng in Dongguan.[698] In the ninth year of Yuanjia [432–433] the older sister was nine years old and the younger was eight. They were coarse and ignorant, knowing nothing of sutras or the Dharma. Suddenly on the

---

695. Source texts: *Fayuan zhulin* 18.418c (section "honoring the Dharma" [*jing fa* 敬法]); Lu, *Gu xiaoshuo gouchen*, 429; Wang Guoliang, *Mingxiang ji yanjiu*, 84. Additional texts: *Fahua zhuanji* 3.59c; *Taiping guangji* 116.2.

696. In what is now Linzhang district, Henan province.

697. Source texts: *Fayuan zhulin* 5.304a–b (section "the six paths [of rebirth]" [*liudao* 六道]); *Fayuan zhulin* 22.453b (section "entering the [monastic] path" [*ru dao* 入道]); Lu, *Gu xiaoshuo gouchen*, 430; Wang Guoliang, *Mingxiang ji yanjiu*, 85; Wakatsuki, Hasegawa, and Inagaki, *Hōon jurin no sōgō teki kenkyū*, 42–45. Additional texts: *Biqiuni zhuan* 3.941c–942a (trans. Tsai, *Lives of the Nuns*, 67–68); *Ji shenzhou sanbao gantong lu* 3.433c. Previously discussed in Campany, "Buddhist Revelation and Taoist Translation," 3–4.

698. Dongguan was at the time a commandery in what is now Guangdong province.

eighth day of the second month[699] they both disappeared. After three days they returned, saying something rather confusedly about having seen the Buddha. On the fifteenth day of the ninth month they vanished again. When they returned ten days later they spoke in a foreign tongue and could recite sutras and even write Sanskrit. Upon meeting a monk from the Western regions, the girls and the monk were indeed able to understand each other.

The next year, on the fifteenth day of the first month, they suddenly disappeared once more. Workers in nearby fields said they saw them floating up into the sky on the wind. Their parents wailed in fear, sacrificing to the gods to beg their favor. Only after a month did the girls return home this time. They came back with their heads shaved as nuns, wearing monastic robes and carrying their hair. They said they had seen the Buddha as well as a nun, who had told them, "Because of your karma from former lives, it is appropriate that you become my disciples." With that the nun had raised her hand and rubbed their heads, whereupon their hair had fallen off. She had given them Dharma names: the older sister's name was Fayuan 法緣, the younger's Facai 法綵. Upon sending them back she had told them, "You should build an oratory. I will then transmit to you sutras and the Dharma."

The girls then had returned home. At once they dismantled and got rid of their family's altar to spirits[700] and set up in its place an oratory.[701] At night[702] they practiced abstinence there and recited sutras.[703] Each night there appeared a multicolored light that flowed around and encircled them like candle flames.[704] From this time forward, both girls were elegant in appearance, their speech ordered and perfect, so much so that even the most refined and elegant [ladies] of the capital could not surpass them. The regional inspectors Wei Lang 韋朗 and Kong Mo 孔默,[705] along with others,

---

699. This was one of two dates on which the birthday of Gautama Buddha was commemorated with festival observances. This and the other two dates mentioned below—the fifteenth day of the ninth month and the fifteenth day of the first month—were also days on which Buddhist laymen and laywomen, as well as monks and nuns, practiced abstinence ceremonies.

700. *Fayuan zhulin* 5, *Fayuan zhulin* 22, and *Ji shenzhou sanbao gantong lu* alike call this destroyed structure a *guizuo* 鬼座.

701. *Fayuan zhulin* 5 at this point terms this a *jinglu* 精廬, *Fayuan zhulin* 22 a *jingshe* 精舍. Both passages give *jingshe* three sentences above.

702. *Fayuan zhulin* 22 has "day and night."

703. In their behavior they thus replicated the central activities of the *zhai* ceremonies mentioned above.

704. *Fayuan zhulin* 5 here has, but *Fayuan zhulin* 22 lacks, the phrase "the girls said," which seems out of place. I follow *Fayuan zhulin* 22 in omitting it.

705. *Fayuan zhulin* 5 mentions only Wei Lang; I follow *Fayuan zhulin* 22 in including Kong Mo. Both men are mentioned in *Song shu*: Wei Lang at 5.79 and 5.82, and Kong Mo at 5.78, 42.1318, 64.1699, and 92.2270. According to *Song shu* 5.82, Wei Lang was appointed inspector of Guangzhou in Yuanjia 10 [433–434]; according to *Song shu* 5.78, Kong Mo[zhi] was inspector of Guangzhou in Yuanjia 6 [429–430].

went to their village to call on them and make merit donations. When these visitors heard the girls' speech, they were struck with wonder. Because of these events, everyone in the village learned to uphold the Dharma.[706]

Comments

This story's portrayal of the destruction of the household altar to spirits in favor of an oratory is its contribution to the Buddhist attempt to replace sacrificial modes of religion with its own systems for the production of merit and fortune. The particular dates on which the revelatory transmission of long-distance religious instruction to the girls is said to have occurred are not random: they suggest that the girls were being mysteriously elevated to some sort of celestial or Pure Land abstinence ceremony (or perhaps we should understand that they were whisked to an imagined India and back), able on their return to chant the scriptures they had heard recited there and speak the sacred language of the sutras. The final lines allow us to glimpse a community of onlookers and interlocutors whose impressions of the girls are what led to this story's preservation.

85[707]

During the Song there lived Wang Qiu 王球, styled Shuda 叔達,[708] a native of Taiyuan. He served as governor of Fuling.[709] Because in Yuanjia 9 [432–433] he was derelict in his duties in the commandery,[710] he was imprisoned and encumbered with a heavy chain that was fastened down tightly. Qiu had earlier been vigorous in his [Buddhist] practice; now that he was incarcerated he applied his mind diligently [in devotion]. There were over a hundred persons imprisoned with him, and many of them were hungry. Each time Qiu was given a meal, he distributed his food among them, meanwhile himself observing a fast[711] and concentrating his mind to the utmost on Guanshiyin. One night he dreamed he ascended a high seat,

---

706. *Fayuan zhulin* 22 and *Ji shenzhou sanbao gantong lu* both end with ellipses, omitting this final sentence. In *Biqiuni zhuan* it is said that Fayuan died at age fifty-five in the Jianyuan period.

707. Source texts: *Fayuan zhulin* 23.459b–c (section "exhortation and guidance" [*jiang-dao* 獎導]); Lu, *Gu xiaoshuo gouchen*, 430; Wang Guoliang, *Mingxiang ji yanjiu*, 86; Wakatsuki, Hasegawa, and Inagaki, *Hōon jurin no sōgō teki kenkyū*, 158–160. Additional texts: *Xi Guanshi-yin yingyanji* 23 (Makita, *Rikuchō kōitsu Kanzeon ōkenki no kenkyū*, 36); *Fayuan zhulin*, as cited in *Taiping guangji* 110.26; *Guanshiyin chiyan ji* 1.95c; *Guanyin cilin ji* 2.91a; *Fahua zhuanji* 5.71c. Previously translated and discussed in Teiser, *Reinventing the Wheel*, 121–126; my translation differs from Teiser's in ways noted below.

708. The byname varies across several textual sources.

709. Located in modern Fuling district, Sichuan province.

710. There is an apparent mention of this incident in *Song shu* 5.81.

711. *Chi zhai* 持齋. Here, given the context, *zhai* must be taken in the narrower sense of "fast" (from food) rather than as indicating the broader list of abstinences in the Buddhist periodic observance also often summarily referred to as *zhai*.

where he saw a monk who handed him a scroll of scripture. The titles on it read "Chapter on Light" and "Chapter on Comfortable Conduct,"[712] and it also had the names of various bodhisattvas. Qiu took and unrolled it. He forgot [on waking] the first bodhisattva's name but remembered that the second was Guanshiyin and the third was Mahāsthāmaprāpta.[713] He also saw a wheel, and the monk said, "This is the wheel of the five paths."[714] He then woke to find the chain severed. In his mind Qiu knew it had happened due to divine power, so he redoubled his concentration, and because of this[715] he refastened the chain. After three days of this,[716] he was pardoned.[717]

---

712. *Guangming anle xing pin* 光明安樂行品. "Comfortable Conduct" is the name of a chapter of Kumārajīva's translation of the *Lotus Sutra* (*Miaofa lianhua jing*, ch. 14), and it is very close in wording to the title of the corresponding chapter in Dharmarakṣa's translation (*Zheng fahua jing*). Teiser (*Reinventing the Wheel*, 124 n11) makes a "guess" that the other title may refer to a chapter in *Pusa yingluo jing*, translated by Zhu Fonian around 365. I am less certain than Teiser is that two titles are indicated in this phrase, rather than one, but it makes little difference to the story's import. Indeed I am not certain that the passage is intended to refer to (one or two) particular, *known* texts at all.

713. Or Dashizhi 大勢至. On this bodhisattva and his role in Chinese Buddhist devotion, see Mochizuki, *Bukkyō daijiten*, 3294b–3297a; Hou Xudong, "The Buddhist Pantheon," 1123; Hureau, "Translations, Apocrypha, and the Buddhist Canon," 770; and Wong, *Chinese Steles*, 145–147, 172, 177.

714. That is, the five paths of rebirth (sometimes counted as six paths). For studies of this textual and visual motif in Buddhist sources and physical culture, see Teiser, *Reinventing the Wheel*, and Teiser, "The Local and the Canonical."

715. That is, because he knew that he had divine protection and would eventually be freed.

716. Punctuating differently from the *Fayuan zhulin* text.

717. Teiser, *Reinventing the Wheel*, 123, translates the final lines thus: "When Qiu woke up, his chains were torn asunder. Qiu's power of mind was vast, and his spiritual strength was concentrated. Because he unlocked his own chains, after three days he was pardoned." I disagree with this translation on several points. First, in tales of this genre (and in many other kinds of texts from early medieval times), the phrase *xin zhi* 心知 is very often used verbally to mean "in his heart (or mind) he knew (or realized)" and rarely if ever to mean something like "the knowledge in his heart (or mind)" or, in Teiser's looser understanding, "power of mind." An example may be seen in item 49 above (translating *Fayuan zhulin* 17.410a15). Second, *ding zhi* 釘治 cannot mean "unlocked": *ding* 釘 means "to lock" or "to fasten," and *zhi* 治 is an all-purpose verb meaning "to manage." Third, simply in terms of narrative logic, prisoners do not normally get pardoned for unlocking their own chains. We are not told why Wang Qiu is pardoned. That moral or legal calculus happens offstage. What we are told of is Wang's own state of mind, which is one of confidence because he knows that the severing of his chains is an auspicious response by the Bodhisattva Sound Observer to his devotion and that he therefore only has to wait in order to be freed through proper channels. Typically in stories of this type that are set in the south, a pardon arrives. (See, e.g., item 53, though it is set in the west, and compare items 120, in which a prisoner's shackles are at first refastened by the jailer after being loosened by Guanshiyin, and 123, in which a prisoner is clearly said to have refastened his miraculously loosened fetters to wait for a pardon.) In stories where there was little hope of administrative pardon, such as those set in the north or those in which the prisoner is being held by bandits (as in item 73, in which a woman re-

Comments

This is a rather unusual Guanshiyin story in its mention of two quasi revealed scriptures and the wheel of rebirth, all of which appear as instructional props.

The Wang clan of Taiyuan was well-known in aristocratic circles, almost as prestigious as the Wangs of Langye.[718] Wang Yan's own clan hailed from Taiyuan, and it is possible that this Wang Qiu was his own ancestor, though in that case we would expect him to mention this.

86[719]

Liu Ling 劉齡 lived during the Song; his family's place of origin is unknown. He lived in Lucheng village in eastern Jinling.[720] He was quite observant of the Dharma. In his home he established an oratory, and he sometimes hosted abstinence gatherings. On the twenty-seventh day of the third month of the ninth year of Yuanjia [15 May 432] his father suddenly fell ill and died. A spirit-medium and an invocator[721] both warned that his family would soon experience three more deaths.

In a neighboring family there was a libationer who served the Dao named Wei Po 魏叵. He often made petitions and talismans so as to hoodwink and win over the villagers. He told Ling, "The disasters due to befall your family are not yet over. They are due to your having served a Western barbarian god. If instead you serve the great Dao, you will surely receive fortune; but if you do not change your ways, your entire family will be wiped out." So Ling began to perform libations with wine and no longer observed the Dharma. Po told him, "You should rid yourself of all your sutras and images. In this way further calamity can be avoided." So Ling closed up the doors to his oratory and started a fire inside it. The fire burned for several days. But only the room was burned; the sutras, images,

---

fastens her miraculously loosened fetters to avoid detection while waiting for her cell door to be miraculously opened as well), the prisoner has the bars of his cell miraculously opened so as to make his escape. My thanks to Stephen Bokenkamp for discussing this passage with me.

718. See Mather, "Intermarriage as a Gauge of Family Status," 215.

719. Source texts: *Fayuan zhulin* 62.760c (section "divination and physiognomy" [*zhan xiang* 占相]); Lu, *Gu xiaoshuo gouchen*, 431; Wang Guoliang, *Mingxiangji yanjiu*, 87. Additional texts: *Fayuan zhulin*, as cited in *Taiping guangji* 113.8. Previously discussed in Campany, "Notes on Sutra Texts," 42.

720. Jinling was a district in what is now Wujin district, Jiangsu province.

721. Translating *wuzhu* 巫祝. It is possible, though unlikely, that *wuzhu* here functions as a compound term somewhat redundantly denoting one person, not two. Often the roles were understood as distinct, with the *zhu* functioning as a sort of priest or master of sacred ceremonies and the *wu* as an entranced medium channeling communication with spirits—as seen today (under different nomenclature) in many ritual performances. See von Falkenhausen, "Spirit Mediums in Early China," 293, and Harper, "Contracts with the Spirit World," 243.

banners, and hanging scrolls remained completely intact, and the images moreover glowed brightly at night.

At the time there were over twenty libationers nearby. Some of them, awed and cowed by this numinous confirmation,[722] snuck away. But Po and his disciples were determined and were not to be deterred. He let down his hair, performed the steps of Yu,[723] and, brandishing his ritual sword and whip, said that the Buddha was ordered to return to his barbarian country, that he was forbidden to remain in China harming the people. That night Ling felt as if someone were raining blows on him, and he fell to the floor. When family members lifted him up, he was still breathing, but he was henceforth crippled and could no longer walk. As for the master of the Dao[724] Wei Po, he developed internal ulcers at that same time. Each day he lost two liters [of blood], and within a month he had died a very painful death. All of his followers developed leprosy.

One of Ling's neighbors, the governor of Dong'an,[725] Shui Qiuhe 水丘和, transmitted this story to Dongyang Wuyi 東陽無疑.[726] And there were many who saw the events at the time.

Comments

This is perhaps the most vividly contestational story in *Signs from the Unseen Realm*. Petitions and talismans (*zhang fu* 章符) were the classic Celestial Master Daoist way of relating to the gods. The story shows how a typical argument against Buddhism found in texts circulated among the educated elite—that it was a foreign import, or, as our text puts it, that the Buddha was a "Western barbarian god" (*hu shen* 胡神)—played out at the levels of the local community and ritual in much less abstract ways.[727]

---

722. "Numinous confirmation" translates *lingyan* 靈驗.

723. The "steps of Yu" (*Yu bu* 禹步) was an exorcistic dance modeled on the myth of the ancient thearch Yu and his taming of the cosmic flood (on which see most recently Lewis, *The Flood Myths of Early China*). The dance, long (and still today) associated with Celestial Master and other Daoist ritual, is thought to have originated with shamans as early as the Warring States period. See Andersen, "Practice of *Bugang*"; Harper, "Warring States, Qin, and Han Manuscripts," 240–243; Harper, "Warring States Natural Philosophy," 872–873; and Campany, *To Live as Long as Heaven and Earth*, 250.

724. Throughout, "master of the Dao" translates *daoshi* 道士, and "libationer" translates *jijiu* 祭酒. The terms both designated performers of Daoist liturgy; *daoshi*, which had earlier been a broader designation for practitioners of a larger range of loosely Daoist techniques, began to be used as a rough substitute for *jijiu* around the time these stories were formed, in the fifth century.

725. Located in what is now Zheshui district, Shandong province.

726. Dongyang Wuyi was the compiler of a *zhiguai* collection titled *Qi Xie ji* 齊諧記 (*Qi Xie's Records*), on which see Wang Guoliang, *Wei Jin nanbeichao zhiguai xiaoshuo yanjiu*, 323; Li Jianguo, *Tang qian zhiguai xiaoshuo shi*, 387–389; and Campany, *Strange Writing*, 80–81.

727. For a survey of this sort of anti-Buddhist argument and pro-Buddhist responses to it, see Zürcher, *The Buddhist Conquest of China*, 264–280.

87[728]

During the Song there lived one Ma Qianbo 馬虔伯, a native of Langzhong in western Ba.[729] In his youth he had believed in the Dharma of Buddha. He was serving as magistrate[730] of Yihan district[731] when, one night in the seventh month of the twelfth year of Yuanjia [August 435], he had a dream in which he saw three persons in the sky, some twenty feet tall, of serious and elegant mien, looking down on him from the clouds. Celestial music filled the air. They said to him, "Your peril lies in Jingchu.[732] In the fifteenth year [438], on the fourth day of the eighth month, if you head into the mountains and marshes the misfortune will dissipate. You are also excused from the abstinences and prohibitions that are observed among people [around that day]. If you can pass safely through that period, then you will awaken to the Path." As he looked upward he then caught sight of Yang Xian 楊暹 and others, eight in all, whom he knew; all were in shackles and chains. He also saw the master of the Dao Hu Liao 胡遼, his body half submerged in the ground. Divine personages in the heavens were calculating the year and month on which the allotted life spans of the eight of them would run out; it was only to Liao that they said, "If you can cultivate yourself and establish merit, you can lengthen your life further." Yang Xian and the others all [later] died according to the schedule he [Qianbo] had overheard. Hu Liao, for his part, grew even more frightened, and so he upheld the Dharma, lived in the mountains, and practiced [Buddhism] with great diligence to the utmost.

Qianbo later worked in the Western Section of the administration of Liangzhou[733] under the governor Xiao Sihua 蕭思話 [406–455].[734] Xiao was then transferred to the region of the Southern Man 南蠻[735] and ordered to serve there as acting administrator. When Qianbo heard the Jingchu dialect he was greatly apprehensive and asked Xiao to be relieved of his duties and posted to Hengshan, but Xiao steadfastly refused. It was the

---

728. Source texts: *Fayuan zhulin* 32.536c–537a (section "transformations" [*bianhua* 變化]); *Taiping guangji* 113.10; Lu, *Gu xiaoshuo gouchen*, 431; Wang Guoliang, *Mingxiang ji yanjiu*, 88; Wakatsuki, Hasegawa, and Inagaki, *Hōon jurin no sōgō teki kenkyū*, 204–206.

729. Langzhong was a district in what is now still known as Langzhong district, Sichuan province.

730. The term used is an informal one; see Hucker, *A Dictionary of Official Titles*, 514, s.v. *tsai-chün*.

731. A district located in what is now Dongxiang district, Sichuan province.

732. An old name for the region of Chu in the south, comprising modern Hubei and Hunan provinces.

733. Liangzhou was located in what is now Nanzheng district, Shaanxi province.

734. Mentions of Xiao may be found in sprinkled throughout the *Song shu* and *Nan shi*. His official biography appears at *Song shu* 78.2011 and *Nan shi* 18.933.

735. *Man* 蠻 was a general, vague designation for any of a variety of southern, non-Han ethnic groups.

fifteenth year [of Yuanjia, 438], an *wuyin* 戊寅 year; at the end of the sixth month Qianbo fell ill. By the fourth day of the eighth month the illness was grave, and his life hung in the balance. At dusk that evening, he suddenly in the distant sky to the west caught sight of three persons, perhaps sixteen feet tall. The one in front wore a lined robe[736] and a beard, with a round halo over his head; the two behind wore brilliant raiments of gold. They stood dignified, arrayed in the air several dozen feet above the ground. Qianbo scrutinized them carefully and confirmed they were the ones he had dreamed of earlier. Soon they vanished, but a fragrance persisted, and all who lived in the area, young and old, could smell it. After this, Qianbo perspired heavily, and his condition seemed to improve slightly. His living quarters were lowly, but during this time it seemed to him that he was living in a palace with walls covered in precious stones. Afterward his illness completely dissipated, and he returned to normal.

Comments

Are we to understand the three dream-figures here—later also glimpsed in a confirmatory waking vision—as some of the "spirits of goodness" (*shanshen*) we read of elsewhere? Like the *shanshen*, in any case, they function as overseers and protectors of a pious layman.

88[737]

During the Song there lived the monk Zhu Huiqing 竺惠慶, a native of Guangling.[738] He constantly practiced to cultivate insight. In the twelfth year of Yuanjia [435–436] there was general flooding in Jing;[739] rivers and

---

736. There are textual variants which could indicate a sort of headgear, but what seems to be meant is *jia* 袷, glossed in many sources as *jiayi* 夾衣 and meaning a doubled or two-layered robe or gown (but without padding or collar), similar to the even simpler *danyi* 單衣, a single-layer gown or robe that seems to have connoted *official attire* to contemporary readers. (See, for example, the sumptuary regulations for various grades of officials in *Song shu* 18.510–524, where *danyi*, along with *ze* 幘, some sort of turban, headcloth, or tight-fitting cap [see Dien, *Six Dynasties Civilization*, 313], is almost uniformly the prescribed attire for many ranks of officials from the central court to the provinces and districts.) We are in need of a specialized study of the many terms for items of clothing and headgear, their precise designations, and their broader cultural associations in both secular and Daoist and Buddhist canonical sources in this period.

737. Source texts: *Fayuan zhulin* 65.785c–786a (section "saving from danger" [*jiu wei* 救厄]); Lu, *Gu xiaoshuo gouchen*, 432; Wang Guoliang, *Mingxiang ji yanjiu*, 89. Additional texts: *Meisōden shō*; *Gaoseng zhuan* 12.407b; *Guanshiyin chiyan ji* 1.95a; *Guanyin cilin ji* 2.91b; *Xi Guanshiyin yingyan ji* 29 (Makita, *Rikuchō kōitsu Kanzeon ōkenki no kenkyū*, 29), where the inclusion of a version of the same story in Liu Yiqing's *Xuanyan ji* is mentioned.

738. He has a brief biography in *Gaoseng zhuan* 12.407b, where his monastic name is given as Shi Huiqing 釋慧慶. He is there grouped among monks skilled at sutra recitation, and essentially the same story is given.

739. An old name for the region of Chu in the south.

dry land were as one. Huiqing was on his way to Mount Lu. His boat was exceedingly small. A violent wind suddenly arose. Other travelers had managed to put in to shore, but Huiqing's boat had not yet been able to drop anchor. The wind on the river was ferocious, and the waves were towering to the point where there was nothing to do but quietly wait for the boat to capsize and sink. Huiqing concentrated his mind and focused his thought, chanting the *Guanshiyin Sutra*. Others nearby watched as his boat was suddenly propelled through the water as if pulled by several dozen men. His boat thus reached the riverbank, and everyone on the boat was saved.

89[740]

During the Song, there lived Ge Jizhi 葛濟之, a native of Jurong and descendant of Ge Zhichuan 稚川.[741] His wife was a member of the Ji 紀 clan from the same commandery; she was beautiful and elegant, an excellent wife. Jizhi and his family for generations had served divine transcendents.[742] So had the Ji clan, but [Jizhi's wife] in her heart had long delighted in the law of Buddha without flagging. In the thirteenth year of Yuanjia [436–437] she was working at her loom when she suddenly noticed that the clouds were parting and the sky was brilliantly clear. She put down her basket and shuttle and looked up in all directions. In the west she saw the perfected form of the Tathāgata,[743] along with bejeweled canopies, banners, and scrolls arrayed across the sky. In her heart she rejoiced, thinking, "The scriptures speak of the Buddha of Limitless Lifespan. Is this he?" She then made obeisance. Jizhi, surprised[744] to see her doing this, got up and went over to her. She took his hand and pointed to where the Buddha was, and Jizhi was then able to look up and see half the Buddha's body and the banners and canopies. After a short while they faded away. Afterward the sky was streaked with a brilliant array of radiant colors, noticed by many neighbors and relatives nearby. Only after the span of two or three meals' time did the radiant colors also fade away.

Because of this, many in this hamlet took refuge in the Dharma.

---

740. Source texts: *Fayuan zhulin* 15.399c–400a (section "honoring Buddhas" [*jing Fo* 敬佛]); *Taiping guangji* 114.5; Lu, *Gu xiaoshuo gouchen*, 432; Wang Guoliang, *Mingxiang ji yanjiu*, 90; Wakatsuki, Hasegawa, and Inagaki, *Hōon jurin no sōgō teki kenkyū*, 74–76. Additional texts: *Fozu tongji* 28.289c; *Wangsheng ji* 3.151c. Discussed: Soper, *Literary Evidence for Early Buddhist Art*, 167; Hou Xudong, *Wu liu shiji beifang minzhong Fojiao xinyang*, 142.

741. I.e., Ge Hong 洪, author of *The Master Who Embraces the Unhewn*, *Traditions of Divine Transcendents*, and other works. See Campany, *To Live as Long as Heaven and Earth*, and Campany, "Two Religious Thinkers."

742. Following the phrasing in *Taiping guangji*, *shi shi shenxian* 世事神仙, rather than *Fayuan zhulin*'s *shi shi xianxue* 世事仙學, which would yield "for generations had served the practice of transcendence."

743. That is, the body of the Buddha. "Perfected form" translates *zhenxing* 真形.

744. Reading 驚 for 敬. The *Taiping guangji* version omits these few sentences.

Comments

In its co-optation of a member by marriage of the Ge lineage so highly esteemed by many Daoists, including both participants in the quest for transcendence and admirers of the Lingbao revelations and rituals of the early fifth century,[745] this story very clearly engages in pro-Buddhist contestation with those traditions. It is also an excellent example of the intrafamily tensions that were sometimes triggered by Buddhist practice.

90[746]

During the Song there lived the nun Huimu 慧木, whose natal surname was Fu 傅. She left the household[747] at eleven, receiving and observing the precepts of a novice.[748] She resided at Zhuyi 築弋 monastery in Liang commandery. She began by reciting the *Larger Perfection of Wisdom Sutra*; each day she would chant two scrolls of it. Her master, Huichao 慧超, had had a sutra hall[749] constructed. Each time Huimu went there to do obeisance, a monk appeared in the northeast corner of the room, his body golden, his robe black, his feet not touching the floor. Huimu would also continue chanting [sutras] when lying down for the night. She [once] dreamed she went to the Western land, where she saw a pool filled with lotus blossoms, each blossom giving birth by transformation to a person, the people all arrayed seated on the blossoms. There was one large blossom that had no one sitting in it. Huimu tried to climb up into the blos-

---

745. On which see Bokenkamp, "Sources of the Ling-pao Scriptures."

746. Source texts: *Fayuan zhulin* 15.400a (section "honoring Buddhas" [*jing Fo* 敬佛]); Lu, *Gu xiaoshuo gouchen* 433; Wang Guoliang, *Mingxiang ji yanjiu*, 91; Wakatsuki, Hasegawa, and Inagaki, *Hōon jurin no sōgō teki kenkyū*, 76–78. Additional texts: *Biqiuni zhuan* 2.938c (trans. Tsai, *Lives of the Nuns*, 45–48). Tsai also translates the *Mingxiang ji* story; my translation differs considerably. Discussed: Mai, "Visualization Apocrypha," 21.

747. "To leave the household" is the literal meaning of *chujia* 出家 and the way in which I have consistently translated this expression. Note, however, that a few lines down Huimu appears to be still living at home with her mother; she takes up residence in a monastery only after her mother's death. In the Dunhuang region three and more centuries later it was common for monks and nuns to live with their families, going to monasteries only on special occasions, and the same may have been true in some (or many) areas in south China in the fifth century. See Hao Chunwen, "The Social Life of Buddhist Monks and Nuns," 82–89.

748. *Shouchi xiaojie* 受持小戒, literally "received and observed the lesser [set of] precepts." Wang Guoliang improbably takes "lesser" to indicate "the precepts of the Lesser Vehicle." Here this expression must mean the ten precepts undertaken by a novice upon his or her initial monastic ordination, which were the five lay precepts (to abstain from taking life, stealing, sexual misconduct, lying, and intoxicants) plus refraining from all sexual activity and five additional rules (to abstain from eating after midday; from singing, dancing, and music; from wearing jewelry and using perfumes; from sleeping on elevated, luxurious beds; and from handling gold and silver).

749. "Sutra hall" translates *jingtang* 經堂.

som, and as she was exerting herself in doing so [in her dream] she was unconsciously chanting sutras in a loud voice. Huimu's mother, thinking she must be suffering fright from a nightmare, got up and called out to her.

Huimu's mother was decrepit. She had no teeth left, so Huimu would always chew her mother's food for her and then feed it to her; in doing so she broke the prohibition against eating after midday. Since she was unable to maintain ritual purity, she passed the age of thirty without yet having received the full monastic precepts.[750] After her mother died, Huimu personally cleared away brush, built an [ordination] platform, and asked to receive the precepts from her master. Suddenly the air and ground around the platform were flooded with a golden radiance. Looking up toward the southwest, she saw a celestial person wearing a brocade robe of crimson and yellow, sometimes nearer to Huimu and sometimes farther away. In a little while the person vanished.

Each time she saw numinous anomalies such as this, she would keep them secret, telling no one. Her elder brother, who had also left the household [to become a monk], got wind of them and wished to know about them, so he tried to coax them out of her by saying, "You have been on the path for many years, but with no discernible results. You could let your hair grow back out and marry." When Huimu heard this she was very apprehensive,[751] so she told him in rough terms what she had seen. It was only the nun Jingcheng 靜稱[752] who, hearing of her virtue, went to make inquiries of her, so that Huimu told her everything in detail.

Later, Huimu, along with her monastic colleagues, was [once] paying obeisance to Amitābha Buddha. In doing so she prostrated herself on the floor without rising, so that everyone thought she must be asleep. Even when nudged and questioned, Huimu made no response. When Jingcheng persistently sought her attention, Huimu finally answered, "As I was lying on the floor, I dreamed I went to the Anyang realm 安養國[753] and saw the Buddha there. He was expounding the *Smaller Perfection of Wisdom Sutra* for us and had already progressed up to the fourth scroll. I was then awakened by your nudging, which I deeply regret!"

In the fourteenth year of Yuanjia [437–438] Huimu was sixty-nine years old.

---

750. *Dajie* 大戒, literally "the greater [set of] precepts," here meaning the entire set of over two hundred monastic rules. For convenient discussions of the basic monastic ordination ceremony and the rules of monastic life, see Lamotte, *History of Indian Buddhism*, 54–65, and Hureau, "Buddhist Rituals."

751. Lest her older brother attempt to compel her to quit the monastic path and marry.

752. The nun Jingcheng is the subject of a biography in *Biqiuni zhuan* 2.940a, translated in Tsai, *Lives of the Nuns*, 55–56.

753. Literally "the realm [where one is] at peace and cared for," a common epithet for the Pure Land (and one that recurs in item 126 below).

Comments

In the *Traditions of Nuns* (*Biqiuni zhuan*) version of her story, Huimu does not construct her own ordination platform: instead she sees it, along with the divine monk, in a vision. The ordination platform was a ritual prop laden with religious significance, as recent studies have shown.[754] This story is another example of the confirmation of Pure Land scriptural depictions by means of the reported experiences of an individual in China.

91 [755]

During the Song there lived the monk Shi Sengyu 釋僧瑜, a native of Yu-hang in Wuxing.[756] His original surname was Zhou 周. He left the household while still a youth and was remarked as having unusual spiritual discernment. He devoted himself intensely and fully to his cultivational practice, never flagging from start to finish. In Yuanjia 15 [438–439] he traveled to Mount Lu; among his companions were [the monks] Tanwen 曇溫, Huiguang 慧光, and others. They all practiced with the utmost strictness and maintained pure discipline at their retreat. To this end they built a structure on the south side of the mountain. It is the one known today as Zhaoyin 招隱 monastery.

Sengyu often considered that being bound to the three unfortunate paths of rebirth[757] was the result of attachment and bodily form,[758] and that attachment must therefore be expunged and form reduced. How could the precedent set by the Medicine King be uniquely unattainable?[759] And so Sengyu uttered an oath to burn his body. At age forty-three, on the third day of the sixth month of Xiaojian 2 [3 July 455], he set about fulfilling his aim. Monks and laypersons came to watch, their vehicles and mounts amassed nearby. Sengyu led all others in his practice of the path and adhered strictly to the scriptural precepts. On the day in question it was overcast and about to rain. Sengyu uttered a vow: "If what I intend is to be fulfilled, then let the sky clear. If [my vow] is an insufficient stimulus, then let it pour rain. Let this assembled community see that divine response is

---

754. See McRae, "Daoxuan's Vision of Jetavana"; Hureau, "Buddhist Rituals," 1212; and Chen, *The Revival of Buddhist Monasticism*, 100.

755. Source texts: *Fayuan zhulin* 63.770a–b (section "gardens and fruits" [*yuanguo* 園果]); Lu, *Gu xiaoshuo gouchen*, 434; Wang Guoliang, *Mingxiang ji yanjiu*, 92. Additional texts: *Gaoseng zhuan* 12.405a–b, which is quoted in *Fayuan zhulin* 96.992a–b (section "giving up life" [*she shen* 捨身]), although the attribution there is unclear; *Hongzan fahua zhuan* 5.24a; *Fahua zhuanji* 10.94b; *Fahua jing chiyan ji* 1.68a; *Meisōden shō*. Discussed in Benn, *Burning for the Buddha*, 35–36 (with a partial translation of the *Gaoseng zhuan* text).

756. Yuhang district, still today so named, is in Zhejiang province.

757. The *santu* 三途, meaning rebirth as an animal, a hungry ghost, or a purgatory dweller.

758. Translating *qing xing* 情形.

759. See comments.

no lie." Soon after he finished speaking the clouds parted, and the sky cleared. Come nightfall he mounted the pyre, joined his palms together, and sat motionless while reciting the "Medicine King" chapter.[760] When the flames reached him he remained seated with his palms joined, composed. When monastics and laypersons heard of it, they rushed to the site, bowed, and made obeisance, wishing to create a karmic tie to his act.[761] All present saw purple *qi* rise into the air, lingering a long time before dissipating.[762]

Two weeks later a pair of paulownia trees sprang up in the chamber where Sengyu had lived, the roots and branches intertwining as if from a single tree. They grew through the thatch roof and kept on growing until they formed one giant tree. Experts said they were *suoluobao* trees,[763] that Sengyu had attained *nirvāṇa*,[764] and that his achievement resulted in this manifestation of verifying signs. Sengyu thus came to be called the Paired Paulownia Monk.

Zhang Bian 張辯 of Wuxing[765] was serving as administrator on the staff of the [General Who] Pacifies the South[766] at the time. He witnessed these events personally and recounted them in detail in a eulogy....[767]

Comments

This is our text's only mention of self-immolation as an extreme devotional act—not surprisingly, given the lay point of view of the stories it collects.[768] As our story indicates, one scriptural inspiration and model for this act was the chapter of the *Lotus Sutra* devoted to the Bodhisattva Med-

---

760. That is, the famous chapter of the *Lotus Sutra* that created the main scriptural warrant for the sort of self-immolation described here. Other accounts of such acts frequently mention that the self-immolator chanted this *Lotus* chapter as the flames rose.

761. This phrase translates rather literally *yuan jie yinyuan* 願結因緣. In these few sentences I follow the *Gaoseng zhuan* version; the *Fayuan zhulin* version lacks these sentences, jumping from the advancing flames to the purple smoke with no mention of the *Lotus* chapter or the crowd's reaction.

762. *Gaoseng zhuan* here has "He was forty-four at the time," but this sentence does not appear in *Fayuan zhulin* (and is inconsistent with information given earlier in the story). From this point on I revert to the *Fayuan zhulin* text.

763. *Suoluobao shu* 娑羅寶樹 often designates teak trees, but that makes no sense in the context.

764. This is the only instance in our text in which a Buddhist practitioner is explicitly claimed to have attained *nirvāṇa* so denoted (as mentioned in Liu Yuanru, *Chaoxiang shenghuo shijie*, 287–288).

765. According to *Song shu* 53.1509, he was the fourth son of Zhang Yu 裕 (styled Maodu 茂度, a figure mentioned repeatedly in the same history) and held a series of offices.

766. Based on *Song shu* 6.119, Wang Guoliang surmises that this must be Liu Hui 劉褘, prince of Donghai.

767. Ellipsis in the original. The eulogy is quoted in the *Gaoseng zhuan* version of the story.

768. For a comprehensive study of the complex and highly controversial act of self-immolation in Buddhist circles in early medieval China, see Benn, *Burning for the Buddha*.

icine King.[769] In demographic terms, self-immolation was a vanishingly rare (and, to my knowledge, exclusively monastic) act in early medieval China, but records of its performance understandably drew much attention and controversy.

92[770]

During the Song there lived one Ruan Zhizong 阮稚宗, a native of Hedong.[771] In the sixteenth year of Yuanjia [439–440] he was serving in Zhongli[772] under the governor Ruan Yin 阮愔 in the commandery headquarters. The governor sent Zhizong on a mission to a distant hamlet, escorted by subofficial functionaries Gai Gou 蓋茍 and Bian Ding 邊定. When they had reached the homes of the villagers there, Zhizong was suddenly as if asleep and could not be awakened. The people assumed he had died. They carried him outside and were about to encoffin him when, after a night had passed, he was able to speak.

He said that at first a hundred-odd people arrived, bound him, and led him away. After going several dozen *li* they arrived at a stupa[773] to which an assembly of monks was presenting offerings, just as in this world. One monk said, "You enjoy hunting and fishing. Now you will receive the retribution for these." With that Zhizong was taken and flayed in exactly the manner in which animals are butchered. He was then thrown into deep water, hooked in the mouth, pulled out, sliced open, and minced, as sashimi is prepared. Next he was thrown into a hot cauldron over a stove and cooked, turned over three times. The pain was unbearable. He was then asked, "Do you want to live?" Zhizong knocked his head on the ground and begged for his life. The monk ordered him to crouch down and then poured water over him, saying, "One ablution will remove five hundred sins." Zhizong pleaded for more ablutions, but the monk said, "Three is enough."

Zhizong then saw several ants. The monk pointed to them and said, "Although these are only tiny creatures, even they may not be killed, not to mention living beings larger than this. Of fish and meat, you may eat only from those animals that have died naturally. On days of abstinence cere-

---

769. Trans. Hurvitz, *Scripture of the Lotus Blossom*, 293–302.

770. Source texts: *Fayuan zhulin* 64.772b (section "fishing and hunting" [*yulie* 漁獵]); Lu, *Gu xiaoshuo gouchen*, 434; Wang Guoliang, *Mingxiang ji yanjiu*, 93. Additional texts: *Xiangyi ji* 祥異記, cited in *Taiping guangji* 131.10, previously translated in Campany, "Return-from-Death Narratives," 119–120 (where Yuan's surname is erroneously given as 元). Discussed: Mai, "Visualization Apocrypha," 86 n54.

771. Hedong was a commandery in what is now northern Xia district, Shanxi province.

772. Zhongli was a commandery in what is now northeastern Fengyang district, Anhui province.

773. The term *fotu* 佛圖 is sometimes used (in this text and elsewhere) to designate a monastery, but here a stupa is clearly intended.

mony gatherings, you must wear new clothes, or, if not new, they should be freshly washed."[774]

Zhizong then asked, "There were three of us traveling together, but I am the only one who received punishment. Why?" The monk answered, "Those two are already aware of sin and merit, yet despite being aware of it, they still commit offenses. Only you were ignorant of karmic retribution, so we did this to warn you."

At this point Zhizong revived. After several days he was able to rise. Henceforth he gave up fishing and hunting.

Comments

Among other things, this story illustrates the degree to which sin and merit were conceived as quantifiable, as well as contingent on intention. None of the regulations taught by the monk to Zhizong would have seemed new or surprising to even moderately well-informed Buddhist readers (whether lay or monastic), but the story graphically demonstrates their gravity.

93[775]

Xing Huaiming 邢懷明 was a native of Hejian;[776] during the Song he served as an adjutant under the general-in-chief [Liu Yikang 劉義康 (409–451)]. He once followed governor Zhu Xiuzhi 朱修之 on his northern campaign, which ended in utter defeat.[777] After this the men [including Huaiming] were looking for opportunities to escape back southward. They would travel by night and hide during the day. Three days later they were still fearful of being caught, so they sent someone ahead to scout for signs of enemy presence. Several days passed, and the man did not return. Then one night, when it was very dark and cloudy, the scout suddenly returned just before daybreak. Surprised, the man said, "Just now I could see a very bright firelight, so I headed toward it, but now that I've arrived here, I find it's dark." Xiuzhi and the others were amazed. Huaiming had previously been observant of the Dharma, and ever since the beginning of the campaign he had constantly carried a copy of the *Guanshiyin Sutra* on his head and had recited it without cease. That night, too, he had been quietly chanting it, so ev-

---

774. These are not new or unusual injunctions. Xi Chao's *Fengfa yao*, for example, mentions the total prohibition on killing, even insects, and on accepting meat that has been specifically slaughtered for the practitioner; see Zürcher, *The Buddhist Conquest of China*, 165.

775. Source texts: *Fayuan zhulin* 23.459b (section "exhortation and guidance" [*jiangdao* 奬導]); Lu, *Gu xiaoshuo gouchen*, 435; Wang Guoliang, *Mingxiang ji yanjiu*, 94; Wakatsuki, Hasegawa, and Inagaki, *Hōon jurin no sōgō teki kenkyū*, 155–158. Additional texts: *Xi Guanshiyin yingyanji* 57 (Makita, *Rikuchō kōitsu Kanzeon ōkenki no kenkyū*, 50–51); *Fayuan zhulin*, cited in *Taiping guangji* 110.25; *Guanyin cilin ji* 2.91a. Previously translated in Campany, "Notes on Sutra Texts," 37–38 (translating only the *Xi Guanshiyin yingyanji* version, and only partially).

776. A commandery in what is now Shandong province.

777. A campaign mentioned in passing in *Song shu* 97.2397.

eryone thought the event must be due to divine power. Because of this they together maintained prayerful hearts,[778] and thus they were able to escape.

Huaiming [then] lived in the capital. In the seventeenth year of Yuan-jia [440–441] a monk called on Huaiming and said, "I see that this lane, including your home, has a strong aura of blood. You should move away so as to avoid it." When he had said this, he departed. Huaiming followed behind and watched him; as soon as the monk had passed through the outer gate, he vanished. He regarded it as deeply inauspicious. Two weeks later his neighbor Zhang Jingxiu 張景秀 attacked his father and killed his father's concubine. Huaiming took this event as what had been meant by the "aura of blood" and assumed he was in the clear. At the time Liu Bin 劉斌 and Liu Jingwen 劉敬文 were neighbors with properties abutting Huaiming's on the same lane. That year, they were all taken to be involved in the Liu Zhan 劉湛 cabal and were thus all executed....[779]

94[780]

During the Song there lived one Cheng Dedu 程德度, a native of Wuchang. His father, Daohui 道惠, had served as regional inspector in Guangzhou.[781] Dedu was serving as adjutant under the prince of Linchuan [Liu Yiqing 劉義慶, 403–444][782] and was at the time in Xunyang. At his home there was a swallow nest. One night he saw his room suddenly brighten and a small, immaculate lad, perhaps a foot tall, emerge from the nest, come to his bedside, and say, "Three years from now you will attain a way of long life." The next moment he vanished. Dedu secretly wondered at it.

In the seventeenth year of Yuanjia [440–441] he followed the prince on his campaign in Guangling and while doing so met a meditation master named Shi Daogong 釋道恭.[783] He went to him to study meditation, resulting in a great advance in his understanding.

---

778. Translating *yu shi chang gong qixin* 於是常共祈心.

779. Ellipsis in the original. These figures and events are mentioned multiple times in *Song shu* (e.g., at 26.747, 52.1497, 58.1595). I know of no Western-language discussion of them.

780. Source texts: *Fayuan zhulin* 28.492b (section "numinous anomalies" [*shenyi* 神異]); Lu, *Gu xiaoshuo gouchen*, 436; Wang Guoliang, *Mingxiang ji yanjiu*, 95; Wakatsuki, Hasegawa, and Inagaki, *Hōon jurin no sōgō teki kenkyū*, 199–200. Additional texts: *Xuanyan ji* 11 (cited in *Taiping yulan* 922.3a).

781. This is also reported in *Song shu* 5.77. Cheng Daohui is the protagonist of item 44 above.

782. Liu Yiqing, an imperial prince, is best known for having ordered his officials to compile the collection of witty anecdotes known as *Shishuo xinyu* 世說新語, or *Recent Anecdotes from the Talk of the Age*, on which see Mather, *Shih-shuo Hsin-yü*. My translation of the title of the work is borrowed from Jack Chen. Liu is mentioned at several points elsewhere in our text as well, sometimes as an interlocutor or witness to events narrated there. For a recent biographical sketch, see Knechtges and Chang, *Ancient and Early Medieval Chinese Literature*, 588–590.

783. It might be this same monk who is mentioned in passing in *Xu gaoseng zhuan* 19.580b26, a biography set in the Eastern Jin period.

In the spring of the nineteenth year [442], in his home in Wuchang, there was suddenly an unusual fragrance in the empty abstinence [hall],[784] dispersing out into the street so that neighbors came to see what it was. Only after three days did it dissipate.

Comments

This item appears to be a collection of very brief (perhaps summarized) anecdotes of miracles transmitted by or associated with a known individual, which suggests one way in which the tales in *Signs from the Unseen Realm* came to be transmitted.

95[785]

During the Song there was one Liu Chenzhi 劉琛之, a native of Pei commandery. In Guangling he once met a monk who told him, "You have the *qi* of one who is ill, but you should not expect to die from it. You can offer a feast worth 100 or 200 in cash for the assembly of monks and thereby avoid this trouble." Chenzhi had never believed in the Buddha's Dharma, and in his mind there arose resistance. The monk said, "You should have more faith, rather than getting angry." When the monk had walked twenty paces away, he suddenly vanished. Chenzhi fell ill seven days later. He was weak and near death. On the ninth day, as if in a dream yet not in a dream, he saw a five-story Buddha stupa atop his heart. There were twenty or more monks circumambulating the stupa paying obeisance. At this he awoke and felt great relief. The sickness gradually subsided.

Later, he was residing in the capital when an unfamiliar monk walked directly in through his door and said to him, "You, sir, have the karmic destiny to practice Dharma. Why do you not exert yourself in it?" Chenzhi then told him of his previous encounter [with a monk], and this monk said, "That was Piṇḍola." When the monk had said these words, he suddenly departed, it was unclear in which direction.

In the summer of Yuanjia 17 [440] Chenzhi was in Guangling when he saw from afar, before the Huiwang monastery, banners and canopies in great profusion, but without any [Buddha] image. He hurried forward for a closer look, but as he approached the gate the whole scene suddenly vanished.

Comments

Here again we see spirit-monks offering advice and hovering near the devotee to protect him—unless the monks he sees circumambulating the

---

784. *Kongzhai* 空齋, which here can only mean an empty chamber for abstinence observances—short, that is, for the usual *zhaitang* 齋堂.

785. Source texts: *Fayuan zhulin* 36.569a15ff. (section "hanging banners" [*xuanfan* 懸幡]); Lu, *Gu xiaoshuo gouchen* 436; Wang Guoliang, *Mingxiang ji yanjiu*, 96; Wakatsuki, Hasegawa, and Inagaki, *Hōon jurin no sōgō teki kenkyū*, 209–211.

stupa over his heart are to be understood instead as beneficent spirits (*shanshen*).[786] This stupa over the devotee's heart and the spirit-monastery are further cases of elements of the unseen world suddenly glimpsed in a fleeting but vivid vision thanks to devotional acts.

One of the circle of senior arhats who were the initial followers of Gautama Buddha, Piṇḍola (a name variously transliterated in Chinese texts—here it is Bintoulu 賓頭盧), about whom many legends accreted over the centuries in India and East Asia, was also "regarded as one of the [a]rhats who had voluntarily remained in the world to protect the [Dharma] until the coming of Maitreya"[787] (the next, future Buddha). This story illustrates this idea by showing Piṇḍola still active in the world. He also figured importantly in Chinese Buddhist legend and ritual practice—as, for example, the devotional focus of a rite of "bathing the monk" (*yu seng* 浴僧), as well as in the practice of leaving the highest-ranking seat for him at merit feasts hosted by lay families for monastic and lay guests during abstinence ceremonies, at which feasts he was also represented by an image. Both customs are prescribed in the brief mid-to-late-fifth-century ritual text *Method for Inviting Piṇḍola* (*Qing Bintoulu fa* 請賓頭盧法).[788]

96[789]

During the Song there lived one Fu Wanshou 伏萬壽, a native of Pingchang.[790] In the nineteenth year of Yuanjia [442–443] he was serving as military adjutant in Guangling.[791] He asked for leave to return home. As he

786. Or unless this is, in some cases, a distinction without a difference.

787. Zürcher, *The Buddhist Conquest of China*, 391 n73.

788. These same customs were treated in texts listed by Sengyou in his catalogue, including his now-lost compendium on Buddhist ritual practices. See for example *Chu sanzang jiji* 4.23b24, listing *Qing Bintoulu fa*; 4.33a24, listing a *Bintoulu qupen jing* 賓頭盧取鉢經 in one scroll; and 4.4.35c28, listing a *Yuseng gongde jing* 浴僧功德經 in one scroll. In the table of contents of his now-lost *Fayuan zayuan yuanshi ji* 法苑雜緣原始集 preserved in chapter 12 of the same work are listed several other relevant texts from which Sengyou had excerpted passages on the origins of customs, such as the *Yuseng yuan ji* 浴僧緣記, listed as extracted from a *Wenshi jing* 溫室經 [12.92a6], and a *Gongyang shengseng yuanji* 供養聖僧緣記, listed as extracted from *Bintoulu jing* 賓頭盧經 [12.92a8]. See also Lévi and Chavannes, "Les seize arhat protecteurs de la loi"; Strong, "The Legend of the Lion-Roarer"; Georgieva, "Buddhist Nuns in China," 148–149, 167; Lamotte, *History of Indian Buddhism*, 243–244; Shinohara, "Taking a Meal at a Lay Supporter's Residence," 28–35; Zürcher, *The Buddhist Conquest of China*, 194; Link, "The Biography of Shih Tao-an," 34–35; Mochizuki, *Bukkyō daijiten*, 4333–4335; Joo, "The Ritual of Arhat Invitation," 85–86; and Ch'en, *Buddhism in China*, 100–101.

789. Source texts: *Fayuan zhulin* 27.484b (section "utmost sincerity" [*zhicheng* 至誠]); Lu, *Gu xiaoshuo gouchen*, 437; Wang Guoliang, *Mingxiang ji yanjiu*, 97; Wakatsuki, Hasegawa, and Inagaki, *Hōon jurin no sōgō teki kenkyū*, 169–171. Additional texts: *Xi Guanshiyin yingyanji* 7 (Makita, *Rikuchō kōitsu Kanzeon ōkenki no kenkyū*, 28–29); *Fayuan zhulin*, cited in *Taiping guangji* 111.6; *Guanshiyin chiyan ji* 1.96a; *Guanyin cilin ji* 2.90b.

790. Pingchang was a commandery in what is now Anqiu district, Shandong province.

791. *Xi Guanshiyin yingyanji* 7 further specifies that he was adjutant to the prince of Linchuan, Liu Yiqing.

was returning by boat, he was crossing the river one night at the beginning of the fourth watch. The waves and current were normal when they set out, but at midstream a wicked wind rose up. It was also pitch black, and no one knew which direction to steer toward. Wanshou had earlier been a strict observer of Dharma. Now he single-mindedly entrusted his life to Guanshiyin, concentrating on him without pause. In a little while, several persons on the boat saw lights on the north bank resembling the home fires of a village; they rejoiced, saying, "Those must be bonfires."[792] So they steered the boat accordingly, reaching shore before daybreak. When they asked people on shore about it, they said, "No one lit a fire here last night." Only then did they realize [the light] had been due to divine power. When he arrived at his destination Wanshou sponsored an abstinence-ceremony gathering.

Comments

The motif of the apparent firelight that suddenly materializes (after invoking Guanshiyin) to guide travel by night, which later turns out to have been of a miraculous nature, is also seen in items 31 and 92. We have here an example of a story type that traveled and was repeated, in modular fashion, in the creation and propagation of new experiences and stories about them.

97[793]

During the Song, there was one Gu Mai 顧邁,[794] a native of Wu commandery. He was a strict upholder of Dharma and served as a military adjutant. In year 19 of Yuanjia [442–443], he was returning [with a party of officials] from the capital to Guangling. They had just left Shitou city[795] when they encountered crosscurrents and unfavorable winds. The wind had not yet subsided when the people on the boats had exhausted all available measures. When they reached the middle of the river, the waves were even larger. Mai's boat was the only one still upright. The peril was extreme, and there were no alternatives, so he recited the *Guanshiyin Sutra*. He had completed over ten cycles of recitation when the wind gradually subsided and the waves calmed. At that point a fragrance resembling a strange type of

---

792. Following *Taiping guangji* and not *Fayuan zhulin* here.

793. Source texts: *Fayuan zhulin* 27.484b16ff. (section "utmost sincerity" [*zhicheng* 至誠]); Lu, *Gu xiaoshuo gouchen*, 437; Wang Guoliang, *Mingxiang ji yanjiu*, 98; Wakatsuki, Hasegawa, and Inagaki, *Hōon jurin no sōgō teki kenkyū*, 171–172. Additional texts: *Guanyin cilin ji* 2.90b; *Xi Guanshiyin yingyan ji* 8 (Makita, *Rikuchō kōitsu Kanzeon ōkenki no kenkyū*, 29), where the inclusion of a version of the same story in Liu Yiqing's *Xuanyan ji* is mentioned. That version is no longer extant but was probably a source for this *Mingxiang ji* item.

794. Gu Mai is mentioned in *Song shu* 42.1309, 77.2006, 100.2462; *Nan Qi shu* 42.752; and *Nan shi* 15.428.

795. Located near Qingliangshan in today's city of Nanjing, Jiangsu province.

incense could be detected in midstream, powerful and lasting. Mai was secretly glad in his heart, and he kept reciting without cease, and so he reached shore safely.

98⁷⁹⁶

During the Qin period[797] there lived the monk Daojiong 道冏. His place of origin and family name are given in a previous record.[798] In the eighteenth year of the Hongshi period of the Yao Qin 姚秦 [416],[799] his master Daoyi 道懿 sent him to Mount Huo 霍山[800] in Henan to gather stalactites.[801] He went together with four others, including fellow disciple Daolang 道朗. Carrying torches, they entered a cave. They had gone a distance of three *li* when they reached a deep stream, which they [planned to] cross on a wooden beam. Jiong was the first across. The others all fell from the beam and died. The torches also were extinguished, so that it was now pitch black. Jiong could only weep, thinking his life was over. But he called "Guanshiyin" single-mindedly, vowing[802] that if he was able to get out he would offer a gathering for a hundred guests[803] as his recompense to the great deity.[804] After passing a night, he saw a tiny light flickering; it looked like a firefly. Suddenly the cave was flooded with light. He was thus able to see a way out and managed to exit the cave.

Because of this experience his belief and understanding deepened, and he witnessed a succession of miraculous events. In Yuanjia 19 [442–443] Prince Kang of Linchuan [Liu Yiqing][805] was serving as defense commander in Guangling and invited Jiong to a merit feast. In the ninth month

796. Source texts: *Fayuan zhulin* 65.784c–785a (section "saving from danger" [*jiu wei* 救厄]); Lu, *Gu xiaoshuo gouchen* 437; Wang Guoliang, *Mingxiang ji yanjiu*, 99. Additional texts: *Xi Guanshiyin yingyan ji* 60 (Makita, *Rikuchō kōitsu Kanzeon ōkenki no kenkyū*, 52); *Fayuan zhulin*, quoted in Taiping guangji 111.5. Note: Item 76 above (based on the passage cited from *Mingxiang ji* in *Fayuan zhulin* 17) is another story about Shi Daojiong. Both were clearly included—but separately—in Wang Yan's text (or at least in some early version of *Mingxiang ji*), and the second story alludes to the first. See the first note to item 76 for a synopsis of the contents of the various sources.

797. The events in the ensuing narrative span the northern dynasties later known as the Later Qin (384–417), Western Qin (385–431), and beyond. From 446 to 452 there was a major persecution of Buddhism in the north, particularly in the capital, Chang'an; see Liu Shufen, "Art, Ritual, and Society," 29–30, and Liu Shufen, "Ethnicity and the Suppression of Buddhism."

798. Item 76 above.

799. That is, the northern Qin dynasty founded and ruled by members of the Yao clan.

800. In Linru district, Henan province.

801. Stalactites were ground into powder and used medicinally. See Unschuld, *History of Pharmaceutics*, 232–233.

802. *Shiyuan* 誓願.

803. *Xi Guanshiyin yingyan ji* 60 has "one hundred monks."

804. *Biao bao weishen* 表報威神.

805. On whom see note above in item 93 and below, item 98.

of that year, [Jiong] was performing a ten-day Guanshiyin abstinence ceremony in [his host's] western abstinence hall.[806] It was the ninth day. That night, when the fourth watch was ending, all the monks were sleeping. Jiong rose and performed obeisance.[807] Returning, he was about to begin sitting meditation when he suddenly saw monks without number, their bodies half protruding from the four walls, and a Buddha with a conch topknot,[808] all very distinct and clear. There was one tall personage who wore a pillbox-shaped cap and a jacket-and-trousers ensemble made of sheer cloth,[809] brandishing a sword, his countenance very imposing and strange. He plucked out a stick of incense [from a bundle] and handed it to Jiong, who, however, hesitated to take it. The monks in the wall responded, "Master Jiong, you should accept the incense for the benefit of your host." Then in a moment they all faded away and were no more to be seen. While this was happening, he looked but could see none of the monks in the assembly. All he could see was the processional image[810] of Śākyamuni that had been placed there.

99[811]

During the Song there was the nun Tanhui 曇輝, a native of Chengdu in Shu commandery.[812] Her secular surname was Qingyang 青陽, and her given name was Baiyu 白玉. At the age of six she already took delight in sitting in meditation. Each time she did so, her consciousness would reach some place that she did not recognize; she simply said it must be a dream. One night when she was sleeping together with her older sister, she entered

---

806. We are probably to understand that the host implied here is Liu Yiqing, but the wording leaves this less than clear.

807. Presumably to the image installed on the altar for this ritual—probably in this case an image of Sound Observer.

808. *Luoji* 螺髻, that is, with his hair tied atop his head in a spiral-shaped topknot resembling a conch shell, in the style of South Asian monarchs. This passage could describe quite well the cave chapels carved into hillsides and riverbanks by artisans hired by medieval Chinese Buddhist donors.

809. "Sheer cloth" again (as above in item 76) translates *jianbu* 箋布. "Jacket-and-trousers ensemble" renders *kuxi* 褲褶, a fashionable style of dress during the period, probably introduced by the Xianbei people who ruled northern China for much of this era but soon popular even among civil and military officials in the south; see Dien, *Six Dynasties Civilization*, 319–320.

810. *Xingxiang* 行像. A processional image was lighter than permanent images, designed to be carried by one person in religious processions, and thus appropriate for use during a periodic ceremony such as the one described here.

811. Source texts: *Fayuan zhulin* 22.453a19ff. (section "entering the [monastic] path" [*ru dao* 入道]); Lu, *Gu xiaoshuo gouchen* 438; Wang Guoliang, *Mingxiang ji yanjiu*, 100; Wakatsuki, Hasegawa, and Inagaki, *Hōon jurin no sōgō teki kenkyū*, 151–154. Additional texts: *Biqiuni zhuan* 4.945c–946b, trans. Tsai, *Lives of the Nuns*, 92–95 (this version is a bit longer and more detailed than the one translated here); *Gaoseng zhuan* 3.343c.

812. Present-day Chengdu, capital of Sichuan province.

a trance state.[813] Her sister found her in a corner of the screen, her body like wood or stone, not breathing. Terrified and alarmed, the sister summoned other family members, all of whom shook her but were unable to rouse her even when morning came. They rushed to ask shamans what to do, and they all said that she was possessed by a ghost or spirit.[814]

When she was ten, the foreign meditation master Kālayaśas[815] arrived in the region of Shu. Tanhui asked him for an audience. Kālayaśas, in consideration of the level she had already reached in meditation, encouraged her to leave her family [to become a nun]. At that time Tanhui was about to be married; a day had been set [for the wedding]. [Meanwhile the nun] Fayu 法育, without consulting with Tanhui's family, had been secretly inviting her to the monastery. Once Tanhui's family learned of this, they tried to force her to marry, but Tanhui refused to budge, announcing this solemn oath: "If my intention to enter the Path is not to be recognized, but if instead I am to be compelled [to marry], then I will burn this body of mine or feed it to tigers. Having then rid myself of this vile form,[816] I vow to ascend by the utmost in mental concentration to see all the Buddhas of the ten directions."

Regional Inspector Zhen Fachong 甄法崇,[817] who was a Buddhist believer, when he heard of Tanhui's determination went to call on her. He furthermore summoned officials and monks and nuns to a meeting in which she was questioned and objections were raised, but she would not be moved. All those seated at the time sighed in wonder. Fachong then gave permission for her to leave her family and receive the monastic precepts. In year 19 of Yuanjia [442–443], Prince Kang of Linchuan [Liu Yiqing] invited her to Guangling.

Comments

We note here again the use of shamans—in depicted practice, and in narrative—to confirm Buddhist representations. The familial tensions result-

---

813. In sutras, this term, *ding* 定, is normally used to render *samādhi*, represented in texts as a complex type of trancelike absorption with many stages, levels, and aspects. See Harrison, "*Buddhānusmṛti*"; Harrison, "Commemoration and Identification in *Buddhānusmṛti*"; Harrison, *The Pratyutpanna Samādhi Sūtra*; Stevenson, "The Four Kinds of Samādhi"; and Zürcher, *The Buddhist Conquest of China*, 194, 222–223.

814. *Guishen suo ping* 鬼神所憑.

815. Jiangliangyeshe 畺良耶舍. His name seems to have been a transliteration of the Sanskrit Kālayaśas; he arrived in Nanjing in 424 and is credited with the translation of a small number of sutras, including the *Sutra on Visualizing the Buddha of Limitless Life Span* mentioned elsewhere in this text (although scholars now doubt that that sutra is in fact a translation from an Indic original). He is the subject of a biography in *Gaoseng zhuan* 3.343c–344d.

816. Rebirth as a woman was presented in many—but not all—Buddhist texts as less desirable than rebirth as a man. For a critical reassessment of the relevant sources and their actual impact on women's practice in medieval East Asia, see Meeks, *Hokkeji*. Compare item 117.

817. He is mentioned at several points in the official histories: see *Song shu* 5.81, 29.862, 45.1384, and 64.1699; for a biography, see *Nan shi* 70.1705.

ing from the appeal of the monastic vocation to young women are in clear evidence; here, an official becomes involved as mediator.

100[818]

During the Song period, Zhao Xi 趙習 of Huainan in the twentieth year of Yuanjia [443–444] was serving as assistant to the commander of the guard. He had a long-standing illness from which he feared he would not recover. With utmost mind he took refuge in the Buddha. That night he dreamed of a man of extraordinary appearance, like a god, who handed him from the rafter beam a small packet and a razor and said, "Take this medicine and use this razor,[819] and your illness will certainly be cured." Xi then woke up with a start, and he actually had possession of the medicine and the razor. He at once took the medicine, and his sickness was dispelled. He left the household and took the Dharma name Sengxiu 僧秀. He lived past the age of eighty, and only then died.

101[820]

During the Song there lived the monk Shi Huiquan 慧全, a meditation master from Liangzhou.[821] He taught and bestowed teachings on many; he had five hundred followers. There was one disciple who by nature was rather uncivil and deviant.[822] Huiquan refused to instruct him. Later the man suddenly proclaimed that he had attained the third fruit of the path.[823] Huiquan, because the disciple had never engaged in any prac-

---

818. Source texts: *Fayuan zhulin* 22.453b (section "entering the [monastic] path" [*ru dao* 入道]); Lu, *Gu xiaoshuo gouchen*, 439; Wang Guoliang, *Mingxiang ji yanjiu*, 101; Wakatsuki, Hasegawa, and Inagaki, *Hōon jurin no sōgō teki kenkyū*, 154–155.

819. The razor is presumably to be used for shaving the head prior to monastic ordination. It functions, in other words, as a synecdochic suggestion to leave the household.

820. Source texts: *Fayuan zhulin* 19.429a (section "honoring the order of monks" [*jing seng* 敬僧]); Lu, *Gu xiaoshuo gouchen*, 439; Wang Guoliang, *Mingxiang ji yanjiu*, 102; Wakatsuki, Hasegawa, and Inagaki, *Hōon jurin no sōgō teki kenkyū*, 147–149. Additional texts: *Ji shenzhou sanbao gantong lu* 3.433c–434a; *Shimen zijing lu* 2.824a; *Fanwang jing pusa xin dipin xia lue shu* 6.749c. Discussed: Mai, "Visualization Apocrypha," 383.

821. Liangzhou was a commandery located in what is now Wuwei district, Gansu province.

822. Following the well-attested variant reading given in *Ji shenzhou sanbao gantong lu*, I translate *yi* 異, in preference to *Fayuan zhulin*'s *bao* 暴, though either would make sense in the context.

823. *San daoguo* 三道果, that is, the status of a "non-returner," one who will not again be reborn as a human being but rather into one of several "pure abodes" where he will gain final awakening. See Gethin, *The Foundations of Buddhism*, 194; and Buswell and Gimello, introduction to *Paths to Liberation*, 8. These stages of progress toward the status of arhat were already laid out in China in the indigenously composed *Sutra in Forty-Two Sections*, as well as in many early-translated sutras; see Sharf, "The *Scripture in Forty-Two Sections*," 364–365, and Heng-ching Shih, *Sutra of Forty-Two Sections*, 33–34.

tice, never acknowledged his claim. Later Huiquan fell ill. When the disciple in question came one night to ask after him, the door to Huiquan's chamber remained shut as it had been. Huiquan was amazed. Wishing to test him further, he told him to return the next night. He then secretly had all the windows and doors sealed. That night the disciple arrived, proceeding right up to Huiquan's bedside, and said, "Now the *ācārya* should be convinced!" He then told Huiquan, "When, *ācārya*, you cross over to your next life, you will be reborn in a brahman household." Huiquan said, "I have accumulated much practice in meditation. How would I come to be reborn in such a status?" The disciple said, "*Ācārya*, your faith in the path is not steadfast, and you have never completely broken with your study of outside texts.[824] Although you have merited fortune and rewards, you cannot yet transcend [rebirth]. If you were to sponsor a large assembly and were thereby able to feed one sage, you would achieve a fruit of the path."

Because of this, Huiquan hosted an assembly. The disciple then again spoke to him: "You should distribute monastic robes. If there are any who are in need of them, do not discriminate between senior and junior monks." When the assembly was concluding and the robes were being distributed, a *śrāmaṇera* [novice] approached Huiquan seeking a robe. Realizing it was his disciple, Huiquan said, "I intended to present this to a sagely monk! Why should I give it to you?" But then he recalled the admonition not to distinguish between senior and junior, so he joyfully presented the robe.

Another day when Huiquan saw this novice, he asked him, "Are you not going to wear the robe I gave you?" The novice said, "Not only did I not receive a robe, I had business to attend to and was ashamed not to be able to make your assembly." Only then did Huiquan realize that the novice at the assembly was a sage transformed.

It was many years before the disciple passed on from this world. At the time of his passing, there were no further anomalies, except that on all sides of his tomb there sometimes appeared white lights. As for Huiquan, he was still alive in Yuanjia 20 [443–444], residing in Jiuyuan.[825]

Comments

Unlike most stories in *Signs*, this one concerns only monks, not laypersons. It is also one of our text's very few mentions of a monk hosting an abstinence ceremony.

---

824. "Study of outside texts" translates *wai xue* 外學, here meaning the study of non-Buddhist texts and methods of various sorts.

825. Jiuyuan was a commandery in what is now Jiuyuan district, Gansu province.

102[826]

During the Song there lived one Wang Hu 王胡, a native of Chang'an. His uncle had been dead for several years when, in the twenty-third year of Yuanjia [446–447], his form suddenly appeared and returned to his former household. He accused Hu of lax conduct and of letting family affairs become disordered, and he caned him five times as punishment. Bystanders and neighbors all heard his voice and the sounds made by the caning, and they saw the wounds made by the beating, but they could not see the uncle's form; only Hu could see it. The uncle told Hu, "I should not have died yet, but the spirits needed me to perform calculations in the registers of the dead. Today I am followed by a large detachment of [spirit] officers and troops, but I was afraid they would frighten and decimate the populace of the village, so I did not bring them in with me." Hu could indeed see a large mass of ghosts milling about just outside the village.

Soon thereafter, his uncle took his leave, saying, "I will return again briefly next year on the seventh day of the seventh month.[827] At that time I intend to take you on a tour of the byways of the unseen realm, so that you will know of the retribution that follows upon sins and fortunate acts. You need not set out any expensive offerings at that time, but if this makes you uneasy, you can simply set out some tea." On the day in question he did indeed return, saying to the Hu family, "I am about to take Hu on a sightseeing tour. When it is completed, I will return him here. Don't worry." Hu then abruptly lay down on his bed and seemed to black out and pass away. At this the uncle took him to see a succession of mountains, glimpsing all the ghostly anomalies on each one. The last mountain they visited was Mount Song.[828] When the ghosts encountered Hu, they would all offer him refreshments. For the most part they did not differ in flavor from those of this world, except that the ginger there was far superior. Hu wanted to take some of the ginger back with him, but those nearby laughed and told him, "You can only eat it here. You can't take it back with you."

At the very end of his tour Hu saw a place with richly decorated rooms and well-appointed pavilions, inhabited by two monks. Hu called on them, and the monks set out various fruits and areca nuts for him. Hu wandered

---

826. Source texts: *Mingbao ji*, as cited in *Fayuan zhulin* 6.314c–315a (section "the six paths [of rebirth]" [*liudao* 六道]); Lu, *Gu xiaoshuo gouchen*, 440; Wang Guoliang, *Mingxiang ji yanjiu*, 103; Wakatsuki, Hasegawa, and Inagaki, *Hōon jurin no sōgō teki kenkyū*, 48–51. Like Lu Xun and Wang Guoliang, I take this to be a *Mingxiang ji* story (see Wang Guoliang, *Mingxiang ji yanjiu*, 25, for a brief discussion). Additional texts: *Gaoseng zhuan* 10.392b; *Yiyuan*, as cited in *Taiping guangji* 323.13 (Wang Guoliang, p. 25, incorrectly says that *Taiping guangji* fails to cite its source for this story); *Shenseng zhuan* 2.956a; *Mingbao ji ji shumu* 310a.

827. See comments.

828. A noted mountain located in Henan province.

about this area for a long time, seeing all the punishments and rewards that are given in recompense for sins and fortunate acts, respectively. He then took his leave. The uncle told him, "Now you realize that goodness must be cultivated. Why, then, would you wish to remain in the household? The 'White-Footed Reverend'[829] is a strict and eminent practitioner of the precepts. You should serve him as your master." This Chang'an monk's feet were light in color, hence at the time people called him White-Footed *alian* 白足阿練. He was deeply respected by the Wei caitiffs, and the circle of men surrounding the caitiff ruler all treated him as their master. Hu thereupon followed these instructions. In [Tanshi's] monastery he saw the two young monks whom he had encountered the previous year on Mount Song. Astounded, he took them aside and asked, "When did you come here?" They answered, "We have all along resided at this monastery, and we have no recollection of having ever seen you before!" Hu again spoke of their encounter on Mount Song, but the monks said, "You are mistaken, sir. How could this be?" The next day, the monks left the monastery for no apparent reason. Hu then went around to all the other monks in residence there, telling them of what he had previously seen on Mount Song. They were all astonished to hear of it and set off after the two monks to catch up to them, but they were unable to locate them. At this they realized the two monks must have been divine persons.

At the end of the Yuanjia period, the Chang'an monk Shi Tanshuang 釋曇爽 came traveling through Jiangnan and told of all of this in detail.

Comments

We see in this story another fascinating admixture of indigenous and Buddhist themes, with indigenous ones predominating here. The seventh day of the seventh month had long been a point in the calendar at which contact between the seen and unseen worlds was especially fluid, and item 26 above similarly features a deceased person visiting his living family on this date.[830] It is unusual for a living human traveler in the other world to be described as receiving food from his spirit-hosts, although this motif recurs in item 119.

---

829. *Baizu alian* 白足阿練; *alian* was apparently a respectful term of address for monks (but it had a range of meanings; see *Yiqie jing yinyi* 5.335b). *Baizu alian* was the nickname of a monk, Shi Tanshi 曇始, known from several other sources. He is the subject of a hagiography in the section of *Gaoseng zhuan* devoted to wonder-working monks (10.392b). But there seem to have been more than one monk with this or a very similar sobriquet: see *Ji shenzhou sanbao gantong lu* 3.434a; *Poxie lun* 1.481a; *Xu gaoseng zhuan* 1.428a; and *Guang hongming ji* 2.102a.

830. For further treatment see Campany, *To Live as Long as Heaven and Earth*, 266–269.

103[831]

During the Song there lived the layman Bian Yuezhi 卞悅之, a native of Ji-yin.[832] He served as audience attendant and lived beside the Chao canal.[833] At fifty he did not yet have a son. His wife chose a concubine for him, but several years went by without her having conceived. In order to pray for descendants, he recited the *Guanshiyin Sutra* one thousand times. When he had completed this number of recitations, the concubine conceived and bore him a son. This occurred in the eighteenth year of Yuanjia [441–442], a *xinyi* year....[834]

Comments

Compare item 70 above.

104[835]

During the Song, when the monk Shi Tandian 釋曇典 was still a layman aged twenty-nine, he suddenly fell ill and died, then revived after seven days. He said that when he first died he saw two men rush up to take him away. They made him grind grain.[836] There must have been a group of several thousand persons all grinding grain day and night without stop. Then he saw two monks, who said to him, "We are your original five-precept masters."[837] They had come to ask after him and comfort him. They took him to see the official in charge, saying, "He is our disciple. Furthermore, he has committed no grave sins. And his life span count[838] is not yet used up." So he was released and sent back.

The two monks escorted Tandian back to his home, stopping above his

---

831. Source texts: *Fayuan zhulin* 52.678b (section "family" [*juanshu* 眷屬]); *Taiping guangji* 111.2; Lu, *Gu xiaoshuo gouchen*, 441; Wang Guoliang, *Mingxiang ji yanjiu*, 104. Additional texts: *Guanshiyin chiyan ji* 1.96a; *Guanyin cilin ji* 2.91b. Wang Guoliang, *Mingxiang ji yanjiu*, 20, says that a version of the story appears in *Xuanyan ji*, but I do not find it in Lu Xun's compilation of quotations from that work.

832. Jiyin was a district in what is now Dingtao district, Shandong province.

833. Chaogou 潮溝, a canal in northern Jiankang, mentioned in *Jiankang shilu* 2.

834. Ellipsis in the original. The *Taiping guangji* version omits the ellipsis and places the event in Yuanjia 14 (without giving a cyclical designation in the sexagenary cycle). Wang Guoliang emends the sexagenary correlate, and I follow his emendation.

835. Source texts: *Fayuan zhulin* 90.953c (section "breaking the precepts" [*pojie* 破戒]); Lu, *Gu xiaoshuo gouchen*, 441; Wang Guoliang, *Mingxiang ji yanjiu*, 105. Discussed: Mai, "Visualization Apocrypha," 119–120.

836. Following Wang Guoliang and the variants given in the Taishō edition.

837. *Wo shi ru wujie benshi* 我是汝五戒本師. Contrary to what Wang Guoliang says (*Mingxiang ji yanjiu*, 215 n2), this must mean that they were his masters in a former life as a layman (not that they are Buddhas or bodhisattvas). If they were his masters from his present lifetime, then he should have recognized them when they appeared.

838. Translating *li suan* 曆筭.

house. They admonished him, "You should become a monk and diligently cultivate the work of the path." When they had spoken these words, they descended into the house, and the monks pushed Tandian back into his body through his armpit.[839] He then revived.

Afterward he left the household. Twenty years later, in Yuanjia 14 [437–438], he died.

Comments

The monks cite three distinct reasons for return to life, all of them classic, two Buddhist and one not unique to Buddhism. One of the things this story does is argue again forcefully for the benefits of having Buddhist masters. Not only do they look out for you in this world, they are also your advocates in the next. And the next world is most certainly a place where one has need of advocates.

The scene in which ghosts grind grain is reminiscent of a humorous story, reproduced in more than one tale collection from our period, in which a new ghost is put to work grinding grain, first by a Buddhist and then by a Daoist household, until it learns it must cause frightening anomalies at the homes of "commoners" (*baixing* 百姓) if it wants to cajole sacrifices from terrified living families.[840]

105[841]

During the Song, one Wang Huaizhi 王淮之, styled Yuanzeng 元曾,[842] was a native of Langye. For generations his family had been staunch classicists[843] and did not believe in the Dharma of Buddha. He often said, "The body and spirit both perish; how can there exist the 'three times'?"[844] During the Yuanjia period he served as magistrate of Danyang. In the tenth year [433–434] he fell ill and stopped breathing. After a short while he briefly re-

---

839. In Buddhist legend Siddhārtha's mother was said to have delivered him via her armpit. This particular point for the soul's reentry into the body is unusual in stories of this type.

840. See *Bianzheng lun* 7.538b and *Youming lu* item 256 (Lu, *Gu xiaoshuo gouchen*, 274–275).

841. Source texts: *Fayuan zhulin* 79.875a14ff. (section "the ten evil acts" [*shi e* 十惡]); Lu, *Gu xiaoshuo gouchen* 441; Wang Guoliang, *Mingxiang ji yanjiu*, 107.

842. In *Song shu* 42.1313 and 42.1318, and *Nan shi* 21.570 and 21.649, his name is given as Wang Zhunzhi 准之 and his byname as Yuanlu 魯.

843. *Ru* 儒, scholars especially learned in the classics—works that later, through complex historical processes and interactions with Western assumptions, came to be identified with the "Confucian" tradition. On the senses of *ru*, see Nylan, *The Five "Confucian" Classics*, 2 n and 364–365. The Wang clan of Langye was one of the most famous and powerful clans during these centuries.

844. In Buddhist doctrine this generally refers to the past, present, and future; here, more specifically, it means past, present, and future lives in the courses of rebirth.

vived. At that time the magistrate of Jiankang, He Daoli 賀道力,[845] was among the others there calling on the family. Huaizhi told Daoli, "Now I know that Buddhist teachings are not false. When people die, their spirits survive; this belief can be confirmed." Daoli said, "All your life you argued against this view. Why have you now changed your mind?" Huaizhi knitted his brow and said, "The spirit truly does not die. Buddhist teachings must be believed." When he had said this, he expired.

Comments

Here we see a relatively unusual bit of contestation: classicist versus Buddhist. The story co-opts a member of the powerful Langye Wang family of southern Shandong—a family known to have produced adherents of Daoism and Buddhism as well as of the classicist tradition—into the Buddhist community.[846]

106[847]

During the Song, the monk Huihe 慧和 resided at Zhongzao monastery 眾造寺 in the [southern] capital. At the time of the disorder of the Yijia period [466],[848] Huihe was still a layman and was serving as a clerk on the staff of Liu Hu 劉胡. Hu at one point led a raiding party of several dozen men to carry out reconnaisance to the east. Huihe was among them. They got as far as Que[wei] island[849] when they were met by imperial troops on the west bank. The raiding party dispersed, each man fleeing into the countryside and marshes. Huihe managed to reach the outskirts of Xinlin[850] undetected. There he met an old peasant whose clothes were tattered. He exchanged his intact trousers and jacket for this man's clothes, and he carried a shoulder pole and thus resembled a farmer of the area. At the time detachments of troops were moving about, rounding up members of the scattered raiding party. Examining Huihe's appearance closely, they grew suspicious and questioned him, and Huihe's answers gave him away. He was further interrogated under torture and slated for immediate execution. Now, ever since Huihe had fled the raiding party he had been silently

---

845. He is mentioned in the official histories: see *Nan Qi shu* 33.598 and *Nan shi* 22.604. On Jiankang, the southern capital, in this period see Liu Shufen, "Jiankang," and Dien, *Six Dynasties Civilization*, 34–45, 356–357.

846. On this family, see Mather, "Intermarriage as a Gauge of Family Status."

847. Source texts: *Fayuan zhulin* 27.484b–c (section "utmost sincerity" [*zhicheng* 至誠]); Lu, *Gu xiaoshuo gouchen*, 442; Wang Guoliang, *Mingxiang ji yanjiu*, 113; Wakatsuki, Hasegawa, and Inagaki, *Hōon jurin no sōgō teki kenkyū*, 172–174. Additional texts: *Xi Guanshiyin yingyanji* 18 (Makita, *Rikuchō kōitsu Kanzeon ōkenki no kenkyū*, 33); *Fayuan zhulin*, cited in *Taiping guangji* 111.8; *Guanshiyin chiyan ji* 1.95b; *Guanyin cilin ji* 2.90c.

848. The fullest account of this rebellion may be found in *Song shu* 84.2129–2135. The Liu Hu mentioned in the next sentence is also mentioned in these same pages of *Song shu*.

849. Located in what is now Wuwei district, Anhui province.

850. In today's Jiangning district, Jiangsu province.

reciting the *Guanshiyin Sutra* continuously. When it came time for his execution, his earnest prayers were answered. The executioner brought down the blade three times, and each time it broke. Alarmed, the executioner released him.

After this, Huihe left the household and carried out his practice vigorously.

107[851]

During the Song the monk Huiyuan 慧遠[852] resided at the Changsha monastery 長沙寺 in Jiangling.[853] His teacher, Huiyin 慧印, excelled at meditation methods; he was often referred to simply as the Master of Meditation. Huiyuan had originally been Huiyin's servant, and his original name was Huang Qian 黃遷, but when he was twenty, each time Huiyin entered a meditative trance[854] he saw that Qian in their previous lives had been his teacher, so he released Qian and made him his disciple. He often sent Huiyuan to the home of Yang Daochan 楊道產, located west of the Jiangling market. [Huiyuan] practiced *pratyutpanna* with utmost strictness for over a year, and because of this he obtained some anomalies in response.

Once, in the space of a single day, he attended the abstinence ceremony in more than ten locations at once, and although that night he continued by circumambulating and reciting sutras,[855] at each household Huang Qian was seen to be present.[856] The community gradually began to wonder at him, suspecting he must have attained [some stage on] the Path.[857]

In the second year of Xiaojian [455] he suddenly one day announced the time of approaching death. He said to Yang Daochan, "Tomorrow eve-

---

851. Source texts: *Fayuan zhulin* 97.1003c29–1004a (section "mortuary practices" [*song zhong* 送終]), 19.428c29–429a10 (section "honoring the order of monks" [*jing seng* 敬僧]); Lu, *Gu xiaoshuo gouchen*, 442; Wang Guoliang, *Mingxiang ji yanjiu*, 108; Wakatsuki, Hasegawa, and Inagaki, *Hōon jurin no sōgō teki kenkyū*, 145–147. Additional texts: *Gaoseng zhuan* 10.393c; *Ji shenzhou sanbao gantong lu* 3.434a–b.

852. He is not to be confused with the famous, earlier monk also named Huiyuan (of Lushan, 334–417), who is mentioned in items 14 and 55 above.

853. Its founding is narrated in *Gaoseng zhuan* 3.342c, and it is mentioned elsewhere in that text (5.355c–356a, 8.377a, 10.393c, 11.399a, 13.416b), in *Guang hongming ji* (15.202b, 24.277a), in *Ji shenzhou sanbao gantong lu* (2.416a–b, where it is mentioned as having temporarily housed an "Aśokan image," on which see Zürcher, *The Buddhist Conquest of China*, 279), and multiple times in *Fayuan zhulin*. A disciple of the famed monk Dao'an once served as its abbot (see Zürcher, *The Buddhist Conquest of China*, 190, 199).

854. *Ruding* 入定, or "entered *samādhi*," on which see the note to item 99 above.

855. *Xingdao zhuanjing* 行道轉經.

856. This simultaneous multilocality is a feat often attributed to several kinds of ascetic practitioners in early medieval China, including seekers of transcendence; for examples, see Campany, *To Live as Long as Heaven and Earth*, 86–87, 96, 154, 169–172, 281, 283, 286.

857. *Yi wei de dao* 以為得道. Implied here is that he was suspected of having reached some stage on the path to arhatship.

ning I will surpass this era[858] at your home." The next day, Daochan hosted an eightfold abstinence ceremony and kept lamps lit all night long. Early in the evening and at midnight Qian was still in the midst of the assembly circumambulating, joyful as usual. After the fourth watch, he said he was tired and lay down. His expression changed slightly, and a moment later he expired. The entire area participated in a twenty-one-day abstinence ceremony for him and raised a stupa [over his remains]; the stupa still stands today.

A while after his death, he manifested his form at Duobao monastery,[859] telling the monk Tanxun 曇珣, "Next year on the twenty-third day of the second month, I will come in the company of many other celestial persons to welcome you." After he had spoken these words, he departed. Tanxun then in a meditation chamber in Changsha carried out a ninety-day period of abstinence; he "abandoned his body" and distributed alms.[860] On the expected day, his breathing became labored, and he knew he must soon die. He invited many monks and laypersons and hosted a bountiful Dharma assembly. During the third watch he called out to ask the other monks, "Do you see and hear that?" None of them was aware of anything unusual. Xun said, "In the air, there is the sound of music being played. The incense fragrance is extraordinary. What Huang Qian predicted is now being fulfilled!" All the monks began returning to the hall to draw close to his mat, but by the time they reached him Xun had already expired.

Comments

This story includes telling details on devotional practice, including the practice of the abstinence ceremony. The monk's multilocality and foreknowledge of his own date of death are feats that, like many other extraordinary feats attributed to monks in this text, match up against similar deeds attributed to transcendence seekers. The dramatic deathbed scene may be compared to item 82 above.

---

858. Or "surpass this world," translating *guo shi* 過世: that is, he will die. "Era" captures the temporal sense of *shi* that, in a Buddhist (and some other) contexts, implies crossing from this "lifetime" to the next. Elsewhere I sometimes render *guo shi* as "pass away." This was relatively new usage in this period; see Zhou Junxun, *Wei Jin nanbeichao zhiguai xiaoshuo cihui*, 417–418.

859. Located in Jiankang.

860. "Abandoned his body and distributed alms" translates *sheshen bushi* 捨身布施: in preparation for death he rid himself of all possessions and maintained strict discipline. The summer retreat, a period of intensified practice for monks and nuns, traditionally lasted ninety days; cf. *Gaoseng zhuan* 406b26 (biography of Shi Tansui 釋曇邃) and Daoxuan's *Sifen lü shanfan buque xingshi chao* 42b7.

108[861]

Empress Dowager Lu Zhao 路昭太后 of the Song,[862] in the fourth year of Daming [460], fashioned [an image of] Bodhisattva Samantabhadra[863] seated on a bejeweled saddle atop a white elephant. She had it placed in the meditation chamber in Zhongxing 中興 [monastery],[864] and it was thus often set up for lectures in the monastery. That year, on the eighth day of the tenth month, the abstinence ceremony was concluding, and the altars were being taken down; two hundred monks had been present at the assembly. The monastery at the time had just begun to be built. The Empress Dowager[865] was very involved in the construction, coming personally several times a week, and the monks and [lay] followers conducted themselves in strict concordance with the regulations. On that day the order of monks' names was fixed. Long after they had taken their seats [in strict order], a monk suddenly came in and inserted himself into the ranks of seats. His manner was dignified and refined. The entire hall stared at him in amazement. The master of the abstinence ceremony spoke with him; they exchanged perhaps a hundred words, and then the monk suddenly disappeared. Everyone present in the assembly saw it. They realized he must have been a divine personage.

Comments

See the next item.

---

861. Source texts: *Fayuan zhulin* 17.408c (section "honoring Buddhas" [*jing Fo* 敬佛]); *Sanbao ganying yaolue lu* 3.850a; Lu, *Gu xiaoshuo gouchen*, 443; Wang Guoliang, *Mingxiang ji yanjiu*, 109. Additional texts: *Chu sanzang jiji* 12.92c15 (citing Seng Zhao's *Fayuan zayuan yuanshi ji* 法苑雜緣原始集, which is now lost except for its table of contents; here is given the title of a memorial submitted to the Empress Dowager, a document that was probably a source for the ornate language of our *Mingxiang ji* entry); *Gaoseng zhuan* 7.372b–373a; *Hongzan fahua zhuan* 1.14a (giving details on the Samantabhadra image mentioned in the story, as well as the monk who fashioned it). Discussed: Mai, "Visualization Apocrypha," 290.

862. Lu Zhao was a consort of Song Emperor Wen, with whom she conceived the future Emperor Xiaowu. A biography appears in *Song shu* 41.1286–1287; nothing is said there of her Buddhist inclinations or of an image of Samantabhadra.

863. See the comments to item 76 above.

864. This monastery is mentioned numerous times in *Gaoseng zhuan*, and its founding is briefly mentioned at 4.350c.

865. The text has *di* 帝, but this term must refer here to the Empress Dowager. In the next item, oblique reference is made to visits she paid to the monastery.

109[866]

During the Daming period of the Song [457–465] there lived the Dharma master and abbot Daowen 道溫.[867] He resided in Moling district.[868] Having seen [the event recorded above], he reported [to the empress] as follows:[869] "Your highness' perspicacity reflects profound insight, and your sagacity tallies with hidden concord. Your cleansed thoughts purify the ritual space,[870] and your studious mind reaches to our realm. Truly your voice and literary elegance shake the Central Realm, and the efficacy of your deeds reaches beyond the land of brahmans. Then you conceived the thought of casting and cutting, to give expression to divine splendor. They replicated and fashioned Samantabhadra, a splendid statue in a variegated form. The lecture and abstinence halls that you established are now completed. During the lecture and abstinence ceremony that you sponsored on the eighth day of this month, the register of names [of those attending] had been fixed, and all were seated according to rank; there were just enough mats for the number of guests present. When the sutra recitation was halfway completed, at midnight, we suddenly saw a strange monk appear amid the seats. He was of refined appearance and a very dignified air. All present stared at him; no one recognized him. The host of the abstinence ceremony asked him, 'What is your name?' He replied, 'My name is Huiming 慧明.' 'At which monastery do you reside?' 'I come from Tian'an 天安.' As they were speaking, the strange monk suddenly vanished. All present in the hall were stunned and considered that the event must have been an auspicious responsive sign from the unseen realm. The purple mountain may be glimpsed; the floral platform is not far away![871] I have heard that on account of being moved by utmost sincerity, the sun has been known to reverse its course, and that on account of a

---

866. Source texts: *Fayuan zhulin* 17.408c (section "honoring Buddhas" [*jing Fo* 敬佛]); Lu, *Gu xiaoshuo gouchen*, 443; Wang Guoliang, *Mingxiang ji yanjiu*, 110; Wakatsuki, Hasegawa, and Inagaki, *Hōon jurin no sōgō teki kenkyū*, 86–88. Additional texts: *Song shu* 97; *Gaoseng zhuan* 7.372b–373a (a somewhat clearer version); *Wei shu* 114.

867. He has a biography in *Gaoseng zhuan* 7.372b–373a, which gives an only slightly different version of his communication to the Empress Dowager Lu Zhao. He was abbot of the temple that is the setting of the narrative in item 108.

868. Located in present-day Jiangning district, Jiangsu province.

869. The language of the ensuing passage is honorific to the point of obscurity. My thanks are due to David Knechtges for his invaluable help in translating it. I have followed the text in *Fayuan zhulin*, but there are significant variants in the *Gaoseng zhuan* version.

870. *Chang* 場 here is probably short for *daochang* 道場, a common translation of *bodhimaṇḍa*, or "place of religious practice." The term has a very broad range of reference in medieval Chinese. See Mochizuki, *Bukkyō daijiten*, 3897a–3898b.

871. These are apparent references to Vulture Peak, on which Gautama Buddha was said to have resided, and the decorated "high seats" from which Buddhas and bodhitsattvas preach—the point being that Buddhas and bodhisattvas are in fact near at hand through such miracles as the visitation by the mysterious monk.

purified mind a rock, on being struck, has been known to produce a spring.[872] How much the more is this true in the case of a monarch's pure virtue! A ruler's kindness and righteousness stir the unseen world to respond. Thus it was that, when the exalted ruler established the Great Brilliance [*daming* 大明] reign, this moved the wondrous personage to appear in the same chamber where Your Highness had visited, as if to say that, since Your Highness's wisdom is as brilliant as the sun and moon, [the personage] took Brilliance of Wisdom [Huiming 慧明] as his name. To continue, since the flourishing of your reign knows no bounds, [the personage] gave Celestial Peace [Tian'an 天安] as the name of his monastery, indicating that [your reign] enjoys the security of divine favor, that the realm is at peace and all under heaven are pleased. These messages were carefully arrayed in our district in such a way as to make clear Heaven's favor."

Comments

This and the previous item prominently feature the motif of the spirit-monk who appears to break standard seating order at the abstinence-ceremony meal. These narratives are another example of Buddhists' inserting themselves into the process of arguing dynastic legitimacy via the discourse of auspicious omens and portents; in this light, they may be read alongside items 41 and 63 above. The spirit-monk apparition is here decoded by the temple's abbot in such a way that it becomes a manifested sign of Heaven's approval of the Empress Dowager's reign.

---

872. This sentence alludes to two exemplary cases of "utmost sincerity" known in the indigenous canon. The first is the story of the Duke of Luyang 魯陽公 in the "Lanming" 覽冥 (Peering into Things Unseen) chapter of the second-century-BCE *Huainanzi* 淮南子, or *Masters of Huainan* (adopting the translation of the title employed by Mark Csikszentmihalyi in *Readings in Han Chinese Thought*, viii), translated thus by Charles Le Blanc: "The Duke of Luyang was locked in battle with Han. As the fighting became the fiercest, the sun began to set. He (the Duke) raised his spear and waved at the sun, and the sun reverted three mansions on his behalf" (Le Blanc, *Huai-nan tzu*, 105–106; cf. *Huainanzi jishi* 6.447). This chapter of *Masters of Huainan* is in fact a magisterial summation of pre-Buddhist Chinese notions of "stimulus-response" (*ganying* 感應) and the power of people's "utmost sincerity" (*jingcheng* 精誠) to move other beings and things, and was thus a most apt text for Daowen to allude to. The duke's story is also mentioned twice by Wang Chong 王充 in *A Balance-Beam for Arguments* (*Lunheng* 論衡); see *Lunheng jiaoshi* 5.230 (trans. Forke, *Lun-hêng*, 2.173) and 29.1183 (trans. in ibid., 1.89). The second allusion is to a regional myth preserved in chapter 4 of Chang Qu's 常璩 *Huayangguo zhi* 華陽國志, the mid-fourth-century treatise on Shu topography and culture: a figure called the Bamboo King 竹王, to whom one or more temples were dedicated, born of the union of a floating bamboo staff and a woman washing clothes in a river, anciently lived with his people on a great rock; when they complained of lack of water, he struck the rock with his sword, and a spring emerged, which still runs today (*Huayangguo zhi jiaozhu*, 339–340; for an example of a sixth-century reception of the myth, see Campany, *Strange Writing*, 230, and for another version of the story, see *Yiyuan* 5.4).

110[873]

During the Song there lived Jiang Xiaode 蔣小德, a native of Jiangling. He served as office attendant in the audience chamber of Zhu Xiu 朱脩 when the latter was regional inspector of Yuezhou.[874] As a youth he was pious and practiced more diligently than anyone else. Xiu delighted in this; each time there was to be a Dharma ceremony he informed Xiaode of it. In the last year of Daming [464–465] Xiaode fell ill and died. That same night, at the third watch, others were about to encoffin him when he revived. He said an envoy came, announcing that the king had summoned him, and took Xiaode away. When they arrived, the king said, "You, sir, are vigorous, diligent, attentive, and reverent in your practice of the great Dharma. Indra therefore ordered that you be specially brought here and granted an accelerated rebirth in a place of goodness.[875] But since your life span count is still quite long, I was sent to summon you first. You will now receive the joys of heaven for your delight." Xiaode happily agreed. The king said, "You may temporarily return home, attend to your affairs, and perform acts of merit. But do these quickly, because in seven days you will return here."

Xiaode, following these instructions, set off for home. By the roadside he came upon a small, isolated, dilapidated dwelling. At this dwelling he met [the monk] Master Nan 難公, formerly of Xin monastery; as they had previously been acquainted, they asked each other's news. Master Nan said, "Ever since I had left the household, I had never imbibed wine. But when I went to visit Master Lan 蘭公, he insisted strongly that I drink and compelled me to down a liter or so. I was summoned by the king for this reason. If I hadn't done this, I would have been reborn in the heavens, but instead I was ordered to live in this run-down dwelling. Only after three years will I be allowed to ascend."

When Xiaode reached home, he wanted to confirm[876] what the monk had said, so he sent someone to make inquiries. It turned out that Master Nan had indeed on such-and-such a day gone to sleep at the residence of Master Lan and died that same night.

Once Xiaode had recovered completely, within seven days he hosted a great gathering to make donations and generate fortune. At the appointed time he abruptly died. Zhu Tiao exempted Xiaode's family from militia

---

873. Source texts: *Fayuan zhulin* 94.978b (section "wine and meat" [*jiu rou* 酒肉]); Lu, *Gu xiaoshuo gouchen*, 444; Wang Guoliang, *Mingxiang ji yanjiu*, 111. Additional texts: *Shimen zijing lu* 2.814c.

874. Zhu Yuezhi 之, as he is identified in the histories, has biographies in *Song shu* 76.1969–1971 and *Nan shi* 16.462–464. I here follow Wang Guoliang's suggested punctuation and not that in the Taishō edition of *Fayuan zhulin*.

875. *Yi shu sheng shandi* 宜速生善地.

876. *Yan* 驗.

service. The two monks Lan and Nan both continued to live at Xin monastery. Master Nan was thenceforth spirited in his practice, not like other monks.

Comments

This is another story involving an early death summons, as well as another critique of monastic laxity—here, loose observance of the prohibition against consumption of alcohol.[877]

111[878]

During the Song there was a certain Shen Sengfu 沈僧覆 of Wuxing. Late in the Daming period [ca. 462–465] there was a famine in the area, so he went to Shanyang [district] in search of food. During the days he would enter villages and hamlets to beg for meals; at night he would return to stay in one or another temple or monastery. At that time there were a great many small metal [Buddha] images in the temples of Shanyang. Sengfu and several others from his home area over time stole quite a few of these, until they had accumulated bags and boxes full of them. So they took them all back home, where they melted them down for cash.

Once the affair had become known and he was being led out of the city [under arrest], upon boarding the boat he said he saw people burning him with torches. Day and night he cried out, screaming, "I can't take the pain!" He died before he could be executed. His entire body was covered with burn marks that seemed to have been made by torches.

Wu Heng 朱亨 of Wu commandery knew Sengfu personally and saw all these things with his own eyes.

112[879]

During the Song there lived the nun Shi Huiyu 釋慧玉, a native of Chang'an. She was strict in her practice and mastered both sutras and precepts. Once in the Xueshangshu monastery 薛尚書寺 in Chang'an[880] she saw a red and white light over a ten-day period. On the eighth day of the

877. On the prohibition, see Benn, "Buddhism, Alcohol, and Tea."

878. Source texts: *Fayuan zhulin* 79.874b26ff. (section "the ten evil acts" [*shi e* 十惡]); Lu, *Gu xiaoshuo gouchen* 445; Wang Guoliang, *Mingxiang ji yanjiu*, 112.

879. Source texts: *Fayuan zhulin* 16.407b (section "honoring Buddhas" [*jing Fo* 敬佛]); Lu, *Gu xiaoshuo gouchen*, 445; Wang Guoliang, *Mingxiang ji yanjiu*, 106; Wakatsuki, Hasegawa, and Inagaki, *Hōon jurin no sōgō teki kenkyū*, 83–85. Additional texts: *Biqiuni zhuan* 2.937c–938a (trans. Tsai, *Lives of the Nuns*, 39–40); *Ji shenzhou sanbao gantong lu* 2.418b; *Fahua jing chiyan ji* 1.68a.

880. So far as I am aware, this and the other two monasteries mentioned are attested in extant textual sources only in witnesses to this nun's story.

fourth month, a monk from Liuchong monastery 六重寺 visited this monastery and, at the place where the light was, found a metal image of Maitreya, about a meter tall.[881]

Huiyu later traveled south to the cities of Fan 樊城 and Ying 郢城[882] and resided in Lingshou monastery 靈收寺 in Jiangling. One night in the tenth month of Yuanjia 14 [late November or early December 437], she saw a purple light radiating from a tree on the east side of the monastery. It illuminated the entire grove around it. She told her fellow practitioner Miaoguang 妙光 and others about it, but none of them could see it. Huiyu saw it continuously for more than twenty days. Later the abbess Shi Fahong 釋法弘 was about to construct the foundation for a meditation hall under the tree when, looking up into the branches, she found a gilded image. This one was also about a meter tall.

113[883]

During the Song there lived one Fei Chongxian 費崇先, a native of Wuxing. When young he believed in the Dharma, and up into his thirties he was a diligent and vigorous practitioner. In the third year of Taishi [467–468] he received the bodhisattva precepts[884] and was observing the abstinence ceremony as a guest in the home of Xie Huiyuan 謝惠遠. Throughout the twenty-four days he was attentive day and night. Each time he listened to the sutra recitation, he placed a magpie tailfeather incense burner before his knees. During the first three evenings of the abstinence ceremony he saw a person of unusual countenance and clothing come toward him, pick up the incense burner, and take it away. Chongxian could see that the incense burner in front of his knees was still there in its correct place. Yet when he looked again closely at the man, he distinctly saw him pick it up and take it. Only then did Chongxian realize this was a divine anomaly. He reflected on the fact that the man's robe was newly washed, with not a spot of dirt on it anywhere. Beside his seat was a spittoon. He tried removing the spittoon, and upon doing so he again saw the man return the incense burner to its spot in front of his seat. Before he reached his mat, it was as if he saw two incense burners, but once he was in his seat they joined to form

---

881. The date is doubly significant: not only is it the date on which Gautama Buddha's birthday was often celebrated, but it is also the date on which the future Buddha Maitreya was predicted to attain awakening, as seen, for example, in *Mile laishi jing* 434c21.

882. Both were located in what is now Hubei province.

883. Source texts: *Fayuan zhulin* 24.467a–b (section "speaking and listening" [*shuo ting* 說聽]); *Chuxue ji* 25.606 (only a very truncated excerpt of the story is given here); Lu, *Gu xiaoshuo gouchen*, 445; Wang Guoliang, *Mingxiang ji yanjiu*, 114; Wakatsuki, Hasegawa, and Inagaki, *Hōon jurin no sōgō teki kenkyū*, 160–162. Additional texts: *Fayuan zhulin*, cited in *Taiping guangji* 114.1.

884. See the note to item 82 above.

one. It must, then, have been the case that what the divine man was picking up was the shadow of the incense burner![885]

Chongxian had also often heard people say that in the Fuyuan monastery 福遠寺 there resided a nun named Sengqin 僧欽, a rigorous practitioner who had obtained the path. He was delighted and wanted to meet her but had not yet had the opportunity to go, even though doing so was very much on his mind. He was once attending the abstinence ceremony at someone else's home when, in the third watch of the night, he suddenly saw a nun, her expression and comportment strict and correct, wearing a *kaṣāya*[886] of crimson cloth, standing upright before the area where the abstinence ceremony was being conducted. In the space of a meal she vanished. Later, when Chongxian met this nun, he saw that her face and clothes were those of the nun he had seen outside the window that night.

114[887]

He Jingshu 何敬叔 of Donghai had venerated the Buddha since his youth. In the Song Taishi period [465–472] he followed the regional inspector of Xiangzhou, Liu Yun 劉韞,[888] on an inspection tour. Along the way Jingshu found some sandalwood and carved it into an image. It was almost complete, lacking only the final layer.[889] Jingshu was very careful and deliberate, but in his temporary quarters there was no place to store the image.[890] He was anxiously mulling this over when, dozing off, he saw a monk in a robe, bearing a staff, coming toward him and saying, "Sandalwood is unobtainable; it is in any case an inelegant wood that does not last. In the district here there is a family named He; they have a paulownia shield that you could use for the outer layer. They value it very highly, but if you plead for it hard enough they will give it to you." Jingshu, on waking, made inquiries

---

885. My translation of much of this paragraph is tentative.

886. That is, a *jiasha* 袈裟, or monastic robe. On the semiotics of this garment see Kieschnick, "The Symbolism of the Monk's Robe."

887. Source texts: Unattributed citation in *Fayuan zhulin* 14.388b (section "honoring Buddhas" [*jing Fo* 敬佛]); *Taiping guangji* 276.50; *Taiping yulan* 357.3b–4a; Lu, *Gu xiaoshuo gouchen*, 446; Wang Guoliang, *Mingxiang ji yanjiu*, 116. Additional texts: *Ji shenzhou sanbao gantong lu* 2.418c.

888. Liu Yun is mentioned multiple times in *Song shu*, e.g., at 8.160–166, 9.179, 10.194–195, 28.806, and 83.2113.

889. In *Fayuan zhulin* and *Ji shenzhou sanbao gantong*, this is simply *guang* 光, and in *Taiping guangji* it is not a question of the final coating—He Jingshu is there still searching for wood to carve an image from in the first place. Wang Guoliang gives *guangcai* 光材, on what basis I am not sure. I do not know whether *guang* 光 in this context indicates pigment (paint or dye), gilding, or an outer layer of fine-quality wood or other material. *Grand dictionnaire Ricci de la langue chinoise* defines *guangcai* 光材 as "bois de finition."

890. Wang Yan's own preface to this work (see above) recounts—in parallel terms—a similar concern he had at one point in his life.

in the district and found that there was indeed a He family. So he sought to buy the shield from them. Members of the He family said, "We do in fact have such a shield. We are very fond of it. Fearing that someone would ask for it, we have never shown it to anyone. How did you learn of it, sir, and know to come directly here and ask for it?" Jingshu told them of his dream. The He family were both stunned and delighted. They contributed it to be used as the outer layer [of the image].

115[891]

During the Song there lived Yuan Bing 袁炳, styled Shuhuan 叔煥,[892] a native of Chen commandery. At the end of the Taishi period [ca. 471] he served as district magistrate of Linxiang.[893] Several years after he had died, his friend Sima Xun 司馬遜, as if in a dream, saw him approach near daybreak. They exchanged greetings and asked each other's news. Then Bing said to Xun, "When I was alive, you and I often agreed that life was haste and toil, and death was rest. Now I know this is, in fact, not true. I constantly worry that in the world there are people who toil and rush after money and possessions, giving and taking from each other, and all the while it is the same in the unseen world." Xun asked, "What do the realities of recompense for sins and fortunate acts turn out to be?" Bing answered, "According to my former understanding, they would not completely match what the scriptures and teachings say, that the sayings of the sage had perhaps been pulled and tugged somewhat. But according to the understanding I have today, the great orderings of [recompense for] good and evil do not differ at all [from the scriptures].[894] Mind you, the prohibition against killing living things is the most grave of all. You must take care not to violate it!"

Xun then said, "Your admonition is marvelous! I must pass it along to the minister." Bing replied, "Excellent! When you do, please convey my regards." At that time, Director of Public Works Wang Sengqian 王僧虔 was serving as director of the ministry of personnel; Bing and Xun had both been his guests, and that is why they touched on him now. The two conversed a while longer, and then, when Bing began to take his leave, Xun said, "We have been apart for so long, and I have constantly longed to see

---

891. Source texts: *Fayuan zhulin* 21.441a–b (section "refuge in faith" [*guixin* 歸信]); *Taiping guangji* 326.1; Lu, *Gu xiaoshuo gouchen*, 446; Wang Guoliang, *Mingxiang ji yanjiu*, 117; Wakatsuki, Hasegawa, and Inagaki, *Hōon jurin no sōgō teki kenkyū*, 149–151.

892. Yuan has a biography in *Nan Qi shu* 52.897, where his style is given as Shuming 叔明.

893. Located in what is now Changsha district, Hunan province.

894. One could argue that it is linguistically possible to read these lines as meaning that there is no great difference in the unseen world (except in the case of killing living beings) between how merit and sin are treated. But this reading is so deeply at variance with what is tirelessly argued elsewhere in this text that I have chosen to translate as indicated.

you. Meeting each other is now very difficult. Can you not stay a while longer?" But Bing replied, "I only came for a short while. I cannot linger. I am also not permitted to speak of details in this sort of conversation."[895] With that he departed. Bing had first arrived in the dark of night. Without Xun's having noticed exactly how, there had been enough light to see by [during their conversation]. As Bing was leaving, Xun got down from his couch to see him off, and when he started walking it was dark again. But he noticed that between Bing's feet there was a cone of light that illuminated the area below him. The surrounding ground was still dark....[896]

116[897]

During the Song there lived the monk Daozhi 道志, who resided at Duobao monastery 多寶寺 in Jiankang.[898] Once, having been informed by other monks of the location of a richly appointed stupa, he stole a large number of jewels and other ornaments from the canopies; later he even stole the pearl[899] from between the eyes of the image. Because he broke open a hole in the wall, as if thieves had entered from outside the building, the monks had no way of finding out [who the real thief was].

Over a week later, Daozhi fell ill. He then saw a strange man stabbing him with a spear; he would come, then depart, then come again. Each time the man arrived Daozhi would be terrified; he would cry out and bleed. At first this happened once or twice a day. Later, as the illness worsened, the stabbings grew more frequent, until he had wounds all over his body and screamed constantly from the pain. The monks of his monastery suspected he had sinned and wanted to induce him to confess and apologize. When they first questioned him, he continued to deceive and did not speak of his trangression, but after two or three more days he told them all of it. Sobbing, he begged to be saved, saying, "In my stupidity I told myself that there is in fact no unseen world.[900] Due to a lapse of thought I committed a sin and summoned this misfortune on myself. While alive, I

---

895. *Qie ci bei yu yi bu rong de weixi* 且此輩語亦不容得委悉.

896. Ellipsis in the original.

897. Source texts: *Fayuan zhulin* 79.874c (section "the ten evil acts" [*shi e* 十惡]); *Taiping guangji* 116.6; Lu, *Gu xiaoshuo gouchen*, 447; Wang Guoliang, *Mingxiang ji yanjiu*, 118. Additional texts: *Shimen zijing lu* 51.804c.

898. As we have seen above, Wang Yan himself in his preface tells of visiting this monastery, located in the southern capital of Jiankang, to retrieve his image of the Bodhisattva Sound Observer. The monastery is also mentioned in item 107.

899. Here and below, the term used for gems taken from the Buddha image is *xiang zhu* 相珠—literally "*lakṣaṇa* pearl," perhaps actually pearls or more likely gems of many and varied sorts that were affixed to images to represent the special *lakṣaṇas* (*xiang* 相), or markings unique to Buddhas' bodies.

900. "Unseen world" translates *youtu* 幽途, literally "dark paths" or "paths in the unseen realm."

am suffering this torment; after death I will undergo the sword and the cauldron. Have pity on this poor derelict of a person. I have nothing left now except my robe, blanket, and shoes. Maybe they would be enough to sponsor one assembly. May I also trouble you to sponsor a confession on my behalf?[901] Earlier I stole two gems from the image. One already belongs to an old woman and cannot be recovered. I exchanged the other one for cash; it is at the home of Chen Zhao 陳照, and you can go now and buy it back."

Daozhi then died. The monks pooled together and bought back one of the gems for the image. They also sponsored an abstinence and confession ceremony.[902] At first, when the artisan tried to reattach the gem to the image, it would not fit no matter how he turned it about. Only after the monks had again performed obeisance and burned incense before the image would the gem attach properly.

Over a year later some of his fellow monks heard a voice in midair one night. On listening closely they recognized it as Daozhi's voice. He said that ever since he had died he had undergone terrible suffering and would continue to do so for a very long time, with no end in sight. But he was grateful to the assembly of monks for their compassion on his behalf in having bought back the stolen gem for the image; because of this he had been granted a temporary reprieve from punishment. Being moved by gratitude for their generous act, he had returned briefly to express his thanks. He said only this. During the time he spoke, there was the stench of rotting flesh, so strong that it was hard to bear. After he finished speaking, a long time passed before the stench dissipated.

These events happened in the last year of Taishi [471–472]. Someone in the monastery who was fond of accounts of such affairs made a detailed record of these matters.

117[903]

During the Song period, there was a certain Chen Xiuyuan 陳秀遠 of Yingchuan. He once served in the western section of Xiang region,[904] during which time he resided as a guest in Linxiang district. In his youth he be-

---

901. The language is precise and telling: he is now enacting a *yuan* 願—a *vow* or *wish*, a solemn expression of intent—that a confession be performed; the other monks will later *perform* it ritually *on his behalf* (the "on his behalf" indicated by the word *wei* 為).

902. *Bing she zhai chan* 并設齋懺.

903. Source texts: *Fayuan zhulin* 32.536b (section "transformations" [*bianhua* 變化]); *Taiping guangji* 114.4; Lu, *Gu xiaoshuo gouchen* 448; Wang Guoliang, *Mingxiang ji yanjiu*, 119; Wakatsuki, Hasegawa, and Inagaki, *Hōon jurin no sōgō teki kenkyū*, 201–203.

904. The western section was an administrative unit at the level of region and commandery; see Hucker, *Dictionary of Official Titles*, 229, s.v. *hsi-ts'ao*.

lieved in the three treasures,[905] and on passing the age of sixty he still diligently practiced [Buddhist precepts] without flagging. One day in the middle of the seventh month of the Song Yuanwei period [August 474], at dusk, as he reclined but had not yet fallen asleep, he sighed in wonderment to think of the births and deaths of the myriad beings, flowing and changing without cease. He contemplated his own person: Where had he come from? With a concentrated mind he prayed and wished to have a dream in response [to this question]. It had just grown dark at the time, and there were not yet any candles or lamps lit in the room. In a moment he noticed something like a firefly's glow beside his pillow; it grew brighter, then flew away. Moments later the entire room was illuminated as brightly as if by daylight. Xiuyuan quickly rose and joined his palms, breathless from excitement. Soon he saw in midair forty or fifty feet above him a bridge with red patterned railings.[906] Without being aware of climbing up to it or moving, Xiuyuan saw himself seated at the side of the bridge. On it he saw [two] women walking back and forth, their clothing and ornaments no different from those of people in this world. One was perhaps thirty years of age. She wore a blue jacket and a white cotton skirt. She walked to Xiuyuan's left side and stood. In a moment, the other woman, dressed entirely in white cotton, with an elaborate one-sided circular coiffure[907] and carrying flowers and incense, came and stood before him. She said to Xiuyuan, "You wanted to see your previous self. I am she. Because I offered this flower to Buddha, I was able to be reborn as you."[908] Then she turned, pointed to the other woman, and said, "This lady, in turn, is my own former self." When she had spoken these words they both departed, and after they had left, the bridge also vanished. Without realizing how, Xiuyuan had redescended to the ground. The light was gone as well.

Comments

This is one of the most vivid and personalized rebirth narratives recorded in early medieval China. Knowledge of one's previous rebirths was normally reckoned to be an advanced spiritual attainment. Here it is granted to a pious layman.

---

905. This is simply a way of saying that, in the modern way of putting it, Chen "was a Buddhist."

906. On Buddhism and bridges, see Kieschnick, *The Impact of Buddhism*, 203–214.

907. The woman's white attire and the objects she carries mark her as a Buddhist laywoman. Her hairstyle is not atypical for the period; see Dien, *Six Dynasties Civilization*, 313–314, 322–323.

908. Some Buddhist scriptures suggested that, for various reasons, rebirth as a woman was karmically inferior to rebirth as a man. The sense of this statement is therefore that her gift to the Buddha generated sufficient merit for her to achieve better rebirth (as a man) than in her previous life (as a woman). For a convincing demonstration that this assertion of the inferiority of rebirth as a woman was not determinative of much of medieval Buddhist understanding and practice (especially women's practice), see Meeks, *Hokkeji*.

118[909]

During the Song there lived Zhida 智達, a monk who resided at the Suo monastery 索寺 in Yizhou.[910] He was rather lax in his monastic practice, but he excelled at [chanting] sutras and hymns. At age twenty-three, in the sixth month of the third year of the Song Yuanhui period [late July or early August 475], he died of illness. But his body remained warm, so he was not encoffined. Two days later his breathing gradually returned to normal, and he was finally able to speak and see again. He gave the following account. At the outset of his dire situation he saw two men wearing trousers and shirts of yellow cloth. One of them stood outside the door to his cell; the other entered, stood by the bed, and said, "Monk, you must go. Step down onto the floor." Zhida replied, "I am weak and cannot walk very well." The man said, "You will ride in a carriage." As he finished speaking these words, a carriage arrived. So Zhida climbed in. At this point he felt rather dazed and no longer saw his family's house or even the carriage he was riding in. Looking in all directions, he saw only wasteland. The way was perilous and steep, but the two men hurried things along and allowed no chance to rest. They reached a vermilion gate in a [city with] elaborate walls and towers. Zhida went in and arrived in a hall. At the back of the hall was a nobleman in a vermilion gown and hat leaning on a couch. His demeanor was dignified and intimidating. He was attended by a dense array of over a hundred soldiers in vermilion robes, armed with swords. On seeing Zhida, the nobleman collected himself and said in a formal manner, "As a monk, how is it that you have so many sins?" Zhida replied, "I do not recollect having sinned from the time at which I gained knowledge [of right and wrong]." The man asked, "Have you given up reciting the precepts?" Zhida said, "At the time that I first received the precepts, I often recited them. But lately when I have attended the abstinence ceremony lecture, I am always asked to do the sutra recital, and so when it comes time to recite the precepts I sometimes skip them." The nobleman said, "To be a monk and yet not recite the precepts: if this is not a sin, what is? Recite a sutra!" Zhida recited the *Lotus* three times, then stopped.

The nobleman gave orders to the messengers who had brought Zhida in: "Take him to an odious place. Don't allow him to suffer too much." The two men took him away. After they had gone several dozen *li*, he could hear a great clamor, and the road ahead turned dark. They then

---

909. Source texts: *Fayuan zhulin* 90.953a–c (section "breaking the precepts" [*pojie* 破戒]); Lu, *Gu xiaoshuo gouchen*, 449; Wang Guoliang, *Mingxiang ji yanjiu*, 120. Additional texts: *Shimen zijing lu* 1.811b–c; *Hongzan fahua zhuan* 9.40c–41a.

910. In today's Chengdu, Sichuan province. I have no other information on this monastery.

came to a gate several dozen feet tall, solid black—it must have been made of iron. The surrounding walls were similar. Zhida thought to himself: The sutras speak of earth prisons; this must be where we are now. With this he was terrified, regretting that he had not cultivated acts of merit while he had been in the world. They entered through the gate. The clamor grew louder, then after a while subsided, and he realized that what he was hearing were the cries of people. Once inside the gate all was completely dark, and he could see nothing more except for a firelight that would sometimes go out and sometimes reappear. By that light he saw several people tied up and being led backward; behind them were other people shoving them forward with prongs. Their blood flowed like springs. One of them was Zhida's great aunt. When she saw him, she seemed to want to speak to him, but one of the guards prodded her along, so that she was unable to say anything.

Two hundred paces or more inside the gate he saw an object shaped like a granary, about ten feet tall. The two men seized Zhida and threw him up on top of it. Inside the cylinder was a fire. Half of Zhida's body was burned away; the pain was unbearable. He fell from the cylinder to the ground and was unconscious for a long time. The two men then took him away again. He saw a dozen or so iron cauldrons in which sinners were being boiled, bobbing up and down. Beside the cauldrons were men with pitchforks poking at them. One sinner was pulled out of a cauldron. Both eyes hung from their sockets; his tongue protruded a foot from his mouth; all his flesh had been burned away, but he still was not dead. All but one of the cauldrons were full. The two men said to Zhida, "Monk, you must enter this one." When Zhida heard their words, he fell to the ground terror-stricken, begging them, "Please allow me just once to pay obeisance to Buddha!" He bowed with all his might, hoping to avoid this punishment. He remained prostrated on the ground for the space of a meal, intently praying and confessing. He then looked around and saw nothing but a level span of ground and luxuriant trees—a clear, bright scene. But the two men were still leading Zhida along. They arrived at the foot of a tall but narrow tower. Atop it was a man sitting calmly who told Zhida, "Śramaṇa [i.e., monk], you have received a light retribution. You are very fortunate." Without being aware of it, Zhida had gone from being at the bottom of the tower to being back in his former body.

Today Zhida is still residing at Suo monastery. He observes the abstinence regulations with the utmost strictness and applies himself completely each time he meditates and recites.

119[911]

During the Song, Yuan Kuo 袁廓, styled Sidu 思度, was a native of Chen commandery.[912] During the Yuanhui period [473–early 477] he served as aide to the [magistrate of] Wu commandery.[913] He had been ill for a few days when suddenly he was as if dead, only he had not quite stopped breathing. [His family] prepared his coffin and garments, waiting for his breathing to stop before readying him for burial, but after three days he was able to move and look around. He gave the following account of what had happened.

An envoy summoned him. Kuo followed him and departed. They arrived at a large city surrounded by a wall and moat, with fine arrays of towers, battlements, stairways, and gates. Kuo was ordered to go in. His host sat facing south at the top of an imposing series of stairs; a capped attendant brandishing a sword motioned for Kuo to sit. Once he was seated, pleasantries were exchanged, and then wine was served, along with roasted meats, fruits, dumplings, pickled vegetables, sweetmeats, and the like, all of which Kuo sampled. Their types, shapes, and flavors were no different than those of this world. After several rounds of wine, the host said to Kuo: "My assistant magistrate is not well. There is a vacancy on my staff. Because of your ample talent, sir, I wonder if you would condescend to consider it?"

Kuo, realizing this was the other world, firmly declined. "My talents are ordinary, and I would not be able to manage the position. On top of that, my children would be orphaned and my siblings bereft. For reasons both professional and personal I must presume upon your kindness and ask to be excused."

The host said, "It must be because the dark and light worlds are different realms that you decline, sir. But the honors and salary here are ample, and your food and clothing here would probably surpass what you have in the world. I cherish the thought that we might work together, and it is my earnest hope that you will accede to my request." But Kuo was steadfast in declining: "My sons and daughters are still young. If I were suddenly to accept this position, they would have no one to see to their upbringing. How

---

911. Source texts: *Fayuan zhulin* 52.678a–b (section "family" [*juanshu* 眷屬]); Lu, *Gu xiaoshuo gouchen*, 450; Wang Guoliang, *Mingxiang ji yanjiu*, 121. Additional texts: *Fayuan zhulin*, cited in *Taiping guangji* 377.2. In translating I have sometimes borrowed phrases from Gjertson, *Ghosts, Gods, and Retribution*, 6–10.

912. Today's Huaiyang county, Henan province. Yuan Kuo has a biography in *Nan shi* 26.708–9, where his name is given (apparently correctly) as Yuan Kuozhi 之. He was the great-grandson of Yuan Hong, mentioned above in item 60.

913. Today's Wu county in Jiangsu province.

can you sever the bonds of affection between a father and his children?" Kuo wept and bowed his head.[914]

The host said, "If you insist on declining, of course I will grant your request. How would I dare compel you? But it is a pity you did not accept my invitation." He then walked to a table, picked up a document, and made some notations on it. Kuo thanked him for his kindness and said his farewell. But the host replied, "Do you not wish, sir, to inquire after your deceased forebears?" With that he sent someone to escort Kuo. They passed by numberless offices until they finally came to a citadel whose gates and railings were black. It must have been a prison. Kuo was taken inside, toward a corner where there were several run-down housing units packed tightly together. They came next to a unit inside of which Kuo saw his mother, née Yang. Her appearance and attire were inelegant, quite different from when she was alive. When she saw Kuo she was startled and delighted. Beside the doorway was someone whose face and body were covered in sores, presenting a very strange appearance. She spoke to Kuo, who, surprised, asked, "Who is she?" His mother replied, "This is Lady Wang. Don't you recognize her?"

Lady Wang said, "When I was in the world, I didn't believe in karmic retribution.[915] Even though I did not amass many sins, I was guilty of whipping the servants too severely, and so I am receiving this punishment. Ever since I died I have had no break in this suffering until today's brief respite. Previously I called for your elder sister to come here, hoping she could replace me,[916] but this proved to be of no benefit and only made matters worse." When she had spoken these words, she wept. (Lady Wang had been the principal wife of Kuo's father, and during that time Kuo's elder sister had served as one of her attendants.)[917]

In a little while Kuo's escort led him away. They passed through many lanes and alleyways in neighborhoods resembling those in which commoners dwell. Lastly they arrived at a thatch house with a bamboo fence, and here Kuo saw his father[918] sitting at a table, wearing a kerchief with a blanket draped over him. Kuo started in through the gate, but his father lifted his hand and sent him away, saying, "Since you have been released, you should leave quickly! There is no need for you to come here!"

---

914. This scene is a common one in Chinese lore of the period, and there is nothing uniquely Buddhist about it: death sometimes resulted from a summons to an otherworld bureaucratic post; premature death could result when an otherworld official particularly desired the services of a well-qualified but not-yet-due-to-die living person. For an example see Campany, "Return-from-Death Narratives," 97–99. For an example of another story in which the just-deceased protagonist appeals for his return to life based on his paternal duties, see ibid., 117–118.

915. Translating *bu xin baoying* 不信報應.

916. Translating *qian huan ru jie lai wang yi zi dai* 前喚汝姊來望以自代.

917. This parenthetical remark is in the original.

918. His father, Yuan Jingjun 袁景儁, served as governor of Huainan and is mentioned in *Song shu* 6.119 and *Nan shi* 26.708–709.

At this Kuo knelt, said goodbye, and returned. The escort brought him all the way back home and then departed. Today Kuo is librarian [in the Editorial Service] of the heir apparent.[919]

Comments

As discussed in part 1, this story is one of the major places in our text where the indigenous culture of afterlife "replacements" (along with the associated phenomenon of "plaints") is argued against. The mention of the whipping of servants provides another indication of the social level of this text's readers and of the circles from which its stories emerged.

120[920]

During the Song there lived one Han Hui 韓徽, his place of origin unknown. He lived in Zhijiang.[921] His uncle, [Han] Youzong 幼宗, served as [commander of] garrison militia in Xiangzhou late in the Song era.[922] In the first year of Shengming [477–478], Jingzhou Regional Inspector Chen Youzhi 沈攸之[923] launched a military uprising in the east. The administrator of Xiangzhou, Yu Peiyu 庾佩玉,[924] organized a defense but was unsure where to deploy his troops. Suspecting Youzong of duplicity, he ordered his execution and those of his wives and offspring. Since Hui was an eldest son,[925] he was imprisoned in the commandery jail and tightly bound in stocks and chains, destined for certain execution along with all the others. He was terrified and had nothing left to do but await his fate. He had once served the Buddha and had had some practice reciting the *Guanshiyin Sutra*, so he began now to recite it day and night, amounting to several hundred repetitions. Just at daybreak his fetters gave forth a sound as if being demolished by smelting and hammering. When he looked at them, he saw that the fetters were opened and that he had been released. Fearing that

---

919. This statement matches information listed about Yuan Kuo in his official biography in *Nan shi* 26.709: 為太子洗馬. On the office mentioned here, see Hucker, *Dictionary of Official Titles*, 242.

920. Source texts: *Fayuan zhulin* 27.484c (section "utmost sincerity" [*zhicheng* 至誠]); Lu, *Gu xiaoshuo gouchen*, 452; Wang Guoliang, *Mingxiang ji yanjiu*, 122; Wakatsuki, Hasegawa, and Inagaki, *Hōon jurin no sōgō teki kenkyū*, 175–177. Additional texts: *Xi Guanshiyin yingyanji* 39 (Makita, *Rikuchō kōitsu Kanzeon ōkenki no kenkyū*, 42–43); *Guanyin cilin ji* 2.90c. Discussed: Campany, "The Real Presence," 246.

921. Located in what is now Jiangling district, Hubei province.

922. He is mentioned in *Song shu* 83.2125 and in *Nan Qi shu* 29.538.

923. Chen Youzhi is mentioned repeatedly in *Song shu* (e.g., in chapters 8 and 9), and an account of his rebellion (with mentions of the other figures mentioned here) is given in at least two sections of that work (10.193–196 and in his biography in 74.1927–1939). Cf. *Nan shi* 37. I know of no discussion in a Western language.

924. Mentioned in *Song shu* 10.196.

925. Earlier the text clearly says that Hui was Youzong's nephew. It may be that the eldest sons of other branches of the clan were rounded up for execution; or perhaps the text is simply corrupt here.

the jailer would think he had loosened the fetters himself, Hui summoned him and told him what had happened. The jailer, although amazed, reaffixed the shackles. Hui chanted as before, and after another day the fetters again made the same sound and came loose, just as before. The jailer told all of this to Peiyu, who personally inspected the fetters and, moved by the sight, released them all.

Hui is still alive today, exerting himself in the practice to an uncommon degree.

121[926]

During the Song there lived the monk Shi Huiyan 釋慧嚴; he was a monk of Dong'an monastery 東安寺 in the capital. His reasoning and thought were thorough and penetrating, and he was admired by laypersons and monks. Once, deploring the large number of characters contained in the *Mahā[pari]nirvāṇa Sutra* (*Daniepan jing* 大涅槃經),[927] he made his own abridgment, cutting it down to several scrolls in length. He made two or three copies and showed them to some of his friends. When he was on the cusp of sleep he suddenly saw a man over sixteen feet tall, very powerful in physique and aspect, saying to him, "The *Nirvāṇa* is a venerated sutra, paramount among all others. How can you, based on your own trifling thoughts, so lightly make changes in it?" Huiyan [on waking] was disconsolate, but he still continued to develop his own ideas, recklessly seeking to increase his knowledge.[928] The next night as he was lying down to sleep he saw the same man again. This time he looked extremely angry and said, "To err but realize and correct it can be said to be not an error. But I specially spoke to you yesterday, and you still do nothing to stop your error? If you do not fail to put this [modified] sutra out of circulation, your ruin will be immediate." Huiyan awoke alarmed at his error. Before dawn had come he dispatched riders with letters [to his friends] to ask for the copies to be returned. He burned them all.

[The monk] Shi Daoyan 釋道儼 of Chenwai oratory 塵外精舍 heard all of this in detail.

---

926. Source texts: *Fayuan zhulin* 18.418c (section "honoring the Dharma" [*jingfa* 敬法]); Lu, *Gu xiaoshuo gouchen*, 452; Wang Guoliang, *Mingxiang ji yanjiu*, 123; Wakatsuki, Hasegawa, and Inagaki, *Hōon jurin no sōgō teki kenkyū*, 132–134. Additional texts: *Gaoseng zhuan* 7.367b–c; *Chu sanzang jiji* 2.12b, 3.21a, 12.83c; *Shimen zijing lu* 1.805c. Discussed: Campany, "Notes on Sutra Texts," 66 n59. For a somewhat similar, later story in a Daoist text of the miracle-tale genre with a decidedly less happy ending for the protagonist, see Mollier, *Buddhism and Taoism Face to Face*, 25–26.

927. On this important sutra and its reception in China, see Williams, *Mahāyāna Buddhism*, 107–109; Ch'en, *Buddhism in China*, 113–118; and comments below. Huiyan is recorded in other sources as well, including his *Gaoseng zhuan* biography (see note above), as having modified this sutra.

928. My thanks to David Knechtges for his suggestion on translating this passage.

Comments

This story may be read, of course, as a stern, general warning against the abridgment of sutras. But there is probably more to it. The particular sutra referred to is the *Dabanniepan jing* 大般涅槃經 (Taishō 375), a modification of the translation by the same title by Dharmakṣema (Taishō 374) carried out in 421 and then introduced into the south sometime in the middle of the Yuanjia era [424–453].[929] Huiyan is recorded elsewhere, and not only in our text, as having been instrumental in this process, along with the noted layman Xie Lingyun 謝靈運. And both were involved in "making alterations in the sectional divisions" of the text.[930] Our story is counterfactual, in that Huiyan's version *did* circulate. The *Mahā[pari]nirvāṇa Sutra* was known in particular for its teachings of the eternal, joyous nature of *nirvāṇa* and of the omnipresence of Buddha-nature in all living beings. It may be that this story was intended, in part, as a defense of these teachings against detractors who were focused on a notion of *nirvāṇa* as extinction or on the realization of emptiness as the practitioner's primary goal. Even controversial or surprising sutra passages, the story may be read as arguing, must be left intact.

122[931]

During the Song there lived the wife of Luo Yu 羅璵, originally of the Fei 費 clan and a native of Ningshu.[932] Her father, Fei Yue 悦, served the Song as regional inspector in Ningzhou. As a girl, Fei was pious and recited the *Lotus Sutra* for several years persistently without flagging. Later in life she suddenly fell ill. She suffered from a pain in her heart and was fighting for her life. Her family grew alarmed, laid a cloth before her face,[933] and waited for her time to come. In her mind Fei thought: I have recited the sutra with great effort and diligence. Some assistance should be coming to me; I should not be allowed to simply die like this. She then lay down to sleep. After the space of a meal, somewhere between waking and dreaming, she

---

929. There had been an earlier translation by Faxian.

930. Ch'en, *Buddhism in China*, 114; cf. Zürcher, *The Buddhist Conquest of China*, 412 n125. Xie Lingyun is mostly—and justly—remembered as a poet and calligrapher, but his Buddhist writings (some of them poems) were extensive; see Zürcher, *The Buddhist Conquest of China*, 412–413; Tang Yongtong, *Han Wei liang Jin nanbeichao fojiao shi*, 308–311; and most recently Knechtges, "Zhongguo zhonggu wenren de shanyue youguan."

931. Source texts: *Fayuan zhulin* 95.988b (section "illness and pain" [*bingku* 病苦]), and *Taiping guangji* 109.4, both citing *Shuyi ji* 述異記 as their source; Lu, *Gu xiaoshuo gouchen*, 453; Wang Guoliang, *Mingxiang ji yanjiu*, 124. Additional texts: *Hongzan fahua zhuan* 6.28c; *Fahua jing chiyan ji* 1.68a; *Fahua lingyan zhuan* 2.15a.

932. A commandery that spanned parts of what are now Guanghan, Guangdu, and other districts in Sichuan province.

933. This was done in the case of those who, on their deathbeds, seemed very near to expiring, to detect when breathing had stopped. The practice is also mentioned in item 33.

saw Buddha in the window of her room. He extended his arm and rubbed her heart with his hand. At once she recovered. The entire room full of people, men and women, servants and slaves, all saw a golden light and smelled a pleasant fragrance.

Luo Yu's cousin, wife of Minister in the Section for Inner Troops Fei Yin 費愔, who was my wife's great-grandfather, was at the time keeping watch over Fei's sickbed and saw and heard these things. This deepened her faith and insight, causing her to maintain the precepts for the rest of her life. She told of this miracle to encourage her children, nephews, and nieces.

Comments

The intrafamilial source of this story of devotion to the entire *Lotus Sutra* (and not just to its chapter on Guanshiyin) is particularly striking. A relative of Wang Yan is implied to be the source of the next story as well.

123[934]

During the Song there lived one Peng Ziqiao 彭子喬, a native of Yiyang district.[935] He served as recorder in his own commandery and also worked on the staff of Governor Shen Wenlong 沈文龍. In the first year of Jian-yuan [479–480] he was arrested for a crime. In his youth Ziqiao had once left the household [to become a monk], and although he had returned to lay life he continued to recite the *Guanshiyin Sutra* often. Wenlong was very angry; he had him tightly bound and certainly intended to kill him. Distraught, and seeing no other alternative, Ziqiao began chanting the sutra with all his might, repeating it more than a hundred times. Tired, he fell asleep one day; the dozen or so others incarcerated with him were also asleep at the time. A subofficial functionary from Xiangxi district, Du Daorong 杜道榮, was also in jail at the time, dozing off and then waking up again, not able to fall soundly asleep. Suddenly a pair of white cranes landed on Ziqiao's screen. In a moment, one of them descended and alighted beside Ziqiao. It seemed [to Daorong] that it was a beautiful person who had landed. In his mind Daorong thought it strange. When he rose, he saw that Ziqiao's fetters were loosened around his feet, though the cangue was still intact. While Daorong was still examining him, Ziqiao woke up. Together they pondered the fetters and sighed. Daorong asked Ziqiao, "Did

---

934. Source texts: *Fayuan zhulin* 27.484c–485a (section "utmost sincerity" [*zhicheng* 至誠]); Lu, *Gu xiaoshuo gouchen*, 453; Wang Guoliang, *Mingxiang ji yanjiu*, 125; Wakatsuki, Hasegawa, and Inagaki, *Hōon jurin no sōgō teki kenkyū*, 177–179. Additional texts: *Xi Guanshiyin yingyanji* 40 (Makita, *Rikuchō kōitsu Kanzeon ōkenki no kenkyū*, 43); *Fayuan zhulin*, cited in *Taiping guangji* 111.7; *Fahua zhuanji* 6.73b; *Guanyin cilin ji* 2.90c–91a; *Guanshiyin chiyan ji* 1.96b.

935. In today's Hanshou district, Hunan province.

you dream of anything?" Ziqiao replied, "No, I didn't dream." Daorong then told him of what he had just seen. Even though Ziqiao knew then that he would be all right, he still feared that the jailers would suspect that he was attempting to escape, so he refastened the fetters on himself. Four or five days later he was pardoned and released.

My cousin, [Wang] Lian 璉,[936] knew Ziqiao and Daorong personally. He heard both men talk of this event in terms similar to the ones related here.

<h1 style="text-align:center">124[937]</h1>

During the Qi there lived one Dong Qingjian 董青建; his place of origin is unknown. His father was styled Xianming 賢明. In the first year of Jian-yuan [479–480][938] he served as a cavalry commandant.

When Qingjian's mother was pregnant with him, she dreamed that someone told her, "You will certainly give birth to a boy. On his body will be a green birthmark. You should name him Qingjian."[939] When the boy was born it was as the dream-figure had said, so she named him accordingly. Handsome, jovial in speech, of a magnanimous character, his family members had never seen him angry, and all who met him found him remarkable.

At fourteen he was appointed to a post as master of records for the region. In the first year of Jianyuan the heir apparent had subdued the Fan and Han river valleys, and Qingjian was appointed administrator in the waterways section. On the sixteenth of the seventh month of the second year [7 August 480] he suddenly fell gravely ill, and he told himself, "I cannot be saved." On the eighteenth, approaching the moment of his death, he got up and said to his mother: "My sin has been expunged. Good fortune will arrive. Our karmic bond is now forever severed. It is my wish that you cut yourself off [from attachment to me] and not be sorrowful." He then emitted seven cries and died.

His body was laid out before the abstinence hall to be prepared for

---

936. Unfortunately I have not found any other information about Wang Lian, who is also mentioned in this same capacity in the *Xi Guanshiyin yingyan ji* version of this story.

937. Source texts: *Fayuan zhulin* 52.677b–c (section "family" [*juanshu* 眷屬]); Lu, *Gu xiaoshuo gouchen*, 454; Wang Guoliang, *Mingxiang ji yanjiu*, 126. Additional texts: *Fayuan zhulin*, as quoted in *Taiping guangji* 114.6; *Liudao ji* 1.112c. Translated: Mai, "Visualization Apocrypha," 356–360; my translation borrows some phrasing from Mai's and differs mostly in the translation of a few technical terms.

938. *Fayuan zhulin* gives the dynasty as the Jin, whose brief Jianyuan reign-era lasted from 343 to 344; *Taiping guangji* gives the dynasty as Qi, of which the Jianyuan dates are as given in my text in brackets. I follow Wang Guoliang's suggestion in dating this story to the Qi, not the Jin, and there are two other stories with internal dates during the Qi (see below). It remains possible that the events narrated here were held to have occurred in the Jin.

939. This is not our text's only reference to physiognomy; see also item 51.

burial. That night a spirit-medium said,[940] "The paths of the living and dead diverge. Do not place him before the abstinence hall. An image-making monk will soon come and retrieve the body for burial." The next day, a monk by the name of Tanshun 曇順 did indeed arrive. Following the numinous communication,[941] they told the monk what had happened. Tanshun said, "I reside at Nanlin monastery 南林寺.[942] I have almost finished fashioning a sixty-foot-tall image. Since your worthy son had this miraculous response, we should bury him in the vacant plot to the west of the monastery." So it was that he came to be buried there beside the monastery.

Three days later his mother led a dozen or so relatives to make offerings at the grave. East of the grave they saw Qingjian just as he had been while alive. He said, "It is my wish that you cut yourself off [from attachment to me] and return home. I have now returned to reside at the monastery." His mother stopped wailing and went back home, where the whole family commenced eating a vegetarian diet and performing the long abstinence ceremony.[943] On the eleventh day of the intercalary month, [Qingjian's father] Xianming saw Qingjian in a dream; Qingjian said to him, "It is my wish that you go out to [reside in] the eastern abstinence hall for a short time." Xianming then bathed himself in fragrant water, observed the abstinence prohibitions, and went out [to stay in] the eastern abstinence hall. On the night of the fourteenth,[944] while sleeping, he could hear Qingjian calling him. Sitting up with a start, he saw Qingjian before the abstinence hall, just as he had been in life. His father asked, "Where have you gone to?" Qingjian replied, "Since my death I have resided in the palace for the refinement of spirits.[945] After I have completed one hundred days

---

940. Translating *lingyu yun* 靈語云. This phrase might perhaps indicate (though I doubt it) not a spirit-medium proper but a message derived from the spirit world in any fashion— for example, by some method of divination. The speaker might be understood as Qingjian or as the medium channeling his message; thus the ensuing statement may be read in either the first or the third person. Cf. the similarly worded passage in item 78 above.

941. Translating *yi lingyu* 依靈語.

942. Located in Jiankang.

943. The same phrase occurs in a passage in the *Consecration Sutra* (*Guanding jing* 12.533c–534a) instructing the reader on how to attain rebirth in the heavens.

944. Note that this is three days after the dream. Three-day liminal periods were very common in rebirth situations and in contact between the living and the dead. Note further that the fourteenth of any month would have been a night of abstinence-ceremony observance. As I have remarked elsewhere above, such periods are often represented in our text as particularly suited for communication between the seen and unseen realms.

945. Translating *lianshen gong* 練神宮, a term (given in both *Fayuan zhulin* and *Taiping guangji*) I find attested nowhere else except in iterations of this same story, and one that attests in interesting ways to the interweaving of indigenous and Buddhist themes. One finds numerous mentions of the "refinement" of spirits in texts such as the *Xiang'er* 想爾 commentary to the *Daode jing*; see Bokenkamp, *Early Daoist Scriptures*, 46–48, 102, 135, and Rao Zongyi, *Laozi Xiang'er zhu jiaozheng*, 21 (where the very similar phrase *lianshen zhi gong* 練神之宮 is used).

there, I am to be reborn in the *trāyastriṃśa* heaven.[946] I cannot bear to see you, Mother, and my brothers weeping and in such pain. On the twenty-first day [in the sequence of funeral rites] you should pay obeisance to all Buddhas and bodhisattvas, invite the Four Celestial Kings,[947] and I will thus be able to return temporarily. It is my wish that you and Mother from now on cease wailing and making sacrificial offerings for me. Mother has already made a vow seeking to see me, and her allotted life span is due to expire soon, after which she and I will be reborn together in the same place. You, Father, will live to the old age of seventy-three. After your allotted life span ends, you are scheduled to receive three years of retribution for your sins, but if you apply yourself to practicing the path with diligence, you will be able to avoid this." His father asked, "You arrived here in the middle of the night. What do you use for light?" Qingjian answered, "I descended today with many bodhisattvas and celestial beings. Their bodies give off light." His father asked again, "Whom have you recognized in the heavens?" Qingjian said, "I have seen Cavalryman Wang 王, a Zhang of Wuxing, and my maternal grandfather from Xihe."

Qingjian continued: "But it is not merely in our family that I have been reborn. Over the past forty-seven years I have died and been reborn seven times. I have attained the fourth fruit of the path.[948] Earlier I had made seven vows to be reborn in the human realm; that is why I passed through those [seven] births and deaths. From this point on my births and deaths will be forever terminated, as I have gained release from those seven rounds of suffering. As I was dying I saw these seven sites of my former births and deaths, and that is why I gave seven cries, because I was separating from my seven families." His father asked, "Which other families were you born into?" Qingjian said, "I was born into the family of Minister of Personnel Jiang 江, the Yang 羊 family of Guangzhou, the Zhang 張 family of Wuxing, the family of Chariot and Horse General Wang 王, the Xiao 蕭 family of Wuxing, the family of Palace Steward Liang 梁, and the family of cavalryman Dong Yue 董越. It was only in this [last] interval that I lived

---

946. See the note in item 8 above.

947. That is, the *si tianwang* 四天王. In China, these were conceived as celestial beings who personally or via envoys checked on the merits and sins of living persons on the days of *zhai* observances; hence the rationale for holding those observances on their particular days of the calendar. They functionally paralleled the indigenous Director of Allotted Life Span, or Siming 司命, and, before him, Heaven 天 itself: all of them adjusted human life span (and, in the Buddhist case, additionally meted out reward or punishment) in accordance with the noted and recorded sins of individuals, and all depended on a system of regular reportage of sins upward. The Four Kings' activities were presented in detail in the *Da loutan jing*, as well as in a fifth-century indigenous scripture, the *Sutra of the Four Celestial Kings*, or *Si tianwang jing* 四天王經, on which see the study and translation in Sørensen, "Divine Scrutiny of Human Morals."

948. *Yi de si dao guo* 已得四道果; that is to say, he has become an arhat. See Gethin, *The Foundations of Buddhism*, 194; Buswell and Gimello, introduction to *Paths to Liberation*, 8; and cf. items 64 and 101 above.

seventeen years; in other cases it was only for three or five years. From this point on, the years of suffering [for you] will be many. You should cultivate merit assiduously. I have observed that many people in this world, when they die, fall into the three evil paths of rebirth, while those reborn in the heavens are few. Practice with vigor, that you may obtain release and deliverance. Vow to be reborn in the heavens, and we may then see each other again; otherwise we will not."

His father asked further: "Your mother is worried about you. She is near death. Can you allow her to see you?" Qingjian said, "We should not see each other. It would only deepen her misery. Just tell her what I have told you. The celestial persons have already departed; I am not permitted to stay here much longer." He wore a sad expression, and then suddenly he vanished. After he left, a fragrance of incense lingered in the bamboo grove nearby; other family members could smell it as well.[949]

Xianming thereupon left the household, taking the Dharma name Fazang 法藏.

Comments

This complex rebirth story, like some others above, seems concerned to confront the familial lineage system and its attendant cult of ancestors, which had existed in China for hundreds of years prior to Buddhism's advent, with the Buddhist teaching of rebirth—specifically cross-family rebirth. Family members' wish to be reborn together in subsequent lives is attested in many "prayer" (*yuanwen* 願文) sections of memorial liturgies and in many dedications inscribed on Buddhist images.[950] We note yet again the use of shamans (or at least of some sort of vehicle for the conveyance of the speech of the dead to the living) to confirm Buddhist teaching.[951]

125[952]

During the Qi there lived a woman originally of the Wang 王 clan named Siniang 四娘. In the third year of Yongming [485–486] she died of illness. Her corpse was laid out on the floor, but when she was being prepared for burial it was noticed that her heart was still warm, so she was not yet encof-

949. There appears in the text at this point a re-enumeration of the seven families into which Dong Qingjian claimed to have been reborn (with some added personal names), a sentence seemingly added later. I omit it here.

950. See Hou Xudong, *Wu liu shiji beifang minzhong Fojiao xinyang*, 87–248.

951. Liu Yuanru, *Chaoxiang shenghuo shijie*, 266, points out that this story may also be read as a concrete expression of conditioned co-production. She also notes (p. 290) that the ritual service of *seven generations* of ancestors long predated Buddhism's arrival in China, so that the number of rebirths mentioned in this story is hardly accidental.

952. Source texts: *Fayuan zhulin* 91.958b–c (section "breaking the abstinence [regulations]" [*po zhai* 破齋]); Lu, *Gu xiaoshuo gouchen*, 456; Wang Guoliang, *Mingxiang ji yanjiu*, 127.

fined. Two days later her body gradually began to warm up, her breathing slowly returned to normal, and soon she regained the ability to speak. She gave the following account.

Two persons arrived to apprehend and take her away. They reached a large gate where a monk sat on a Western seat.[953] On seeing her he was startled and asked, "Why have you come?" He then scolded the two persons, saying, "You apprehended the wrong person! Forty lashes for each of you!" To Siniang he said, "Lady, you may go." She replied, "Just now I was confused, and I do not know the way back. I would ask for someone to show me the way." The monk then ordered a guard to escort her.

When they had gone some distance, she saw her former servant leaning against a tall tower. The servant asked in surprise, "Siniang, why have you suddenly come here? Did you come to see your younger brother's wife?" Siniang answered, "I do not know where she is." She asked her servant to take her there, but the servant said, "I cannot take you there, but if you just go along, the road will take you straight to her." She handed Siniang a horse whip and said, "Take care to hold onto this whip, and you will know which way to go."

She went maybe several *li* and saw the woman in question. It turned out to be the wife of Siniang's *husband's* younger brother. She was in the midst of undergoing punishment. Her four limbs were tied back in the way that geese and ducks are dressed for the table, and she was hanging by the side of the road. They cried out in sorrow when they saw each other. The woman said, "When I was alive, I sinned. Now I am undergoing this punishment." She tried to move her hands to plead for help, but they were lashed to a post; she was unable to join them together. Siniang could hear the sounds of others being punished nearby, but she could not see their forms. Siniang asked, "What is that sound?" The other woman responded, "Those are monks who did not practice properly, who broke the abstinence rules and violated the precepts.[954] They cry out in pain upon receiving their punishment as recompense."

Siniang continued on her way back and soon arrived at her home. Upon seeing her corpse she felt overwhelming disgust and did not want to return to it. Someone pushed her from behind so that she stumbled and fell, and thus she reentered her body and revived. She is still alive today.

Comments

In the last sentence we note the temporal proximity of the persons and events recounted to the formation of the text. Some protagonists of *Mingxiang ji* stories were still living when the stories were compiled and circulated in this form.

---

953. See the note to item 6 above.
954. *Po zhai fan jie* 破齋犯戒.

126[955]

During the Yongming period of the [southern] Qi [483–493] the monk Shi Huijin 釋慧進 resided at Gaozuo monastery 高座寺 in Yangdu.[956] In his younger days he was brash and traveled about as an adventurer, but at forty he realized the impermanence of things and so left the household. He kept a vegetarian diet, dressed plainly, and vowed to recite the *Lotus Sutra*.[957] He applied his mind and with utmost diligence held a copy of the sutra, but he then fell ill. He vowed to produce one hundred copies of the sutra to repent of his former [karmic] impediments.[958] So he began, and had progressed as far as [copying] sixteen hundred words when thieves entered, demanding his goods. When Huijin showed them the money for [buying materials to copy] the sutra,[959] they felt ashamed and left. Later he completed one hundred copies and recovered from illness as a result. His reciting of the sutra now complete and his vow fulfilled, he transferred the karmic merit from the recitation,[960] vowing to be reborn in the Anyang realm.[961] He then heard a voice from midair proclaim: "Your vow is already fulfilled. You will certainly be reborn there."[962] He died without any sign of illness at an age past eighty.

---

955. Source texts: *Fayuan zhulin* 95.989a28–b6 (section "illness and pain" [*bingku* 病苦]); *Taiping guangji* 109.6; Lu, *Gu xiaoshuo gouchen*, 456; Wang Guoliang, *Mingxiang ji yanjiu*, 128. Additional texts: *Gaoseng zhuan* 12.407c–408a; *Xiangyi ji* 2 (Lu, *Gu xiaoshuo gouchen*, 432, based on *Taiping guangji* 109.6); *Ji shenzhou sanbao gantong lu* 3.427a; *Fahua zhuanji* 4.63b; *Hongzan fahua zhuan* 6.28a; *Wangsheng ji* 1.129a. Translated: Mai, "Visualization Apocrypha," 78; my translation borrows some phrasing and does not differ in any important way. Discussed: Campany, "Notes on Sutra Texts," 32; Campany, "The Real Presence," 249 n40.

956. The *Fahua zhuanji* version indicates he was originally surnamed Yao 姚 and was a native of Wuxing. The story of the founding of this monastery is briefly recounted in *Gaoseng zhuan* 1.328a, and the temple is mentioned elsewhere in that and a few other early medieval texts as well.

957. Although it is only implied here, I believe we are to understand that he vowed to recite the sutra not once, but repeatedly or constantly. Such recitation is reported elsewhere in this period and genre.

958. "[Karmic] impediments" here translates *zhang* 障, literally "earthworks" but often used metaphorically (and technically) for residual karmic "blockages" from former lives, the specific causes of which are unknown to the person in question but the effects of which are manifest in his life. The term was frequently used (with *fannao* 煩惱) to translate the Sanskrit *āvarṇa*. See Mochizuki, *Bukkyō daijiten*, 2543c–2544c.

959. In the *Fahua zhuanji* text, this episode is more clearly narrated: "Huijin said, 'All I have is money for copying the sutra.'"

960. Translating *hui ci song ye* 迴此誦業. *Fahua zhuanji* has *chang hui zhu fuye* 常迴諸福業. While the language of "transferring" merit to oneself for use in future rebirths may seem odd, it was in fact quite common. For examples, see Nattier, *A Few Good Men*, 114–115, and Teiser, *The Scripture on the Ten Kings*, 27–30, 121–128. The merit produced by a ritual performance could also be transferred to multiple parties; for examples, see Teiser, "Ornamenting the Departed," 230–231.

961. That is, the Pure Land. See the note in item 90 above.

962. The *Fahua zhuanji* version places this episode at a time shortly before Huijin's death.

127[963]

Shi Jun 史儁,[964] who had considerable learning, venerated the Dao and ridiculed the Buddha. He often told people, "Buddha is a minor deity not worth serving." Each time he saw an image of the Venerable One, he would treat it disrespectfully and upbraid it. Because of this he later contracted a foot deformity. Of all the prayers and acts of fortune he carried out, none proved effective. A friend of his, Zhao Wen 趙文, told him, "Among paths leading to fortune, the fortune of the Buddha is foremost. You should fashion an image of Guanyin."[965] Because his illness was acute, Jun did as Wen had said and made an image. When it was complete, Jun dreamed of Guanyin, and afterward he recovered.

128[966]

The wife of Chen Xuanfan 陳玄範, originally surnamed Zhang 張, dedicatedly venerated the Buddha. For a long time she had wanted to make a metal image with her own hands and then present offerings to it for the rest of her life. She wanted to do this but had never found the means. She worried at how much time was passing without her having done it. Suddenly a metal image of Guanyin, five feet tall and completely painted, appeared atop the high seat [in her home].

129[967]

During the Jin the monk Daotai 道泰 resided at the Hengtang 衡唐 oratory on Mount Chang. During the Jin Yixi period [405–419] he once dreamed of a man who told him, "Your remaining life span will run out in six or

---

963. Source texts: *Bianzheng lun* 7.539c; *Xuanyan ji* 9, as collected in Lu, *Gu xiaoshuo gouchen,* 438; Wang Guoliang, *Mingxiang ji yanjiu,* 130. Additional texts: *Xuanyan ji* 9 (as quoted in *Taiping guangji* 111.16 and *Bianzheng lun* 7.539c, which cites its source thus: 出宣驗冥祥等記 [and this is not the only example of such]). Discussed: Campany, *Strange Writing,* 334.

964. *Bianzheng lun* writes the Jun of his name as 俊; *Taiping guangji,* as 儁.

965. This is the first point in our text at which this bodhisattva's name is given as Guanyin 觀音, not Guanshiyin 觀世音, reflecting the uptake of a rendition that began with Kumārajīva.

966. Source texts: *Bianzheng lun* 7.539c; Lu, *Gu xiaoshuo gouchen,* 458; Wang Guoliang, *Mingxiang ji yanjiu,* 131. Additional texts: *Xuanyan ji* 29 (collected in Lu, *Gu xiaoshuo gouchen,* 444, from the *Bianzheng lun* passage noted above; Lu Xun, because of the vagueness of *Bianzheng lun*'s manner of citation, collected the story under both *Xuanyan ji* and *Mingxiang ji*).

967. Note: This item is out of chronological order, because I only discovered it late in the writing process. Source texts: *Fayuan zhulin* 17.410b; Wakatsuki, Hasegawa, and Inagaki, *Hōon jurin no sōgō teki kenkyū,* 108–109. This item is not collected by Lu Xun (as noted by Wakatsuki, Hasegawa, and Inagaki, *Hōon jurin no sōgō teki kenkyū,* 27) or Wang Guoliang. Additional texts: *Xu Guangshiyin yingyanji* 5 (Makita, *Rikuchō kōitsu Kanzeon ōkenki no kenkyū,* 21); *Xu gaoseng zhuan* 25.645b; *Taiping guangji* 110.11 (citing *Fayuan zhulin*).

seven more years." When Daotai had reached the age of forty-two, he contracted a grave illness. He thought he would not recover. He entrusted the benefit of his robe and bowl as a generous bestowal of fortune. He also gave himself over to reciting the [name or scripture of] Sound Observer. For four days and nights he kept it up, never once flagging. Some persons who were sitting at his bedside before the bed curtain suddenly saw beneath the curtain that a man had jumped in through the window. His feet and lower legs were of a golden color, and light from them illuminated the room. Daotai lifted the curtain to afford them a quick glimpse, but the figure suddenly vanished. Astonished and delighted, they conferred about it. Daotai then broke out in a great sweat, after which he felt lighter. His illness was cured.

APPENDIX 1

Fragments and Questionable Items

I briefly list here two sorts of passages attributed in collectanea to *Mingxiang ji*. One type consists of fragments of text so brief that no story line is discernible. The other type consists of whole stories that I doubt—either on the basis of their content or on the lateness of the anthology (combined with the absence of earlier attributions of the story in question to *Mingxiang ji*)—were part of Wang Yan's text (at least autograph versions of it), despite the attribution. This is by no means an exhaustive list, and ongoing research may well turn up additional items to be added either to the text itself or to this list of questionably attributed passages.

1. An Fakai 安法開

Source texts: *Taiping yulan* 946; Lu, *Gu xiaoshuo gouchen*, 533; Wang Guoliang, *Mingxiang ji yanjiu*, 129.
   This is a mere fragment. It concerns centipedes.

2. Jin Jianwen di 晉簡文帝

Source texts: *Ji shenzhou sanbao gantong lu* 1; Wang Guoliang, *Mingxiang ji yanjiu*, 33.
   This is a two-sentence fragment stating that the emperor in question had wanted to build a stupa at the Changgan temple but died before doing so.

3. Wang Huan 王奐[1]

Source text: *Fayuan zhulin* 75.852a5–22; not collected by Lu Xun or Wang Guoliang.

---

1. On Wang Huan, see Chittick, *Patronage and Community in Medieval China*, 74–75.

This is a story set in the Qi era that describes its protagonist as a profound believer in Buddhist scriptures but also as very jealous and resentful, often without due cause. It mentions that he had his concubine comb his moustache in his abstinence hall (!) and later had her unfairly executed. She filed a complaint in the unseen world, and he later paid the price of his unjust act. This appears to be more a classic story of ghostly revenge than the sort of tale attested elsewhere in *Mingxiang ji*, and I suspect it is misattributed.

4. Sengmiao 僧妙

Source text: *Shimen zijing lu* 1.811a–b.

Additional texts: *Tang Gaoseng zhuan*, as cited in *Fayuan zhulin* 35.559c.

This story is attributed to *Mingxiang ji* in *Shimen zijing lu*, but the lack of any earlier attributions of it to Wang Yan's text leads me to believe that it is probably wrongly attributed.[2]

---

2. However, it has been argued that *Shimen zijing lu* was in fact compiled not by Huixin 懷信 in the mid-ninth century but by Huixiang 惠祥 (?–706), author of *Hongzan fahua zhuan*, sometime between 698 and 704. See Zheng, "*Mingxiang ji* buji," 172, and Chen Jinhua, *Philosopher, Practitioner, Politician*, 21. If this argument about the date of the compendium is correct—but the evidence is ambiguous at best (the work is differently attributed in various Chinese and Japanese sources)—it would place it only about forty years later than Daoshi's *Fayuan zhulin*. Zheng, "*Mingxiang ji* buji," argues that this story should be restored to *Mingxiang ji*.

APPENDIX 2
List of Major Motifs

The following lists the item numbers of stories in which a select set of motifs appear.[1] Other, more specific listings of the occurrences of certain themes and ideas may be found in part 1 and in the index.

Bodhisattva Sound Observer responds to devotion and saves devotee from distress: 13, 28, 31, 32, 33, 42, 46, 47, 48, 49, 50, 51, 52, 53, 58, 61, 62, 70, 73, 74, 85, 88, 93, 96, 97, 98, 103, 106, 120, 123, 129

Healing, miraculous: 23, 24, 33, 71, 87, 100, 122, 126, 127, 129

Heavens and Pure Lands, depictions of: 22, 72, 82, 87, 89, 90, 107

Image, miracles associated with: preface, 1, 19, 58, 112, 114, 128

Mountain as place of monastic habitation: 7, 9, 10, 14, 15, 41, 55, 56, 60, 91

Pilgrimage: 1, 4, 12

Punishment for desecration of images or sutras, theft of Buddhist property, or assault on Buddha: 75, 79, 83, 86, 111, 116, 121, 127

Purgatories, depictions of: 5, 6, 23, 44, 45, 59, 65, 66, 67, 77, 92, 102, 118, 119, 125

Rain produced miraculously: 14, 56

Rebirth, with recall of former lives or prediction of future ones: 3, 30, 34, 45, 57, 69, 81, 101, 117, 124

Return from death: 5, 6, 23, 30, 35, 44, 45, 59, 65, 66, 77, 92, 104, 105, 110, 118, 119, 125

Revelation of sutra or teaching: 2, 45, 84

Spirit-monks appear: 11, 12, 16, 18, 19, 20, 25, 27, 39, 43, 66(?), 76, 87(?), 90, 95, 98, 101, 102, 104, 108, 109, 113

---

1. For very different sorts of classification of the work's contents, see Zhou Ciji, *Liuchao zhiguai xiaoshuo yanjiu*, 116–118, and Xiong Daolin, "*Mingxiang ji* yanjiu," 244–255.

Bibliography

Primary sources

A. Buddhist Canonical Sources Cited by Title

Numbers given in the middle column are the serial numbers assigned to the text in modern Sino-Japanese editions. Numbers not preceded by a letter are found in *Taishō shinshū daizōkyō* 大正新脩大藏經 (*Re-edited Canon of the Taishō Era*), ed. Takakusu Junjirō 高楠順次郎, Watanabe Kaigyōku 渡辺海旭, and Ono Gemmyō 小野玄妙, 100 vols. (Tokyo: Taishō Issaikyō Kankōkai, 1924–1935; repr., Taipei: Xinwen feng, 1983). Numbers preceded by the letter Z are found in *Dainippon zoku zōkyō* 大日本續藏經 (*Supplement to the Canon*), ed. Maeda Eun 前田慧雲 and Nakano Tatsue 中野達慧, 750 vols. in 150 boxes (Kyoto: Zōkyō Shoin, 1905–1912). Numbers in the right column indicate volume numbers in the two respective collections. Passages in these works are generally cited by scroll, page, register, and (sometimes) line number; thus, "5.2a6–7" would indicate lines 6–7 on register a (the topmost of the three horizontal registers) of page two in the fifth scroll. (The alternate edition of the canon that is mentioned in Conventions is *Zhonghua dazangjing* 中華大藏經 [*Hanwen bufen* 漢文部分], 106 vols. [Beijing: Zhonghua shuju chubanshe, 1984–1996].)

Baguan zhai fa 八關齋法	Z1130	60
Bannihuan jing 般泥洹經	6	1
Banzhou sanmei jing 般舟三昧經	417	13
Beishan lu 北山錄	2113	52
Bianzheng lun 辯正論	2110	52
Biqiuni zhuan 比丘尼傳	2063	50
Chanfa yaojie 禪法要解	616	15
Chang ahan jing 長阿含經	1	1
Chan yao jing 禪要經	609	15
Chengju guangming dingyi jing 成具光明定意經	630	15
Chu sanzang jiji 出三藏記集	2145	55
Chu yao jing 出曜經	212	4
Dabanniepan jing 大般涅槃經	374	12
Dabanniepan jing 大般涅槃經	375	12
Da loutan jing 大樓炭經	23	1
Daoxing banruo jing 道行般若經	224	8

Da Tang xiyu ji 大唐西域記	2087	51
Fahua jing chiyan ji 法華經持驗記	Z1541	78
Fahua lingyan zhuan 法華靈驗傳	Z1539	78
Fahua zhuanji 法華傳記	2068	51
Fangguang banruo jing 放光般若經	221	8
Fanwang jing 梵網經	1484	24
Fanwang jing pusa xin dipin xia lue shu 梵網經菩薩心地品下略疏	Z695	38
Fayuan zhulin 法苑珠林	2122	53
Fozu tongji 佛祖統紀	2035	49
Gaoseng zhuan 高僧傳	2059	50
Guangding jing 灌頂經	1331	21
Guang hongming ji 廣弘明集	2103	52
Guan Puxian pusa xingfa jing 觀普賢菩薩行法經	277	9
Guanshiyin chiyan ji 觀世音持驗紀	Z1542	78
Guan wuliangshoufo jing 觀無量壽佛經	365	12
Guanyin cilin ji 觀音慈林集	Z1644	88
Guiyuan zhizhi ji 歸元直指集	Z1156	61
Hailong wang jing 海龍王經	598	15
Hongming ji 弘明集	2102	52
Hongzan fahua zhuan 弘贊法華傳	2067	51
Jinglü yixiang 經律異相	2121	53
Jingtu lun 淨土論	1963	47
Jingtu shengxian lu 淨土聖賢錄	Z1549	78
Jingtu wangsheng zhuan 淨土往生傳	2071	51
Jinguang ming jing 金光明經	663	16
Ji shenzhou sanbao gantong lu 集神州三寶感通錄	2106	52
Jushi zhuan 居士傳	Z1646	88
Kaiyuan shijiao lu 開元釋教錄	2154	55
Liudao ji 六道集	Z1645	88
Luoyang qielan ji 洛陽伽藍記	2092	51
Lushan ji 廬山記	2095	51
Meisōden shō 名僧傳抄	Z1523	77
Miaofa lianhua jing 妙法蓮華經	262	9
Mile laishi jing 彌勒來時經	457	14
Mingbao ji ji shumu 冥報記輯書目	Z1648	88
Mohe jiaye dubinmu jing 摩訶迦葉度貧母經	497	14
Pinimu jing 毘尼母經	1463	24
Poxie lun 破邪論	2109	52
Pusa chutai jing 菩薩處胎經	384	12
Pusa yingluo jing 菩薩瓔珞經	656	16
Qing Bintoulu fa 請賓頭盧法	1689	32
Renwang banruo poluomi jing 仁王般若波羅蜜經	245	8
Sanbao ganying yaolue lu 三寶感應要略錄	2084	51
Shenseng zhuan 神僧傳	2064	50
Shimen zijing lu 釋門自鏡錄	2083	51
Shishi yaolan 釋氏要覽	2127	54
Shisong lü 十誦律	1435	23

Shizhu duanjie jing 十住斷結經	309	10
Shoulengyan sanmei jing 首楞嚴三昧經	642	15
Sifen lü 四分律	1428	22
Sifen lü shanfan buque xingshi chao 四分律刪繁補闕行事鈔	1804	40
Si tianwang jing 四天王經	590	15
Taizi ruiying benqi jing 太子瑞應本起經	185	3
Tiecheng nili jing 鐵城泥犁經	42	1
Wangsheng ji 往生集	2072	51
Wangsheng xifang ruiying zhuan 往生西方淨土瑞應傳	2070	51
Wuliangshou jing 無量壽經	360	12
Xiuxing benqi jing 修行本起經	184	3
Xu gaoseng zhuan 續高僧傳	2060	50
Yiqie jing yinyi 一切經音義	2128	54
Yu ye jing 玉耶經	143	2
Zhancha shan'e yebao jing 占察善惡業報經	839	17
Zheng fahua jing 正法華經	263	9
Zhujing yaoji 諸經要集	2123	54
Zuochan sanmei jing 坐禪三昧經	614	15

B. Daoist Canonical Sources Cited by Title

Numbers given in the right column are those assigned the text in Schipper and Verellen, *The Taoist Canon*, in which further information on each text can be found. Passages are cited by scroll and page number (the letters a and b here indicating recto and verso).

Daojiao lingyan ji 道教靈驗記	590
Huayang Tao yinju ji 華陽陶隱居集	1050
Sandong zhunang 三洞珠囊	1139
Santian neijie jing 三天內解經	1205
Taishang cibei jiuyou bazui chan 太上慈悲九幽拔罪懺	544
Taishang dongshen dongyuan shenzhou zhibing kouzhang 太上洞神洞淵神咒治病口章	1290
Wudang fudi zongzhen ji 武當福地總真集	962
Yunji qiqian 雲笈七籤	1032
Zhengyi fawen taishang wailu yi 正一法文太上外籙儀	1243
Zhou shi mingtong ji 周氏冥通記	302

C. Other Chinese Texts Cited by Title

Passages are cited by scroll and page number unless otherwise indicated, except for passages from Lu Xun's *Gu xiaoshuo gouchen*, which are cited by page number (sometimes with the serial number of the cited passage also indicated as "item such-and-such").

Chuxue ji 初學記 by Xu Jian 徐堅 et al. 3 vols. continuously paginated. Beijing: Zhonghua shuju, 1962.

Fengsu tongyi 風俗通義 by Ying Shao 應劭
   Fengsu tongyi jiaozhu 風俗通義校注. Ed. Wang Liqi 王利器. 2 vols. continuously paginated. Beijing: Zhonghua shuju, 1981.
Hou Han shu 後漢書. Zhonghua shuju ed.
Huainan zi 淮南子
   Huainan zi jishi 淮南子集釋. Ed. He Ning 何寧. 4 vols. Beijing: Zhonghua shuju, 1998.
Huayangguo zhi 華陽國志 by Chang Qu 常璩
   Huayangguo zhi jiaozhu 華陽國志校注. Ed. Liu Lin 劉琳. Chengdu: Bashu shushe, 1984.
Jiankang shilu 建康實錄. Siku quanshu zhenben liuji ed.
Jingyi ji 旌異記. Compiled in Lu, *Gu xiaoshuo gouchen.*
Jin shu 晉書. Zhonghua shuju ed.
Liang shu 梁書. Zhonghua shuju ed.
Linggui zhi 靈鬼志. Compiled in Lu, *Gu xiaoshuo gouchen.*
Lunheng 論衡 by Wang Chong 王充
   Lunheng jiaoshi 論衡校釋. Ed. Huang Hui 黃暉. 4 vols. continuously paginated. Beijing: Zhonghua shuju, 1990.
Nan Qi shu 南齊書. Zhonghua shuju ed.
Nan shi 南史. Zhonghua shuju ed.
Qi Xie ji 齊諧記. Compiled in Lu, *Gu xiaoshuo gouchen.*
Shuijing zhu 水經注. By Li Daoyuan 酈道元. Ed. Dai Zhen 戴震. Taibei: Shijie shuju, 1988.
Song shu 宋書. Zhonghua shuju ed.
Soushen houji 搜神後記. Ed. Wang Shaoying. *Gu xiaoshuo congkan* series. Beijing: Zhonghua shuju, 1981. Cited by scroll and serial item number (not page number).
Soushen ji 搜神記. *Xinjiao soushen ji.* Ed. Yang Jialuo. Taipei: Shijie shuju, 1982. Cited by scroll and serial item number (not page number).
Sui shu 隋書. Zhonghua shuju ed.
Taiping guangji 太平廣記. Comp. Li Fang 李昉 et al. 4 vols. Shanghai: Shanghai guji chubanshe, 1990. Cited by scroll and serial position of the cited item in the scroll (e.g. "387.1" indicates the first passage anthologized in scroll 387).
Taiping yulan 太平御覽. Comp. Li Fang 李昉 et al. Facsimile repr. of Shāngwu yinshuguan 1935 printing from a Song copy. 4 vols. Beijing: Zhonghua shuju, 1992.
Wei shu 魏書. Zhonghua shuju ed.
Xuanyan ji 宣驗記. Compiled in Lu, *Gu xiaoshuo gouchen.*
Xu Qi Xie ji 續齊諧記. Compiled in Lu, *Gu xiaoshuo gouchen.*
Yiwen leiju 藝文類聚. Comp. Ouyang Xun et al. Modern recension by Wang Shaoying. 2 vols. continuously paginated. Beijing: Zhonghua shuju, 1965.
Yiyuan 異苑. Baibu congshu jicheng ed. Ed. Yan Yiping 嚴一萍. N.p.: Yiwen yinshuguan, n.d. Cited by scroll and serial item number (not page number).
Youming lu 幽明錄. Compiled in Lu, *Gu xiaoshuo gouchen.*

Secondary sources

Abe, Stanley K. *Ordinary Images.* Chicago: University of Chicago Press, 2002.
———. "Provenance, Patronage, and Desire: Northern Wei Sculpture from Shaanxi Province." *Ars Orientalis* 31 (2001): 1–30.

Andersen, Poul. "The Practice of *Bugang.*" *Cahiers d'Extrême-Asie* 5 (1990): 15–53.

Bai Bin. "Religious Beliefs as Reflected in the Funerary Record." In *Early Chinese Religion, Part Two: The Period of Division (220–589 AD),* ed. John Lagerwey and Lü Pengzhi, 989–1073. Leiden: Brill, 2010.

Bakhtin, M. M., and P. N. Medvedev. *The Formal Method in Literary Scholarship: A Critical Introduction to Sociological Poetics.* Trans. A. J. Wehrle. Cambridge, Mass.: Harvard University Press, 1985.

Balazs, Stefan. "Der Philosoph Fan Dschen und sein Traktat gegen den Buddhismus." *Sinica* 7 (1932): 220–234.

Beal, Samuel. *Si-yu ki: Buddhist Records of the Western World.* 2 vols. London, 1884. Repr. Delhi: Motilal Banarsidass, 1981.

Beckwith, Christopher I. *Empires of the Silk Road: A History of Central Eurasia from the Bronze Age to the Present.* Princeton: Princeton University Press, 2009.

Bell, Alexander Peter. *Didactic Narration: Jataka Iconography in Dunhuang with a Catalogue of Jataka Representations in China.* Münster: LIT Verlag, 2000.

Benn, James A. "Another Look at the Pseudo-*Śūraṃgama sūtra.*" *Harvard Journal of Asiatic Studies* 68 (2008): 57–90.

———. "Buddhism, Alcohol, and Tea in Medieval China." In *Of Tripod and Palate: Food, Politics, and Religion in Traditional China,* ed. Roel Sterckx, 213–236. New York: Palgrave Macmillan, 2005.

———. *Burning for the Buddha: Self-Immolation in Chinese Buddhism.* Kuroda Institute Studies in East Asian Buddhism 19. Honolulu: University of Hawai'i Press, 2007.

Beyer, Stephan. "Notes on the Vision Quest in Early Mahayana." In *Prajnaparamita and Related Systems: Studies in Honor of Edward Conze,* ed. Lewis Lancaster, 329–340. Berkeley Buddhist Studies Series. Berkeley: Institute of East Asian Studies, University of California, 1977.

Birnbaum, Raoul. *The Healing Buddha.* Rev. ed. Boston: Shambhala, 1989.

———. "The Manifestation of a Monastery: Shen-ying's Experiences on Mount Wu-t'ai in T'ang Context." *Journal of the American Oriental Society* 106 (1986): 119–137.

Bivar, A. D. H. "Hāritī and the Chronology of the Kuṣāṇas." *Bulletin of School of Oriental and African Studies* 33 (1970): 10–21.

Bloss, Lowell W. "Ancient Indian Folk Religion as Seen through the Symbolism of the Nāga." Ph.D. diss., University of Chicago, 1971.

———. "The Buddha and the Nāga: A Study in Buddhist Folk Religiosity." *History of Religions* 13 (1973): 36–53.

Bodde, Derk. *Festivals in Classical China.* Princeton: Princeton University Press, 1975.

Bokenkamp, Stephen R. *Ancestors and Anxiety: Daoism and the Birth of Rebirth in China.* Berkeley: University of California Press, 2007.

———. "Answering a Summons." In *Religions of China in Practice,* ed. Donald S. Lopez Jr., 188–202. Princeton: Princeton University Press, 1996.

———. *Early Daoist Scriptures.* With a contribution by Peter S. Nickerson. Berkeley: University of California Press, 1997.

———. "The Silkworm and the Bodhi Tree: The Lingbao Attempt to Replace Buddhism in China and Our Attempt to Place Lingbao Daoism." In *Ancient and Medieval China,* vol. 1 of *Religion and Chinese Society,* ed. John Lagerwey, 317–339. Hong Kong: Chinese University of Hong Kong Press and Ecole Française d'Extrême-Orient, 2004.

————. "Simple Twists of Fate: The Daoist Body and Its *Ming*." In *The Magnitude of Ming: Command, Allotment, and Fate in Chinese Culture*, ed. Christopher Lupke, 151–168. Honolulu: University of Hawai'i Press, 2005.

————. "Sources of the Ling-pao Scriptures." In *Tantric and Taoist Studies in Honour of R. A. Stein*, ed. Michel Strickmann, 2:434–486. Bruxelles: Institut Belge des Hautes Études Chinoises, 1983.

————. "The Yao Boduo Stele as Evidence for 'Dao-Buddhism' of the Early Ling-bao Scriptures." *Cahiers d'Extrême-Asie* 9 (1996–1997): 55–67.

Boucher, Daniel. *Bodhisattvas of the Forest and the Formation of the Mahāyāna: A Study and Translation of the Rāṣṭrapālaparipṛcchā-sūtra*. Honolulu: University of Hawai'i Press, 2008.

————. "Buddhist Translation Procedures in Third-Century China: A Study of Dharmarakṣa and His Translation Idiom." Ph.D. diss., University of Pennsylvania, 1996.

————. "Dharmarakṣa and the Transmission of Buddhism to China." *Asia Major*, 3rd ser., 19 (2006): 13–38.

————. "Gāndhārī and the Earliest Chinese Buddhist Translations Reconsidered: The Case of the Saddharmapuṇḍarīkasūtra." *Journal of the American Oriental Society* 118 (1998): 471–506.

————. "On *Hu* and *Fan* Again: The Transmission of 'Barbarian' Manuscripts to China." *Journal of the International Association of Buddhist Studies* 23 (2000): 7–28.

————. "Sutra on the Merit of Bathing the Buddha." In *Buddhism in Practice*, ed. Donald S. Lopez Jr., 59–68. Princeton: Princeton University Press, 1995.

Brandes, Stanley H. "The Creation of a Mexican Memorate." *Journal of American Folk-Lore* 87 (1974): 162–164.

Brashier, K. E. "Text and Ritual in Early Chinese Stelae." In *Text and Ritual in Early China*, ed. Martin Kern, 249–284. Seattle: University of Washington Press, 2005.

Brown, Robert L. "Expected Miracles: The Unsurprisingly Miraculous Nature of Buddhist Images and Relics." In *Images, Miracles, and Authority in Asian Religious Traditions*, ed. Richard Davis, 23–35. Boulder: Westview, 1998.

Buswell, Robert E., Jr., and Robert M. Gimello. Introduction to *Paths to Liberation: The Mārga and Its Transformations in Buddhist Thought*, ed. Robert E. Buswell Jr. and Robert M. Gimello, 1–36. Kuroda Institute Studies in East Asian Buddhism 7. Honolulu: University of Hawai'i Press, 1992.

Cahill, Suzanne E. *Transcendence and Divine Passion: The Queen Mother of the West in Medieval China*. Stanford: Stanford University Press, 1993.

Campany, Robert Ford. "À la recherche de la religion perdue: 'Aśokan Stupas,' Images, and the Cult of Relics in Early Medieval China." Paper presented to the Seminar on Buddhist Relic Veneration, American Academy of Religion, 1995.

————. "Buddhist Revelation and Taoist Translation in Early Medieval China." *Taoist Resources* 4 (1993): 1–29.

————. "Chinese History and Writing about 'Religion(s)': Reflections at a Crossroads." In *Opening Conference of the Consortium "Dynamics in the History of Religions between Asia and Europe,"* ed. Marion Steinicke and Volkhard Krech. Leiden: Brill, forthcoming.

————. "The Dreamscape of Early Medieval China." Unpublished manuscript.

————. "The Earliest Tales of the Bodhisattva Guanshiyin." In *Religions of China in*

Practice, ed. Donald S. Lopez Jr., 82–96. Princeton: Princeton University Press, 1996.

———. "Ghosts Matter: The Culture of Ghosts in Six Dynasties *Zhiguai.*" *Chinese Literature: Essays, Articles, Reviews* 13 (1991): 15–34.

———. "Living off the Books: Fifty Ways to Dodge *Ming* in Early Medieval China." In *The Magnitude of Ming: Command, Allotment, and Fate in Chinese Culture*, ed. Christopher Lupke, 129–150. Honolulu: University of Hawai'i Press, 2005.

———. *Making Transcendents: Ascetics and Social Memory in Early Medieval China.* Honolulu: University of Hawai'i Press, 2009.

———. "The Meanings of Cuisines of Transcendence in Late Classical and Early Medieval China." *T'oung Pao* 91 (2005): 126–182.

———. "Notes on the Devotional Uses and Symbolic Functions of Sutra Texts as Depicted in Early Chinese Buddhist Miracle Tales and Hagiographies." *Journal of the International Association of Buddhist Studies* 14 (1991): 28–72.

———. "On the Very Idea of Religions (in the Modern West and in Early Medieval China)." *History of Religions* 42 (2003): 287–319.

———. "The Real Presence." *History of Religions* 32 (1993): 233–272.

———. "Return-from-Death Narratives in Early Medieval China." *Journal of Chinese Religions* 18 (1990): 91–125.

———. *Strange Writing: Anomaly Accounts in Early Medieval China.* Albany: State University of New York Press, 1996.

———. *To Live as Long as Heaven and Earth: A Translation and Study of Ge Hong's "Traditions of Divine Transcendents."* Berkeley: University of California Press, 2002.

———. "Two Religious Thinkers of the Early Eastern Jin: Gan Bao and Ge Hong in Multiple Contexts." *Asia Major*, 3rd ser., 18 (2005): 175–224.

Cao Daoheng 曹道衡. "Lun Wang Yan he ta de *Mingxiang ji*" 論王琰和他的冥祥記. *Wenxue yichan* 文學遺產 1992, issue 1, pp. 26–36.

Capitanio, Joshua. "Dragon Kings and Thunder Gods: Rainmaking, Magic, and Ritual in Medieval Chinese Religion." Ph.D. diss., University of Pennsylvania, 2008.

Carter, Martha L. *The Mystery of the Udayana Buddha.* Supplemento n. 64 agli *Annali Istituto Universitario Orientale* 50 (1990), fasc. 3. Napoli: Istituto Universitario Orientale, 1990.

Cedzich, Angelika. "Corpse Deliverance, Substitute Bodies, Name Change, and Feigned Death: Aspects of Metamorphosis and Immortality in Early Medieval China." *Journal of Chinese Religions* 29 (2001): 1–68.

Chapman, Ian D. "Carnival Canons: Calendars, Geneaology, and the Search for Ritual Cohesion in Medieval China." Ph.D. diss., Princeton University, 2007.

Chard, Robert L. "Rituals and Scriptures of the Stove Cult." In *Ritual and Scripture in Chinese Popular Religion*, ed. David Johnson, 3–54. Berkeley: Institute of East Asian Studies, University of California, 1995.

———. "The Stove God and the Overseer of Fate." In *Minjian xinyang yu Zhongguo wenhua guoji yantao lunwen ji* 民間信仰與中國文化國際研討會論文集, 655–682. Taibei: Hanxue yanjiu zhongxin bian, 1994.

Chatman, Seymour. *Story and Discourse: Narrative Structure in Fiction and Film.* Ithaca: Cornell University Press, 1978.

Chavannes, Édouard. *Cinq cents contes et apologues extraits du Tripiṭaka chinois.* 4 vols. 1910–1935. Repr., Paris: Librairie d'Amérique et d'Orient Adrien-Maisonneuve, 1962.

Chen Guofu 陳國符. *Daozang yuanliu kao* 道藏原流考. Rev. ed. Beijing: Zhonghua shuju.

Chen Hong 陳洪. "Fojiao baguanzhai yu zhonggu xiaoshuo" 佛教八關齋與中古小說. *Jianghai xuekan* 江海學刊 1995, issue 5, pp. 159–163.

Chen Huaiyu. "A Buddhist Classification of Animals and Plants in Early Tang Times." *Journal of Asian History* 43 (2009): 31–51.

―――. *The Revival of Buddhist Monasticism in Medieval China*. New York: Peter Lang, 2007.

Chen Jinhua. "The Indian Buddhist Missionary Dharmakṣema (385–433): A New Dating of His Arrival in Guzang and of His Translations." *T'oung Pao* 90 (2004): 215–263.

―――. *Monks and Monarchs, Kinship and Kingship: Tanqian in Sui Buddhism and Politics*. Italian School of East Asian Studies Essays 3. Kyoto: Scuola Italiana di Studi sull'Asia Orientale, 2002.

―――. *Philosopher, Practitioner, Politician: The Many Lives of Fazang (643–712)*. Leiden: Brill, 2007.

Ch'en, Kenneth K. S. "Anti-Buddhist Propaganda during the Nan-ch'ao." *Harvard Journal of Asiatic Studies* 15 (1952): 166–192.

―――. *Buddhism in China: A Historical Survey*. Princeton: Princeton University Press, 1964.

―――. *The Chinese Transformation of Buddhism*. Princeton: Princeton University Press, 1973.

―――. "Inscribed Stelae during the Wei, Chin, and Nan-ch'ao." In *Studia Asiatica: Essays in Asian Studies in Felicitation of the Seventy-Fifth Anniversary of Professor Ch'en Shou-yi*, 75–84. San Francisco: Chinese Materials Center, 1975.

Chittick, Andrew. "The Development of Local Writing in Early Medieval China." *Early Medieval China* 9 (2003): 35–70.

―――. *Patronage and Community in Medieval China: The Xiangyang Garrison, 400–600 CE*. Albany: State University of New York Press, 2009.

Cohen, Alvin P. *Tales of Vengeful Souls: A Sixth Century Collection of Chinese Avenging Ghost Stories*. Taipei: Institut Ricci, 1982.

Collins, Steven. *Nirvana and Other Buddhist Felicities: Utopias of the Pali Imaginaire*. Cambridge: Cambridge University Press, 1998.

―――. *Selfless Persons: Imagery and Thought in Theravāda Buddhism*. Cambridge: Cambridge University Press, 1982.

Connery, Christopher Leigh. *The Empire of the Text: Writing and Authority in Early Imperial China*. Lanham: Rowan and Littlefield, 1999.

Copp, Paul F. "Notes on the Term *Dhāraṇī* in Medieval Chinese Buddhist Thought." *Bulletin of the School of Oriental and African Studies* 71 (2008): 493–508.

―――. "Voice, Dust, Shadow, Stone: The Makings of Spells in Medieval Chinese Buddhism." Ph.D. diss., Princeton University, 2005.

Csikszentmihalyi, Mark, ed. *Readings in Han Chinese Thought*. Indianapolis: Hackett, 2006.

Davis, Natalie Zemon. *Fiction in the Archives: Pardon Tales and Their Tellers in Sixteenth-Century France*. Cambridge: Cambridge University Press, 1987.

De Crespigny, Rafe. "Recruitment Revisited: The Commissioned Civil Service of Later Han." *Early Medieval China* 13–14 (2008): 1–47.

Dégh, Linda. *Legend and Belief: Dialectics of a Folklore Genre*. Bloomington: Indiana University Press, 2001.

Dégh, Linda, and Andrew Vázsonyi. "The Memorate and the Proto-Memorate." *Journal of American Folk-Lore* 87 (1974): 225–239.

De Jong, J. W. "L'épisode d'Asita dans le Lalitavistara." In *Asiatica: Festschrift Friedrich Weller*, ed. Johannes Schubert, 312–325. Leipzig: Otto Harrassowitz, 1954.

De la Vaissière, Étienne. *Histoire des marchands sogdiens*. 2nd ed. Paris: Collège de France, Institut des Hautes Études Chinoises, 2004.

Deleanu, Florian. "The Transmission of Xuanzang's Translation of the *Yogācārabhūmi* in East Asia." In *Kongōji Issaikyō no sōgōteki kenkyū to Kongōji shōgyō no kisokuteki kenkyū* 金剛寺一切経の総合的研究と金剛寺聖教の基礎的研究, ed. Ochiai Toshinori 落合 俊典, 589–632 (1–44). Koyama: Kabushiki kaisha, 2008.

Delehaye, Hubert. "Les antécédents magiques des statues chinoises." *Revue d'esthétique* 5 (1983): 45–53.

Demiéville, Paul. "Appendice II: Vimalakīrti en Chine." In *L'Enseignement de Vimalakīrti*, by Etienne Lamotte, 438–455. Publications de l'Institut orientaliste de Louvain 35. Louvain: Institut Orientaliste, 1987.

———. "La Yogācārabhūmi de Sangharakṣa." *Bulletin de l'École française d'Extrême-Orient* 44 (1954): 339–436.

———. "Une descente aux enfers sous les T'ang: La biographie de Houang Chek'iang." *Études d'histoire et de littérature chinoises offertes au professeur Jaroslav Prusek*, 71–84. Paris: Presses Universitaires de France, 1976.

De Rauw, Tom. "Baochang: Sixth-Century Biographer of Buddhist Monks…and Nuns?" *Journal of the American Oriental Society* 125 (2005): 203–218.

Despeux, Catherine. "La culture lettré au service d'un plaidoyer pour le bouddhisme: Le 'Traité des deux doctrines' ('Erjiao lun') de Dao'an." In *Bouddhisme et lettrés dans la Chine médiévale*, ed. Catherine Despeux, 145–227. Paris: Editions Peeters, 2002.

———. "Physiognomie." In *Divination et société dans la Chine médiévale*, ed. Marc Kalinowski, 513–555. Paris: Bibliothèque Nationale de France, 2003.

De Visser, M. W. *The Bodhisattva Ti-tsang (Jizō) in China and Japan*. Berlin: Oesterheld Verlag, 1914.

Dhirasekera, J. D. "Hāritī and Pāñcika: An Early Buddhist Legend of Many Lands." In *Malalasekera Commemoration Volume*, ed. O. H. de A. Wijisekera, 61–70. Colombo: Malalasekera Commemoration Volume Editorial Committee, 1976.

Dien, Albert E. "Caravans and Caravan Leaders in Palmyra." In *Les Sogdiens en Chine*, ed. Étienne de la Vaissière and Éric Trombert, 195–206. Paris: École française d'Extrême-Orient, 2005.

———. "Civil Service Examinations: Evidence from the Northwest." In *Culture and Power in the Reconstitution of the Chinese Realm, 200–600*, ed. Scott Pearce, Audrey Spiro, and Patricia Ebrey, 99–121. Cambridge, Mass.: Harvard University Press, 2001.

———. *Six Dynasties Civilization*. New Haven: Yale University Press, 2007.

Drège, Jean-Pierre. *Les bibliothèques en Chine au temps des manuscrits*. Paris: École Française d'Extrême-Orient, 1991.

Dudbridge, Glen. *Lost Books of Medieval China*. London: British Library, 2000.

Durt, Hubert. "The Meaning of Archaeology in Ancient Buddhism: Notes on the Stūpas of Aśoka and the Worship of the 'Buddhas of the Past' according to Three Stories in the *Samguk Yusa*." In *Bulgyo ne sokwahak [Buddhism and Science]*, 1223–1241. Seoul: Tongguk University, 1987.

Ebersole, Gary L. *Captured by Texts: Puritan to Postmodern Images of Indian Captivity.* Charlottesville: University of Virginia Press, 1995.

Ebrey, Patricia. "Patron-Client Relations in the Later Han." *Journal of the American Oriental Society* 103 (1983): 533–542.

————. "Toward a Better Understanding of the Later Han Upper Class." In *State and Society in Early Medieval China*, ed. Albert E. Dien, 49–72. Stanford: Stanford University Press, 1990.

Eichhorn, Werner. "Description of the Rebellion of Sun En and Earlier Taoist Rebellions." *Mitteilungen des Instituts für Orientforschung* 2.2 (1954): 25–53 and 2.3 (1954): 463–476.

Fang Shiming 方詩銘 and Fang Xiaofen 方小芬, eds. *Zhongguo shiliri he zhongxi liri duizhao biao* 中國史歷日和中西歷日對照表. Shanghai: Shanghai cishu chubanshe, 1987.

Faure, Bernard. "Les cloches de la terre: Un aspect du culte des reliques dans le bouddhisme chinois." In *Bouddhisme et lettrés dans la Chine médiévale*, ed. Catherine Despeux, 25–44. Paris: Editions Peeters, 2002.

————. "Space and Place in Chinese Religious Traditions." *History of Religions* 26 (1987): 337–356.

Field, Stephen L. *Ancient Chinese Divination.* Honolulu: University of Hawai'i Press, 2008.

Forke, Alfred. *Lun-hêng.* 2 vols. Repr. of 1907–1911 ed. New York: Paragon Book Gallery, 1962.

Forte, Antonino. *The Hostage An Shigao and His Offspring: An Iranian Family in China.* Italian School of East Asian Studies Occasional Papers 6. Kyoto: Istituto Italiano di Cultura Scuola di Studi sull'Asia Orientale, 1995.

Forte, Antonino, and Jacques May. "Chōsai." In *Hōbōgirin: Dictionnaire encyclopédique du Bouddhisme d'après les sources chinoises et japonaises*, 5:392–407. Paris: Librairie d'Amérique et d'Orient, 1979.

Funayama Tōru 船山徹. "The Acceptance of Buddhist Precepts by the Chinese in the Fifth Century." *Journal of Asian History* 38 (2004): 97–120.

————. "'Kanyaku' to 'Chūgoku senjutsu' no aida: Kanbun Butten ni tokuyūna keitai o megutte" 漢譯と中國撰述の間: 漢文佛典に特有な形態おめぐって. *Bukkyō shigaku kenkyū* 佛教史學研究 45 (2002): 1–28.

————. "Masquerading as Translation: Examples of Chinese Lectures by Indian Scholar-Monks in the Six Dynasties Period." *Asia Major*, 3rd ser., 19 (2006): 39–55.

————. "Rikuchō jidai ni okeru bōsatsukai no juyō katei: Ryū Sō, Nan Sei ki o chūshin ni" 六朝時代における菩薩戒の受容過程: 劉宋, 南齊期お中心に. *Tōhō gakuhō* 東方學報 67 (1995): 1–135.

Garro, Linda C., and Cheryl Mattingly. "Narrative as Construct and Construction." In *Narrative and the Cultural Construction of Illness and Healing*, ed. Cheryl Mattingly and Linda C. Garro, 1–49. Berkeley: University of California Press, 2000.

Georgieva, Valentina. "Buddhist Nuns in China from the Six Dynasties to the Tang." Proefschrift, Universiteit Leiden, 2000.

Gernet, Jacques. *Buddhism in Chinese Society: An Economic History from the Fifth to the Tenth Centuries.* Trans. Franciscus Verellen. New York: Columbia University Press, 1995.

Gethin, Rupert M. L. *The Buddhist Path to Awakening.* Oxford: Oneworld, 2001.

————. *The Foundations of Buddhism.* Oxford: Oxford University Press, 1998.

————. "The *Mātikās*: Memorization, Mindfulness, and the List." In *In the Mirror of Memory: Reflections on Mindfulness and Remembrance in Indian and Tibetan Buddhism*, ed. Janet Gyatso, 149–172. Albany: State University of New York Press, 1992.

Gjertson, Donald E. "The Early Chinese Buddhist Miracle Tale: A Preliminary Survey." *Journal of the American Oriental Society* 101 (1981): 287–301.

————. *Gods, Ghosts, and Retribution: Nine Buddhist Miracle Tales from Six Dynasties and Early T'ang China*. Amherst: University of Massachusetts Press, 1978.

————. *Miraculous Retribution: A Study and Translation of T'ang Lin's "Ming-pao chi."* Berkeley Buddhist Studies Series. Berkeley: Institute of Buddhist Studies, 1989.

————. "Rebirth as an Animal in Medieval Chinese Buddhism." *Bulletin of the Society for the Study of Chinese Religions* 8 (1980): 56–69.

Goodman, Howard L. *Ts'ao P'i Transcendent: The Political Culture of Dynasty-Founding in China at the End of the Han*. Seattle: Scripta Serica, 1998.

Goossaert, Vincent. "The Beef Taboo and the Sacrificial Structure of Late Imperial Chinese Society." In *Of Tripod and Palate: Food, Politics, and Religion in Traditional China*, ed. Roel Sterckx, 237–248. New York: Palgrave Macmillan, 2005.

Graff, David. *Medieval Chinese Warfare, 300–900*. London: Routledge, 2001.

Grafflin, Dennis. "Reinventing China: Pseudobureacracy in the Early Southern Dynasties." In *State and Society in Early Medieval China*, ed. Albert E. Dien, 139–170. Stanford: Stanford University Press, 1990.

Grand dictionnaire Ricci de la langue chinoise. Paris: Institut Ricci, 2001.

Gu Zhengmei 古正美. *Cong tianwang chuantong dao Fowang chuantong: Zhongguo zhongshi Fojiao zhiguo yishi xingtai yanjiu* 從天王傳統到佛王傳統: 中國中世佛教治國意識形態研究. Taibei: Shangzhou chuban, 2003.

Hallisey, Charles, and Anne Hansen. "Narrative, Sub-ethics, and the Moral Life: Some Evidence from Theravāda Buddhism." *Journal of Religious Ethics* 24 (1996): 305–327.

Hanyu dacidian 漢語大辭典. Ed. Luo Zhufeng 罗竹风. Shanghai: Shanghai cishu chubanshe, 1986.

Hao Chunwen 郝春文. "Dunhuang xieben zhaiwen ji qi yangshi de fenlei yu dingming" 敦煌写本斋文及其样式的分类与定名. *Beijing Shifan xueyuan xuebao (Shehui kexue ban)* 北京师范大學院學報 (社会科學版) 1990, no. 3, pp. 91–98.

————. "Guanyu Dunhuang xieben zhaiwen de jige wenti" 關于敦煌写本斋文的几个問題. *Shoudu shifan daxue xuebao (Shehui kexue ban)* 首都师范大學學報（社会科學版) 1996, no. 2, pp. 64–71.

————. "The Social Life of Buddhist Monks and Nuns during the Late Tang, Five Dynasties, and Early Song." *Asia Major*, 3rd ser., 23, no. 2 (2010): 77–96.

Harper, Donald. "A Chinese Demonography of the Third Century B.C." *Harvard Journal of Asiatic Studies* 45 (1985): 459–498.

————. "Contracts with the Spirit World in Han Common Religion: The Xuning Prayer and Sacrifice Documents of A.D. 79." *Cahiers d'Extrême-Asie* 14 (2004): 227–267.

————. *Early Chinese Medical Literature*. London: Kegan Paul, 1998.

————. "Resurrection in Warring States Popular Religion." *Taoist Resources* 5, no. 2 (1994): 13–29.

————. "Spellbinding." In *Religions of China in Practice*, ed. Donald S. Lopez Jr., 241–250. Princeton: Princeton University Press, 1996.

————. "Warring States Natural Philosophy and Occult Thought." In *From the Origins of Civilization to 221 B.C.*, vol. 1 of *The Cambridge History of Ancient China*, ed. Michael Loewe and Edward L. Shaughnessy, 813–884. Cambridge: Cambridge University Press, 1999.

————. "Warring States, Qin, and Han Manuscripts Related to Natural Philosophy and the Occult." In *New Sources of Early Chinese History: An Introduction to the Reading of Inscriptions and Manuscripts*, ed. Edward L. Shaughnessy, 223–252. Berkeley: Society for the Study of Early China and Institute of East Asian Studies, University of California, 1997.

Harrison, Paul M. "*Buddhānusmṛti* in the *Pratyutpanna-buddha-saṃmukhāvasthita-samādhi-sūtra.*" *Journal of Indian Philosophy* 6 (1978): 35–57.

————. "Commemoration and Identification in *Buddhānusmṛti.*" In *In the Mirror of Memory: Reflections on Mindfulness and Remembrance in Indian and Tibetan Buddhism*, ed. Janet Gyatso, 215–238. Albany: State University of New York Press, 1992.

————. "Mañjuśrī and the Cult of the Celestial Bodhisattvas." *Chung-Hwa Buddhist Journal* 13 (2000): 157–193.

————. "Mediums and Messages: Reflections on the Production of Mahāyāna Sūtras." *Eastern Buddhist* 35 (2003): 116–151.

————, trans. *The Pratyutpanna Samādhi Sūtra Translated by Lokakṣema.* BDK English Tripiṭika 25-II. Berkeley: Numata Center for Buddhist Translation and Research, 1998.

Harrist, Robert E., Jr. *The Landscape of Words: Stone Inscriptions from Early and Medieval China.* Seattle: University of Washington Press, 2008.

Harvey, Peter. 1986. "The Between-Lives State in the Pāli Suttas." In *Perspectives on Indian Religion: Papers in Honour of Karel Werner*, ed. Peter Connolly, 175–189. New Delhi: Sri Satguru Publications.

He Jingsong 何勁松. "Han Wei liang Jin nanbeichao shiqi de Jiaozhou fojiao ji qi tong zhongyuan fojiao de guanxi" 漢魏兩晉南北朝時期的交州佛教及其同中原佛教的關係. *Shijie zongjiao yanjiu* 世界宗教研究 36, no. 2 (1989): 69–79.

Helms, Mary W. *Ulysses' Sail: An Ethnographic Odyssey of Power, Knowledge, and Geographical Distance.* Princeton: Princeton University Press, 1988.

Hendrischke, Barbara. "The Concept of Inherited Evil in the *Taiping jing.*" *East Asian History* 2 (1991): 1–30.

Henry, Eric. "The Motif of Recognition in Early China." *Harvard Journal of Asiatic Studies* 47 (1987): 5–30.

Ho Puay-Peng. "Building on Hope: Monastic Sponsors and Merit in Sixth- to Tenth-Century China." *Asia Major*, 3rd ser., 17 (2004): 35–57.

Hōbōgirin 法寶義林: *Dictionnaire encyclopédique du Bouddhisme d'après les sources chinoises et japonaises.* 8 vols. to date. Paris: Librairie d'Amérique et d'Orient; Tokyo: Maison Franco-Japonaise, 1929–2003.

Holcombe, Charles. *In the Shadow of the Han: Literati Thought and Society at the Beginning of the Southern Dynasties.* Honolulu: University of Hawai'i Press, 1994.

Honko, Lauri. "Memorates and the Study of Folk Beliefs." *Journal of the Folklore Institute* 1 (1964): 5–19.

Hou Ching-lang. *Monnaies d'offrande et la notion de tresorerie dans la religion chinoise.* Paris: Collège de France, Institut des Hautes Études Chinoises, 1975.

Hou Xudong 侯旭东. "The Buddhist Pantheon." In *Early Chinese Religion, Part Two:*

The Period of Division (220–589 AD), ed. John Lagerwey and Lü Pengzhi, 1095–1168. Leiden: Brill, 2010.

———. *Wu liu shiji beifang minzhong Fojiao xinyang* 五六世紀北方民众佛教信仰. Beijing: Zhongguo shehui kexue chubanshe, 1998.

Hsieh, Shu-wei. "Writing from Heaven: Celestial Writing in Six Dynasties Daoism." Ph.D. diss., Indiana University, 2005.

Huang Guoan 黃國安. "Zhongguo fojiao zai Jiaozhi de chuanbo yu yingxiang" 中國佛教在交趾的傳播與影響. *Dongnanya zongheng* 東南亞縱橫 68 (1995): 18–21.

Huang, H. T. *Fermentations and Food Science*. Part 5 of *Biology and Biological Technology*, vol. 5 of *Science and Civilisation in China*. Cambridge: Cambridge University Press, 2000.

Hucker, Charles O. *A Dictionary of Official Titles in Imperial China*. Stanford: Stanford University Press, 1985.

Hureau, Sylvie. "Bouddhisme chinois." *Annuaire de l'Ecole Pratique des Hautes Etudes, Sciences religieuses* 115 (2006–2007): 47–52.

———. "Buddhist Rituals." In *Early Chinese Religion, Part Two: The Period of Division (220–589 AD)*, ed. John Lagerwey and Lü Pengzhi, 1207–1244. Leiden: Brill, 2010.

———. "La cérémonie de réception des règlements de *bodhisattva* selon le *Fanwang jing*." Unpublished manuscript.

———. "Preaching and Translating on *Poṣadha* Days: Kumārajīva's Role in Adapting an Indian Ceremony to China." *Journal of the International College for Postgraduate Buddhist Studies* 10 (2006): 86–118.

———. "Réseaux de bouddhistes des Six Dynasties: Défense et propagation du bouddhisme." In *Bouddhisme et lettrés dans la Chine médiévale*, ed. Catherine Despeux, 45–66. Paris: Editions Peeters, 2002.

———. "Translations, Apocrypha, and the Emergence of the Buddhist Canon." In *Early Chinese Religion, Part Two: The Period of Division (220–589 AD)*, ed. John Lagerwey and Lü Pengzhi, 741–774. Leiden: Brill, 2010.

Hurvitz, Leon. "'Render unto Caesar' in Early Chinese Buddhism." *Sino-Indian Studies* 5 (1957): 96–114.

———. *Scripture of the Lotus Blossom of the Fine Dharma*. New York: Columbia University Press, 1976.

Ikehira Noriko 池平紀子. "Butsu Dō ni okeru gokai no judoku to nijugo shin no shugo ni tsuite" 佛道における五戒の受持と二十五神の守護について. *Tōhō gaku* 東方學 106 (2008): 55–73.

Inagaki Hisao and Harold Stewart, trans. *The Sutra on the Contemplation of Amitāyus*. BDK English Tripiṭaka 12-III. Berkeley: Numata Center for Buddhist Translation and Research, 1995.

Jan Yün-hua. 1977. "The Power of Recitation: An Unstudied Aspect of Chinese Buddhism." *Studi storico religiosi* 1:289–299.

Jansen, Thomas. *Höfische Öffentlichkeit im frühmittelalterlichen China: Debatten im Salon des Prinzen Xiao Ziliang*. Rombach Historiae, Band 11. Freiburg: Rombach Verlag, 2000.

Ji Zhichang 紀志昌. "Dong Jin jushi Xie Fu kao" 東晉居士謝敷考. *Hanxue yanjiu* 漢學研究 20 (2002): 55–83.

Joo, Ryan Bongseok. "The Ritual of Arhat Invitation during the Song Dynasty." *Journal of the International Association of Buddhist Studies* 30 (2009): 81–116.

Kanno Ryūshō 菅野 龍清. "Yōshi to Bukkyō" 姚氏と仏教. Ōsaki gakuhō 大崎學報 155 (1999): 209–235.

Kao, Karl S.Y., ed. *Classical Chinese Tales of the Supernatural and the Fantastic: Selections from the Third to the Tenth Century*. Bloomington: Indiana University Press, 1985.

Keenan, John P. *How Master Mou Removes Our Doubts: A Reader-Response Study and Translation of the "Mou-tzu li-huo lun."* Albany: State University of New York Press, 1994.

Khoroche, Peter. *Once the Buddha Was a Monkey: Ārya Śūra's Jātakamālā*. Chicago: University of Chicago Press, 1989.

Kieschnick, John. "Buddhist Monasticism." In *Early Chinese Religion, Part Two: The Period of Division (220–589 AD)*, ed. John Lagerwey and Lü Pengzhi, 545–574. Leiden: Brill, 2010.

———. "Buddhist Vegetarianism in China." In *Of Tripod and Palate: Food, Politics, and Religion in Traditional China*, ed. Roel Sterckx, 186–212. New York: Palgrave Macmillan, 2005.

———. *The Impact of Buddhism on Chinese Material Culture*. Princeton: Princeton University Press, 2003.

———. "The Symbolism of the Monk's Robe in China." *Asia Major*, 3rd ser., 12 (1999): 9–32.

Kleeman, Terry. *Great Perfection: Religion and Ethnicity in a Chinese Millennial Kingdom*. Honolulu: University of Hawai'i Press, 1998.

———. "Land Contracts and Related Documents." In *Makio Ryōkai Hakase shōju kinen ronshu, Chūgoku no shūkyō: Shisō to kagaku* 牧尾良海博士頌壽記念論集，中國の宗教: 思想と科學, 1–34. Tokyo: Kokusho Kankōkai, 1984.

Kloetzli, Randy. *Buddhist Cosmology: From Single World System to Pure Land*. Delhi: Motilal Banarsidass, 1983.

Knechtges, David R. [Kang Dawei 康達維]. "Zhongguo zhonggu wenren de shanyue youguan: Yi Xie Lingyun 'Shanju fu' wei zhu de taolun" 中國中古文人的山嶽遊觀: 以謝靈運 '山居賦' 為主的討論. In *Youguan: Zuowei shenti zhiyi de zhonggu wenxue yu zongjiao* 遊觀: 作為身體技藝的中古文學與宗教 / *Inner Landscape Visualized: Techniques of the Body in Medieval Chinese Literature and Religion*, ed. Liu Yuanru 劉苑如, 1–63. Taibei: Zhongyanyuan wenzhesuo, 2009.

Knechtges, David R., and Taiping Chang, eds. *Ancient and Early Medieval Chinese Literature: A Reference Guide, Part One*. Leiden: Brill, 2010.

Kohn, Livia. "Counting Good Deeds and Days of Life: The Quantification of Fate in Medieval China." *Asiatische Studien / Etudes Asiatiques* 52 (1998): 833–870.

———. *Laughing at the Tao: Debates among Buddhists and Taoists in Medieval China*. Princeton: Princeton University Press, 1995.

———. "Mirror of Auras: Chen Tuan on Physiognomy." *Asian Folklore Studies* 47 (1988): 215–256.

Kominami Ichirō 小南一郎. "Rikuchō Zui Tō shōsetsushi no tenkai to Bukkyō shinkō" 六朝隋唐小説史の展開と仏教信仰. In *Chūgoku chūsei no shūkyō to bunka* 中國中世の宗教と文化, ed. Fukunaga Mitsuji 福永光司, 415–500. Kyoto: Kyoto Daigaku Jinbun kagaku kenkyūsho, 1982.

Kuo Li-ying. *Confession et contrition dans le bouddhisme chinois du Ve au Xe siècle*. Paris: Publications de l'Ecole Française d'Extrême-Orient, 1994.

———. "Divination, jeux de hazard et purification dans le bouddhisme chinois: Autour d'un *sūtra* apocryphe chinois, le *Zhancha jing*." In *Bouddhisme et cultures locales: Quelques cas de réciproques adaptations,* ed. Fukui Fumimasa and Gérard Fussman, 145–167. Paris: École française d'Extrême-Orient, 1994.

———. "La récitation des noms de Buddha en Chine et au Japon." *T'oung Pao* 81 (1995): 230–268.

———. "Sur les apocryphes bouddhiques chinois." *Bulletin de l'École française d'Extrême-Orient, Mélanges du centenaire* 87 (2000): 677–705.

Kuwayama, Shoshin. "Pilgrimage Route Changes and the Decline of Gāndhara." In *Gāndhāran Buddhism: Archaeology, Art, and Texts,* ed. Pia Brancaccio and Kurt Behrendt, 107–134. Vancouver: University of British Columbia Press, 2006.

Lai, Whalen. "The *Chan-ch'a ching*: Religion and Magic in Medieval China." In *Chinese Buddhist Apocrypha,* ed. Robert E. Buswell Jr., 175–206. Honolulu: University of Hawai'i Press, 1990.

———. "Emperor Wu of Liang on the Immortal Soul, *Shen Pu Mieh.*" *Journal of the American Oriental Society* 101 (1981): 167–175.

Lamotte, Etienne. *History of Indian Buddhism.* Trans. Sara Webb-Boin. Publications de l'Institut orientaliste de Louvain 36. Louvain: Institut Orientaliste, 1988.

———. *L'Enseignement de Vimalakīrti.* Publications de l'Institut orientaliste de Louvain 35. Louvain: Institut Orientaliste, 1987.

Lavoix, Valérie. "La contribution des laïcs au végétarisme: Croisades et polémiques en Chine du Sud autour de l'an 500." In *Bouddhisme et lettrés dans la Chine médiévale,* ed. Catherine Despeux, 103–144. Paris: Editions Peeters, 2002.

Le Blanc, Charles. *Huai-nan tzu: Philosophical Synthesis in Early Han Thought.* Hong Kong: Hong Kong University Press, 1985.

Lesbre, Emmanuelle. 2000. "La conversion de Hariti au Buddha: Origine du thème iconographique et interprétations picturales chinoises." *Arts asiatiques* 55:98–119.

Lessa, William. *Chinese Body Divination: Its Forms, Affinity and Function.* Los Angeles: United World Press, 1968.

Lévi, Sylvain, and Edouard Chavannes. "Les seize arhat protecteurs de la loi." *Journal asiatique* 8 (1916): 205–275.

Lewis, Mark Edward. *China between Empires: The Northern and Southern Dynasties.* Cambridge, Mass.: Harvard University Press, 2009.

———. *The Early Chinese Empires: Qin and Han.* Cambridge, Mass.: Harvard University Press, 2007.

———. "The *Feng* and *Shan* Sacrifices of Emperor Wu of the Han." In *State and Court Ritual in China,* ed. Joseph P. McDermott, 50–80. Cambridge: Cambridge University Press, 1999.

———. *The Flood Myths of Early China.* Albany: State University of New York Press, 2006.

Li Gang. "State Religious Policy." In *Early Chinese Religion, Part Two: The Period of Division (220–589 AD),* ed. John Lagerwey and Lü Pengzhi, 193–274. Leiden: Brill, 2010.

Li Jianguo 李劍國. *Tang qian zhiguai xiaoshuo shi* 唐前志怪小說史. Tianjin: Nanhai daxue chubanshe, 1984.

———. *Xinji Soushenji, Xinji Soushen houji* 新輯搜神記, 新輯搜神後記. 2 vols. Beijing: Zhonghua shuju, 2007.

Li Jianmin. "They Shall Expel Demons: Etiology, the Medical Canon and the Transformation of Medical Techniques before the Tang." In *Early Chinese Reli-*

gion, Part One: Shang through Han (1250 BC–220 AD), ed. John Lagerwey and Marc Kalinowski, 1103–1150. Leiden: Brill, 2009.

Li Jung-shi, trans. *Biographies of Buddhist Nuns: Pao-chang's "Pi-chiu-ni chuan."* Osaka: Tohokai, n.d.

Li Yuqun. "Classification, Layout, and Iconography of Buddhist Cave Temples and Monasteries." In *Early Chinese Religion, Part Two: The Period of Division (220–589 AD)*, ed. John Lagerwey and Lü Pengzhi, 575–738. Leiden: Brill, 2010.

Liebenthal, Walter. "The Immortality of the Soul in Chinese Thought." *Monumenta Nipponica* 8 (1952): 327–397.

Lin, Fu-Shih. "Chinese Shamans and Shamanism in the Chiang-nan Area during the Six Dynasties Period (3rd–6th century A.D.)." Ph.D. diss., Princeton University, 1994.

Lin Renyu 林仁昱. *Dunhuang fojiao gequ zhi yanjiu* 敦煌佛教歌曲之研究. Gaoxiong: Foguangshan wenjiao jijinhui, 2004.

Lincoln, Bruce. *Theorizing Myth: Narrative, Ideology, and Scholarship*. Chicago: University of Chicago Press, 1999.

Link, Arthur. "The Biography of Shih Tao-an." *T'oung Pao* 46 (1958): 1–48.

———. "*Cheng-wu lun*: The Rectification of Unjust Criticism." *Oriens Extremus* 8 (1961): 136–165.

Lippiello, Tiziana. *Auspicious Omens and Miracles in Ancient China: Han, Three Kingdoms and Six Dynasties*. Monumenta Serica Monograph Series 39. Sankt Augustin: Institut Monumenta Serica, 2001.

Liu Difan 劉滌凡. *Tang qian guobao xitong de jiangou yu ronghe* 唐前果報系統的建構與融合. Taibei: Xuesheng shuju, 1999.

Liu Shufen [Liu Shu-fen] 劉淑芬. "Art, Ritual, and Society: Buddhist Practice in Rural China during the Northern Dynasties." *Asia Major*, 3rd ser., 8 (1995): 19–49.

———. "Ethnicity and the Suppression of Buddhism in Fifth-Century North China: The Background and Significance of the Gaiwu Rebellion." *Asia Major*, 3rd ser., 15 (2002): 1–21.

———. "Jiankang and the Commercial Empire of the Southern Dynasties: Change and Continuity in Medieval Chinese Economic History." In *Culture and Power in the Reconstitution of the Chinese Realm, 200–600*, ed. Scott Pearce, Audrey Spiro, and Patricia Ebrey, 35–52. Cambridge, Mass.: Harvard University Press, 2001.

———. "The Return of the State: On the Significance of Buddhist Epigraphy and Its Geographic Distribution." In *Early Chinese Religion, Part Two: The Period of Division (220–589 AD)*, ed. John Lagerwey and Lü Pengzhi, 319–342. Leiden: Brill, 2010.

Liu Xinru. *Ancient India and Ancient China: Trade and Religious Exchanges, AD 1–600*. Delhi: Oxford University Press, 1994.

Liu Yuanru [Liu Yuan-ju] 劉苑如. *Chaoxiang shenghuo shijie de wenxue quanshi: Liuchao zongjiao xushu de shenti shijian yu kongjian shuxie* 朝向生活世界的文學詮釋: 六朝宗教敘述的身體實踐與空間書寫. Taibei: Xinwenfeng, 2010.

———. "Cong Xianbei xuji kan nanchao zhiguai zhong yizu xiangxiang yu shidai ganjue" 從鮮卑敘記看南朝志怪中異族想像與時代感覺. *Zhongguo wenzhe yanjiu jikan* 中國文哲研究集刊 20 (2002): 223–262.

———. *Shenti, xingbie, jieji: Liuchao zhiguai de chang yi lunshu yu xiaoshuo meixue* 身體，性別，階級: 六朝志怪的常異論述與小說美學. Taibei: Zhong yanyuan wenzhesuo, 2002.

————. "Xingxian yu mingbao: Liuchao zhiguai zhong guiguai xushu de fengyu—yi ge 'daoyi wei chang' moshi de kaocha" 形見與冥報: 六朝志怪敘述的諷喻——一個 '導異為常' 模式的考察. *Bulletin of the Institute of Chinese Literature and Philosophy (Zhongyang yanjiuyuan zhongguo wenzhe yanjiu jikan* 中央研究院中國文哲研究集刊) 29 (2006): 1–45.

Lo, Yuet Keung. "Recovering a Buddhist Voice on Daughters-in-Law: The *Yuyenü Jing.*" *History of Religions* 44 (2005): 318–350.

Loewe, Michael. *Ways to Paradise: The Chinese Quest for Immortality.* London: George Allen and Unwin, 1979.

Lu Xun 魯迅. *Gu xiaoshuo gouchen* 古小說鉤沈. Beijing: Renmin wenxue chuban-she, 1954.

Ma Shichang. "Buddhist Cave-Temples and the Cao Family at Mogao Ku, Dun-huang." *World Archaeology* 27 (1995): 303–317.

MacWilliams, Mark W. "Kannon *Engi*: The *Reijō* and the Concept of *Kechien* as Strategies of Indigenization in Buddhist Sacred Narrative." *Transactions of the Asiatic Society of Japan*, 4th ser., 5 (1990): 53–70.

Maeda Shigeki. "Between Karmic Retribution and Entwining Infusion: Is the Karma of the Parent Visited upon the Child?" In *Daoism in History: Essays in Honour of Liu Ts'un-yan*, ed. Benjamin Penny, 101–120. London: Routledge, 2006.

Magnin, Paul. "Donateurs et joueurs en l'honneur du Buddha." In *De Dunhuang au Japon: Etudes chinoises et bouddhiques offertes à Michel Soymié*, ed. Jean-Pierre Drège, 103–140. Genève: Droz, 1996.

Mai, Cuong T. "Visualization Apocrypha and the Making of Buddhist Deity Cults in Early Medieval China: With Special Reference to the Cults of Amitābha, Maitreya, and Samantabhadra." Ph.D. diss., Indiana University, 2009.

Mair, Victor H. *Painting and Performance: Chinese Picture Recitation and Its Indian Genesis.* Honolulu: University of Hawai'i Press, 1988.

————. *Tun-huang Popular Narratives.* Cambridge: Cambridge University Press, 1983.

Makita Tairyō 牧田諦亮. *Gikyō kenkyū* 疑經研究. Kyoto: Kyoto University, Jinbun kagaku kenkyūsho, 1976.

————. *Rikuchō kōitsu Kanzeon ōkenki no kenkyū* 六朝古逸觀世音應驗記の研究. Kyoto: Hyōrakuji shoten, 1970.

Martin, François. "Buddhism and Literature." In *Early Chinese Religion, Part Two: The Period of Division (220–589 AD)*, ed. John Lagerwey and Lü Pengzhi, 891–951. Leiden: Brill, 2010.

————. "Les Bouddhistes laïcs, leurs idéaux et leurs pratiques." In *Religion et société en Chine ancienne et médiévale*, ed. John Lagerwey, 531–563. Paris: Éditions du CERF / Institut Ricci, 2009.

Maspero, Henri. "Le songe et l'ambassade de l'empereur Ming." *Bulletin de l'École française d'Extrême-Orient* 10 (1910): 95–130.

Mather, Richard B. *The Age of Eternal Brilliance: Three Lyrical Poets of the Yung-ming Era (483–493).* 2 vols. Leiden: Brill, 2003.

————. "Individualist Expressions of the Outsiders during the Six Dynasties." In *Individualism and Holism: Studies in Confucian and Taoist Values*, ed. Donald Munro, 199–215. Ann Arbor: Center for Chinese Studies, University of Michi-gan, 1985.

————. "Intermarriage as a Gauge of Family Status in the Southern Dynasties." In

State and Society in Early Medieval China, ed. Albert E. Dien, 211–228. Stanford: Stanford University Press, 1990.

———. "The Life of the Buddha and the Buddhist Life: Wang Jung's (468–93) *Songs of Religious Joy (Fa-le tz'u)*." *Journal of the American Oriental Society* 107 (1987): 31–38.

———. *Shih-shuo Hsin-yü: A New Account of Tales of the World*. Minneapolis: University of Minnesota Press, 1976.

———. "Vimalakīrti and Gentry Buddhism." *History of Religions* 8 (1968): 60–73.

———. "Wang Jung's *Hymns on the Devotee's Entrance into the Religious Life*." *Journal of the American Oriental Society* 106 (1986): 79–98.

Mattingly, Cheryl. "Emergent Narratives." In *Narrative and the Cultural Construction of Illness and Healing*, ed. Cheryl Mattingly and Linda C. Garro, 181–211. Berkeley: University of California Press, 2000.

———. *Healing Dramas and Clinical Plots: The Narrative Structure of Experience*. Cambridge: Cambridge University Press, 1998.

McCallum, Donald F. "The Saidaiji Lineage of the Seiryōji Shaka Tradition." *Archives of Asian Art* 49 (1996): 51–67.

McNair, Amy. *Donors of Longmen: Faith, Politics, and Patronage in Medieval Chinese Buddhist Sculpture*. Honolulu: University of Hawai'i Press, 2007.

McRae, John R. "Daoxuan's Vision of Jetavana: The Ordination Platform Movement in Medieval Chinese Buddhism." In *Going Forth: Visions of Buddhist Vinaya*, ed. William M. Bodiford, 68–100. Honolulu: University of Hawai'i Press, 2005.

———. *Seeing Through Zen: Encounter, Transformation, and Genealogy in Chinese Chan Buddhism*. Berkeley: University of California Press, 2003.

Meeks, Lori. *Hokkeji and the Reemergence of Female Monastic Orders in Premodern Japan*. Kuroda Institute Studies in East Asian Buddhism 23. Honolulu: University of Hawai'i Press, 2010.

Miller, Tracy. *The Divine Nature of Power: Chinese Ritual Architecture at the Sacred Site of Jinci*. Cambridge, Mass.: Harvard University Press, 2007.

Miyakawa Hisayuki. "Local Cults around Mount Lu at the Time of Sun En's Rebellion." In *Facets of Taoism: Essays in Chinese Religion*, ed. Holmes Welch and Anna Seidel, 83–102. New Haven: Yale University Press, 1979.

Mochizuki Shinkō 月望 信亨. *Bukkyō daijiten* 佛教大辭典. 10 vols. continuously paginated. Tokyo: Sekai seiten kankō kyōkai, 1933–1936.

Mollier, Christine. *Buddhism and Taoism Face to Face: Scripture, Ritual, and Iconographic Exchange in Medieval China*. Honolulu: University of Hawai'i Press, 2008.

———. "Talismans." In *Divination et société dans la Chine médiévale*, ed. Marc Kalinowski, 403–429. Paris: Bibliothèque nationale de France, 2003.

Murase, Miyeko. "Kuan-Yin as Savior of Men: Illustration of the Twenty-fifth Chapter of the Lotus Sūtra in Chinese Painting." *Artibus Asiae* 33 (1971): 39–74.

Murray, Julia K. "Representations of Hariti, the Mother of Demons, and the Theme of 'Raising the Alms Bowl' in Chinese Painting." *Artibus Asiae* 43 (1981–82): 253–268.

Nattier, Jan. "Avalokiteśvara in Early Chinese Buddhist Translations: A Preliminary Survey." In *Bodhisattva Avalokiteśvara (Guanyin) and Modern Society: Proceedings of the Fifth Chung-Hwa International Conference on Buddhism*, ed. William Magee and Yi-hsun Huang, 181–212. Taipei: Dharma Drum, 2007.

————. *A Few Good Men: The Bodhisattva Path according to "The Inquiry of Ugra (Ugraparipṛcchā)."* Honolulu: University of Hawai'i Press, 2003.

————. *A Guide to the Earliest Chinese Buddhist Translations: Texts from the Eastern Han and Three Kingdoms Periods.* Bibliotheca Philologica et Philosophica Buddhica X. Tokyo: International Research Institute for Advanced Buddhology, Soka University, 2008.

————. *Once Upon a Future Time: Studies in a Buddhist Prophecy of Decline.* Berkeley: Asian Humanities Press, 1991.

————. "Re-evaluating Zhu Fonian's *Shizhu duanjie jing* (T309): Translation or Forgery?" *Annual Report of the International Research Institute for Advanced Buddhology at Soka University* 13 (2010): 231–258.

Nickerson, Peter S. "The Great Petition for Sepulchral Plaints." In *Early Daoist Scriptures*, by Stephen R. Bokenkamp, 230–274. Berkeley: University of California Press, 1997.

————. "Taoism, Death, and Bureaucracy in Early Medieval China." Ph.D. diss., University of California, Berkeley, 1996.

Ning, Qiang. *Art, Religion and Politics in Medieval China: The Dunhuang Cave of the Zhai Family.* Honolulu: University of Hawai'i Press, 2004.

Nussbaum, Martha. *Love's Knowledge: Essays on Philosophy and Literature.* New York: Oxford University Press, 1990.

Nylan, Michael. *The Five "Confucian" Classics.* New Haven: Yale University Press, 2001.

————. "Wandering in the Ruins: The *Shuijing zhu* Reconsidered." In *Interpretation and Literature in Early Medieval China*, ed. Alan K. L. Chan and Yuet-Keung Lo, 63–102. Albany: State University of New York Press, 2010.

Obeyesekere, Gananath. *Imagining Karma: Ethical Transformation in Amerindian, Buddhist, and Greek Rebirth.* Berkeley: University of California Press, 2002.

Ochs, Elinor, and Lisa Capps. *Living Narrative: Creating Lives in Everyday Storytelling.* Cambridge, Mass.: Harvard University Press, 2001.

Ōfuchi Ninji 大淵忍爾. *Shoki no dōkyō* 初期の道教. Tokyo: Sōbunsha, 1991.

Ortner, Sherry B. "Patterns of History: Cultural Schemas in the Foundings of Sherpa Religious Institutions." In *Culture Through Time: Anthropological Approaches*, ed. Emiko Ohnuki-Tierney, 57–93. Stanford: Stanford University Press, 1990.

Orzech, Charles D. *Politics and Transcendent Wisdom: The Scripture for Humane Kings in the Creation of Chinese Buddhism.* University Park: Pennsylvania State University Press, 1998.

Owen, Stephen. "The Manuscript Legacy of the Tang: The Case of Literature." *Harvard Journal of Asiatic Studies* 67 (2007): 295–326.

Pagel, Ulrich. *The Bodhisattvapiṭaka.* Buddhica Britannica Series Continua V. Tring: Institute of Buddhist Studies, 1995.

Palumbo, Antonello. "Dharmarakṣa and Kaṇṭhaka: White Horse Monasteries in Early Medieval China." In *Buddhist Asia 1: Papers from the First Conference of Buddhist Studies Held in Naples in May 2001*, ed. Giovanni Verardi and Silvio Vita, 167–216. Kyoto: Italian School of East Asian Studies, 2003.

Pan Guiming 潘桂明. *Zhongguo jushi fojiao shi* 中國居士佛教史. Beijing: Zhongguo shehui kexue chubanshe, 2000.

Pearce, Scott, Audrey Spiro, and Patricia Ebrey. Introduction to *Culture and Power in the Reconstitution of the Chinese Realm, 200–600*, ed. Scott Pearce, Audrey

Spiro, and Patricia Ebrey, 1–32. Cambridge, Mass.: Harvard University Press, 2001.

Pelliot, Paul. "Meou-tseu ou les doutes levés." *T'oung Pao* 19 (1920): 255–433.

Peri, Nöel. "Hârîtî, la Mère-de-démons." *Bulletin de l'École française d'Extrême-Orient* 17 (1917): 1–102.

Pregadio, Fabrizio. "The Notion of 'Form' and the Ways of Liberation in Daoism." *Cahiers d'Extrême-Asie* 14 (2004): 95–130.

———, ed. *The Encyclopedia of Taoism.* 2 vols. London: Routledge, 2007.

Pu Chengzhong. "Kindness toward Animals in Early Chinese Buddhist History." Ph.D. diss., School of Oriental and African Studies, University of London, 2005.

———. "Notes on the *Chengju guangming jing, Sūtra* of Achieving the Bright Light Concentration." *Buddhist Studies Review* 25 (2008): 27–53.

Pu Muzhou [Poo Mu-chou] 浦慕州, ed. *Guimei shenmo: Zhongguo tongsu wenhua zexie* 鬼魅神魔: 中國通俗文化側寫. Taibei: Maitian chubanshe, 2005.

Pulleyblank, Edwin G. *Lexicon of Reconstructed Pronunciation in Early Middle Chinese, Late Middle Chinese, and Early Mandarin.* Vancouver: University of British Columbia Press, 1991.

———. "The Origins and Nature of Chattel Slavery in China." *Journal of Economic and Social History of the Orient* 1 (1958): 185–220.

Rao Zongyi 饒宗頤. *Laozi Xiang'er zhu jiaozheng* 老子想爾注校證. Shanghai: Shanghai guji chubanshe, 1991.

———. "Tan fojiao de fayuan wen" 談佛教的發願文. *Dunhuang Tulufan yanjiu* 敦煌吐魯番研究 4 (1999): 477–487.

Raz, Gil. "Daoist Sacred Geography." In *Early Chinese Religion, Part Two: The Period of Division (220–589 AD),* ed. John Lagerwey and Lü Pengzhi, 1399–1442. Leiden: Brill, 2010.

Ren Jiyu 任繼愈, ed. *Zhongguo daojiao shi* 中國道教史. Shanghai: Shanghai renmin chubanshe, 1990.

Rhie, Marylin Martin. *The Eastern Chin and Sixteen Kingdoms Period in China and Tumshuk, Kucha and Karashahr in Central Asia—Text.* Vol. 2 of *Early Buddhist Art of China and Central Asia.* Leiden: Brill, 2002.

———. *The Eastern Chin and Sixteen Kingdoms Period in China and Tumshuk, Kucha and Karashahr in Central Asia—Illustrations.* Vol. 2 of *Early Buddhist Art of China and Central Asia.* Leiden: Brill, 2002.

———. *Later Han, Three Kingdoms and Western Chin in China and Bactria to Shan-shan in Central Asia.* Vol. 1 of *Early Buddhist Art of China and Central Asia.* Leiden: Brill, 1999.

Richter, Antje. "Letters and Letter Writing in Early Medieval China." *Early Medieval China* 12 (2006): 1–29.

———. "Notions of Epistolarity in Liu Xie's *Wenxin diaolong.*" *Journal of the American Oriental Society* 127 (2007): 143–161.

Robert, Jean-Noël. *Le sûtra du Lotus.* Paris: Fayard, 1997.

Robinson, Richard H., Willard L. Johnson, and Thanissaro Bhikkhu [Geoffrey DeGraff]. *Buddhist Religions: A Historical Introduction.* 5th ed. Belmont, Calif.: Thomson Wadsworth, 2005.

Robson, James. "Buddhist Sacred Geography." In *Early Chinese Religion, Part Two: The Period of Division (220–589 AD),* ed. John Lagerwey and Lü Pengzhi, 1353–1398. Leiden: Brill, 2010.

———. "Monastic Spaces and Sacred Traces: Facets of Chinese Buddhist Monastic

Records." In *Buddhist Monasticism in East Asia: Places of Practice*, ed. James A. Benn, Lori Meeks, and James Robson, 43–64. New York: Routledge, 2010.

———. "'Neither Too Far, Nor Too Near': The Historical and Cultural Contexts of Buddhist Monasteries in Medieval China and Japan." Introduction to *Buddhist Monasticism in East Asia: Places of Practice*, ed. James A. Benn, Lori Meeks, and James Robson, 1–17. New York: Routledge, 2010.

———. *Power of Place: The Religious Landscape of the Southern Sacred Peak (Nanyue 南嶽) in Medieval China*. Harvard East Asian Monographs 316. Cambridge, Mass.: Harvard University Press, 2009.

———. "Signs of Power: Talismanic Writing in Chinese Buddhism." *History of Religions* 48 (2008): 130–169.

Rogers, Michael C. *The Chronicle of Fu Chien: A Case of Exemplar History*. Berkeley: University of California Press, 1968.

Rong Xinjiang 榮新江. "*Sabao* or *Sabo*: Sogdian Caravan Leaders in the Wall-Paintings in Buddhist Caves." In *Les Sogdiens en Chine*, ed. Étienne de la Vaissière and Éric Trombert, 207–230. Paris: École française d'Extrême-Orient, 2005.

Rotman, Andy. *Divine Stories: Divyāvadāna, Part I*. Boston: Wisdom, 2008.

———. "Monks, Merchants, and a Moral Economy: Visual Culture and the Practice of Faith in the *Divyāvadāna*." Ph.D. diss., University of Chicago, 2003.

Ruppert, Brian O. "Buddhist Rainmaking in Early Japan: The Dragon King and the Ritual Careers of Esoteric Monks." *History of Religions* 42 (2002): 143–174.

Salguero, C. Pierce. "Buddhist Medicine in Medieval China: Disease, Healing, and the Body in Crosscultural Translation (Second to Eighth Centuries C.E.)." Ph.D. diss., Johns Hopkins University, 2010.

Salomon, Richard. *Ancient Buddhist Scrolls from Gandhāra: The British Library Kharoṣṭhī Fragments*. Seattle: University of Washington Press, 1999.

Sano Seiko 佐野誠子. "Ō En *Meishoki* to Riku Kō *Kei Kanzeon ōkenki*" 王琰 '冥祥記' と陸杲 '繫觀世音應驗記.' *Bulletin of the Faculty of Representational Studies / Wakō daigaku hyōgen gakubu* 和光大学表現学部 10 (2009): 1–11.

Sawada Mizuhō 澤田瑞穗. *Jigoku hen: Chūgoku no meikai setsu* 地獄變: 中國の冥界說. Kyoto: Hōzōkan, 1968.

Schaberg, David. "Prose and Authority, 100–300 C.E." In *China's Early Empires: A Re-appraisal*, ed. Michael Nylan and Michael Loewe, 505–516. Cambridge: Cambridge University Press, 2010.

Schafer, Edward. *The Golden Peaches of Samarkand: A Study of T'ang Exotics*. Berkeley: University of California Press, 1963.

———. "The Stove God and the Alchemists." In *Studia Asiatica: Essays in Asian Studies in Felicitation of the Seventy-Fifth Birthday of Professor Ch'en Shou-yi*, ed. Laurence G. Thompson, 261–266. San Francisco: Chinese Materials Center.

Schipper, Kristofer, and Franciscus Verellen, eds. *The Taoist Canon: A Historical Companion to the Daozang*. Chicago: University of Chicago Press, 2004.

Schopen, Gregory. "The Buddha as an Owner of Property and Permanent Resident in Medieval Indian Monasteries." *Journal of Indian Philosophy* 18 (1990): 181–217.

———. "The Buddhist 'Monastery' and the Indian Garden: Aesthetics, Assimilations, and the Siting of Monastic Establishments." *Journal of the American Oriental Society* 126 (2006): 487–505.

———. *Buddhist Monks and Business Matters: Still More Papers on Monastic Buddhism in India*. Honolulu: University of Hawai'i Press, 2004.

————. *Figments and Fragments of Mahāyāna Buddhism in India: More Collected Papers*. Honolulu: University of Hawai'i Press, 2005.

Seidel, Anna. "Datsueba." In *Hōbōgirin: Dictionnaire encyclopédique du Bouddhisme d'après les sources chinoises et japonaises*, 8:1159–1169. Paris: Librairie d'Amérique et d'Orient, 2003.

————. "Geleitbrief an die Unterwelt: Jenseitsvorstellungen in den Graburkunden der späteren Han Zeit." In *Religion und Philosophie in Ostasien: Festschrift für Hans Steininger*, ed. G. Naundort, 161–183. Würtzburg: Königshausen und Neumann Verlag, 1985.

Sharf, Robert H. *Coming to Terms with Chinese Buddhism: A Reading of the Treasure Store Treatise*. Kuroda Institute Studies in East Asian Buddhism 14. Honolulu: University of Hawai'i Press, 2002.

————. "The Scripture in Forty-Two Sections." In *Religions of China in Practice*, ed. Donald S. Lopez Jr., 360–371. Princeton: Princeton University Press, 1996.

————. "The Scripture on the Production of Buddha Images." In *Religions of China in Practice*, ed. Donald S. Lopez Jr., 261–267. Princeton: Princeton University Press, 1996.

Sheng, Angela. "From Stone to Silk: Intercultural Transformation of Funerary Furnishings among Eastern Asian Peoples around 475–650 C.E." In *Les Sogdiens en Chine*, ed. Étienne de la Vaissière and Éric Trombert, 141–180. Paris: École française d'Extrême-Orient, 2005.

Sheng Kai 聖凱. *Zhongguo fojiao chanfa yanjiu* 中國佛教懺法研究. Beijing: Zongjiao wenhua chubanshe, 2004.

Shih, Heng-ching, trans. *The Sutra of Forty-Two Sections*. In *Apocryphal Scriptures*, 27–46. BDK English Tripiṭaka 25-I, 25-V, 25-VI, 29-I, 104-VI. Berkeley: Numata Center for Buddhist Translation and Research, 2005.

Shih, Robert. *Biographies des moines éminents (Kao seng tchouan) de Houei-kiao*. Louvain: Université de Louvain, Institut Orientaliste, 1968.

Shinohara Koichi. "Changing Roles for Miraculous Images in Medieval Chinese Buddhism: A Study of the Miracle Image Section in Daoxuan's 'Collected Records.'" In *Images, Miracles, and Authority in Asian Religious Traditions*, ed. Richard H. Davis, 141–188. Boulder: Westview, 1998.

————. "Ji shenzhou sanbao gantong lu: Some Explanatory Notes." In *Kalyana-Mitta: Professor Hajime Nakamura Felicitation Volume*, ed. V. N. Jha, 203–224. Delhi: Sri Satguru, 1991.

————. "Taking a Meal at a Lay Supporter's Residence: The Evolution of the Practice in Chinese *Vinaya* Commentaries." In *Buddhist Monasticism in East Asia: Places of Practice*, ed. James A. Benn, Lori Meeks, and James Robson, 18–42. New York: Routledge, 2010.

————. "Two Sources of Chinese Buddhist Biographies: Stupa Inscriptions and Miracle Stories." In *Monks and Magicians: Religious Biographies in Asia*, ed. Phyllis Granoff and Koichi Shinohara, 119–228. Oakville, Ont.: Mosaic, 1988.

Shirkey, Jeffrey C. "The Moral Economy of the *Petavatthu*: Hungry Ghosts and Theravāda Buddhist Cosmology." Ph.D. diss., University of Chicago, 2008.

Shōji Kakuichi 莊司格一. "*Meishoki* ni tsuite" 冥祥記について. *Tōyōgaku shūkan* 東洋學集刊 22 (1969): 41–65.

Shryock, J. K., trans. *The Study of Human Abilities: The "Jen wu chih" of Liu Shao*. Ann Arbor: University Microfilms, 1937.

Silk, Jonathan A. *Managing Monks: Administrators and Administrative Roles in Indian Buddhist Monasticism.* Oxford: Oxford University Press, 2008.

Skilling, Peter. "*Dharma, Dhāraṇī, Abhidharma, Avadāna*: What Was Taught in Trayastriṃśa?" *Annual Report of the International Research Institute for Advanced Buddhology at Soka University* 11 (2008): 37–60.

Smith, Barbara Herrnstein. "Narrative Versions, Narrative Theories." *Critical Inquiry* 7 (1980): 213–236.

Smith, Jonathan. *Drudgery Divine: On the Comparison of Early Christianities and the Religions of Late Antiquity.* Chicago: University of Chicago Press, 1990.

Smith, Richard J. *Fortune-Tellers and Philosophers: Divination in Traditional Chinese Society.* Boulder: Westview, 1991.

Soper, Alexander Coburn. *Literary Evidence for Early Buddhist Art in China.* Ascona: Artibus Asiae, 1969.

Sørensen, Henrik. "Divine Scrutiny of Human Morals in an Early Chinese Buddhist Sutra: A Study of the *Si tianwang jing* (T. 590)." *Studies in Central and East Asian Religions* 8 (1995): 44–83.

Soymié, Michel. "Biographie de Chan Tao-k'ai." *Mélanges publiés par l'Institut des Hautes Études chinoises* 1 (1957): 415–422.

———. "Les dix jours de jeûne de Kṣitigarbha." In *Contributions aux études sur Touen-houang*, ed. Michel Soymié, 1:135–159. Génève: Librairie Droz, 1979.

———. "Quelques representations de statues miraculeuses dans les grottes de Touen-houang." In *Contributions aux études de Touen-houang*, ed. Michel Soymié, 3:77–102. Paris: École Française d'Extrême-Orient, 1984.

———. "Sources et sourciers en Chine." *Bulletin de la Maison Franco-Japonaise*, n.s., 7 (1961): 1–56.

———. "Un calendrier de douze jours par an dans les manuscrits de Touen-houang." *Bulletin de l'École française d'Extrême-Orient* 69 (1981): 209–228.

Stein, Rolf A. "Remarques sur les mouvements du taoïsme politico-religieux au IIe siècle ap. J.C." *T'oung Pao* 50 (1963): 1–78.

Stevenson, Daniel B. "Buddhist Practice and the *Lotus Sūtra* in China." In *Readings of the Lotus Sūtra*, ed. Stephen F. Teiser and Jacqueline I. Stone, 132–150. New York: Columbia University Press, 2009.

———. "Death-Bed Testimonials of the Pure Land Faithful." In *Buddhism in Practice*, ed. Donald S. Lopez Jr., 592–602. Princeton: Princeton University Press, 1995.

———. "The Four Kinds of Samādhi in Early T'ien-t'ai Buddhism." In *Traditions of Meditation in Chinese Buddhism*, ed. Peter N. Gregory, 45–98. Kuroda Institute Studies in East Asian Buddhism 4. Honolulu: University of Hawai'i Press, 1986.

———. "Tales of the Lotus Sūtra." In *Buddhism in Practice*, ed. Donald S. Lopez Jr., 427–451. Princeton: Princeton University Press, 1995.

———. "Visions of Mañjusrī on Mount Wutai." In *Buddhism in Practice*, ed. Donald S. Lopez Jr., 203–222. Princeton: Princeton University Press, 1995.

Stone, Jacqueline I. "By the Power of One's Last Nenbutsu: Deathbed Practices in Early Medieval Japan." In *Approaching the Land of Bliss: Religious Praxis in the Cult of Amitābha*, ed. Richard K. Payne and Kenneth K. Tanaka, 77–119. Kuroda Institute Studies in East Asian Buddhism 17. Honolulu: University of Hawai'i Press, 2004.

———. "Do *Kami* Ever Overlook Pollution? *Honji suijaku* and the Problem of Death Defilement." *Cahiers d'Extrême-Asie* 16 (2006–2007): 203–232.

Strickmann, Michel. *Chinese Magical Medicine.* Ed. Bernard Faure. Stanford: Stanford University Press, 2002.

———. *Chinese Poetry and Prophecy: The Written Oracle in East Asia.* Ed. Bernard Faure. Stanford: Stanford University Press, 2005.

———. "The *Consecration Sūtra*: A Buddhist Book of Spells." In *Chinese Buddhist Apocrypha*, ed. Robert E. Buswell Jr., 75–118. Honolulu: University of Hawai'i Press, 1990.

———. *Le taoïsme du Mao Chan: Chronique d'une révélation.* Mémoires de l'Institut des Hautes Études Chinoises 17. Paris: Collège de France, 1981.

———. *Mantras et mandarins: Le bouddhisme tantrique en Chine.* Paris: Editions Gallimard, 1996.

Strong, John S. "The Legend of the Lion-Roarer." *Numen* 26 (1979): 50–88.

———. *Relics of the Buddha.* Princeton: Princeton University Press, 2004.

Sutherland, Gail Hinich. *The Disguises of the Demon: The Development of the Yakṣa in Hinduism and Buddhism.* Albany: State University of New York Press, 1991.

Tai Shiwen 太史文 [Stephen F. Teiser]. "Shilun zhaiwen de biaoyanxing" 試論齋文的表演性. *Dunhuang Tulufan yanjiu* 敦煌吐魯番研究 10 (2007): 295–308.

———. "Wei wangzhe yuan: Dunhuang yishi wenlei dingyi chutan" 為亡者願: 敦煌儀式文類定義初探. Trans. Xie Huiying 謝惠英. In *Shengzhuan yu chanshi: Zhongguo wenxue yu zongjiao lunji* 聖傳與禪詩: 中國文學與宗教論集, ed. Li Fengmao 李豐楙 and Liao Zhaoheng 廖肇亨, 284–307. Taibei: Zhongyang yanjiuyuan Zhongguo wenzhe yanjiusuo, 2007.

Takeda Akira 竹田晃. *Chūgoku no setsuwa to kōshōsetsu* 中国の說話と古小說. Tokyo: Daizō shōin, 1992.

Tang Changru. "Clients and Bound Retainers in the Six Dynasties Period." In *State and Society in Early Medieval China*, ed. Albert E. Dien, 111–138. Stanford: Stanford University Press, 1990.

Tang Yongtong 湯用彤. *Han Wei liang Jin nanbeichao fojiao shi* 漢魏兩晉南北朝佛教史. Shanghai, 1938. Repr., Beijing: Beijing daxue chubanshe, 1997.

Tangherlini, Timothy R. "'It Happened Not Too Far from Here...': A Survey of Legend Theory and Characterization." *Western Folklore* 49 (1990): 371–390.

Teiser, Stephen F. *The Ghost Festival in Medieval China.* Princeton: Princeton University Press, 1988.

———. "Ghosts and Ancestors in Medieval Chinese Religion: The Yü-lan p'en Festival as Mortuary Ritual." *History of Religions* 26 (1986): 47–67.

———. "'Having Once Died and Returned to Life': Representations of Hell in Medieval China." *Harvard Journal of Asiatic Studies* 48 (1988): 433–464.

———. "The Local and the Canonical: Pictures of the Wheel of Rebirth in Gansu and Sichuan." *Asia Major*, 3rd ser., 17 (2004): 73–122.

———. "Ornamenting the Departed: Notes on the Language of Chinese Buddhist Ritual Texts." *Asia Major*, 3rd ser., 22 (2009): 201–237.

———. *Reinventing the Wheel: Paintings of Rebirth in Medieval Buddhist Temples.* Seattle: University of Washington Press, 2006.

———. *The Scripture on the Ten Kings and the Making of Purgatory in Medieval Chinese Buddhism.* Kuroda Institute Studies in East Asian Buddhism 9. Honolulu: University of Hawai'i Press, 1994.

————. "T'ang Buddhist Encyclopedias: An Introduction to *Fa-yuan chu-lin* and *Chu-ching yao-chi.*" *T'ang Studies* 3 (1985): 109–128.

Teiser, Stephen F., and Jacqueline I. Stone. "Interpreting the *Lotus Sūtra.*" In *Readings of the Lotus Sūtra*, ed. Stephen F. Teiser and Jacqueline I. Stone, 1–61. New York: Columbia University Press, 2009.

Tessenow, Hermann, and Paul U. Unschuld. *A Dictionary of the Huang Di nei jing su wen.* Berkeley: University of California Press, 2008.

Tian, Xiaofei. *Beacon Fire and Shooting Star: The Literary Culture of the Liang (502–557).* Cambridge, Mass.: Harvard University Asia Center, 2007.

————. *Tao Yuanming and Manuscript Culture: The Record of a Dusty Table.* Seattle: University of Washington Press, 2005.

Tokuno, Kyoko. "The Evaluation of Indigenous Scriptures in Chinese Buddhist Bibliographical Catalogues." In *Chinese Buddhist Apocrypha*, ed. Robert E. Buswell Jr., 31–74. Honolulu: University of Hawai'i Press, 1990.

Tsai, Katherine. *Lives of the Nuns: Biographies of Chinese Buddhist Nuns from the Fourth to Sixth Centuries.* Honolulu: University of Hawai'i Press, 1994.

Tsiang, Katherine R. "Embodiments of Buddhist Texts in Early Medieval Chinese Visual Culture." In *Body and Face in Chinese Visual Culture*, ed. Wu Hung and Katherine R. Tsiang, 49–78. Cambridge, Mass.: Harvard University Asia Center, 2004.

Tsien, Tsuen-hsuin. *Written on Bamboo and Silk: The Beginnings of Chinese Books and Inscriptions.* 2nd ed. Chicago: University of Chicago Press, 2004.

Tsukamoto Zenryū 塚本善隆. *A History of Early Chinese Buddhism.* Trans. Leon Hurvitz. 2 vols. Tokyo: Kodansha, 1985.

Twitchett, Denis. *The Writing of Official History under the T'ang.* Cambridge: Cambridge University Press, 1992.

Unschuld, Paul U. *Medicine in China: A History of Ideas.* Berkeley: University of California Press, 1985.

————. *Medicine in China: A History of Pharmaceutics.* Berkeley: University of California Press, 1986.

Verellen, Franciscus. "'Evidential Miracles in Support of Taoism': The Inversion of a Buddhist Apologetic Tradition in Late Tang China." *T'oung Pao* 78 (1992): 217–263.

————. "The Heavenly Master Liturgical Agenda according to Chisong zi's Petition Almanac." *Cahiers d'Extrême-Asie* 14 (2004): 291–343.

Vetch, Hélène. "Lieou Sa-ho et les grottes de Mo-kao." In *Nouvelles contributions aux études de Touen-houang*, ed. Michel Soymié, 137–148. Génève: Librairie Droz, 1981.

————. "Liu Sahe: Traditions et iconographie." In *Les peintures murales et les manuscrits de Dunhuang: Colloque franco-chinois organisé par la Fondation Singer-Polignac à Paris, les 21, 22 et 23 fevrier 1983*, ed. Michel Soymié, 61–78. Paris: Editions de la Fondation Singer-Polignac, 1984.

Vogel, P. "The Past Buddhas and Kāśyapa in Indian Art and Epigraphy." In *Asiatica: Festschrift Friedrich Weller*, 808–816. Leipzig: Harassowitz, 1954.

Von Falkenhausen, Lothar. "Reflections on the Political Role of Spirit Mediums in Early China: The *Wu* Officials in the *Zhou li.*" *Early China* 20 (1995): 279–300.

Von Hinüber, Oskar. "Three New Bronzes from Gilgit." *Annual Report of the Interna-*

tional Research Institute for Advanced Buddhology at Soka University 10 (2007): 39–44.

Wakatsuki Toshihide 若槻俊秀, Hasegawa Makoto 長谷川慎, and Inagaki Akio 稲垣淳央, eds. *Hōon jurin no sōgōteki kenkyū: Omo to shite Hōon jurin shoroku Meishoki no honbun kōtei narabi ni senchū senyaku* 法苑珠林の總合的研究: 主として法苑珠林所錄冥祥記の本文校訂竝びに選注選譯. *Shinshū Sōgō Kenkyū Sho kenkyū kiyō* 真宗総合研究所研究紀要 (*Annual Memoirs of the Otani Shin Buddhist Comprehensive Research Institute*) 25 (2007): 1–224.

Wang, Eugene Y. "Pictorial Program in the Making of Monastic Space: From Jing'aisi of Luoyang to Cave 217 at Dunhuang." In *Buddhist Monasticism in East Asia: Places of Practice*, ed. James A. Benn, Lori Meeks, and James Robson, 65–106. New York: Routledge, 2010.

———. *Shaping the Lotus Sutra: Buddhist Visual Culture in Medieval China*. Seattle: University of Washington Press, 2005.

Wang Guoliang 王國良. *Liuchao zhiguai xiaoshuo kaolun* 六朝志怪小說考論. Taibei: Wenshizhe chubanshe, 1988.

———. "*Mingxiang ji* xiao kao" 冥祥記小考. *Dong Wu zhongwen xuebao* 東吳中文學報 3 (1997): 271–284.

———. *Mingxiang ji yanjiu* 冥祥記研究. Taibei: Wenshizhe chubanshe, 1999.

———. *Wei Jin nanbeichao zhiguai xiaoshuo yanjiu* 魏晉南北朝志怪小說研究. Taibei: Wenshizhe chubanshe, 1984.

———. *Xu Qi Xie ji yanjiu* 續齊諧記研究. Taibei: Wenshizhe chubanshe, 1987.

Wang Juan 汪娟. *Dunhuang lichanwen yanjiu* 敦煌禮懺文研究. Taibei: Fagu wenhua, 1998.

———. *Tang Song guyi fojiao chanyi yanjiu* 唐宋古逸佛教懺儀研究. Taibei: Wenjin chubanshe, 2008.

Wang Li 王力. *Wang Li gu hanyu zidian* 王力古漢語字典. Beijing: Zhonghua shuju, 2000.

Wang Qing 王青. "Jinyang Wang shi de jiashi menfeng yu *Mingxiang ji* de chuangzuo" 晉陽王氏的家世門風與冥祥記的創作. In *Zhongguo gudai wenxue wenxian xue: Guoji xueshu yantaohui lunwenji* 中國古代文學文獻學: 國際學術研討會論文集, ed. Cheng Zhangcan 程章灿, 142–159. Nanjing: Fenghuang chubanshe, 2006.

Wang Sanqing 王三慶. *Cong Dunhuang zhaiyuan wenxian kan fojiao yu Zhongguo minsu de ronghe* 從敦煌齋願文獻看佛教與中國民俗的融合. Taibei: Xinwenfeng, 2009.

———. *Dunhuang fojiao zhaiyuan wenben yanjiu* 敦煌佛教齋願文本研究. Taibei: Xinwenfeng, 2009.

Wang Yi-t'ung. *A Record of Buddhist Monasteries in Lo-yang by Yang Hsüan-chih*. Princeton: Princeton University Press, 1984.

Wang-Toutain, Françoise. "Entre spéculation métaphysique et dévotion: La doctrine bouddhique en Chine avant le VIIe siècle." In *Religion et société en Chine ancienne et médiévale*, ed. John Lagerwey, 601–641. Paris: Éditions du CERF / Institut Ricci, 2009.

———. *Le Bodhisattva Kṣitigarbha en Chine du Ve au XIIe siècle*. Paris: École française d'Extrême-Orient, 1998.

———. "Le bol du Buddha: Propagation du bouddhisme et légitimé politique." *Bulletin de l'École française d'Extrême-Orient* 81 (1994): 59–82.

Wayman, Alex. "Contributions Regarding the Thirty-Two Characteristics of the Great Person." *Sino-Indian Studies* 5 (1957): 243–260.

Wechsler, Howard. *Offerings of Jade and Silk: Ritual and Symbol in the Legitimation of the T'ang Dynasty.* New Haven: Yale University Press, 1985.

Whitfield, Roderick. "The Monk Liu Sahe and the Dunhuang Paintings." *Orientations* 3 (1989): 64–70.

Williams, Paul. *Mahāyāna Buddhism: The Doctrinal Foundations.* 2nd ed. London: Routledge, 2009.

Wilson, Liz. *Charming Cadavers: Horrific Figurations of the Feminine in Indian Buddhist Hagiographic Literature.* Chicago: University of Chicago Press, 1996.

Wong, Dorothy C. *Chinese Steles: Pre-Buddhist and Buddhist Use of a Symbolic Form.* Honolulu: University of Hawai'i Press, 2004.

Wright, Arthur F. *Studies in Chinese Buddhism.* Ed. Robert M. Somers. New Haven: Yale University Press, 1990.

———. *The Sui Dynasty: The Unification of China, A.D. 581–617.* New York: Knopf, 1978.

Wu Hung. "Buddhist Elements in Early Chinese Art (2nd and 3rd Centuries A.D.)." *Artibus Asiae* 47 (1986): 263–352.

———. "On Tomb Figurines: The Beginning of a Visual Tradition." In *Body and Face in Chinese Visual Culture,* ed. Wu Hung and Katherine R. Tsiang, 13–47. Cambridge, Mass.: Harvard University Asia Center, 2004.

———. "Rethinking Liu Sahe: The Creation of a Buddhist Saint and the Invention of a 'Miraculous Image.'" *Orientations* 27 (1996): 32–43.

———. "What Is *Bianxiang* 變相? On the Relationship between Dunhuang Art and Dunhuang Literature." *Harvard Journal of Asiatic Studies* 52 (1992): 111–192.

Xiao Dengfu [Hsiao Deng-fu] 蕭登福. *Han Wei liuchao Fo dao liang jiao zhi tiantang diyu shuo* 漢魏六朝佛道兩教之天堂地獄說. Taibei: Xuesheng shuju, 1989.

Xie Mingxun 謝明勳. *Liuchao xiaoshuo benshi kaosuo* 六朝小說本事考索. Taibei: Liren shuju, 2003.

Xiong Daolin 熊道麟. "*Mingxiang ji* yanjiu" 冥祥記研究. *Xingda zhongwen xuebao* 興大中文學報 6 (1993): 239–265.

Xiong, Victor Cunrui. *Emperor Yang of the Sui Dynasty.* Albany: State University of New York Press, 2006.

Xu Yanling 徐燕玲. "*Mingxiang ji* ji qi sengren xingxiang tanxi" 冥祥記及其僧人形象探析. *Zhongguo wenhua yuekan* 中國文化月刊 277 (2004): 102–121.

Xue Huiqi 薛惠琪. *Liuchao fojiao zhiguai xiaoshuo yanjiu* 六朝佛教志怪小說研究. Taibei: Wenjin chubanshe, 1995.

Yoshikawa Kōjirō 吉川辛次郎. "The *Shih-shuo Hsin-yü* and Six Dynasties Prose Style." Trans. Glen W. Baxter. *Harvard Journal of Asiatic Studies* 18 (1955): 124–141.

Yoshikawa Tadao 吉川忠夫. "'Seishitsu' ko" '靜室' 考. *Tōhō gakuhō* 東方學報 59 (1987): 125–162.

Yü, Chün-fang. *Kuan-yin: The Chinese Transformation of Avalokiteśvara.* New York: Columbia University Press, 2001.

Yü Ying-shih. "Individualism and the Neo-Taoist Movement in Wei-Chin China." In *Individualism and Holism: Studies in Confucian and Taoist Values,* ed. Donald Munro, 121–156. Ann Arbor: Center for Chinese Studies, University of Michigan, 1985.

Zacchetti, Stefano. "Teaching Buddhism in Han China: A Study of the *Ahan koujie shi'er yinyuan jing* T 1508 Attributed to An Shigao." *Annual Report of the International Research Institute for Advanced Buddhology at Soka University* 7 (2004): 197–224.

Zhang Guangda 張廣達. "'Tan fo' yu 'tan zhai': Guanyu Dunhuang wenshu zhong de 'zhaiwanwen' de jige wenti" '嘆佛'與'嘆齋': 關於敦煌文書中的齋琬文的幾個問題. In *Qingzhu Guangming jiaoshou jiushi huadan lunwen ji* 慶祝鄧廣銘教授九十華誕論文集, 60–73. Shijiazhuang: Hebei jiaoyu chubanshe, 1997.

Zheng Yong 鄭勇. "*Mingxiang ji* buji" 冥祥記補輯. *Wenxian jikan* 文學季刊 2007, no. 3, pp. 171–174.

Zhiru. *The Making of a Savior Bodhisattva: Dizang in Medieval China*. Kuroda Institute Studies in East Asian Buddhism 21. Honolulu: University of Hawai'i Press, 2007.

Zhou Ciji 周次吉. *Liuchao zhiguai xiaoshuo yanjiu* 六朝志怪小說研究. Taipei: Wenjin chubanshe, 1990.

Zhou Junxun 周俊勛. *Wei Jin nanbeichao zhiguai xiaoshuo cihui yanjiu* 魏晉南北朝志怪小說詞彙研究. Chengdu: Ba Shu shushe, 2006.

Zhu Pingyi 祝平一. *Handai de xiangrenshu* 漢代的相人術. Taibei: Xuesheng shuju, 1990.

Zürcher, Erik. *The Buddhist Conquest of China*. Leiden: Brill, 1959.

———. "Buddhist Influence on Early Taoism: A Survey of Scriptural Evidence." *T'oung Pao* 66 (1980): 84–147.

———. "A New Look at the Earliest Chinese Buddhist Texts." In *From Benares to Beijing: Essays on Buddhism and Chinese Religion*, ed. Koichi Shinohara and Gregory Schopen, 277–304. Oakville: Mosaic, 1991.

———. "Prince Moonlight." *T'oung Pao* 68 (1982): 1–75.

Zysk, Kenneth G. *Asceticism and Healing in Ancient India: Medicine in the Buddhist Monastery*. New York: Oxford University Press, 1991.

Index

abstinence ceremony (*zhai*), 31, 107; as
  depicted in miracle tales, 51–55, 114,
  144, 192, 193, 226, 233, 239; halls for,
  in private homes, 53, 103, 145, 192,
  204, 223, 253, 254; importance of, in
  Buddhist communities in early
  medieval China, xiii; regulations for,
  217, 257
accounts of anomalies (*zhiguai*), 22; and
  Buddhist miracle tales, 2; as designed
  to demonstrate regularities in the
  workings of the unseen world, 13, 14;
  and fiction, 13, 17
allotted life span (*ming*), 41, 82, 83, 87, 116,
  135, 168, 177, 182, 187, 196, 209, 229,
  237, 255, 259
alms bowls, 103–104, 106, 107, 109, 151, 260
Amitābha, 50, 101, 116, 188, 211, 213
An Fakai, 261
An Shigao, 1, 2, 68
An Xuan, 1
ancestors, 9, 39, 59, 74, 122, 201, 256
animals: categories of, 137–138; mastery of,
  88, 91, 92, 93, 163; releasing, as act of
  merit, 197
anomalies. *See* accounts of anomalies;
  miraculous
Apang, 183
arhat path, 33, 136, 174, 225, 232, 255
Aśoka, 57, 61, 66, 79, 94, 151, 152, 153
audience for miracle narratives, 20, 25,
  29–30, 205
authenticity, 61–62, 77, 152, 180, 246
avadāna literature, 2–3, 33–34

baguanzhai (eightfold abstinence ceremony), 104, 107, 189, 196
Bamboo King, 236

banners: as devotional ornaments and
  merit-making gifts, 79, 113, 208; seen
  in visions, 211; as signs of office in the
  unseen realm, 128, 195
Bannihuan jing, 43
bathing: Buddha images, 52, 57, 121, 149,
  150; the monk, rite of, 220
beef taboo, 162
Bi Lan, 171–172
Bian Yuezhi, 229
Biqiuni zhuan, 214
bodhisattva precepts, 201, 239
bodhisattvas, role of, in miracle tales, 32
bodily marks of divine beings, 65–66, 151
Bokenkamp, Stephen R., xv, 43, 143, 207,
  212
Buddhism: essentialist, monolithic views of,
  30, 36; particular idiom of, as reflected in Chinese miracle tales, 30–43;
  sinicization of, and miracle tales,
  37–43
Buxu Mingxiang ji, 3, 28

caitiffs, definition of, 157–158
canopies (*zhang*), 103, 191, 193, 211
caps, 113, 146, 181, 182, 195, 210, 223, 247
celestial kings (*tianwang*), 53–54, 162, 255
Celestial Master Daoism: charity lodges in,
  80; compared to the Buddhism seen in
  miracle tales, 35, 36; contested in
  miracle tales, 39, 42, 57, 145, 176, 179,
  183, 186, 195, 207–208
Changle Gong, 158
chanhui. See confession
Chen Anju, 41, 174–180
Chen Xiuyuan, 243–244
Chen Xuanfan, 259
Cheng Daohui, 145–147, 218

Yuan Bing, 241–242
Yuan Hong, 16, 170

zhai. See abstinence ceremony
Zhang Chong, 142–143
Zhang Xing, 189
Zhang Yan, 4, 28
Zhang Ying, 114–116
Zhao Tai, 19–20, 23–24, 77–84, 147
Zhao Xi, 225
Zheng Xianzhi, 196–197
Zhengwu lun, 43
Zhengying zhuan, 3
Zhenyi zhuan, 13
Zhi Daoshan, 21, 125
Zhi Dun, 102, 104, 126, 137–138
Zhi Fashan, 112, 168
Zhi Qian, 1, 50
Zhida, 245–246
zhiguai. See accounts of anomalies
Zhitong, 203

Zhonghua dazangjing, xviii
Zhou Dang, 119–120
Zhou Min, 110–112
Zhou Zong, 197
Zhoushi mingtong ji, 14
Zhu Changshu, 98–99
Zhu Daorong, 104–106
Zhu Fahu, 101–102
Zhu Fajin, 109–110
Zhu Fatun, 154–155
Zhu Fayi, 132
Zhu Fodiao, 91–93
Zhu Huichi, 184–185
Zhu Huiqing, 210–211
Zhu Tangai, 163–165
zhuangyan (ornamentation), 79
Zhuangzi, 35, 49
zombie, 175
Zong Xie, 160–162
Zu Chongzhi, 13
Zürcher, Erik, xiii, 2, 8, 34–35, 69

About the Author

Robert Ford Campany is Gertrude Conway Vanderbilt Chair in the Humanities and professor of Asian studies at Vanderbilt University. He is co-editor of *Early Medieval China: A Sourcebook* (Columbia University Press, 2014) and the author of three previous books, including *Making Transcendents: Ascetics and Social Memory in Early Medieval China* (University of Hawai'i Press, 2009), which won the American Academy of Religion Award for Excellence in the Study of Religion and honorable mention in the Association for Asian Studies Joseph Levenson Prize competition.